M000252170

Psychological Practice With Women

PSYCHOLOGY OF WOMEN BOOK SERIES

Psychological Practice With Women

Guidelines, Diversity, Empowerment

Edited by
Carolyn Zerbe Enns, Joy K. Rice, and Roberta L. Nutt

American Psychological Association · *Washington, DC*

Copyright © 2015 by the American Psychological Association. All rights reserved. Except as permitted under the United States Copyright Act of 1976, no part of this publication may be reproduced or distributed in any form or by any means, including, but not limited to, the process of scanning and digitization, or stored in a database or retrieval system, without the prior written permission of the publisher.

Published by
American Psychological Association
750 First Street, NE
Washington, DC 20002
www.apa.org

To order
APA Order Department
P.O. Box 92984
Washington, DC 20090-2984
Tel: (800) 374-2721; Direct: (202) 336-5510
Fax: (202) 336-5502; TDD/TTY: (202) 336-6123
Online: www.apa.org/pubs/books
E-mail: order@apa.org

In the U.K., Europe, Africa, and the Middle East, copies may be ordered from
American Psychological Association
3 Henrietta Street
Covent Garden, London
WC2E 8LU England

Typeset in Goudy by Circle Graphics, Inc., Columbia, MD

Printer: Maple Press, York, PA
Cover Designer: Naylor Design, Washington, DC

The opinions and statements published are the responsibility of the authors, and such opinions and statements do not necessarily represent the policies of the American Psychological Association.

Library of Congress Cataloging-in-Publication Data

Psychological practice with women : guidelines, diversity, empowerment / edited by Carolyn Zerbe Enns, Joy K. Rice, and Roberta L. Nutt. — First edition.
    pages cm
Includes bibliographical references and index.
ISBN-13: 978-1-4338-1812-7
ISBN-10: 1-4338-1812-4
1. Women—Psychology. 2. Women—Cross cultural studies. 3. Feminist psychology.
4. Feminist therapy. I. Enns, Carolyn Zerbe. II. Rice, Joy K. III. Nutt, Roberta Lynn, 1944-

HQ1206.P746 2015
155.3'33—dc23
                                    2014012300

British Library Cataloguing-in-Publication Data
A CIP record is available from the British Library.

Printed in the United States of America
First Edition

http://dx.doi.org/10.1037/14460-000

CONTENTS

CONTRIBUTORS

Rosalie J. Ackerman, PhD, ABackans DCP, Inc., Akron, OH
Martha E. Banks, PhD, ABackans DCP, Inc., Akron, OH
Linda J. Beckman, PhD, California School of Professional Psychology, Alliant International University, Los Angeles
Kathleen S. Brown, PhD, Health Psychology Associates, Honolulu, HI
Carrie L. Castañeda-Sound, PhD, Pepperdine University, Encino, CA
Khanh T. Dinh, PhD, University of Massachusetts, Lowell
Carolyn Zerbe Enns, PhD, Cornell College, Mount Vernon, IA
Pilar E. Gauthier, MS, Great Lakes–Native American Research Center for Health, Lac Du Flambeau, WI
Dianna Marisol González, PhD, New Mexico State University, Las Cruces
Phi Loan Le, PsyD, Santa Ana College, Santa Ana, CA
Sayaka Machizawa, PsyD, The Chicago School of Professional Psychology, Chicago, IL
Connie R. Matthews, PhD, New Perspectives, LLC, State College, PA
Linda R. Mona, PhD, VA Long Beach Healthcare System, Long Beach, CA
Rachel L. Navarro, PhD, University of North Dakota, Grand Forks
Roberta L. Nutt, PhD, ABPP, University of Houston, Houston, TX

Wendy M. K. Peters, PhD, University of North Dakota School of Medicine and Health Sciences, Grand Forks

Joy K. Rice, PhD, University of Wisconsin–Madison

Kee J. E. Straits, PhD, Department of Psychology, University of New Mexico, Albuquerque

Wendi S. Williams, PhD, Long Island University–Brooklyn, Brooklyn, NY

SERIES FOREWORD

Applying a feminist lens to current concerns facing individuals, families, schools, communities, and nations can provide deeper insight into and understanding of contemporary social issues, including poverty, immigration, violence toward and abuse of women and children, and physical and mental health disparities. Most important, such work can identify and promote interventions and solutions that improve women's status in society and advance social justice. The American Psychological Association's (APA's) Psychology of Women Book Series is designed to support and disseminate feminist scholarship on education, research, and practice that can contribute to advocacy and social activism on behalf of women and other disempowered groups. It reflects a primary principle of feminist psychology: the application of knowledge through action.

Whereas consciousness of women's issues and the psychology of women began with emphasis primarily on White, middle-class women, the series extends scholarship and concerns about diversity and the intersectionality of multiple social identities of individuals, highlighting not only demographic trends in the United States but also the interplay between national and global concerns. The interacting identities considered include race, ethnicity, gender, sexual orientation, nationality, socioeconomic status, religion, ability, and age. Specific objectives are to synthesize, integrate, and apply empirical knowledge and clinical perspectives for women who represent dimensions of diversities previously ignored or underrepresented in research and clinical application and to extend psychological theory on women and gender so that it is both more diverse and inclusive of all groups of women.

Some of the outstanding books in the series grew out of APA or divisional task forces set up to investigate and summarize current knowledge about socially relevant concerns. The editors of this volume were co-chairs of the APA task force that developed the 2007 "Guidelines for Psychological Practice With Girls and Women." Beginning with the framework of the 2007 Guidelines, the book provides valuable examples of how these aspirational guidelines can be applied to clinical practice and the provision of mental health services to women and girls. Its focus on the intersection and multiple layers of women's social identity is unique and should provide many insights for those interested in working with diverse groups. Each of the chapters that focus on a particular population includes extensive consideration of feminist scholarship (both research and theory) relevant to the group identity, applies the relevant scholarship, explores a variety of therapeutic approaches through the use of case studies, and considers possibilities for advocacy and social change. Moreover, the chapter authors highlight positive approaches based on resiliency and targeted toward the empowerment of women.

The editors begin and end the book by emphasizing the theme of the transformation of psychology and the necessity of inclusion of essential feminist perspectives. They see the book as an effort to promote such a "transformation on how we understand, conceptualize and treat diverse groups of women" (p. 4). Transforming the knowledge, norms, and practices of a profession requires a great deal more than one book. Nonetheless, through the presentation of up-to-date culturally based research, current feminist theory, and their application to clinical practice, this book will help to advance and transform the practice of psychology.

Linda J. Beckman, PhD
Series Editor

ACKNOWLEDGMENTS

This book project would not have been possible without the vision of the former president of the Society for the Psychology of Women (APA Division 35), Janice Yoder, and the former president of the Society of Counseling Psychology (APA Division 17), Nadya Fouad, who both appointed us as cochairs of the task force that crafted the APA "Guidelines for Psychological Practice With Girls and Women." We are also extremely grateful to the many task-force members who contributed to the Guidelines. Their names are listed on the first page of the Guidelines, which appeared in the December 2007 issue of *American Psychologist*. We also thank Pamela Remer and Connie Matthews for their helpful efforts to disseminate the Guidelines.

We wish to acknowledge and thank Linda Beckman, American Psychological Association Division 35 book series editor, who encouraged us to propose this book. The persistent efforts of our acquisitions editor, Maureen Adams, the thoughtful facilitation of Beth Hatch, development editor, Liz Brace, production editor, and Christina Edwards, copy editor, and the creative supervision of our design editor, Ron Teeter, have been invaluable. We are grateful for their efforts and those of other reviewers who read and reviewed chapters and provided constructive feedback. We also appreciate the support of interest group sections within the Society for the Psychology of Women in Division 35 and the Section for the Advancement of Women in Division 17, which were central to identifying the dedicated group of authors who wrote chapters about women's diversity and psychological practice. Of course, the value of this book and its contribution to the field of psychological practice are largely due to the great and varied contributions of the many writers who volunteered for this project, who took great care in writing their chapters, and who were willing to write multiple drafts in response to our feedback. Finally, as we look back over the preparation of this book, we also wish to thank and acknowledge the importance of our families, friends, and professional colleagues who have been unfailingly supportive and encouraging throughout this project.

Psychological Practice With Women

1

TRANSFORMING PSYCHOLOGICAL PRACTICE WITH WOMEN: AN INTRODUCTION

JOY K. RICE, CAROLYN ZERBE ENNS, AND ROBERTA L. NUTT

There are hundreds, maybe thousands, of books on diversity urging psychologists and others to become more knowledgeable and sensitive to diverse populations of people. So why read yet another book on diversity? How is this book different, and how will it help psychologists in practice, be it clinical, research, or teaching? Our aim here is ambitious. We believe psychology and its practitioners need to understand, appreciate, and put into practice the complexities of working with groups of women and girls who embody and live with multiple layers of diverse identities. And this situation is far more common than one would first anticipate in working with women. As but one example, a clinician can explore a layer of identity with a Latina woman and find a Puerto Rican, bisexual mother who has decided her Latina identity takes precedence over her gender and openly embraces that identity, but hides her sexual orientation. In this book, our authors tackle the complexities of working with women and girls who live at the "borders," negotiating

http://dx.doi.org/10.1037/14460-001
Psychological Practice With Women: Guidelines, Diversity, Empowerment, C. Z. Enns, J. K. Rice, and R. L. Nutt (Editors)
Copyright © 2015 by the American Psychological Association. All rights reserved.

multiple identities related to race, ethnicity, class, geography, sexual orientation, and disability. It is not an easy task to help these clients not only to understand their complex path, but also to choose the right interventions, assessments, and resources. This book is chock full of helpful perspectives, techniques, and case studies for psychologists and practitioners who want to be more effective and knowledgeable about working with diverse groups of women. Further, we believe if these issues and knowledge base are centralized in psychological practice, there will be a real transformation on how we understand, conceptualize, and treat diverse groups of women and girls.

Transformation has been a central goal within the psychology of women for many years (Crawford & Marecek, 1989). As early as 1968, Weisstein (1993) declared that "psychology has nothing to say" (p. 197) about women's experiences. She criticized psychologists for ignoring the social context of women's lives and relying on speculative theories that were not supported by evidence. Twenty years after Weisstein's famous speech, Crawford and Marecek (1989) defined the goal of transformation as requiring self-reflective attitudes and changing the norms, practices, and content of psychology.

This book represents an effort to further this transformation in a variety of ways. *Diversity* and *empowerment*, two words that are highlighted in the subtitle of this book, are sometimes identified as buzzwords that have been overused or have limited meaning. We use these words deliberately and purposefully. By using the word *diversity*, we aim to underline the importance of all women's experiences. Diversity involves centralizing the experiences, strengths, and struggles of women of color and from other marginalized groups, drawing our attention to the social-ecological context and complexities of their lives. This book uses an intersectional perspective, often referred to as *intersectionality*, to explore, highlight, and clarify women's multiple and intersecting identities (Shields, 2008), encouraging readers to think in more complicated and nuanced ways about all women's lives. Second, many chapters in this book are written primarily by authors of diverse backgrounds who have lived and studied the social identities they discuss, and thus they convey a depth of understanding of women's experiences as "outsiders-within" (Dill & Zambrana, 2009, p. 6). In their roles as psychologists, these authors have knowledge of psychology as "insiders"; however, they also speak with the authority of "outsiders" who have experienced many of the challenges of the women they discuss. As a result, they are especially well-prepared to see diversity as manifested in interconnected structures of inequality and privilege that often remain invisible to those who have limited personal experience with injustice. Through illustrative case studies, they unveil power issues, reveal sources of women's resilience, and provide ecologically sound recommendations for psychotherapy. A third contribution to transformation is supported by each chapter's attention to social change practices and community resources that reinforce personal change and holistic empowerment that can further lead to the renewal of practice. Much of the literature on women's empowerment emphasizes personal change alone (Becker, 2005), and in contrast, this volume focuses on the importance of both personal change and systemic change that address inequities.

The framework for organizing these transformative applications is the American Psychological Association's (APA's) "Guidelines for Psychological Practice With Girls and Women" (APA, 2007), hereafter referred to as the Guidelines (see https://www.apa.org/practice/guidelines/girls-and-women.pdf). The Guidelines represent the culmination of approximately 40 years of scholarship and research about the contemporary lives of women and girls. Although the 2007 Guidelines were designed and written to apply to both women and girls, the primary focus was on women, and that is true for this book as well. This book highlights specific implications of the Guidelines for working with very diverse groups of adult women. There is vast literature on how gender stereotyping and social location affect the lives, welfare, and mental health of young girls and adolescents that would require another book specifically focused on the application of this literature to psychotherapy and psychological practice with diverse girls and female adolescents. The reader will find, however, several rich case studies that include helpful applications of the Guidelines in working with girls of diverse backgrounds and social identities.

BACKGROUND AND HERSTORY

Beginning in the 1960s and 1970s, psychology as a discipline was widely criticized for its biases with regard to gender, race, ethnicity, class, and sexual orientation. A number of classic studies and publications focused on these limitations. This literature challenged the extent to which existing psychological theories were androcentric and did not adequately describe women's psychological development and behavior including women of color and lesbians (APA, 1975; Chesler, 1972; Gilligan, 1982; Rawlings & Carter, 1977; Rice & Rice, 1973; Weisstein, 1968). Analytical scrutiny of various theories of psychotherapy, research on psychological development, existing diagnostic systems, and assessment procedures and measures revealed problems with noninclusive versions of mental health and gender and ethnic biases (Brown, 1994; Worell & Remer, 2003).

In recent times, gender bias has been observed to be more covert—but still a detectable and powerful—force in psychological theory and practice. Particular areas of concern include the presence of gender bias as well as bias in other social constructs such as ethnicity, age, race, body size and appearance, disability, and social class as they appear within diagnostic criteria, labeling, theoretical conceptualizations of interventions, and testing (Ballou & Brown, 2002; Caplan & Cosgrove, 2004; Enns, 2004; Klonoff, Landrine, & Campbell, 2000; Martens, Johns, Greenberg, & Schimel, 2006; Worell & Goodheart, 2006). Thus, the aim of the 2007 Guidelines was and is to articulate general principles that will enhance gender- and culture-sensitive psychological practice with women and girls from all social classes, ethnic and racial groups, sexual orientations, and ability/disability statuses in the United States. The 2007 Guidelines provide general recommendations for psychologists who seek to increase their awareness, knowledge, and skills in psychological practice with women and girls. The beneficiaries include all consumers of psychological practice, including clients, students, supervisees, research participants, consultees, and other health professionals. Although the Guidelines and supporting literature place substantial emphasis on psychotherapy practice, the general Guidelines are applicable to psychological practice in its broadest sense.

Recently, scholarship by and about women has also increasingly embraced a "complexity paradigm" (Reid, 2002; Silverstein, 2006), and the goal of this volume is to consider some of the major implications of a complex intersectional perspective for psychological practice with diverse groups of women (Cole, 2009; Josselson & Harway, 2012). The editors of this volume were privileged to co-chair the APA task force that developed the 2007 Guidelines and believed it was time to consider their application in the context of expanding feminist perspectives on the critical importance of understanding social intersectionality and the social identities that shape diverse women's self-images, life experiences, and mental health. Although the 2007 Guidelines make reference to the complexities of assessing *social location*, scholarship and practice have considerably expanded our conceptions about the issues involved in working with women who have multiple, layered social identities that are influenced by a myriad of demographic, cultural, historical, and ecological variables. Such a realization makes for a daunting task for the culturally sensitive clinician who desires to work successfully with diverse women.

As previously noted, the Guidelines that provide a foundation for this book have evolved since the social justice and human rights movements of the 1960s. A lengthy list of scholarship in this area is presented in the Introduction to the 2007 Guidelines (APA, 2007). A notable precursor to the current Guidelines, which provided direction for the first wave of nonsexist and feminist psychologists, was the "Principles Concerning the Counseling and Psychotherapy of Women" (APA, 1979; Fitzgerald & Nutt, 1986). The Principles encouraged psychologists to

- become aware of their values, attitudes, and socialization and their implications for working with women;

- gain knowledge of the unique concerns and issues of women and approaches designed to support women's potential;
- work to eliminate oppression, power abuses, and gendered interpersonal violence; and
- establish therapeutic relationships and use communication skills and interventions that facilitate shared responsibility and power, support growth, recognize women as full adults, and transcend gender role restrictions.

Although the 1979 Principles informed gender-fair practice, just 7 years after their publication, Fitzgerald and Nutt (1986) noted the challenges of being attentive to diversities among and between women, stating:

> The theories that are only now being constructed about female psychology are often, ironically, as irrelevant to the description and explanation of the experience and behavior of black, Chicano, poor, elderly, and gay women as were the androcentric formulations of mainstream psychology to the behavior of white, middle-class women a decade ago. (p. 189)

During the decades following the publication of the Principles, problems associated with a "White woman as normative" approach were discussed widely (e.g., Yoder & Kahn, 1993), and 21st-century psychologists are increasingly cognizant of the complex, diverse, and intricate variety of life experiences that result from intersections between gender and social identities such as race/ethnicity, sexual orientation, disability, and numerous other social categories. Whereas during the 1980s, few publications focused on the intersection of identities, a recent computerized search of materials on intersectionality that had been published from 2005 to 2010 uncovered an average of 266 items per year (Fischer & DeBord, 2012). Also evident is growing knowledge of the varieties of oppression, bias, and privilege in 21st-century life. Although research studies and reviews conclude that blatant forms of individual prejudice and bias have decreased since the 20th-century civil rights movements (Enns, 2012), researchers have also concluded that although more difficult to recognize and more easily denied, complex subtle and insidious biases such as stereotype threat, ambivalent forms of sexism/racism, and micro-aggressions contribute to a variety of problems such as performance deficits, lowered confidence, and self-questioning (e.g., Rudman & Glick, 2008).

Emphasis on intersectionality has also contributed to the recognition that multiple forms of discrimination or oppression may not only be multiplicative, but may also be fused, resulting in hybrid "isms," such as gendered racism. For example, a study of White and African American women firefighters revealed that whereas White women were more likely to experience overprotection and paternalism that are consistent with stereotypes of fragility, African American women were more likely to be treated as "beasts of burden" who were expected to carry heavy loads (Yoder & Berendsen, 2001, p. 32). Although knowledge of intersectionality can contribute to enhanced knowledge and respect for the life experiences of individuals, Purdie-Vaughns and Eibach (2008) proposed that persons with multiple subordinate group identities often experience "intersectional invisibility" (p. 377). Persons with multiple social identities may not fit prototypical exemplars or cultural schemas associated with specific identity groups (e.g., Asian American, African American), and thus, their unique concerns may become invisible to the beholder. A biracial Latina college student, for example, may present a Caucasian middle class appearance, and yet be negotiating identities as a Black, a Latina, a woman, and a former child of poverty.

Whereas much of the aforementioned scholarship comes from the United States and a Western perspective, there is also a growing global literature that discusses the complexities of addressing women's mental health, assessment, and practice from international, cross-cultural, and cross-national perspectives. These global perspectives, too, increasingly emphasize an approach that analyzes the layers of social identity, social location, and social intersection in the lives and experiences of diverse groups of women (Rice & Russo, 2010).

As part of this introductory chapter, we wish to acknowledge some of the many psychologists who have contributed to inclusive psychological practice with women. For example, Laura Brown (1994) spoke of the importance of a holistic perspective and criticized approaches that "would require someone to choose which aspect of her identity is the one to be liberated while others lie silenced, unattended to, or rendered marginal" (p. 69). Her biopsychosocial approach has effectively integrated themes related to trauma, cultural competence, and multiple social identities (Brown, 2008, 2010). Ellyn Kaschak (1992), long-standing editor of the journal *Women and Therapy*, has contributed a contextual approach that highlights aspects that range from the physical to the sociocultural dimensions of women's lives, including transnational themes (e.g., Norsworthy & Kaschak, 2011). Lillian Comas-Díaz's (1994, 2000) ethnocultural approach emphasizes the need to integrate all aspects of diversity in the service of transformative healing, and Oliva Espín (1994, 1999, 2013) has addressed therapeutic issues related to intersecting themes associated with immigration, sexual orientation, ethnicity, language, and social class. In related work, Jean Chin (2000) challenged assumptions embedded in European American psychology and expanded our views of cultural competence. Beverly Greene (2000, 2010) has advanced our understanding of psychology practice by exploring the interplay of institutionalized heterosexism, racism, and sexism as well as interactions among multiple minority group statuses. Judith Worell and Pamela Remer (2003) have also explored multiple identities, privileges, and oppressions of women and integrated them within an empowerment model.

Each of the persons identified above, as well as many others who are not identified in this section, have contributed to knowledge of the complexity of women's concerns and their diverse identities (see Barrett et al., 2005, and Porter, 2005, for more detail). The brief illustrations of intersectional realities outlined in this chapter underline the importance of implementing complexity paradigms in psychological practice with women. Chapter 2 and later sections of this book discuss approaches to assessment and social identity analysis that are likely to enhance intersectional knowledge and contribute to optimal interventions.

All the groundbreaking and sustained theoretical, research, practice, and social justice efforts of multicultural and feminist psychologists during the past 40 years have increased the likelihood that women will encounter positive experiences as they seek the services of psychologists. Despite this progress, the need for guidelines remain important for a variety of reasons, including understanding and addressing (a) contemporary biases in diagnosis, treatment, and prognoses for women; (b) the impact of trauma, abuse, and related stressors in women's lives; and (c) the diversities among women that require cultural sensitivity, knowledge, and practice skills for addressing their varied concerns and realities (APA, 2007). Furthermore, many contemporary social forces also contribute to the challenges women face in their daily lives, such as living with the day-to-day realities of terrorism and war, encountering media influences that convey cultural stereotypes, and facing increasingly complex choices and issues related to the biopsychosocial aspects of women's reproductive lives.

THE GUIDELINES: DEVELOPMENT AND OVERVIEW

The 26-member task force that crafted the statements and literature review for the "Guidelines for Psychological Practice With Girls and Women" was highly aware of the issues discussed in the previous section, and members were particularly cognizant of needing to create guidelines that were multicultural, feminist, and attentive to multiple intersecting identities. Consistent with their multifaceted and diverse identities and life experiences, members of the task force held differing perspectives about how to frame and approach guidelines development and the integration of multicultural and feminist approaches. Some members had experienced feminism as a major form of personal consciousness-raising and used their feminist understandings to enrich and expand their understanding of the complexities and diversity of women's rich social identities and multicultural experiences. Other task force members, especially women of color, had often experienced and understood oppression and abuses of power through the lens of race/ethnicity. For these members, multiculturalism was the central reference point and also encompassed a commitment to understanding diverse gender cultures. In this case, culture provided an overarching framework, and inclusive and multicultural feminisms provided a vehicle and methodology for generating social change and equality. Following substantial discussion, task force members concluded that the diverse positionalities and perspectives of participants were valuable assets to the work of crafting guidelines, and could be used to inform, enrich, and test the work of the task force at all levels. An initial set of 11 statements emerged at the end of an intensive working weekend. Orienting statements were crafted, discussed, and refined in small groups, larger group plenary sessions, and process-oriented sessions designed to ensure that the diverse perspectives of task force members were honored in the basic structure that emerged.

The 11 Guidelines are organized into three broad categories: (a) diversity, social context, and power; (b) professional responsibility; and (c) practice applications. The Guidelines reflect 21st-century understandings and expand on previous products (e.g., the 1979 Principles) in a variety of ways. First, these Guidelines emphasize the diversity among girls and women and interactions among multiple social identities such as gender, race/ethnicity, sexual orientation, religion, disability, and social class. Embedded in the Guidelines is the assumption that the impact, importance, and salience of specific social identities (e.g., class, gender) can vary over time, circumstance, and within and between girls and women. There is no singular category of "woman." The privilege that some women and girls experience due to White or middle class status or heterosexual identity is acknowledged within the document, as is the higher likelihood of experiencing oppression if one is a person of color. Gender-related oppression is not understood as an either-or experience. Depending on her mix of identities, a woman may experience privilege in some contexts and bias, prejudice, or oppression in others. This understanding requires substantial knowledge of the specific life experiences, perceptions, values, and contexts of a person.

A second feature of the Guidelines is their emphasis on documenting power differences in society and highlighting ecological perspectives as well as social change, justice, and activism. Implementing gender-neutral or gender-fair practices with individual clients, which was an emphasis in previous documents, is not sufficient for eradicating enduring problems and barriers such as interpersonal violence, classism, racism, heterosexism, and other biases and oppressions. Psychologists are encouraged to "acquaint themselves with and utilize mental health, education, and community resources for girls and women" (APA, 2007, p. 968, Guideline 10) and to "understand and work to change institutional and systemic bias" (APA, 2007, p. 969). The Guidelines are built on the assumption that gender and intersecting social identities are socially constructed and influenced by power structures that place constraints or offer opportunities with regard to "doing" or enacting gender in interactions with many other social identities associated with higher and lower levels of social and personal power.

Third, assessment and diagnosis of problems as well as strengths and resilience of women and girls receive explicit attention. In addition to enumerating the many systems and contexts in which bias and discrimination occur (see Guideline 3), the Guidelines also articulate a "positive" feminist psychology that addresses the strengths, resources, creativity, and resilience of women and girls. A biopsychosocial, ecological framework is prioritized, and the intrapsychic framework of the *Diagnostic and Statistical Manual of Mental Disorders* (5th ed.; American Psychiatric Association, 2013) is seen as one of many potential frameworks that contribute to conceptualizing life difficulties.

It should be noted here that the term *guidelines* refers to:

> statements that suggest or recommend specific professional behavior, endeavors, or conduct for psychologists. Guidelines differ from standards in that standards are mandatory and may be accompanied by enforcement mechanisms. Thus, guidelines are *aspirational* in intent. They are intended to facilitate the continued systematic development of the profession and to help assure a high level of professional practice by psychologists. (APA, 2002, p. 1048)

A list of the 11 Guidelines follows.

Diversity, Social Context, and Power

Guideline 1: Psychologists strive to be aware of the effects of socialization, stereotyping, and unique life events on the development of girls and women across diverse cultural groups.

Guideline 2: Psychologists are encouraged to recognize and utilize information about oppression, privilege, and identity development as they may affect girls and women.

Guideline 3: Psychologists strive to understand the impact of bias and discrimination upon the physical and mental health of those with whom they work.

Professional Responsibility

Guideline 4: Psychologists strive to use gender and culturally sensitive, affirming practices in providing services to girls and women.

Guideline 5: Psychologists are encouraged to recognize how their socialization, attitudes, and knowledge about gender may affect their practice with girls and women.

Guideline 6: Psychologists are encouraged to employ interventions and approaches that have been found to be effective in the treatment of issues of concern to girls and women.

Guideline 7: Psychologists strive to foster therapeutic relationships and practices that promote initiative, empowerment, and expanded alternatives and choices for girls and women.

Guideline 8: Psychologists strive to provide appropriate, unbiased assessments and diagnoses in their work with women and girls.

Guideline 9: Psychologists strive to consider the problems of girls and women in their sociopolitical context.

Guideline 10: Psychologists strive to acquaint themselves with and utilize relevant mental health, education, and community resources for girls and women.

Guideline 11: Psychologists are encouraged to understand and work to change institutional and systemic bias that may impact girls and women.

More detail and representative statements relevant to each of the Guidelines are included in Appendix 1.1. We encourage readers to gain a more complete understanding of the Guidelines by reading the full text, which is published in *American Psychologist* (APA, 2007) and is available in pdf format on the website of the American Psychological Association (see http://www. apa.org/practice/guidelines/girls-and-women.pdf). A variety of other APA guidelines emphasize the importance infusing diversity in all facets of psychological practice. In keeping with the intersectional approach of this book, we encourage psychologists to become familiar with these Guidelines, which include the "Guidelines for Multicultural, Training, Research, Practice, and Organizational Change for Psychologists" (APA, 2003), "Guidelines for Psychological Practice With Lesbian, Gay, and Bisexual Clients" (APA, 2012b), "Guidelines for Psychological Practice With Older Adults" (APA, 2004a), and "Guidelines for Assessment of and Intervention With Persons With Disabilities"(APA, 2012a).

CONTENTS OF THIS VOLUME

The Guidelines are intended to provide guidance to psychologists in a broad array of practice areas, including clinical and counseling practice, teaching and pedagogy, social policy and advocacy activities, consultation, leadership and administration, research and scholarly writing, and other relevant activities in which psychologists engage on behalf of women and girls. The primary purpose of this volume, however, is to discuss the relevance of the Guidelines to counseling and psychotherapy practice with diverse groups of women and to expand the knowledge base relevant to these groups of women. More specifically, the authors consider the diversities among women within social categories related to ethnicity and race, national identity, sexual orientation, and disability. They emphasize the roles that cultural values, power, privilege, and inequality play in the lives of women. In addition, the authors discuss the specific and unique issues faced by women within the identity category; the strengths and resilience of these women; and intersections among multiple identities such as gender, ethnicity and race, sexual orientation, and other social categories. The range of social identities highlighted in this volume's chapters is not comprehensive, but rather, illustrates the type of thinking and practice that supports optimal psychological practice that attends to women's diversities and intersections among their multiple social identities. We are hopeful that future work will continue to build on themes introduced in this book and extend the scholarship of this volume's authors.

Most chapters contain background and literature reviews that focus on the three domains of (a) diversity, social context, and power (Guidelines 1–3); (b) professional responsibility and practice applications (Guidelines 4–9); and (c) community resources and social activism (Guidelines 10–11). A case example or two is included in each chapter. Case studies typically emphasize intersectional themes and complexities associated with multiple identities and focus on the application of the Guidelines to the case scenario.

In Chapter 2, "Working With Diverse Women: Tools for Assessment and Conceptualization," the editors present various conceptual formulations and assessment tools that can generally be used by readers and clinicians interested in applying the Guidelines and in exploring and addressing social intersectionality in their practice. The "Diversity, Social Context, and Power" section of the Guidelines speaks to the importance of centralizing women's diversity and emphasizing the ecological contexts of women's lives. This chapter builds on these themes by providing information about methods that support individualized assessment of the multiple and intersecting social identities of clients. It discusses the limitations of traditional diagnosis and provides practical tools for assessing social identities and the related oppressions and privileges experienced by women, gathering information about clients' strengths and resilience and reframing problems as coping efforts. The importance of psychologist self-awareness is also emphasized.

The succeeding Chapters 3 through 9 present in-depth discussions and analyses of the relevant research, conceptual, and practice issues, and case studies related to applying the Guidelines to diverse groups of women, namely, Black/African descent; Latina; Asian Pacific; East Asian; indigenous women; lesbian, bisexual, and transgender women; and women with disabilities. Each chapter ends with a case study or two that gives the reader practical applications of how these issues play out in counseling and psychotherapy and how clinicians can address the complexities of social location and social intersectionality.

Women of Black/African Descent

In Chapter 3, "Women and Girls of Black/African Descent," Wendi S. Williams presents an insightful exploration of how the life experiences of Black/African descent women and girls are influenced by the intersections of race, ethnicity, class, and gender (Guidelines 1 and 2). She specifically focuses on the process of identity development and mental health, but also discusses the multiple stresses these women face in terms of multiple roles, role confusion, and the often conflicting messages and expectations imposed by traditional gender role expectations of Black women and girls. Williams documents how the issue of identity for Black/African women and girls is often very challenging. Our culture and society disparage the image of femaleness in the form of a Black body, yet African/Black descent women are expected to develop positive, healthy racial and gender ideas about themselves while also conforming to the so-called politics of respectability. Black/African girls may adapt by adopting androgynous attitudes and behaviors that are protective both physically and psychologically. They often enact a kind of "bi-genderism," a form of double consciousness that allows them to gain inclusion and meet complicated expectations in both their gendered worlds and the Black/African American community.

In discussing practice issues, Williams presents several culturally relevant and gender-appropriate practices for Black/African women that emphasize empowerment and resilience (Guidelines 3, 4, 6, 7, and 9). She concludes her chapter with a case study that integrates the use of community-based and alternative resources (Guidelines 10 and 11) and suggests some social activism practices and advocacy to address and change systemic bias and promote institutional change.

Latinas

Latinas now comprise 15% of all women in the United States (U.S. Census Bureau, 2010), making them the largest female ethnic group. However, Latinas represent a broad variety of racial, ethnic, and national origins, and psychologists and practitioners need to appreciate the diversity of Latinas' intersecting identities (Guideline 2) and the unique experiences of gender socialization within the Latina/o culture (Guideline 1). In Chapter 4, Dianna Marisol González, Carrie L. Castañeda-Sound, and Rachel L. Navarro make use of the concept of *borderlands* to explain how Latinas cope with the ambiguity and contradictions inherent in holding multiple social identities and being able to do so without conflict or distress (Anzaldúa, 1987). In the borderlands, Latinas strive to make sense of their intersecting identities, ones that may be associated with privilege and honor (e.g., Whiteness, upper social class, able-bodied, heterosexual attraction) and those that may be associated with bias and oppression (e.g., gender, indigenous descent, same-gender attraction, working class, non–able-bodied).

Traditional views of Latina/o patriarchal culture have assigned positions of power and privilege to Latinos and positions of subordination to Latinas. *Marianismo* is a set of norms that guides subordinate and self-sacrificing female gender role behavior, but also may incorporate positive attributes of the Virgin Mary, namely, assertiveness, courage, and leadership (Guzmán, 2011). The authors note that Latinas' traditional gender roles often tie them closely to their families. These close ties may promote the retention of the Spanish language and propel Latinas into the role of language broker/interpreter for their families at a greater rate than their male peers. Language brokering is also positively related to biculturalism or *cultural frame-switching*, which can be another protective factor for Latinas (Schwartz & Unger, 2010). Cultural adaptation in therapy with Latinas might include conducting the treatment in Spanish. Monolingual, bilingual, and multilingual clients may have complicated presentations of linguistic fluency and literacy.

An informative case study concludes the chapter. Comprehensive assessment and analysis reveals that the young Latina has also been socialized through a framework of *marianismo*. The additive effect of the stressors associated with intersecting bicultural and biracial identities has made this borderland experience particularly distressing for her. Culturally sensitive assessment and interventions for working with her are discussed, which capitalize on skills fostered by experiencing duality and multiplicity.

Lesbian, Bisexual, and Transgender Women

Chapter 5 focuses on issues and considerations in applying the Guidelines to lesbian, bisexual, and transgender women. Sexual minority women face unique challenges that go beyond the marginalization they might face in being women, and mental health professionals are not always prepared to work with them. This group can be called a "hidden minority," for we are all expected by our culture to be heterosexual, and there is the mandate to portray "compulsory heterosexuality" (Fassinger, 1991). Consistent with Guideline 1, then, it is important to assess the client's status early in the therapeutic process, entering every clinical situation with an open mind regarding the client's sexual orientation and gender identity rather than assuming heterosexuality status unless and until the client reveals something different (Matthews, 2007).

In Chapter 5, Connie R. Matthews presents an informative discussion of the various multiple components of identity related to sex and gender, including biological sex, gender identity, gender role, gender expression, gender orientation, and gender behavior. These aspects of identity may or may not be consistent with each other within any given individual. Thus, consistent with Guideline 2, it is vital that therapists have a working knowledge of lesbian, bisexual, and transgender identity development. Lesbian identity development is generally more complicated than most would assume and is a part of a fluid and evolving process as one gives up a privileged identity for a more marginalized one. A lot of stress may occur in the process, including both physical and mental problems (Cochran, Sullivan, & Mays, 2003). Furthermore, for most sexual minority women, minority stress related to sexual orientation or gender identity might represent only part of the overall minority stress they experience. In the case study for this chapter the therapist has to deal effectively with the complexities of multiple minority identities for the bisexual client and her lesbian partner. The case offers helpful insights on how to deal with intimate partner abuse, parenting issues in a lesbian/bisexual relationship, isolation stress associated with one partner "out" and the other closeted, and dealing with the consequences of internalized homophobia.

Affirmative practice with lesbian, bisexual, and transgender women may also pose challenges for some psychologists whose own cultural background and traditions promote different perspectives on sexual identity and gender identity. Self-awareness about one's own deep-seated attitudes must involve serious self-examination that goes beyond general proclamations of being unbiased or believing that any nonheterosexual orientation is morally wrong. Referral to another therapist is not intended to be a substitute for gaining the competence necessary to work with diverse clients, including those whose value systems might differ from the psychologist's. Another good option, which may be even more appropriate, is to work collaboratively with local resources. It is also recommended that, when possible, psychologists apply Guideline 11, advocating for social justice at both the individual and systems levels.

Asian–Pacific Islander American Women

In Chapter 6, Phi Loan Le and Khanh T. Dinh discuss the intersection of gender and ethnicity and the complexities of practice with Asian-Pacific Islander American women. Although they are generally classified as a single group due to common geographical origins in Asia, like Latina women, Asian–Pacific Islander American women actually represent very diverse historical, cultural, and sociopolitical experiences. Furthermore, like Latinas and other minorities, there are, in addition, distinct multiple and intersecting identities that encompass other variables such as ethnicity, sexual orientation, religion, and socioeconomic status. Le and Dinh note that the diverse experiences of these women cannot be captured in one chapter. As a beginning step, however, they explore some relevant issues for Asian-Pacific Islander American women in general and use case studies to demonstrate some essential considerations necessary for clinicians working with this group.

Because of their cultural emphasis on education, filial obedience, and hard work, Asians are mythologized as protected from conflicts, difficulties, and discrimination. Asian–Pacific Islander American women have to confront not only harmful stereotypes from Western culture but also gender oppression from traditional Asian cultures that tend to emphasize Confucian patriarchal influences and the valuing of gendered virtues (True, 1997). Asian–Pacific Islander women living in American culture may experience shifting gender norms that may act to embolden them to defy traditional cultural expectations and to become more individually assertive and outspoken, but likely not without some personal cost and stress as they negotiate what we call in this book "intersecting identities."

Severe conflict engendered from living with competing cultural expectations can be addressed in counseling and therapy. Asian–Pacific Islander American women, however, underutilize mental health treatment, despite the fact that Asian American women between the ages of 15 and 24 and over 65 have the highest suicide rates of all racial/ethnic groups (National Center for Health Statistics, 2011). Cultural norms, mistrust of Western values and approaches, and historical experiences of oppression by Euro Americans may also act to suppress help-seeking behavior outside the family for Asian Americans and Asian–Pacific Islander Americans.

The authors emphasize that psychological practice grounded in Western worldviews and concepts increases the challenge of applying culturally sensitive approaches (Guideline 4). They offer several approaches that are sensitive to this dilemma including relational-cultural theory (Jordan, 2010) and adaptations of mindfulness and acceptance psychotherapies that offer treatment approaches more consistent with Asian American cultural values (Hall, Hong, Zane, & Meyer, 2011). Le and Dinh present two case studies in their chapter. The first highlights the themes and issues related to the sections on diversity and social context and professional responsibility and practice. The second beautifully illustrates the centrality of the therapeutic relationship in the gender and cultural affirming approach of a feminist psychologist working with a Vietnamese female client. The detailed descriptions present an opportunity to bring to life and demonstrate the integration of the Guidelines in providing culturally nuanced woman-oriented therapy.

Women With Disabilities

Chapter 7, by Martha E. Banks, Kathleen S. Brown, Linda R. Mona, and Rosalie J. Ackerman, provides an overview of APA's (2007) "Guidelines for Psychological Practice With Girls and Women" as supplemented by the APA's (2012a) "Guidelines for Assessment of and Intervention With Persons With Disabilities" and discusses how the Guidelines apply to affirmative practice with women and girls with disabilities.

One important contribution of this chapter is the addressing of the very complex intersectionality of disability and color. Women of color with disabilities must cope not only with challenges directly related to their particular disabilities, but also with social, economic, and cultural factors that can impede their healthy being and welfare. As one example, lower wages and higher unemployment rates found among people with disabilities are barriers to affordable, quality health care. Thus, part of practice with women with disabilities (WWD) involves understanding the experience of disability in the context of discrimination. This chapter is based on a *social model of disability* that asserts that socioeconomic effects of disability are experienced by persons with disabilities when they are disabled by a lack of resources to meet their needs. This paradigm changes the conceptualization of disability from a solely medical model to a socioecological approach that emphasizes the context(s) in which disablement occurs (Pledger, 2003).

Lack of basic research, limited inclusion of WWD in clinical trials, and wide variations in manifestations of disability make it difficult to determine which treatments are most effective for WWD (Banks, 2012). Furthermore, psychologists are generally unprepared to practice with people with disabilities and may not engage in examination of their own biases toward persons with disabilities. It is important not to minimize an invisible or relatively unknown disability and to be aware that some clients with disabilities have practiced "passing" as able as a way of coping with society's expectations and discrimination. Passing is often discussed with regard to racism and heterosexism, but applies also to WWD.

The authors conclude that appreciating the responses of WWD to societal stigma, pressures, and discrimination, while attending to the strengths and weaknesses of individual WWD, is the bedrock of affirmative psychological practice with WWD. The chapter ends with a fascinating, detailed case study of a woman with a traumatic brain injury and posttraumatic stress disorder who struggled with adapting to her disability and the conflicting responses of her partner and family. Her comprehensive and multifaceted treatment incorporated many of the issues and considerations presented in this chapter and offers clinicians a rare insight into the issues and challenges of practice with WWD.

Native Women

Chapter 8, "Psychological Practice With Native Women," is written by Wendy M. K. Peters, Kee J. E. Straits, and Pilar E. Gauthier, Native women who bring "organic, bottom-up lived experiences to bear on psychological practice." Their collaborative endeavor, they believe, is indicative of the wisdom and insights that can be found through interactions and intersections of diverse Native experiences. They emphasize that the lives of most Native women and girls are bound to particular historical realities and fundamental cultural constructs such as collective, communal forms of society and *monism*, the philosophy that all things are interconnected and all life is sacred. The forced assimilation of Native peoples completely disregarded the long-standing social and cultural structures that Native peoples had established over many generations and even millennia (Campbell & Evans-Campbell, 2011). This deep cultural displacement has had important consequences for Native women who in most instances had enjoyed relatively equal status with males in their tribes and nations before colonization. Eurocentric views of proper gender roles imposed white male dominance, patriarchy, and disruption of the Native communal family systems. Forced separation from their children in boarding schools left deep "soul wounds" among Native women (Duran, 2006).

Historical trauma or intergenerational trauma (HT/IT) is a key theme in understanding the Native experience as an outcome of societal oppression and socialization. This perspective is consistent with the emphasis of Guidelines 2 and 3, which recognize how discrimination and oppression affect women and girls. The authors point out that HT/IT can also pervade whole communities, even entire societies, and will persist over generations until it is acknowledged and resolved in an appropriate manner (Brave Heart, 2003).

Two very interesting case studies in this chapter demonstrate how many of the Guidelines apply to Native life ways, as well as how they might not be applicable when Native culture and values are in conflict with the systems, guidelines, and ethical codes under which professional practice and responsibilities have originated. The first case underscores the importance of appreciating that more traditional Native clients are usually highly communal and value relationships, especially those of family, over their own individualism. In counseling or therapy, this would mean encountering much more than an individual client and possibly the need to work with a complex family system and its multiple members.

The second case pointedly illustrates the barriers, lack of accessibility, and inappropriateness of mental health care for Native Americans, such as the fact that the client may be given only a pharmacological option for treatment rather than a psychotherapeutic one. The authors conclude by urging clinicians to foster the self-empowerment of Native women by honoring their sovereignty and to appreciate a worldview that may be very different from their own.

Transnational Practice

In Chapter 9, "Transnational Psychological Practice With Women: Perspectives From East Asia and Japan," Sayaka Machizawa and Carolyn Zerbe Enns explore the applicability of the Guidelines to global or international contexts. They also discuss the importance and features of egalitarian collaboration between psychologists from different countries and speak about the value of these partnerships for articulating culture-specific knowledge and research about the lives and experiences of women.

As noted earlier in this chapter, the Guidelines were originally intended to address psychological practice with diverse women, including immigrant women, who reside within North America. In an effort to extend the Guidelines, a 2008 working group that was co-led by Enns and Machizawa worked toward integrating the Guidelines with the International Committee for Women position paper (Rice & Ballou, 2002) and the related APA (2004b) resolution on gender and cultural awareness. The working group identified these documents as compatible and complementary, and also concluded that the general themes articulated in the Guidelines statements are useful for supporting ethical and competent transnational psychological practice. They also concluded, however, that some concepts, such as empowerment, identity development, and assertiveness, need to be framed in more culture-specific ways, often in a manner that is more consistent with collective cultural patterns. In addition, knowledge specific to the lives of women in transnational contexts needs to be explored and disseminated more fully. These knowledge areas include cultural values, philosophical and religious beliefs, social and family systems, education and work, government and legal systems, feminist and other social justice movements, and colonialism and other forms of discrimination.

This chapter also provides background about woman-centered and feminist practice in Japan and indigenous psychotherapies that can be used to enrich psychological practice with women. The case study of a Japanese middle-aged woman who followed her businessman husband to the United States describes dilemmas that reflect her cultural background and illustrates the ways in which she experienced greater confidence and empowerment through her work with a therapist with a Japanese background. A second case study features a young woman who returned to her home country of Japan after completing her undergraduate college education in the United States. In this scenario, the therapist assists the client as she integrates her years in North America with her cultural values and life options as an adult Japanese woman.

Inclusive Psychological Practice

The final chapter, "Inclusive and Affirmative Psychological Practice: Unifying Themes," by the volume editors, brings all the themes in the book together. In this chapter, we attempt to review and integrate the major issues, themes, and concepts discussed throughout the book and speak to future directions that will further enhance psychological practice with women. Major themes that merit exploration include paradoxes, contrasts, and conflicts that arise when women of diverse racial/ethnic/nation groups have different perspectives and traditions. Intersectionality, social location, multiple and intersecting identities, and a complexity paradigm receive emphasis and discussion throughout the book. It is the editors' hope that discussion and clinical illustration of these complex issues will help psychologists engage in affirmative practice with diverse groups of women and girls.

CONCLUDING THOUGHTS

The topics addressed in this chapter represent a brief introduction to the rich material that follows in the next nine chapters. The contents of these chapters are based on contemporary scholarship emerging from theory, research, and practice relevant to the lives of diverse groups of women. As the volume editors, we hope that readers find that the information in this book furthers their understanding of diversity and intersectionality as they relate to all aspects of psychological practice with women and girls, especially in the areas of training, psychotherapy, and advocacy. Likewise, we hope that readers are challenged to re-analyze and expand their own perspectives about the complex gender issues and life concerns presented in this volume, and that they use this intersectional framework to guide their current and future practice. We look forward to future expansion of the topics and complex concerns that are introduced in these chapters.

APPENDIX 1.1: GUIDELINES FOR PSYCHOLOGICAL PRACTICE WITH GIRLS AND WOMEN

Section One: Diversity, Social Context, and Power

Guideline 1: Psychologists strive to be aware of the effects of socialization, stereotyping, and unique life events on the development of girls and women across diverse cultural groups.

Excerpt from the text: "Each girl and woman is socialized within a unique cultural milieu and set of visible and invisible social group memberships that may include, but are not limited to, gender, race/ethnicity, class, age, sexual orientation, SES, spiritual orientation, nationality, physical or cognitive ability, and body size. The multiple group memberships of girls and women intersect and influence each other and are enacted within the family and cultural institutions (schools, religion), through peer influences, and within media."

Guideline 2: Psychologists are encouraged to recognize and utilize information about oppression, privilege, and identity development as they may affect girls and women.

Excerpt from the text: "Because girls and women have multiple personal and social group memberships, they may simultaneously belong to both socially privileged and disempowered groups (e.g., White, heterosexual, lower SES, and female) or to multiple socially oppressed groups (e.g., African American, female, lesbian, disabled). . . . Saliency of a particular identity is determined by several factors, including socialization experiences and the amount of social support received in a particular situation. . . . Psychologists are encouraged to identify the social group memberships of girls and women, the extent to which they accept or deny these memberships, their experiences of oppression and/or privilege within the context of these memberships, and their abilities to resist confining or oppressive messages."

Guideline 3: Psychologists strive to understand the impact of bias and discrimination on the physical and mental health of those with whom they work.

Excerpt from the text: "Bias and discrimination are embedded in and driven by organizational, institutional, and social structures. These dynamics legitimize and foster inequities, influence personal relationships, and affect the perception and treatment of a person's mental and behavioral

---

Excerpts are from "Guidelines for Psychological Practice With Girls and Women," by the American Psychological Association, 2007, *American Psychologist, 62*, pp. 949–979. Copyright 2007 by the American Psychological Association.

problems." The text related to this guideline elaborates further on the impact of the following systems: health, education, the workplace, religious institutions, legal systems, family and couple systems, and research methods and language.

Section Two: Professional Responsibility

Guideline 4: Psychologists strive to use gender sensitive and culturally sensitive, affirming practices in providing services to girls and women.

Excerpt from the text: "Psychologists strive to be knowledgeable about the theoretical and empirical support for the assessment, treatment, research, consultation, teaching, and supervision practices they use with girls and women. Psychologists are encouraged to be aware of assumptions in theory, research, and practice that are noninclusive and to use theories and practices that pay equal attention to relational and autonomous qualities. . . . They are urged to show caution when using methods that have not been developed with the specific needs of diverse groups of girls and women in mind."

Guideline 5: Psychologists are encouraged to recognize how their socialization, attitudes, and knowledge about gender may affect their practice with girls and women.

Excerpt from the text: "The practice of psychologists is likely to be influenced by their culture, values, biases, socialization, and experiences of privilege and oppression or disempowerment. Limited self-knowledge may contribute to subtle belief systems that can be potentially harmful to girls and women with diverse social identities. . . . Psychologists are encouraged to gain specialized education, training, and experience with issues particularly relevant to the experiences and problems of women and girls."

Section Three: Practice Applications

Guideline 6: Psychologists are encouraged to use interventions and approaches that have been found to be effective in the treatment of issues of concern to girls and women.

Excerpt from the text: "Psychologists are therefore encouraged to (a) implement interventions that encourage the development of protective factors, such as healthy relationships and body image, (b) reframe girls' and women's concerns from a coping and ecological perspective, and (c) emphasize a strength and empowerment perspective in psychotherapy treatment, research, advocacy, teaching, consultation, and supervision."

Guideline 7: Psychologists strive to foster therapeutic relationships and practices that promote initiative, empowerment, and expanded alternatives and choices for girls and women.

Excerpt from the text: "Cooperative mutuality and connection facilitate psychotherapy, supervision, teaching, and consultation. . . . Empowerment flourishes in an environment of safety, and this condition is protected by appropriate boundaries. . . . Psychologists are encouraged to make efforts to help women develop an improved sense of initiative, resilience, and personal power and to help them expand their nonstereotyped alternatives and choices."

Guideline 8: Psychologists strive to provide appropriate, unbiased assessments and diagnoses in their work with girls and women.

Excerpt from the text: "Psychologists, therefore, strive to make unbiased, appropriate assessments and diagnoses by considering . . . the following: developmental experiences, physical and psychological health, violence and other traumatic events, life history (including experiences of privilege and discrimination), social and kinship support systems, educational and work experiences, geographical and national affiliation influences, various multiple group memberships, and other relevant aspects related to the cultural context as it uniquely interacts with gender. Assessment tools, such as social, cultural, and gender-role identity analyses, may be especially useful. . . . Psychologists are also urged to show caution when using assessment procedures and tests developed in the United States in countries in which cultural differences and norms have not been considered."

Guideline 9: Psychologists strive to consider the problems of girls and women in their sociopolitical context.

Excerpt from the text: "To support the personal growth, independence, and empowerment of girls and women, psychologists strive to integrate cultural and contextual information into their conceptualizations and interventions. Such contextual factors include immigration, race, ethnicity, geography (e.g., rural or urban residence), sexual orientation, disability, SES, age, and other sociocultural influences."

Guideline 10: Psychologists strive to acquaint themselves with and utilize relevant mental health, education, and community resources for girls and women.

Excerpt from the text: "Psychologists strive to become knowledgeable about community resources and to consult others with expertise about community resources."

Guideline 11: Psychologists are encouraged to understand and work to change institutional and systemic bias that may impact girls and women.

Excerpt from the text: "Psychologists are encouraged to participate in prevention, education, and social policy as forms of psychological practice that improve the mental health and lives of women and girls . . . [and] to support their clients' contributions to positive microlevel and/or macrolevel actions that increase a sense of empowerment and influence."

REFERENCES

American Psychiatric Association. (2013). *Diagnostic and statistical manual of mental disorders* (5th ed.). Washington, DC: American Psychiatric Association Press.

American Psychological Association. (1975). Report of the Task Force on Sex Bias and Sex-Role Stereotyping in Psychotherapeutic Practice. *American Psychologist, 30*, 1169–1175. doi:10.1037/0003-066X.30.12.1169

American Psychological Association. (1979). Principles concerning the counseling and therapy of women. *The Counseling Psychologist, 8*, 21. doi:10.1177/001100007900800113

American Psychological Association. (2002). Criteria for practice guideline development and evaluation. *American Psychologist, 57*, 1048–1051. doi:10.1037/0003-066X.57.12.1048

American Psychological Association. (2003). Guidelines on multicultural education, training, research, practice, and organizational change for psychologists. *American Psychologist, 58*, 377–402. doi:10.1037/0003-066X.58.5.377

American Psychological Association. (2004a). Guidelines for psychological practice with older adults. *American Psychologist, 59*, 236–260. doi:10.1037/0003-066X.59.4.236

American Psychological Association. (2004b). *Resolution on cultural and gender awareness in international psychology*. Washington, DC: Author. Retrieved from http://www.apa.org/about/governance/council/policy/gender.aspx

American Psychological Association. (2007). Guidelines for psychological practice with girls and women. *American Psychologist, 62*, 949–979. doi:10.1037/0003-066X.62.9.949

American Psychological Association. (2012a). Guidelines for assessment of and intervention with persons with disabilities. *American Psychologist, 67*, 43–62. doi:10.1037/a0025892

American Psychological Association. (2012b). Guidelines for psychological practice with lesbian, gay, and bisexual clients. *American Psychologist, 67*, 10–42. doi:10.1037/a0024659

Anzaldúa, G. (1987). *Borderlands/la frontera: The new Mestiza*. San Francisco, CA: Spinsters/Aunt Lute Book Company.

Ballou, M., & Brown, L. S. (Eds.). (2002). *Rethinking mental health and disorder: Feminist perspectives*. New York, NY: Guilford Press.

Banks, M. E. (2012). Multiple minority identities and mental health: Social and research implications of diversity within and between groups. In R. Nettles & R. Balter (Eds.), *Multiple minority identities: Applications for practice, research, and training* (pp. 35–58). New York, NY: Springer.

Barrett, S. E., Chin, J. L., Comas-Diaz, L., Espín, O., Greene, B., & McGoldrick, M. (2005). Multicultural feminist therapy: Theory in context. *Women & Therapy, 28*(3–4), 27–61. doi:10.1300/J015v28n03_03

Becker, D. (2005). *The myth of empowerment: Women and the therapeutic culture in America*. New York: New York University Press.

Brave Heart, M. Y. H. (2003). The historical trauma response among natives and its relationship with substance abuse: A Lakota illustration. *Journal of Psychoactive Drugs, 35*, 7–13. doi:10.1080/02791072.2003.10399988

Brown, L. S. (1994). *Subversive dialogues: Theory in feminist therapy*. New York, NY: Basic Books.

Brown, L. S. (2008). *Cultural competence in trauma therapy: Beyond the flashback*. Washington, DC: American Psychological Association. doi:10.1037/11752-000

Brown, L. S. (2010). *Feminist therapy*. Washington, DC: American Psychological Association.

Campbell, C. D., & Evans-Campbell, T. (2011). Historical trauma and Native American child development and mental health: An overview. In M. C. Sarche, P. Spicer, P. Farrell, & H. E. Fitzgerald (Eds.), *American Indian and Alaska Native children and mental health: Development, context, prevention, and treatment* (pp. 1–26). Santa Barbara, CA: Praeger/ABC-CLIO.

Caplan, P. J., & Cosgrove, L. (Eds.). (2004). *Bias in psychiatric diagnosis*. Northvale, NJ: Jason Aronson.

Chesler, P. (1972). *Women and madness*. Garden City, NY: Doubleday.

Chin, J. L. (Ed.). (2000). *Relationships among Asian American women*. Washington, DC: American Psychological Association. doi:10.1037/10349-000

Cochran, S. D., Sullivan, J. G., & Mays, V. M. (2003). Prevalence of mental disorders, psychological distress, and mental health service use among lesbian, gay, and bisexual adults in the United States [Electronic version]. *Journal of Consulting and Clinical Psychology, 71*, 53–61. doi:10.1037/0022-006X.71.1.53

Cole, E. R. (2009). Intersectionality and research in psychology. *American Psychologist, 64*, 170–180. doi:10.1037/a0014564

Comas-Díaz, L. (1994). An integrative approach. In L. Comas-Díaz & B. Greene (Eds.), *Women of color: Integrating ethnic and gender identities in psychotherapy* (pp. 287–318). New York, NY: Guilford Press.

Comas-Díaz, L. (2000). An ethnopolitical approach to working with people of color. *American Psychologist, 55*, 1319–1325. doi:10.1037/0003-066X.55.11.1319

Crawford, M., & Marecek, J. (1989). Psychology reconstructs the female: 1969–1988. *Psychology of Women Quarterly, 13*, 147–165. doi:10.1111/j.1471-6402.1989.tb00993.x

Dill, B. T., & Zambrana, R. E. (2009). Critical thinking about inequality: An emerging lens. In B. T. Dill & R. E. Zambrana (Eds.), *Emerging intersections: Race, class, and gender in theory, policy, and practice* (pp. 1–21). New Brunswick, NJ: Rutgers University Press.

Duran, E. (2006). *Healing the soul wound: Counseling with American Indians and other native peoples*. New York, NY: Teachers College Press.

Enns, C. Z. (2004). *Feminist theories and feminist psychotherapies: Origins, themes, and diversity* (2nd ed.). Binghamton, NY: Haworth.

Enns, C. Z. (2012). Gender: Women—theories and research. In N. A. Fouad, J. E. Carter, & L. M. Subich (Eds.), *APA handbook of counseling psychology: Vol. 1. Theories, research, and methods* (pp. 397–422). Washington, DC: American Psychological Association.

Espín, O. (1994). Feminist approaches. In L. Comas-Díaz & B. Greene (Eds.), *Women of color: Integrating ethnic and gender identities in psychotherapy* (pp. 265–286). New York, NY: Guilford Press.

Espín, O. (1999). *Women crossing boundaries: A psychology of immigration and transformation of sexuality.* New York, NY: Routledge.

Espín, O. (2013). "Making love in English:" Language in psychotherapy with immigrant women. *Women & Therapy, 36,* 198–218. doi:10.1080/02703149.2013.797847

Fassinger, R. E. (1991). The hidden minority: Issues and challenges in working with lesbian women and gay men. *The Counseling Psychologist, 19,* 157–176. doi:10.1177/0011000091192003

Fischer, A. R., & DeBord, K. A. (2012). Critical questioning of social and feminist identity development literature: Themes, principles, and tools. In C. Z. Enns & E. N. Williams (Eds.), *Oxford handbook of feminist multicultural counseling psychology* (pp. 87–111). New York, NY: Oxford.

Fitzgerald, L. F., & Nutt, R. (1986). The Division 17 principles concerning the counseling/psychotherapy of women: Rationale and implementation. *The Counseling Psychologist, 14,* 180–216. doi:10.1177/0011000086141019

Gilligan, C. (1982). *In a different voice.* Cambridge, MA: Harvard University Press.

Gordon, C. N. Hall, Hong, J. J., Zane, N., & Meyer, O. L. (2011). Culturally competent treatments for Asian Americans: The relevance of mindfulness and acceptance-based psychotherapies. *Clinical Psychology: Science and Practice, 18,* 215–231. doi:10.1111/j.1468-2850.2011.01253.x

Greene, B. (2000). African American lesbian and bisexual women in feminist-psychodynamic psychotherapy: Surviving and thriving between a rock and a hard place. In L. Jackson & B. Greene (Eds.), *Psychotherapy with African American women: Innovations in psychodynamic perspectives and practice* (pp. 82–125). New York, NY: Guilford.

Greene, B. (2010). 2009 Carolyn Wood Sherif Award Address: Riding Trojan horses from symbolism to structural change: In feminist psychology, context matters. *Psychology of Women Quarterly, 34,* 443–457. doi:10.1111/j.1471-6402.2010.01594.x

Guzmán, C. E. (2011). *Toward a new conceptualization of marianismo: Validation of the Guzmán Marianismo Inventory.* (Unpublished dissertation). New Mexico State University: Las Cruces.

Jordan, J. (2010). *Relational-cultural therapy.* Washington, DC: American Psychological Association.

Josselson, R., & Harway, M. (Eds.). (2012). *Navigating multiple identities: Race, gender, culture, nationality, and roles.* New York, NY: Oxford University Press. doi:10.1093/acprof:oso/9780199732074.001.0001

Kaschak, E. (1992). *Engendered lives.* New York, NY: Basic Books.

Klonoff, E. A., Landrine, H., & Campbell, R. (2000). Sexist discrimination may account for well-known gender differences in psychiatric symptoms. *Psychology of Women Quarterly, 24,* 93–99. doi:10.1111/j.1471-6402.2000.tb01025.x

Martens, A., Johns, M., Greenberg, J., & Schimel, J. (2006). Combating stereotype threat: The effect of self-affirmation on women's intellectual performance. *Journal of Experimental Social Psychology, 42,* 236–243. doi:10.1016/j.jesp.2005.04.010

Matthews, C. R. (2007). Affirmative lesbian, gay, and bisexual counseling with all clients. In K. J. Bieschke, R. M. Perez, & K. A. DeBord (Eds.), *Handbook of counseling and psychotherapy with lesbian, gay, bisexual, and transgender clients* (2nd ed., pp. 201–219). Washington, DC: American Psychological Association. doi:10.1037/11482-008

National Center for Health Statistics. (2011). *Health, United States, 2011: With special feature on socioeconomic status and health.* Hyattsville, MD: Author.

Norsworthy, K. L., & Kaschak, E. (2011). Border crossings: Feminist activists and peace workers collaborating across cultures. *Women & Therapy, 34,* 211–222. doi:10.1080/02703149.2011.580661

Pledger, C. (2003). Discourse on disability and rehabilitation issues: Opportunities for psychology. *American Psychologist, 58,* 279–284. doi:10.1037/0003-066X.58.4.279

Porter, N. (2005). Location, location, location: Contributions of contemporary feminist theorists to therapy theory and practice. *Women & Therapy, 28,* 143–160. doi:10.1300/J015v28n03_07

Purdie-Vaughns, V., & Eibach, R. P. (2008). Intersectional invisibility: The distinctive advantages and disadvantages of multiple subordinate-group identities. *Sex Roles, 59,* 377–391. doi:10.1007/s11199-008-9424-4

Rawlings, E. I., & Carter, D. K. (1977). Feminist and nonsexist psychotherapy. In E. I. Rawlings & D. K. Carter (Eds.), *Psychotherapy for women* (pp. 49–76). Springfield, IL: Charles C. Thomas.

Reid, P. T. (2002). Multicultural psychology: Bringing together gender and ethnicity. *Cultural Diversity and Ethnic Minority Psychology, 8,* 103–114. doi:10.1037/1099-9809.8.2.103

Rice, J., & Ballou, M. (2002). *Cultural and gender awareness in international psychology.* Washington, DC: American Psychological Association, Division 52, International Psychology, International Committee for Women.

Rice, J. K., & Rice, D. G. (1973). Implications of the women's liberation movement for psychotherapy. *The American Journal of Psychiatry, 130,* 191–196.

Rice, J. K., & Russo, N. K. (2010). International perspectives on women and mental health. In M. Paludi (Ed.), *Handbook of feminism and women's rights worldwide, Vol. 2, Mental and physical health* (pp. 1–24). New York, NY: Praeger.

Rudman, L. A., & Glick, P. (2008). *The social psychology of gender: How power and intimacy shape gender relations*. New York, NY: Guilford Press.

Schwartz, S. J., & Unger, J. B. (2010). Biculturalism and context: What is biculturalism, and when is it adaptive? *Human Development, 53*, 26–32. doi: 10.1159/000268137

Shields, S. A. (2008). Gender: An intersectionality perspective. *Sex Roles, 59*, 301–311. doi:10.1007/s11199-008-9501-8

Silverstein, L. B. (2006). Integrating feminism and multiculturalism: Scientific fact or science fiction? *Professional Psychology: Research and Practice, 37*, 21–28. doi:10.1037/0735-7028.37.1.21

True, R. H. (1997). Asian American women. In E. Lee (Ed.), *Working with Asian Americans* (pp. 420–427). New York, NY: Guilford Press.

U.S. Census Bureau. (2010).Current Population Survey. Annual Social and Economic Supplement, 2010). Retrieved from http://www.census.gov/population/age/data/2010comp.html

Weisstein, N. (1968). *Kinder, kirche, kuche as scientific law: Psychology constructs the female*. Boston, MA: New England Free Press.

Weisstein, N. (1993). Psychology constructs the female; or the fantasy life of the male psychologist. *Feminism & Psychology, 3*, 195–210.

Worell, J., & Goodheart, C. R. (Eds.) (2006). *Handbook of girls' and women's psychological health: Gender and well-being across the lifespan*. New York, NY: Oxford.

Worell, J., & Remer, P. (2003). *Feminist perspectives in therapy: Empowering diverse women* (2nd ed.). New York, NY: Wiley.

Yoder, J. D., & Berendsen, L. L. (2001). "Outsider within" the firehouse: African American and White women firefighters. *Psychology of Women Quarterly, 25*, 27–36. doi:10.1111/1471-6402.00004

Yoder, J. D., & Kahn, A. S. (1993). Working toward an inclusive psychology of women. *American Psychologist, 48*, 846–850. doi:10.1037/0003-066X.48.7.846

2

WORKING WITH DIVERSE WOMEN: TOOLS FOR ASSESSMENT AND CONCEPTUALIZATION

CAROLYN ZERBE ENNS, JOY K. RICE, AND ROBERTA L. NUTT

Working effectively with clients with diverse and multiple identities is facilitated by attentiveness to the diversity of women throughout the psychotherapy process, beginning with the exploration of women's experiences and assessment. Guideline 8 of the "Guidelines for Psychological Practice With Girls and Women" (American Psychological Association [APA], 2007; hereinafter, the Guidelines), which are discussed in Chapter 1 of this volume, states that "psychologists strive to provide appropriate, unbiased assessments and diagnoses in their work with girls and women" (p. 967), and Guideline 9 indicates that "psychologists strive to consider the problems of girls and women in their sociopolitical context" (p. 968). In addition, optimal assessment practices are built on a foundation of self-awareness. Consistent with this reality, Guideline 5 encourages psychologists to "recognize how their socialization, attitudes, and knowledge about gender may affect their practice" (p. 965). Guideline 2 also encourages psychologists to consider how

http://dx.doi.org/10.1037/14460-002
Psychological Practice With Women: Guidelines, Diversity, Empowerment, C. Z. Enns, J. K. Rice, and R. L. Nutt (Editors)
Copyright © 2015 by the American Psychological Association. All rights reserved.

their self-perceptions and identities may influence their assessments and perceptions.

In this chapter, we discuss a variety of exploration and assessment tools and some applications that are useful for centralizing women's diversity. We describe a variety of open-ended assessment and conceptualization options that lend themselves to gathering information about multiple identities and intersections among these identities. The first of the three major sections of the Guidelines is titled "Diversity, Social Context, and Power" (p. 960). This emphasis on the ecological framework of the client and therapist permeates all aspects of assessment and the psychotherapy experience and is a central foundation for this chapter. Information gained from comprehensive information gathering becomes the basis for framing a client's concerns and choosing interventions. Such assessment also supports the mutual, collaborative understanding of a client's problems, goals, and plans, an approach recommended by Guideline 9. We also propose that as an aspect of preparing for their work with diverse women, psychologists will benefit from applying the chapter's tools to themselves to enhance understanding of their personal, social, and multiple identities. Because there has been much controversy in the appropriate application of tests, measurement tools, and diagnostic labels and procedures for women and girls (APA, 2007; DeBarona & Dutton, 1997), it is important to begin with a critical discussion of some of the challenges in this area that relate to gender and diversity issues.

ON THE CHALLENGES OF CONCEPTUALIZATION AND DIAGNOSIS

The introduction to the Guidelines identifies *bias* in diagnosis and treatment as a major reason why guidelines relevant to girls and women are necessary. Feminist practitioners have often conveyed concern about the adequacy of formal diagnosis (e.g., Rawlings & Carter, 1977; Ussher, 2011), noting that contemporary diagnostic practices can contribute to misdiagnosis, underdiagnosis, overdiagnosis, omission biases, and other biased conceptualizations. According to Ussher (2011), diagnostic labels may also contribute to medicalizing emotional distress, objectifying or distancing the therapist from the client's lived experience, framing the client's survival strategies (or symptoms) in negative terms, and deflecting the therapist's attention from the multiple social and contextual factors that trigger or exacerbate distress. One advantage of diagnosis and conceptualization based on the *Diagnostic and Statistical Manual of Mental Disorders* (DSM) of the American Psychiatric Association (5th ed.; APA, 2013) is its provision of a shared language for conveying information about individual symptoms of distress.

The *DSM*, however, is a not a neutral document and reflects the priorities of powerful institutional healthcare frameworks. For example, approximately 70% of *DSM–5* panel members were reported to have industry ties, typically to pharmaceutical industries (Cosgrove & Krimsky, 2012).

A variety of revisions to the recently published *DSM–5* have been controversial, prompting many members of APA to sign an open letter outlining their concerns. Among concerns about the *DSM–5* are changes to the definition of *mental disorder*, which appears to place greater emphasis on biological theory and less on sociocultural factors (Clay, 2012). The International *DSM–5* Response Committee, which was sponsored by the Society of Humanistic Psychology of the American Psychological Association (http://dsm5response.com), expressed concern about the reliability, validity, and safety of the *DSM–5*, and launched a petition addressing these concerns. The committee focused on the potential for the *DSM–5* to contribute to the mislabeling of distress, unnecessary or potentially harmful use of psychiatric medication in the treatment of clients, and diversion of mental health resources from those who have the greatest need for them.

A second activist group, Counselors for Social Justice (http://dxsummit. org), criticized diagnostic categories in the *DSM–5* for having inadequate empirical support and containing biases with regard to cultural and gender considerations. For example, this committee identified the gender-related diagnostic categories of premenstrual dysphoric disorder and sexual arousal/ interest disorder as potentially contributing to the pathologizing of women's normal experiences. In light of ongoing controversies, we encourage psychologists to become educated about these types of diagnostic concerns when making decisions about conceptual and diagnostic frameworks.

Diagnostic concerns are also being addressed at a global level. Existing classification systems (International Classification of Diseases [ICD]–10 and the *DSM*) have been found to not reflect fully how clinicians across the world think about the mental disorders they find in practice. In a World Health Organization (WHO) study of over 1,300 psychologists and psychiatrists from 64 countries, only moderate correlations between clinician perceptions and current "classification" diagnostic systems were found (Roberts et al., 2012). However, clinician classifications were highly stable across profession, language, and country income level when based on a dimensions approach. Three dimensions were found to be significant in how clinicians group mental and behavioral disorders: externalizing versus internalizing, developmental versus adult onset, and functional versus organic. Based on this approach of incorporating clinicians' intuitivity, the proposed ICD–11 is expected to enhance clinical utility (Roberts et al., 2012).

Psychologists seeking insurance reimbursement for their work with clients are typically expected to use *DSM*-based diagnostic categories and checklists of symptoms. Brown (2006) noted, however, that the feminist psychologist is also a "cultural outsider" (p. 19) who recognizes that a *DSM* diagnosis represents only one component of the complex, informed, and intuitive thinking that is needed to work effectively with clients. As noted by Guideline 9, comprehensive conceptual frameworks are informed by ingredients such as the many contextual factors that impinge on distress, a person's social identities and social locations, developmental factors, a person's life history and coping in response to life challenges, experiences of powerlessness or victimization, competencies and strengths, and health and biological vulnerabilities.

The thoughtful psychologist also considers the meaning and consequences of specific diagnostic labels and asks herself or himself questions such as,

- What are the costs and benefits of applying this label?
- Does this diagnostic category allow for ways to consider how this person's symptoms are adaptive?
- How does this diagnostic label inform interventions that can lead to relief and empowerment?
- How do my client's multiple identities inform how she (or he) experiences distress and empowerment?
- What is the meaning of my client's symptoms within her or his ecological context? (APA, 2007; Ballou, Matsumoto, & Wagner, 2002; Yakushko, Davidson, & Williams, 2009).

Assessing for Diversity and Intersectionality

In general, placing women's issues in the type of ecological, biopsychosocial framework recommended by the Guidelines is an important antidote for counteracting contemporary frameworks that may decontextualize and overmedicalize women's concerns. In this section, we discuss a variety of practical tools for exploring and assessing diversity, including social identity analysis, acronyms for organizing open-ended questions about diversity, identity development, and visual maps and genograms.

Social Identity and Gender Role Analysis

One of the hallmarks of feminist and multicultural approaches to psychotherapy is *social identity analysis* or *gender role analysis* (e.g., Worell & Remer, 2003). We use the term *social identity analysis* to encompass the interconnections among many aspects of identity that are related to a person's social statuses, self-identities, and sources of privilege and disadvantage. Given the fact that personal and social identities are multidimensional, as noted by Guidelines 1 and 2 (APA, 2007), individuals may experience the fusing of social identities and related oppressions (e.g., gendered racism or *rasexism*) or may live on the borders or boundaries between identities, which may contribute to a hybrid identity. In addition, specific identities may be salient in some contexts and not in others. The relevance of any specific social identity may be influenced by the degree to which it is visible and discernable to others (e.g., skin color, disability), or is typically associated with privilege (e.g., White, middle class, Christian, male status) or oppression (nondominant forms of ethnicity/race, sexual orientation, religion, class). Furthermore, one's gender-related identity may be associated with privilege in some situations and disadvantage in others (APA, 2007).

For many persons who seek psychological services, gender-related concerns are not separable from, or may even be experienced as secondary to, other identities, such as age, class, race/ethnicity, sexual orientation, disability, or professional status. The goals of social identity analysis are to develop a clear picture of the unique mosaic of identities and experiences that inform distress and wholeness. The information gained from constructing this mosaic contributes to a comprehensive assessment of a person's strengths and concerns and contributes to consciousness-raising or critical consciousness, which increases both the client's and therapist's awareness of social expectations and roles. In addition, social identity analysis helps clients reframe or redefine distress, which helps to motivate and empower clients. In the sections below, we provide examples of tools for assessing social identity.

Acronyms for Assessing Social Identities

Several authors (D'Andrea & Daniels, 2001; Eriksen & Kress, 2005; Hays, 2008) have proposed the use of acronyms for organizing assessment about the various demographic or social identities. Hays (2008) used the acronym ADDRESSING as a way to gather information about nine relevant factors or identities, which are often associated with specific forms of bias and oppression or sources of privilege. These nine areas can serve as reminders to psychologists to be attentive to both salient and less obvious identities and can be catalysts for generating open-ended assessment questions, such as, "How would you describe your ethnicity, and what does this concept mean to you?" ADDRESSING refers to: Age and generational identity (ageism); Developmental challenges and life transitions, including identity development related to specific social identities (e.g., feminist or ethnic/minority identity); Disability (ableism, bias against disabled persons); Religion and spirituality (religious intolerance/prejudice); Ethnicity/race (racism); Social status (classism); Sexual orientation (heterosexism, antigay bias); Indigenous and cultural heritage (racism, cultural bias); National origin and immigrant status (racism, colonialism, anti-immigration bias); and Gender (sexism).

Brown's (2008) multicultural feminist approach incorporates the ADDRESSING model and adds some additional areas of assessment, such as relationship and parenting statuses, size and attractiveness (and related isms of sizeism and objectified body consciousness), and the traumas of interpersonal violence and combat experience. In addition, Guideline 8 identifies additional domains for assessment such as personal values, family dynamics, life stage, cultural/ethnic background, experiences of trauma, and one's current environment.

A second acronym, RESPECTFUL (D'Andrea & Daniels, 2001), overlaps substantially with the ADDRESSING framework and provides an alternative way of organizing information gathering and interventions related to the following identities: Religion, Ethnic–cultural–racial background, Sexual orientation and identity, Psychological mindedness and maturity, Economic and social class background, Chronological and developmental factors, Threats to health and well-being, Family history and dynamics, Unique physical features and characteristics, and Location and geographical affiliation. For each area, D'Andrea and Daniels (2001) suggested questions for therapist self-assessment as well as client assessment. Examples for potential questions for clients and therapists follow.

With regard to E, ethnic–cultural–racial background, possible questions for the client might include: "How would you describe your culture? What cultural values are important to you?" For the therapist, a related self-reflection question might be: "What values, biases, and preferences have origins in my cultural background? How are these values likely to influence my work with clients?" Client-focused questions related to the second E, economic and social class, might include: "What types of financial pressures do you face in your life?" For the counselor, a relevant related question may be: "How does the socioeconomic class in which I was raised influence my current way of thinking and acting and the way I view clients?"

Because some identities may be more central to the person's self-definition than others, it is useful to listen for clues about the salience, centrality, and context-related aspects of identity as well as ways in which some identities (e.g., gender, ethnicity/race) may be fused. Examples of potential prompts include: "When you think of yourself as a woman (or woman of color, lesbian, woman with a disability, etc.), what sorts of words come to mind that describe your thoughts and feelings about yourself?" "Which identities or aspects of yourself are you most aware of on a daily basis?" When relevant, follow-up questions can focus on specific contexts in which a woman's experiences of herself, as well as privileges and oppressions, may vary. Because assessment is an ongoing process, it may be important to return periodically to discussions about the complexity and multidimensionality of a client's social identities.

Worell and Remer's (2003) approach to social identity and gender assessment encourages individuals to identify the range of social identities listed so far and identify whether a specific facet (e.g., gender, class) confers privilege or a sense of well-being, or whether it has been associated with disadvantage, oppression, or disempowerment. In addition, clients may benefit by creating a personal-social identity timeline, which involves drawing a timeline and identifying important life events or markers. Depending on the client and her priorities, these markers might focus on educational themes, family events, work and professional transitions, relationship history, losses or victimization, or other life changes. The timeline may be divided by decades or other meaningful subjective time periods.

Social Identity Development

As noted in Guideline 2, a variety of identity models propose that individuals encounter developmental phases related to specific dimensions of social development, such as feminist or womanist identity development (e.g., Downing & Roush, 1985; Ossana, Helms, & Leonard, 1992), racial/ethnic identity development (e.g., Cross, 1991), gender transgressive identity development (Fassinger & Arseneau, 2007), or White identity (e.g., Helms, 1995). These models trace typical patterns of movement from internalized oppression (or privilege in the case of White identity), through developmental experiences marked by the salience of the marked identity as well as emotional upheaval. As a way of working through issues, which are often elicited by personal experiences with bias and discrimination (or, in the case of White identity, observations of others' oppression or awareness of one's privilege), individuals tend to move toward seeking personal experiences that enhance knowledge and self-esteem related to the specific identity status.

Although identity development models have provided helpful guides for assessment about single identities (e.g., feminist, lesbian), they may be inadequate for assessing intersectional and multidimensional identities. For example, women and girls may (a) identify with one of their multiple identities; (b) experience a more segmented approach in which specific identities become salient in one or more contexts; or (c) may combine, fuse, or form hybrid identities (Reynolds & Pope, 1991; Root, 2000). Useful questions may focus on themes such as when, how, or where individuals are aware of gender or other identities; or how ethnic/racial identity (or another identity) informs what it means to be a woman. Such social location questions, however, need to be framed in the comfortable and usual language and idioms of the client. Thus, in drawing out a client to think about her experiences of gender, race, or other important social identities, the therapist may find it more useful and successful not to use "research" or "academic speak" but "layperson speak." In other cases, the therapist may gather relevant information by listening carefully to a client's anecdotes and testing observations through the use of tentative reflection statements. The bottom-line task of the psychologist is to be attentive to the fact that social identities often "interact to form qualitatively different meanings and experiences" and that "one cannot reduce identity to a summary of the social groups to which a person belongs" (Warner, 2008, p. 454).

Case Illustration

The following example applies the RESPECTFUL framework (D'Andrea & Daniels, 2001) in therapy with a Black, highly distressed 42-year-old woman. The therapist is attempting both to get a better handle on the specific stressors engendered by this woman's multiple and intersecting social identities as well as gently to urge her to gain a better understanding of how those experiences have impacted her behavior in the past and present.

Joanne is a never-married single mom of two teenage sons who has lost a very good, well-paying job due to high anxiety that led her to make bad decisions in organizing her workload. She compulsively and repeatedly reviewed and changed her work to the point that she could not finish a task, which also severely impeded the production of others on her team. At work and home, Joanne sometimes forgets to eat regularly and is very thin. Her teeth are bad, she has back and hip pain, and she has been medically diagnosed with sciatica, making it hard for her to sit for long periods. Despite an IQ of over 140, she has lost several jobs, and is unable to articulate why in any meaningful way. She now lives in a northern mid-size city, but migrated from the South and presents with a highly verbal and well-mannered speech and demeanor. She is close to her family and active in her church community, whose members helped her when she had gone through her savings and was homeless after a year out of work.

All these factors are dimensions of the RESPECTFUL framework and were assessed by the therapist in the course of the first couple of initial sessions or work with the client, a fairly religious, Black, heterosexual, highly intelligent woman with multiple health issues who has sometimes experienced middle-class living, but now finds herself homeless. A first critical question for the therapist, of course, was could she as a White, older, upper middle-class woman relate to Joanne's problems and identities in a meaningful and respectful way that would help her out of her dilemma.

Whereas the therapist could have made a diagnosis of obsessive–compulsive personality disorder from the description of Joanne's work behaviors, and she indeed kept in mind the symptoms of this anxiety disorder, it was more helpful to understand Joanne's situation by probing into the complexities of her social environment and the intersecting identities with which she lived and coped. Once trust was established in the relationship, the therapist asked several questions over the course of treatment. For example, "Joanne, do you feel you experienced any discrimination or bias in your job?" Note that the question is open-ended and does not directly refer to race, gender, physical appearance, or disabilities, allowing the client to expand on what she felt or thought about her particular situation. A follow-up question asked in several different formats, and over time, was, "How much do you think your own decisions contributed to the situation you are in?" It is critical not to imply blame, but to help the client sort out responsibility for her difficulties while also appreciating and understanding the social forces that impinge on her current and past stress.

When the therapist asked, "How does having been brought up in such a different place affect you now, living in this town?" an insightful discussion began about how hard it was to find reliable social supports, Joanne's unrealistic expectations of others' help, and whether she needed to expand her networks and/or depend more on her own initiative. The question "Why do you think people sometimes underestimate how smart you are?" also was very productive in helping her sort out how people demonstrated mixed messages in approaching her as a Black person, as a woman, as an unemployed person, as a mother, and frequently and unexpectedly, as a very smart person. Given that Joanne's extended family situation and history were also quite complicated, another useful assessment tool that therapist and client might have employed is a genogram. Various kinds of genograms and visual maps are discussed in the next section.

Visual Maps and Genograms for Social Identity Assessment

Genograms (see Figure 2.1) are often used by couples and family therapists to chart family dynamics (McGoldrick, 2011; McGoldrick, Gerson, & Petry, 2008), and they are increasingly being used by ecologically oriented psychologists to explore specific aspects of a person's social identity or ecological space. Genograms are graphic ways of representing a family using a variety of symbols for different family members and various types of relationships. For example, males are represented by squares and females by circles. Marriages may be indicated by joining a couple with a straight line, while one slash through that line can mean a separation and two lines, a divorce. A space in a line in any relationship could mean cut-off communication. Genograms generally include at least three generations and are used to examine family patterns such as communication style, alcohol use and abuse, violence, gender roles, occupational choices, and other relevant information. Standard genogram structures and symbols can be modified to chart nontraditional family dynamics, such as lesbian relationships/marriage, and family structures found within communities that less frequently engage in traditional marriage. Because the genogram structure is factual and graphic, there is no inherent bias that is inconsistent with multicultural, feminist, or other frameworks, especially when genogram symbols are used flexibly. As many themes related to one's culture, identity, ethnicity/race, and sexual orientation are learned and enacted within family environments, recent versions of the genogram lend themselves to social identity assessment. These modified genograms are referred to by titles such as ecograms, ecomaps, flow charts, family maps, family trees, gendergrams, culturagrams (Comas-Díaz, 2011), or mattering maps (Kaschak, 2010).

A variety of authors have provided templates for creating genograms that emphasize specific social identities, such as spirituality (Hodge, 2001; Limb & Hodge, 2011), cultural identity (e.g., Comas-Díaz, 2011; Hardy & Laszloffy, 1995; McGoldrick, 2011), or gender dynamics (White & Tyson-Rawson, 1995). Several genogram approaches seem particularly well-suited for assessing multiple identities as well as oppressions and privileges. The construction of the cultural genogram (Hardy & Laszloffy, 1995) begins with the identification of one's major cultures of origin, followed by the charting of one's personal organizing principles (perceptions, beliefs, and behaviors), symbols, and sources of pride and shame. The culturagram (Comas-Díaz, 2011) resembles the cultural genogram (Hardy & Laszloffy) and includes components that address geopolitics, cultural transitions and translocations, and sociocultural evaluation. The critical genogram (Kosutic et al., 2009) is designed to raise critical consciousness, which is defined as "an ability to recognize, understand, and reflect on interlocking systems of oppression and to take action to resist them" (p. 154).

Typically, the therapist and client construct a genogram together, since the therapist is the expert in using the format and the client is the expert on the family details. They may draw the genogram on paper, chalkboard, on the computer (e.g., http://www.genopro.com), or using whatever medium suits them. Following the construction of a basic critical genogram or chart, the individual is asked to identify and chart the oppressions that are most salient to him or her. Developmental, temporal, and sociopolitical contexts can also be incorporated (see Figure 2.1).

Genograms can also be used to emphasize goal setting, strengths, and ecological contexts. For example, the community genogram (Rigazio-DiGilio, Ivey, Kunkler-Peck, & Grady, 2005) seeks to use a holistic approach to chart multiple sources of strength available to the self and family-in-relation. Developmental themes and interactions with social and personal power bases are also assessed. A primary goal is to create visual images that facilitate clients' re-evaluation of the past and implications for future growth

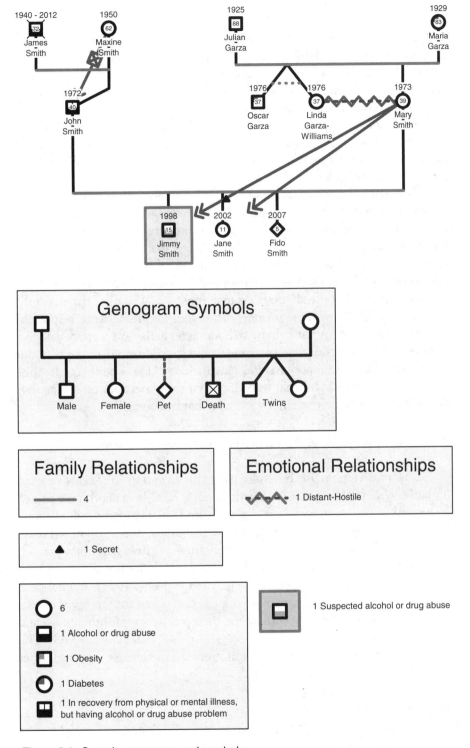

Figure 2.1. Sample genogram and symbols.

and adaptation, referred to as *re-storying*. The community genogram becomes a "flexible blueprint" (Rigazio-DiGilio et al., 2005, p. 31) that may integrate charts, creative elements, and clip art as well as symbols that are associated with more traditional genograms. Yet another alternative, Kaschak's (2011) mattering map, is designed to offer a multidimensional and dynamic approach, or kaleidoscope, to understanding identity and context. Kaschak used the term *mattering* to emphasize what "matters" to the individual. What matters to the individual may vary across contexts, experiences, and the salience of specific identity dimensions.

Following the construction of a genogram, a variety of reflective open-ended questions can be used to further explore areas such as ethnicity, race and skin color, migration, social class, and spirituality (see specific sources for an extended list of questions). Specialized genograms or charts, which can be used as homework between sessions, provide useful foundations for ongoing discussion about themes, events, or people that clients have identified as personally relevant. Potential questions may include: "What are the strengths of your family?" "How have people within your family network responded to challenges?" and "What beliefs, attitudes, and behaviors were developed, affirmed, and maintained across generations?" Additional prompts about social networks and support systems may include "How would you describe your support system?" "In what ways does your social network offer support?" and "How can you use these networks to enhance coping?"

Assessing Strengths and Resilience and Reframing Problems

Positive psychologists have also called for an end to an "exclusive focus on pathology" (Seligman & Csikszentmihalyi, 2000, p. 5) and have placed a renewed emphasis on well-being, growth, and satisfaction as well as topics such as creativity, flourishing, forgiveness, happiness, and resilience (Lopez, 2009; Lopez & Snyder, 2009). Long before these positive psychology trends became popular, feminist and multicultural psychologists advocated for a strength and coping perspective (e.g., Reid & Kelly, 1994). Guideline 8 encourages psychologists "to explore information about the strengths of girls and women, their coping capacities, and their past accomplishments . . . and to help their female clients reframe perceived personal deficits" (p. 968). The following paragraphs focus on assessing strengths to ensure that possibilities for coping and growth are maximized.

Assessing Strengths

Several approaches that are particularly compatible with a strength and resilience approach are discussed briefly in this section. Fredrickson's (2009) "broaden and build" theory emphasizes the value, functions of, and methods for building on positive emotions such as joy, contentment, and interest. Her theory posits that experiencing positive emotion helps individuals see multiple possibilities for themselves, enhance the quality and quantity of positive emotions and personal resources, "undo" the potentially negative effects of stressful or painful events, support creativity and "bigger picture" thinking, and support resilience in the face of difficulty.

A second model, proposed by Keyes (2007), calls for the diagnosis of positive mental health or flourishing. Diagnostic criteria related to flourishing include (a) emotional well-being (positive affect and life satisfaction), (b) psychological well-being (e.g., self-acceptance, life purpose, positive relationships, personal growth), and (c) social well-being (social contribution and social acceptance). Related to the diagnosis of mental health is Peterson and Seligman's (2004) classification of character strengths and the six virtues of wisdom, courage, humanity, justice, temperance, and transcendence.

Another set of useful tools is embedded within the strengths-based therapy model (Jones-Smith, 2014; Smith, 2006). This approach employs the use of multidimensional strength-assessment procedures, including a wheel-of-life exercise and strength charts, which involve identifying emotional, character, creative, educational, analytical/cognitive, financial/economic, survival, social support and community, and wisdom strengths in multiple domains. This assessment also focuses on working through internal and external barriers to change as well as capitalizing on strengths and supporting adaptability and transcendence in one's environment. Some of the open-ended questions that elicit strength-focused thinking include "What are some of your strengths? Accomplishments?" "What do you like about yourself and what do others most like about you?" "What strengths have helped you cope with your current situation?" and "What else do you want for yourself?"

A strength-focused model is also embedded in the relational-cultural model of psychotherapy and development (Miller & Stiver, 1997), which emphasizes the importance of connections in growth. Mutual empathy and mutual empowerment are fostered by "five good things," which consist of zest (feelings associated with authentic connection), the ability to take action in a situation, a sense of knowledge of oneself and others, a sense of worth and validation of one's feelings, and the desire to build more connections. To build on this framework, psychologists can ask clients to elaborate on occasions when they feel zest or a sense of self-worth, and they can be encouraged to use this information to enhance their experiences.

Finally, spirituality is another potential source of strength and resilience. Related to the positive aspect of spirituality, Mattis (2002) found that African American women identified a range of coping functions involving religion and spirituality, such as the recognition and acceptance of reality, the opportunity to deal with existential questions and meaning-making, and methods for finding purpose and transcending current circumstances. Comas-Díaz (2008), who used the term *Spirita* to highlight the spirituality of women of color, proposed that this spirit "nurtures a deepening of women's cultural values and fosters a reconstruction of their identity" (p. 13). According to Comas-Díaz, *Spirita* contributes to women's awareness of oppressive forces while also facilitating racial gender empowerment. It "mobilizes women to take control of their lives, overcome their oppressed mentality, and achieve a critical knowledge of themselves" (p. 13). This womanist worldview can be integrated with a variety of spiritual healing traditions and metaphors and used in the service of bringing women of diverse backgrounds together to "alchemize their oppression into liberation" (p. 17), build alliances among people, and support the construction of a just society.

Reframing and Power Analysis

The preceding paragraphs have focused on the assessment of strengths. Closely related to strength assessment is reframing (Haley, 1985), or identifying and underlining forms of resilience and strength, even when symptoms appear to be signs of pathology. Klein (1976), an influential feminist therapist, redefined emotional pain by stating: "Not all symptoms are neurotic. Pain in response to a bad situation is adaptive, not pathological" (p. 90). Reframing involves providing more contextualized and complete descriptions of behaviors, which are otherwise seen primarily as intrapsychic deficiencies. When clients see how external circumstances and situations are "crazy-making," they are more prepared to consider how their symptoms facilitate coping and to experience decreased self-blame for symptoms. Relevant assessment questions that build on this foundation might include: "What is your pain telling you (about your goals, life circumstances)?" "What information are you gaining from your anxiety or depression (or fill in the blank) about what is important to you?" "Can you think of ways in which your feelings of pain can give your information that will help you cope (with racism, sexism, bias against older women)?" "What is going on around you, and how are your problems an adaptive response to these circumstances?" "How might some of your anxious energy be redirected?" and "What (or who) gives you strength to keep going?"

In responding to questions that facilitate reframing, clients may recontextualize their difficulties and identify how important strengths based on social and cultural traditions can support their coping. For example, Chicana feminists Anzaldúa (1987) and Moya (2001) spoke of the survival value of *la facultad*, which can be defined as a sixth sense that involves paying attention to the power dynamics and potential for marginalization that occur as a part of everyday experiences (see also Chapter 4, this volume, on Latinas). This ability to "read" situations facilitates the ability to adjust to changing and threatening circumstances (*la facultad*), offers a layer of protection and resilience, and allows for creative forms of response. Similarly, Hurtado (1996) spoke of the value of shifting consciousness, which she defined as "the ability of many women of Color to *shift* from one group's perception of social reality to another, and, at times, to be able simultaneously to perceive multiple social realities without losing their sense of self-coherence" (p. 384). These examples point to the value of rich cultural traditions and heritages that can be used to enhance coping and build self-esteem.

Reframing is related to power analysis, a feminist therapy intervention with two purposes: (a) the exploration of power differentials and how they influence one's experiences of privilege and oppression; and (b) the client and therapist's identification of personal, interpersonal, and institutional forms of power that can be used to enhance one's sense of resilience and options for personal and social empowerment (Enns, 2004; Morrow & Hawxhurst, 1998; Worell & Remer, 2003). As part of a comprehensive power analysis, clients and therapists may work to differentiate between power over, power within, and power with. *Power over* involves dominance and control over others and often takes on coercive and destructive forms. In contrast, *power within* reflects the strength, ability, and positive self-identity that support personal growth and empowerment. *Power with* encompasses synergistic, collaborative, relational empowerment, and egalitarian decision-making, which can also provide a foundation for social justice activism.

In general, reframing and power analysis involve redefining and relabeling difficulties so that the political, interpersonal, and social dimensions of an issue as well as one's personal strengths and resilience become more evident. A person moves from personal evaluations that emphasize self-blame toward those that facilitate redefinition, positive self-evaluation, and productive action. The narrative therapy strategy of externalizing one's "problem story" provides one option for reframing and enhancing coping (Brown, 2007). *Externalizing* involves defining a problem such as an eating disorder or depression as an external or vindictive entity that is attacking the person. This strategy frees one to define a problem as external to one's central identity, separate oneself from a "problem story," and map the social-political contexts related to problems. By redefining the problem, clients gain greater freedom to challenge the problem and describe how they might want to re-author a new, healthy story that emphasizes their strengths and coping. A relevant question might be: "How do we challenge the depression or eating disorder that has attacked your life?"

CONCLUSIONS AND RECOMMENDATIONS

This chapter has outlined a variety of practical tools that are designed to enhance psychologists' attentiveness to diverse social identities in order to place women's concerns within an ecological framework. We conclude this chapter by emphasizing the importance of being consistently mindful of one's self in the assessment process and embedding assessment tools within a coherent theoretical framework.

On the Social Identities of the Psychologist

The life experiences and multiple identities of the psychologist inform her or his *positionality*, which can be defined as one's location in social space (APA, 2007; Enns, 2010). Guidelines 2 and 6 emphasize the importance of understanding one's positionality, which involves clarifying the various social identities and forms of social power or disempowerment that have informed one's life and hence one's approach to working with others. As noted in Guidelines 1 and 2, a person's identities are not fixed, but are "situated" and may shift in response to the psychological practice demands, circumstances, and rewards the psychologist encounters. The psychologist is encouraged to consider the potential benefits of disclosing her or his relevant identities, values, and assumptions to those with whom she or he works. This form of disclosure is an extension of informed consent and provides the foundation for a collaborative working relationship.

Important reflection questions for the psychologist include "What are my multiple and intersecting identities, and how are they relevant to my work with others?" "In what ways are power and privilege associated with my identities, and how might these features influence my work with others?" and "How might my age, sexual orientation, ethnicity, health or disability status, religious beliefs, family history, and geographical orientation be related to my preparedness to work with diverse clients?"

A Note on Theoretical Frameworks

A central aspect of a psychologist's work is the development of a theoretical framework that guides exploration, assessment, and conceptualization of a client's concerns. The theory-based assumptions of a psychologist have been shown to have a more significant impact on explanations of problems than *DSM* checklists (Kim & Ahn, 2002). Thus, it is important for the psychologist to be well informed about the theories that inform her or his psychological practice worldview. This theoretical umbrella may encompass psychological, sociological, political, multicultural, and feminist theories (Enns, 2010).

We recommend that psychologists examine carefully the underlying assumptions of the psychological theories they use to assess conceptualize clients' concerns, paying particular attention to elements that are indicative of androcentric, intrapsychic, heterosexist, deterministic, ethnocentric, or monocultural thinking (Worell & Remer, 2003). Guideline 4 (APA, 2007) identifies a variety of theoretical approaches that contain subtle biases or may not be inclusive of the experiences of diverse individuals, including theories that are typically identified as nonsexist (e.g., humanistic, cognitive–behavioral, family therapies, psychodynamic approaches). For example, subtle biases within theory may include

> (a) overvaluing individualism and autonomy and undervaluing relational qualities, (b) overvaluing rationality instead of viewing mental health from a holistic perspective, (c) paying inadequate attention to context and external influences . . . [and] (d) basing definitions of positive mental health on behaviors that are most consistent with masculine stereotypes or life experiences. (p. 964)

Worell and Remer (2003) recommended that psychotherapists evaluate the theories they are drawn to along the following dimensions: (a) the historical evolution of the theory and its key concepts, (b) how problems in living are conceptualized and assessed, (c) the role and functions of the therapist, (d) and major techniques associated with the theory. If biases are identified during this process, psychologists are encouraged to restructure biased or limiting aspects of the theory and transform the approach so that it is consistent with multicultural and feminist criteria. In summary, clarity about one's theoretical framework allows one to organize and implement the tools discussed in this chapter in an effective and inclusive manner.

Concluding Comments

Thoughtful and well-constructed assessments and conceptual frameworks provide the basis for ethical, inclusive, and effective psychotherapy with clients. The tools described in this chapter are likely to demystify the psychotherapy process and provide an egalitarian framework in which clients and therapists work together as partners to resolve clients' issues and build on clients' strengths and resilience. The practices outlined in this chapter also emphasize the importance of therapist awareness and a positive psychotherapy relationship throughout the information-gathering process as well as the centrality of assessment approaches that are ecologically sound and attentive to clients' diverse social identities and the complex contexts in which clients live. In the chapters that follow, the authors will build on these tools and apply them to working with diverse groups of women.

REFERENCES

American Psychiatric Association. (2013). *Diagnostic and statistical manual of mental disorders* (5th ed.). Washington, DC: Author.

American Psychological Association. (2007). Guidelines for psychological practice with girls and women. *American Psychologist, 62,* 949–979. doi:10.1037/0003-066X.62.9.949

Anzaldúa, G. (1987). *Borderlands, la frontera: The new mestiza.* San Francisco, CA: Aunt Lute Books.

Ballou, M., Matsumoto, A., & Wagner, M. (2002). Toward a feminist ecological theory of human nature: Theory building in response to real-world dynamics. In M. Ballou & L. S. Brown (Eds.), *Rethinking mental health and disorder: Feminist perspectives* (pp. 99–141). New York, NY: Guilford Press.

Brown, C. (2007). Talking body talk: Merging feminist and narrative approaches to practice. In C. Brown & T. Augusta-Scott (Eds.), *Narrative therapy: Making meaning, making lives* (pp. 269–302). Thousand Oaks, CA: Sage. doi:10.4135/9781452225869.n14

Brown, L. S. (2006). Still subversive after all these years: The relevance of feminist therapy in the age of evidence-based practice. *Psychology of Women Quarterly, 30,* 15–24. doi:10.1111/j.1471-6402.2006.00258.x

Brown, L. S. (2008). *Cultural competence in trauma therapy: Beyond the flashback.* Washington, DC: American Psychological Association. doi:10.1037/11752-000

Clay, R. A. (2012). Protesting proposed changes to the *DSM. Monitor on Psychology, 43*(2), 42.

Comas-Díaz, L. (2008). 2007 Carolyn Sherif Award Address: *Spirita:* Reclaiming womanist sacredness into feminism. *Psychology of Women Quarterly, 32,* 13–21. doi:10.1111/j.1471-6402.2007.00403.x

Comas-Díaz, L. (2011). *Multicultural care: A clinician's guide to cultural competence.* Washington, DC: American Psychological Association.

Cosgrove, L., & Krimsky, S. (2012). A comparison of *DSM-IV* and *DSM-5* panel members' financial associations with industry: A pernicious problem persists. *PLoS Medicine, 9*(3): e1001190. doi:10.1371/journal.pmed.1001190

Cross, W. (1991). *Shades of black: Diversity in African-American identity.* Philadelphia, PA: Temple University Press.

D'Andrea, M., & Daniels, J. (2001). RESPECTFUL counseling: An integrative model for counselors. In D. Pope-Davis & H. Coleman (Eds.), *The interface of class, culture and gender in counseling* (pp. 417–466). Thousand Oaks, CA: Sage. doi:10.4135/9781452231846.n17

DeBarona, M. S., & Dutton, M. A. (1997). Feminist perspectives on assessment. In J. Worell & N. G. Johnson (Eds.), *Shaping the future of feminist psychology: Education, research, and practice* (pp. 37–56). Washington, DC: American Psychological Association.

Downing, N. E., & Roush, K. L. (1985). From passive acceptance to active commitment: A model of feminist identity development for women. *The Counseling Psychologist, 13*, 695–709. doi:10.1177/0011000085134013

Enns, C. Z. (2004). *Feminist theories and feminist psychotherapies: Origins, themes, and diversity* (2nd ed.). New York, NY: Haworth Press.

Enns, C. Z. (2010). Locational feminisms and social identity analysis. *Professional Psychology: Research and Practice, 41*, 333–339. doi:10.1037/a0020260

Eriksen, K., & Kress, V. E. (2005). *Beyond the DSM story*. Thousand Oaks, CA: Sage.

Fassinger, R. E., & Arseneau, J. R. (2007). "I'd rather get wet than be under that umbrella": Differentiating the experiences and identities of lesbian, gay, bisexual, and transgender people. In K. J. Bieschke, R. M. Perez, & K. A. DeBord (Eds.), *Handbook of counseling and psychotherapy with lesbian, gay, bisexual, and transgender clients* (2nd ed., pp. 19–49). Washington, DC: American Psychological Association. doi:10.1037/11482-001

Fredrickson, B. (2009). *Positivity*. New York, NY: Crown.

Haley, J. (1985). *Conversations with Milton H. Erickson*. New York, NY: Triangle Press.

Hardy, K., & Laszloffy, T. A. (1995). The cultural genogram: Key to training culturally competent family therapists. *Journal of Marital and Family Therapy, 21*, 227–237. doi:10.1111/j.1752-0606.1995.tb00158.x

Hays, P. A. (2008). *Addressing cultural complexities in practice* (2nd ed.). Washington, DC: American Psychological Association.

Helms, J. E. (1995). An update of Helms's White and People of Color racial identity models. In J. G. Ponterotto, J. M. Casas, L. A. Suzuki, & C. M. Alexander (Eds.), *Handbook of multicultural counseling* (pp. 181–198). Thousand Oaks, CA: Sage.

Hodge, D. R. (2001). Spiritual genograms: A generational approach to assessing spirituality. *Families in Society, 82*(1), 35–48. doi:10.1606/1044-3894.220

Hurtado, A. (1996). Strategic suspensions: Feminists of Color theorize the production of knowledge. In N. Goldberger, J. Tarule, B. Clinchy, & M. Belenky (Eds.), *Knowledge, difference, and power: Essays inspired by women's ways of knowing* (pp. 372–392). New York, NY: Basic Books.

Jones-Smith, E. (2014). *Strengths-based therapy: Connecting theory, practice and skills*. Los Angeles, CA: Sage.

Kaschak, E. (2010). The mattering map: Multiplicity, metaphor and morphing in contextual theory and practice. *Women & Therapy, 34*, 6–18. doi:10.1080/02703149.2010.532688

Keyes, C. L. M. (2007). Promoting and protecting mental health as flourishing: A complementary strategy for improving national mental health. *American Psychologist, 62*, 95–108. doi:10.1037/0003-066X.62.2.95

Kim, N. S., & Ahn, W. (2002). Clinical psychologists' theory-based representations of mental disorders predict their diagnostic reasoning and memory. *Journal of Experimental Psychology: General, 131*, 451–476. doi:10.1037/0096-3445.131.4.451

Klein, M. H. (1976). Feminist concepts of therapy outcome. *Psychotherapy: Theory, Research & Practice, 13*, 89–95. doi:10.1037/h0086493

Kosutic, I., Garcia, M., Graves, T., Barnett, F., Hall, J., Haley, E., . . . Kaiser, B. (2009). The critical genogram: A tool for promoting critical consciousness. *Journal of Feminist Family Therapy: An International Forum, 21*, 151–176. doi:10.1080/08952830903079037

Limb, G. E., & Hodge, D. R. (2011). Utilizing spiritual ecograms with Native American families and children to promote cultural competence in family therapy. *Journal of Marital and Family Therapy, 37*, 81–94. doi:10.1111/j.1752-0606.2009.00163.x

Lopez, S. J. (Ed.). (2009). *The encyclopedia of positive psychology* (Vols. 1 & 2). Malden, MA: Wiley-Blackwell.

Lopez, S. J., & Snyder, C. R. (Eds.). (2009). *Oxford handbook of positive psychology.* New York, NY: Oxford University Press. doi:10.1093/oxfordhb/9780195187243.001.0001

Mattis, J. S. (2002). Religion and spirituality in the meaning-making and coping experiences of African American women: A qualitative analysis. *Psychology of Women Quarterly, 26*, 309–321. doi:10.1111/1471-6402.t01-2-00070

McGoldrick, M. (2011). *The genogram journey: Reconnecting with your family.* New York, NY: Norton. doi:10.1037/e579162012-002

McGoldrick, M., Gerson, R., & Petry, S. (2008). *Genograms: Assessment and intervention* (3rd ed.). New York, NY: Norton.

Miller, J. B., & Stiver, I. P. (1997). *The healing connection: How women form relationships in therapy and in life.* Boston, MA: Beacon Press.

Morrow, S. L., & Hawxhurst, D. M. (1998). Feminist therapy: Integrating political analysis in counseling and psychotherapy. *Women & Therapy, 21*(2), 37–50. doi:10.1300/J015v21n02_03

Moya, P. M. L. (2001). Chicana feminism and postmodernist theory. *Signs, 26*, 441–483. doi:10.1086/495600

Ossana, S. M., Helms, J. E., & Leonard, M. M. (1992). Do "womanist" identity attitudes influence college women's self-esteem and perceptions of environmental bias? *Journal of Counseling & Development, 70*, 402–408. doi:10.1002/j.1556-6676.1992.tb01624.x

Peterson, C., & Seligman, M. E. P. (2004). *Character strengths and virtues: A handbook and classification.* Oxford, England: Oxford University Press.

Rawlings, E., & Carter, D. (1977). Feminist and nonsexist psychotherapy. In E. I. Rawlings & D. K. Carter (Eds.), *Psychotherapy for women* (pp. 49–76). Springfield, IL: Charles C. Thomas.

Reid, P. T., & Kelly, E. (1994). Research on women of color: From ignorance to awareness. *Psychology of Women Quarterly, 18*, 477–486. doi:10.1111/j.1471-6402.1994.tb01044.x

Reynolds, A. L., & Pope, R. L. (1991). The complexities of diversity: Exploring multiple oppressions. *Journal of Counseling & Development, 70,* 174–180. doi:10.1002/j.1556-6676.1991.tb01580.x

Rigazio-DiGilio, S. A., Ivey, A. E., Kunkler-Peck, K. P., & Grady, L. T. (2005). *Community genograms: Using individual, family, and cultural narratives with clients.* New York, NY: Teachers College Press.

Roberts, M. C., Reed, G. M., Medina-Mora, M. E., Keeley, J. W., Sharan, P., . . . Saxena, S. (2012). A global clinician's map to improve ICD–11: Analysing meta-structure to improve clinical utility. *International Review of Psychiatry, 24,* 578–590. doi:10.3109/09540261.2012.736368

Root, M. P. P. (2000). Rethinking racial identity development. In P. Spickard & W. J. Burroughs (Eds.), *We are a people: Narrative and multiplicity in constructing ethnic identity* (pp. 206–220). Philadelphia, PA: Temple University Press.

Seligman, M. E. P., & Csikszentmihalyi, M. (2000). Positive psychology: An introduction. *American Psychologist, 55,* 5–14. doi:10.1037/0003-066X.55.1.5

Smith, E. J. (2006). The strength-based counseling model (Major contribution). *The Counseling Psychologist, 34,* 13–79. doi:10.1177/0011000005277018

Ussher, J. M. (2011). *The madness of women: Myth and experience.* New York, NY: Routledge.

Warner, L. R. (2008). A best practices guide to intersectional approaches in psychological research. *Sex Roles, 59,* 454–463. doi:10.1007/s11199-008-9504-5

White, M. B., & Tyson-Rawson, K. J. (1995). Assessing the dynamics of gender in couples and families: The gendergram. *Family Relations, 44,* 253–260. doi:10.2307/585523

Worell, J., & Remer, P. (2003). *Feminist perspectives in therapy: Empowering diverse women* (2nd ed.). Hoboken, NJ: Wiley.

Yakushko, O., Davidson, M. M., & Williams, E. N. (2009). Identity salience model: A paradigm for integrating multiple identities in clinical practice. *Psychotherapy: Theory, Research & Practice, 46,* 180–192. doi:10.1037/a0016080

3

WOMEN AND GIRLS OF BLACK/ AFRICAN DESCENT

WENDI S. WILLIAMS

The concepts of race and gender are integral to the ways Black/African descent women and girls understand themselves and shape their psychological functioning. A review of the literature yields few works that explicitly explore the role of gender in the lives of Black/African women and girls. This chapter fills in gaps by exploring the myriad social contexts that shape the lives of Black/African descent women and girls and inform their within-group diversity. Over the years, scholars have identified problems positioning Black/African descent women and girls relative to feminist or female-focused and race-based debates of fairness, parity, and social experience (Gay & Tate, 1998). Consequently, an *intersectionality* analysis in which systems of race, gender, class, and nation are recognized for shaping the life experiences and the mental health of all persons is recommended and is used in this chapter (Collins, 2000). Additionally, *critical race feminism* has also challenged essentialist notions of race and gender group memberships, ideologies, and

http://dx.doi.org/10.1037/14460-003
Psychological Practice With Women: Guidelines, Diversity, Empowerment, C. Z. Enns, J. K. Rice, and R. L. Nutt (Editors)
Copyright © 2015 by the American Psychological Association. All rights reserved.

consequent attitudes and behaviors (Wing, 2003). Both conceptualizations emphasize the nuances of intersections that shape Black/African descent women's identities, elucidating the actual and varied experiences of Black/African descent women and girls. It should be particularly noted that when applying these lenses, the conceptualization of Black/African descent women's and girls' experience is centered in their phenomenology, rather than in juxtaposition or opposition to Black/African descent men/boys, White women/girls, other women/girls of color, and White men/boys.

These frameworks hold promise for honing in on the experiences of Black/African descent women's and girls' experience of themselves, and consequently, their psychology. The "Guidelines for Psychological Practice With Girls and Women" (APA, 2007; hereinafter the Guidelines) were adopted to promote the understanding of the gender-specific development and concerns of women and girls. Building on these guidelines, the current volume explores themes specific to diverse women and girls, and this chapter focuses on girls and women of Black/African descent (Guidelines 1 and 2). The effects of being a Black/African descent female on mental health (Guideline 3) are considered, and implications for competent and professional practice (Guideline 4) are presented. Specific practice implications are discussed, with a focus on alternative and empowering practices (Guidelines 6 and 7) that are culturally relevant and linked to the community (Guidelines 9 and 10). Further, thorough analysis and application to a case study example, implications for ethical professional practice, and the integration of relevant community resources are explored. Finally, strategies to support social change and challenge institutional and systemic biases, which are consistent with Guideline 11, are also presented. Researchers and practitioners will have a sense of the role of gender in Black/African descent women's and girls' lives, the need to differentiate interventions for specific needs of subgroups within this population, and awareness of innovative alternative methods and community networks for providing client support.

DIVERSITY, SOCIAL CONTEXT, AND POWER

Black/African descent women's and girls' experiences are shaped by social, political, economic, and cultural forces imposed by interlocking matrices of domination such as racism and sexism (Collins, 2000), and these experiences shape their psychological development. In this first section, theories and research of particular relevance to the lives of Black/African descent women and girls are presented with a specific focus on identity development and coping, multiple role stress, traditional gender roles and role confusion, ethnocultural and gendered violence and related trauma, family of origin concerns, and sexuality. The goal of this section is to present a comprehensive view of the ways Black/African descent women's and girls' mental health is shaped by their sociocultural and gendered standpoints.

Identity Development and Coping

Black/African women's and girls' healthy integration of intersecting social identities has come to the forefront of psychological research in the past decade. Essentialist notions that suggest the predominance of one's racial identity over gender or vice versa have been challenged to expand our understanding of the complexity and diversity inherent in Black/African girlhood/ womanhood (Cohen, 1999; Gilroy, 2003, as cited in Shaw, 2005). For example, Gay and Tate (1998) aptly described Black women's political leanings as "doubly bound" because they cope with negotiating their "shared/common" fate with Black/African men due to racism and with women due to sexism. Their analysis concluded that Black/African women's political decision-making is more strongly influenced by race, though the particular framing of the political issue could also connect them with gender-based priorities.

Although the work of Gay and Tate (1998) is often cited, the psychological impact of having to choose one identity over another has only more recently been explored. Williams's (2005) presentation of therapeutic work with a 34-year-old African American lesbian graduate student demonstrates the psychological impact. The client expressed frustration with "always explaining myself" when in various social settings and described a sense of not being accepted by either the Black or women students' organizations in which she sought memberships. She explained that at the Black students' meetings she was viewed suspiciously for the threat that she would subvert the "real" (i.e., Black) agenda. Alternatively, she expressed that at the women students' meetings, White women did not understand the ways White privilege advantaged them over her in the educational setting. Williams's client's inability to find a student group that was relevant to the intersection of her identities may mirror the psychological conflict of some Black/African women and girls who are unable to integrate their racial and gender identities.

In support of the critical role of identity integration, Settles (2006) found that an intersectional identity was more important for Black/African women than being identified primarily by their race or gender alone. Further, she found instances of lower self-esteem and depression to be exhibited by women who described identity "interference," or instances in which their racial or gender identities were not integrated. Racial interference was exhibited in the form of disrupted social connections and networks in the Black community. In contrast, gender interference was related to the enactment of traditional gender role behaviors. As the women in Settles's study indicated, connections to Black social networks and relationships were important, and exhibiting culturally incongruent gendered behaviors in the Black community had the potential to place women at risk for losing or experiencing distress in their relationships and support networks. Settles's work is consistent with other research suggesting racial group membership and identity shapes gender role attitudes and behaviors among Black/African women and girls (Binion, 1990; Brown, 2011; Buckley & Carter, 2005; Jones, 2009; Littlefield, 2004; Miller, 2008; Weekes, 2003).

Identity for Black/African women and girls is often challenging. They are charged with developing healthy racial and gender notions of themselves within a society that continues to contest the legitimacy of femaleness in the form of a Black body and often makes them subject to the "politics of respectability" (Collins, 2005). The politics of respectability can be defined as a set of standards Black/African women and communities have adopted to gain access to political, social, and economic power and to distance themselves from the savagery of slavery (Higginbotham, 1993). Characterized by guidelines for cleanliness of person and property, temperance, thrift, polite manners, and sexual purity, these politics have held promise for African Americans as a way to gain access to the middle class through Black/African women's labor in the home. Black/African women's ability to demonstrate these tenets in their homes and through their families permitted potential access to the "cult of true womanhood." According to Welter (1966), the possession of the four virtues of "piety, purity, submissiveness, and domesticity" represented the hallmarks of the cult of true womanhood. Shaw (2005) argued that these criteria continue to guide notions of femininity and womanhood.

Notions of femininity and definitions of womanhood are contested areas for Black/African women and girls as they strive to define their femaleness. In her revealing essay, Shaw (2005) applied an analysis of gender and race concepts to the question of which type of body can be deemed female. Noting that the controlling image or stereotype of the large and dark body of the Mammy (see Collins, 2000) is the "physical embodiment of features rejected by Western beauty criteria" (p. 146), Shaw's work reminds us of the tenuous inclusion of some Black/African women and girls in a respectable social space. Specifically, she stated that among Black/African women, body size and class distinctions serve as exclusion criteria. Shaw explicates this intersection in an analysis of the "Mammy" stereotype. The Mammy figure is typically a large (she is overweight), Black/African descent woman who serves to provide an endless supply of "strength, love, and other emotional resources that can never be depleted" (p. 146). Shaw stated that this justifies her role as a caretaker to her family and the families for whom she works and negates the need for others to be responsive to her needs. The Mammy's size, race, and socioeconomic status place her outside the definition of what it means to be a woman. Thus she occupies a "subaltern" role in the larger society. She is considered a lesser woman compared with thin Black women of higher social status and any White woman.

The very categorization of femaleness presents a challenge to Black/African girls' and women's identity and requires exploration of their femininity, androgyny, and feminist attitudes in the context of racialized notions of what it means to be a girl or woman. For Black/African girls, this process is engaged in the social context of school and community. Black/African girls form their identity by balancing the demands and expectations of their environments (Weekes, 2003), and this process functions to facilitate their adjustment to environmental demands (Brown, 2011; Jones, 2009). For example, Jones's (2009) qualitative study explored the life of "Kiara," a 22-year-old young woman activist in her San Francisco Bay area community. Kiara described the ways she negotiated gender roles and expectations in an under-resourced, urban context. The article title is taken from a quote of Kiara's that summarizes this negotiation: "I was aggressive for the streets and pretty for the pictures." Depending on the demands of the environment, Kiara portrayed the attitudes and behaviors that were congruent with its expectations of her.

Community context also places demands on Black/African women and girls to find and explore the ways in which they will be perceived as threatening to each other and to Black/African men/boys (Collins, 2005). Weekes (2003) suggested that girls (and by extension women) seek to negotiate the boundary of inclusion and exclusion within the monolithic conceptualization of the "Black Community." These behaviors are accomplished subtly through consideration of both proximity and opposition to Whiteness and through "peer emulation, interracial relationships and appropriate blackness" (p. 48). Black/African girls are tasked to "do gender" in complicated and contextualized ways as they experience inclusion and exclusion within their racial and gender groups. For instance, in the school setting, Black/African girls' risk and resilience is at times overshadowed by a societal preoccupation with the "Black male crisis," which focuses on issues of the achievement gap and the "school to prison" pipeline (see Noguera, 2008, for further discussion about the Black male crisis). Brown (2011) suggested that urban Black/African middle school girls are in the midst of their own developmental crisis. She contended that the perspective of Black/African girls is often overlooked or considered primarily in relation to the challenges Black/African boys face. Brown (2011) and Jones (2009) acknowledged the consequences Black/African girls face when they violate or manipulate normative expectations associated with female gender roles by asserting their needs and rights. These effects are mirrored in the experiences of their adult counterparts (Parks, 2010). Parks (2010) stated, "African American women combine traits that are often perceived as separate; they are whole, nurturing and fierce, caring and commanding. It is an organic feminism, an organic leadership" (p. 204).

The violation of gender roles and expectations implies "bi-genderism." This concept is similar to the biculturalism born out of W. E. B. Dubois's "double consciousness" (1903). Black/African girls adopt androgynous attitudes and behaviors that may be physically and psychologically protective. In one study, Buckley and Carter (2005) found that Black/African girls endorsing androgynous attitudes had higher total self-esteem (which included school, physical attractiveness, anxiety, popularity, and happiness subscales), and these scores correlated with an "internally derived" racial identity status (internalization). Thus, Black/African girls who are exploring the intersection of gender and racial identities face a set of challenges that is two-fold. On the one hand, due to their racial group membership, they may fall outside the parameters of femaleness (the Mammy expectation). Additionally, they also can suffer consequences (rejection by the "Black community") for employing a "functional androgyny" toward gender (i.e., engaging in both traditional male and female behaviors, depending on the needs of the social context). And while Miller (2008) implied that androgyny is associated with positive self-esteem, these multiple and conflicting environmental demands are likely to be confusing.

Similar to their younger counterparts, older Black/African women are often expected to balance androgynous, nontraditional gender roles alongside the endorsement of traditional gender roles and ideals (Binion, 1990; Littlefield, 2004). Stress is associated with multiple role expectations that require a functional identification with both masculine and feminine aspects of Black/African womanhood (Littlefield, 2004). This process is complicated by some Black/African women's desire to achieve traditional gender role developmental milestones such as marriage and motherhood. Consequently, for some Black/African women, the protective androgyny of their youth can conflict with their adult life expectations that call for more traditional gender roles as wives and mothers.

Research studies focused on Black/African women's gender role and sexual identities have borne out the contradictions between the functional necessity of playing androgynous gender roles, which conflict with cultural expectations of enacting traditional gender roles within families and communities (Binion, 1990; Cole & Zucker, 2007; Settles, Pratt-Hyatt, & Buchanan, 2008; Winkle-Wagner, 2008). Binion (1990) found that the majority of women in her study reported androgynous sexual identities with regard to the female role in the family. These women reported strong relationships with both their mothers and fathers. Additionally, Winkle-Wagner (2008) found that a sample of midwestern college participants identified dispositional characteristics such as being silent, passive, motherly, and religious as appropriate for women. Further, these women felt that characteristics such as strength and/or assertiveness, while empowering, could be a liability within their environments. For example, in the context of interactions with men, a woman's assertiveness may be perceived as a threat, and possibly compromise her role in her family, religious community, or heterosexual romantic relationships. Consequently, for some, identifying as "strong" was preferable to "feminist," as a feminist designation was perceived as a potential threat to their relationship with the Black community and men. Collins (2005) underscored the apprehension Black/African women participants expressed in the Winkle-Wagner (2008) study. She contended that economic realities in many Black communities necessitate that working- and middle-class Black/African women work outside the home as well as raise families. As a result, they must exhibit both traditional masculine and feminine gender roles in order to respond to the requirements of multiple relationships and environments. For Black/African women, class status intersects with race/ ethnicity and gender statuses to determine the ways they experience their identity as women and demonstrate traditional gender roles. For example, a college-educated woman married to a man with equal or higher levels of education and career attainment is more likely to demonstrate traditional female gender roles and behaviors in her family than a single mother or a woman with more education and earning potential than her partner. Thus, as Collins (2005) explained, the diminished earning potential of Black men necessitates that Black women earn more outside the home and negotiate the worlds of work and related institutions, while also managing cultural expectations related to their femaleness and interrelationship with the male presence or lack thereof in the home.

Comparing Black/African and White women's ideals of womanhood/ femininity and feminist ideas has been one approach to exploring the influence of race on women's gender ideas. Little difference has been found between Black/African and White women's views of womanhood/femininity (Cole & Zucker, 2007; Settles et al., 2008). Settles et al.'s (2008) qualitative study with a noncollege sample found that both Black/African and White women described experiences of gender-based maltreatment, perceived advantages compared with men, significant support and dependency on friendships with other women and within their community, caretaking responsibilities, and work/family obligations as aspects of womanhood. In contrast to White women, Black/African women identified more negative aspects of their caretaking and work/family responsibilities and endorsed an additional theme, "inner strength," as a coping mechanism. Further, Cole and Zucker (2007) found that although Black/African and White women conceptualized femininity in similar ways (consisting of feminine appearance, feminine traits, and traditional gender role ideology), Black women rated themselves higher on feminism and feminine appearance. Unlike White women, feminism and feminine appearance were correlated, suggesting that Black women did not find feminine behaviors and traits to interfere with their feminist politics and/or values.

Sexuality and Sexual Identity

Black/African women's sexuality and sexual identities are distinctive in the ways gender and race intersect to influence how they experience their bodies and sexual development. Historical and archetypal formulations of Black women's and girls' bodies and the labor and sex extracted from them contribute to complex perceptions through which their attitudes and behaviors are filtered (Collins, 2005; Parks, 2010; Shaw, 2005). Collins (2005) indicated that the contemporary "Jezebel" stereotype serves to justify media and social interactions that sexually exploit Black/African women and girls. Against the backdrop of respectability, politics, and the cult of true womanhood, Black/African women and girls formulate a sexual sense of self accompanied by a constant awareness of the "public gaze," the idea that one's behavior is watched and judged. Scholars have identified this judging gaze as reflecting a heteronormative standard informed by White culture and cultural norms espoused by the Black community (Collins, 2005; Moore, 2006). Careful not to evoke judgment or categorization as oversexed or irresponsible, some Black/African women engage in "silencing" with regard to their sexuality, which has negative implications for optimal sexual development and health (Froyum, 2010; Weekes, 2002; Wyatt, 1997; Wyatt & Lyons-Rowe, 1990).

Sexual intervention research with a focus on decreasing sexually transmitted infections (STIs) and disease has focused on Black/African women's and girls' risk and vulnerability (Williams, Karlin, & Wallace, in press). Although a focus on epidemiology of STIs among Black/African descent women and girls is important, the primary emphasis on disease and risky sexual behaviors pairs the sexuality of Black/African women and girls with ideas of sexual deviance and moral deficits. Collins (2005) suggested that this approach may serve to move the discourse away from a self-determined definition of love, intimacy, and sexuality centered on the Black/African woman's or girl's experience toward a view of sexuality in relationship to and in comparison with others. Weekes (2002) confirmed that this perspective has prompted Black/African women/girls to be silent about their sexual selves and/or to assert their respectability by comparing their chaste behaviors with that of Black/African boys and White girls. She explained that Black girls define their sexuality by what they are not, or at least not in public, and thus develop "excluded sexualities" (p. 252). The following exchange between two girls in her study is explanatory.

Desiree: Check out this, right. He likes the White girls not the Black girls, you get me. He's that type of person. You know what Ian said one time, 'oh I like White girls better than Black girls' 'cause if they put their arm round us or anything, you [sic] take it off. A White girl wouldn't do that so that's why they like the White girls.

Naomi: They're so dirty though. One of them bit her [Mariah's] tits. That's when Mariah kept messing about, 'cause we saw her from up the top. This is when we had detention and Mariah's like this [*makes whining noise*]. (p. 257)

Though defining identity in relation to others is in part normative, one must question the consequences of identifying oneself in opposition to others rather than in affirmation of oneself. Froyum (2010) suggested that this approach has the potential to disenfranchise Black/African girls, and ultimately women, from being active, empowered agents of their sexuality. This approach may also have the potential to compromise healthy sexual decision-making as girls are not engaged in actively deciding the boundaries of their sexuality. Rather, they make declarations and decisions that may not have a basis in the reality of actual sexual experiences. The silencing about sex that Weekes (2002) discussed is unfortunate as it has negative implications for sexual health and development. A lack of fluency about sex-related topics and discussion places women and girls at risk for not actively engaging in sexual decisions relative to (a) whether the act is right for them; (b) whether to use contraception and what type of contraception fits their needs; (c) how to communicate desires and dislikes; and (d) when to discontinue the sexual aspect of a relationship (Wyatt, 1997).

Respectability politics also plays a role in the lack of support and rejection exhibited toward Black/African lesbian, gay, bisexual, and transgendered (LGBT) women and men (Collins, 2005). These politics were disseminated through the conservative values and social control of the Black church that have traditionally promoted a heteronormative ideal (Greene, 2000). Consequently, LGBT Black/African women and girls exhibit, by their very nature, total rejection of the hegemonic masculinity and femininity espoused by conservative Black social institutions, and pose a specific threat to the already tenuous masculinity of Black/African men (Collins, 2005; Moore, 2006). As one woman expressed as part of a study of the multiple identities and oppressions of Black/African lesbians, "Being a lesbian is like an affront to your blackness" (Bowleg, Huang, Brooks, Black, & Burkholder, 2003). This statement underscores the Black community's rejection of its LGBT members (Greene, 2000). Bowleg et al. (2003) explored the "triple jeopardy" of being Black, female, and a lesbian, and the consequent and continuous stress of being unsure whether work, family, and/or community challenges

were related to their race, gender, or sexuality. The persistent stress associated with having social statuses that are undervalued by the dominant White,
heteronormative majority has been described as "insidious trauma" (Root,
1992, as cited in Bowleg et al., 2003), which may result in identity fragmenta-
tion. As a means of coping and protection, Black/African lesbians engage in
self-monitoring and/or in "code switching." For example, Bowleg et al. (2003)
discussed the experience of Cynthia, a 26-year-old physical education teacher.
Cynthia was described as having listened in as a group of all-Black persons
endorsed a Black religious leader with known anti-lesbian/gay ideals. In this
context it was not safe for Cynthia to discuss her counter-narrative as a Black/
African lesbian woman and member of that religious community. Stating her
views may have placed Cynthia's membership in the group in jeopardy and
possibly become a source of distress, as has been found in previous studies
of Black/African women's identity integration. Unfortunately, this type of
maneuvering is psychologically draining. Consistent with Guideline 6, which
recommends the use of interventions that have been found to be effective,
clinicians are encouraged to advocate for client identity integration work to
support the well-being of clients like Cynthia (Williams, 2005).

TRAUMA AND VIOLENCE: ETHNOCULTURAL, FAMILIAL, AND COMMUNITY

Black/African women's and girls' experiences of trauma and violence
are wide and varied. Though the literature aptly documents the experiences
of lower income women and girls in urban and under-resourced communities,
the trauma and violence experiences of middle and upper-middle class and
educated Black/African women and girls are less frequently discussed (West,
2002). In a review of the literature, West (2002) indicated that childhood
sexual abuse, dating violence, intimate partner violence, sexual assault, and
sexual harassment impact the lives of Black/African women and girls and often
are predictive of multiple experiences of varying types of violence across their
lifetime. Violence in the lives of Black/African descent women and girls is gendered and culturally distinguished by the reality that violence against Blacks
and women has often been socially sanctioned (Helms, 2011). Ponterotto
(2006) defined *ethnoviolence* as "an act or attempted act motivated by group
prejudice which is intended to cause physical or psychological injury" (p. 4).
Further, Harrell (2000) suggested that the stress in reaction to race-related
violence intersects with various social identities or statuses and that racism
can be gender-specific. One example is the failure of mainstream media out-
lets to prioritize missing Black/African women and girls in their coverage
(Osunsami, 2012). When a woman or girl is missing, the violence she incurs

tends to be sexual in nature. The lack of media coverage compromises the awareness of her status and impairs the public's ability to provide additional surveillance to facilitate the work of authorities. The virtual lack of media coverage is disproportionately low for Black/African women and girls compared with the coverage about missing White women and girls and thus perpetuates the impact of the ethnoviolence of the initial act (Ehrlich, 2009; Helms, Nicolas & Green, 2012). In light of this wider societal undervaluing of women and girls like them, Black/African women and girls may feel that their vulnerability is enhanced by implicit media messages about who is a "worthy victim" (Ehrlich, 2009).

The "Black Family" and the "Black Community" are often highlighted as sources of support for Black/African women and girls. Yet, it is also in these contexts that the manifestations of collective trauma are demonstrated through the dynamics of internalized oppression, inadequate resources, and a history of enslavement that have fractured family and community processes (Degruy-Leary, 2005). Consequently, dysfunctional family and community dynamics may shape the lives of Black/African girls and women, resulting in transgenerational transmission of internalized racial oppression (Boyd-Franklin, 1991; Degruy-Leary, 2005) and childhood abuse (sexual, battering, and neglect; Boyd-Franklin, 1991). This transmission can set the stage for later experiences of gendered and racialized violence and trauma that uniquely impact Black/African women and girls (Ford, 2002; Helms, 2011). Specifically, repetition of traumatic relational dynamics has the potential to replicate these experiences in future relationships.

Community violence consists of aggression that occurs outside one's home among persons who are not related, but it also often involves known others and possibly family members (Jenkins, 2002). A vicarious experience of community violence creates a sense of being unsafe, which has the effect of essentially preoccupying the psyche of women and girls with fear (Jenkins, 2002; Miller, 2008). Victimization of close others and loss of family and friends carries the threat that one can also be hurt and/or that their environment is inherently dangerous. Furthermore, loss of loved ones has been found to have psychologically distressing effects on those who survive. Their symptoms may be more severe than those of survivors of direct victimization, and their symptoms may not abate over time (Thompson, Norris, & Runback, 1998). In addition, the trauma experienced in these instances is sometimes exacerbated by legal and social systems that are dismissive of the complaints of communities seeking justice for their loved ones (Jenkins, 2002). Consequently, Black/African women attempting to protect themselves and their families have been found to execute "overpunishing" and overprotecting parenting methods to minimize the exposure and vulnerability of their children to violence in their communities (Jenkins, 2002).

Jenkins's (2002) review of the literature highlights the reality that Black/African girls tend to experience exposure to violence at rates comparable to those of boys. However, their attempts to appear tough or able to defend themselves through violent means in their environments do not preclude their vulnerability to threats of physical violence. Their vulnerability also includes sexual harassment and assault (Miller, 2008). Sexual violence in the home and violence at the hands of known perpetrators (e.g., male family members, boyfriends of their mothers, other family friends) place Black/African girls at increased risk in many arenas: sexually transmitted diseases (Josephs & Abel, 2009; Wyatt et al., 2002); psychological sequelae consisting of substance abuse (Dailey, Humphreys, Rankin, & Lee, 2011; Hardy & Qureshi, 2012; West, 2002); depression and anxiety (Dailey et al., 2011; Nicolaidis et al., 2010); posttraumatic and acute stress (Ford, 2002; Jenkins, 2002; Wright, Perez, & Johnson, 2010); and suicide attempts (Kaslow, Jacobs, Young, & Cook, 2006).

Additionally, Black/African women's physical health is often compromised by a lack of self-care as well as violence-avoidant strategies that minimize engagement in a healthy lifestyle (Jenkins, 2002). Larance (2012) underscored the negative impact of violence on physical health, as she has found clients to report high blood pressure and stress-induced asthma at intake. Moreover, Nicolaidis et al.'s (2010) examination of Black/African women's experience with depression and depression care found that distrust of the medical establishment plays a large role in whether participants accessed care. It is likely that similar concerns related to trust are issues for women monitoring their physical health as well.

Women's and girls' experiences with violence are essentially disempowering, and a relationship between experiences of in-home and community violence and compromised sexual health and decision-making has been found (Teitelman, Ratcliffe, Morales-Aleman, & Sullivan, 2008; Wilson, Woods, Emerson, & Donenberg, 2012). Teitelman et al. (2008) found that intimate partner violence among a sample of adolescent girls was associated with inconsistent condom use. Further, Stevens-Watkins, Brown-Wright, and Tyler (2011) found that race-related stress was predictive of the number of sexual partners of African American adolescent girls. These effects of race-related stress are life-long and have the potential to shape Black/African women's coping. In one instance, Kaslow and colleagues (2006) found that Black/African women with a history of childhood trauma were more likely to be "repeat attempters" of suicide as well as to show higher levels of suicidal intent, planning, and lethality. They were also likely to endorse more psychological distress, hopelessness, substance abuse, and childhood trauma. These findings are mirrored by Nicolaidis et al.'s (2010) observation that Black/African women in her study cycled through processes of violence, depression, and drug use that were associated with violence in their lives.

Practice, Application, Resources, and Change

Given the challenges Black/African women and girls experience in the face of integrating a positive, internally-derived personal identity against the backdrop of institutional and systemic restrictions, it is important to develop and implement culturally relevant empowerment-focused interventions to address these concerns (Nicolaidis et al., 2010; Wright et al., 2010). Relevant to the value of empowerment, Wright et al. (2010) found that compared with White residents of a women's shelter, Black/African American residents showed lower rates of posttraumatic stress disorder and depression, which suggests that personal empowerment and resilience may offer a protective factor. They suggested that social cohesion, when enhanced through intervention, plays a large part in developing a sense of personal empowerment among Black/African women as "components that make up a strong sense of community, such as a shared emotional connection, reciprocity, and reinforcement of needs among members, and feelings of trust and belonging" (p. 270). Work with Black/African women and girls should also support the development of healthy notions of their gender and racial/cultural identities (Utsey, Giesbrecht, Hook, & Stanard, 2008; White, 1999). Utsey et al. (2008) indicated that race and cultural aspects of self may make persons more aware of the racism in their environment, thus requiring that they rely on psychological and socio/familial resources to minimize psychological distress and to manage stress associated with race-related stressors. Consistent with Guidelines 10 and 11, Utsey and colleagues recommended collaborating with community and church leaders and engaging in environmental/social change to address concerns.

White also advocated social change strategies and described the integration of race/cultural and gender-centered approaches as aspects of an anti-rape social action campaign in response to the Mike Tyson rape trial (1999). She focused on the need to frame issues appropriately in order to garner community support and understanding. Other scholars have also advocated for the engagement of social action to cultivate a sense of empowerment and control, which are often lacking for Black/African women and girls responding to the injustices they face (Harrell, 2000; Jenkins, 2002; West, 2002). These approaches are consistent with Guideline 11, which advocates for social action in response to oppressive dynamics that shape clients' lives.

Still other researchers have considered the role of traditional therapeutic practices. For example, Hardy and Qureshi (2012) presented the Validation, Challenging and Requesting (VCR) and "Dis" Discourse approaches to working with African American adolescents in an urban context. The VCR model consists of the clinician validating and challenging the concerns of the client and requesting that they engage in a compromise that incorporates their concern(s) while considering the other person's needs and factors about which the client may not be as cognizant (e.g., impact on family members). Hardy's work has focused on feelings of "devaluation" experienced by urban youth (e.g., being dissed), who often complain of not feeling respected, which then becomes an impetus for violence and distress. Thus, the "Dis" Discourse method provides adolescents with an opportunity to process experiences about which they feel disrespected by articulating their discontent rather than stifling their feelings. Although these approaches were originally intended for adolescents, Black/African women may also find them effective in processing their experiences, especially when they face questions about whether they are reading a situation accurately or are making too much of a situation that feels like an ethnoviolent assault. This process is consistent with a Black feminist ethic of using dialogue to assess, test, and validate knowledge claims with a trusted other (Collins, 2000), as well as Guidelines 6 and 7, which endorse employing effective culturally-relevant and empowering interventions.

Other approaches informed by traditional therapeutic processes include general therapy and educational programs (West, 2002), thorough assessment that adequately considers relevant stressors and client strengths/resilience (Harrell, 2000; Helms et al., 2012; Jenkins, 2002; explicated in Guideline 8), the use of role models and development of "oppression-survival" coping strategies (Harrell, 2000; Guidelines 7 and 9), and group work with clients with shared experiences for the purpose of providing therapy and possible consciousness-raising (Harrell, 2000; Jenkins, 2002; Nicolaidis et al., 2010; Short & Williams, 2013; Utsey et al., 2008; Williams, Frame, & Green, 1999), as is also indicated in Guideline 9. For example, groups can be used to process the wide array of concerns Black/African women bring to therapy, with a focus on the spiritual meaning that can be garnered from these experiences (Frame, Williams, & Green, 1999; Williams et al., 1999).

Although various interventions may serve to support the health of clients, not all interventions are appropriate for all clients of racial, ethnic, cultural, or gender groups, even if they are identified as culturally relevant. Larance (2012) advised clinicians to consider "common sense" concerns relative to whether an intervention is appropriate. In her work with women experiencing domestic and/or intimate partner violence, she explained that although using "I" statements is advocated for bolstering abused women's sense of self and empowerment, this language may also place the woman at risk if she is still in contact with her abuser. In this case, her empowerment and "I" statements may be perceived as insubordination. Larance also warned that personal journals, which are sometimes incorporated in traditional therapeutic interventions, may be found by abusers and thus also have the potential to place the client in jeopardy.

Relative to culturally relevant and gender-appropriate practices for Black/African women, Nicolaidis et al. (2010) suggested that clinicians be mindful of the strong Black woman enactment by Black/African women, which may involve playing up their health and strength attributes, when in fact they are scared, tired, and need support. Jones's (2009) work with Black/African adolescents further highlights the need to be vigilant about the vulnerability of youth as well. Larance (2012) suggested the use of multilayered systems of advocacy that are dynamic and responsive to the ever-changing needs of clients as they move through processes of change. For example, for clients managing the complexity of one or more systems (e.g., justice, education, social welfare), it is important to educate them about what they should expect to experience. In addition, providing information about systems and providers of services offers contextual education that enhances the likelihood that treatment will be relevant and effective. Weisz (2005) also suggested advocacy for clients and underscored the importance of providing useful information, emotional support, and consistent advocate services for clients.

Finally, religious and spiritual coping has been identified as important to processing race-related stress, trauma, and psychological distress among Black/African women (Frame et al., 1999; Watlington & Murphy, 2006; Williams et al., 1999). Scholars have recommended outreach to the Black church for support and possible mobilization (Utsey et al., 2008) as well as the integration of spirituality in health interventions because of the relationship of spirituality to positive health outcomes (Musgrave, Allen, & Allen, 2002). Larance's (2012) warnings regarding the appropriateness of interventions are also relevant as the Black community, and Black churches specifically, have been complicit in the rejection of some of their members, namely, LGBT persons (Greene, 2000). Thus, it is possible that work with particular client groups will require a nuanced approach to engaging the religious or spiritual communities that are able to be supportive, while remaining mindful whether spiritual values are salient for the client.

This review of the literature reveals that contextualizing the experiences of Black/African descent women and girls is essential to understanding the ways race, gender, social class, sexual orientation and identity, and other systems shape their psychological functioning and can inform best practices. In the following case study, the experiences of a Black/African adolescent, Geraldine, are explored with a particular focus on using appropriate assessment tools (Guideline 8) and implementing effective interventions that are culturally relevant and empowering (Guidelines 6, 7, and 9). In addition, the case study incorporates the use of alternative and community-based resources (Guidelines 10 and 11) and explores social change and activism practices that can be used to advocate for institutional change and address systemic bias.

CASE STUDY

The case study that follows describes a fictional person based on the author's experiences as a researcher who examines the effects of family acceptance and rejection on gender nonconforming youth. Geraldine represents a composite of various youth. An analysis and commentary of the case as well as potential directions for psychotherapy directly follow the case study.

The Case of Geraldine

Geraldine, who prefers to be called "Gerry," is a 13-year-old African American girl. She lives with her mother and maternal grandmother in the historically African American community of "Eastside Oakland." Gerry presents with a disaffected demeanor, often averting her glance, leaning back in her chair or against a wall/table. Her posture is often closed in unfamiliar settings, with her arms folded close to her. When sitting, however, she tends to spread her legs a bit wider than needed, in an overtly masculine stance, and prefers to wear long silky polyester basketball shorts typical of boys her age. Gerry loves to play basketball with the neighborhood boys who are the children of her mother's contemporaries. Gerry's mother is concerned that she is spending too much time with the boys, and when she questions Gerry about whether she has had any sexual encounters with them, Gerry angrily and with a hint of disgust states, "No, Mama. I don't like those boys like that."

Gerry's mother returned to her childhood home to live with her mother when her relationship with Gerry's father ended during her pregnancy. Beyond infrequent visits during her toddler years, Gerry has not developed a relationship with her father. In a protective effort, her mother has not discussed him. Aside from pictures she has found in her mother's belongings and talk among people in her neighborhood that knew of him, Gerry does not have much information about her father. Though it has never been explicitly stated, she senses she should not ask about him.

Gerry's grandmother has been helping to raise her and is very invested in her development. She prides herself on being able to provide Gerry a solid home guided by "good Christian values." Gerry is in conflict with her mother and grandmother regarding her dress and her preference to be called Gerry over Geraldine. Her mother and grandmother complain that she is too "mannish" and that they prefer she dress more "like a girl." They feel they are losing the battle to get her to want to wear what they deem gender-consistent attire. One area in which they are able to enforce this code of dress is for church services. Sunday mornings are contentious times as Gerry is pressured by her grandmother to wear dresses and the "hard bottom girly shoes" she purchases for Gerry. Gerry's mother and grandmother do not agree about how strict to be with Gerry as her grandmother thinks Gerry's mother is "too soft" and does not enforce "old school" ways of raising children.

Gerry is emotionally distraught by her home experiences and has drifted into a deep depression. The only thing that seems to bring her joy is playing basketball on the school courts after school with her male friends in the neighborhood. Recently, Gerry's mother found her wrapping her breasts down with an Ace bandage to obscure the fact that she has breasts. When her grandmother learned of this, she ordered Gerry to stop going to the courts after school and to come straight home instead. This caused Gerry to sink further into sadness. She has begun to skip school and has begun to smoke marijuana with older boys and men in the neighborhood.

Given Gerry's chronic absence from school, a school-based intervention was initiated by the school counselor and truancy officer. The truancy officer paid a home visit alerting Gerry's mother and grandmother to her absences, and the school counselor followed up with a request for Gerry, her mother, and grandmother to meet with him. As Gerry was reticent to speak openly during the first meeting, the school counselor asked her mother and grandmother to permit him to speak alone with Gerry. Through rapport building, expressing that he understood there may be a lot happening for Gerry that she feels the adults in her life do not understand, the counselor was able to convince Gerry that their attention to her was evidence that they cared for her and were willing to work together on solutions. Gerry, still quiet and guarded, began to tear up. The counselor asked if they could speak more regularly at school. Gerry nodded agreement.

Working slowly with Gerry, the school counselor began the process of initiating a therapeutic relationship that would prepare her to work with her mother and grandmother and a family therapist. Building Gerry's efficacy so that she would begin to feel comfortable talking about her inner world, she and the counselor developed a process for determining what content from their sessions could be shared with her grandmother and mother. The school counselor would meet monthly with Gerry's mother and grandmother to provide updates, follow up on Gerry's behavior at home, and facilitate the transition for their work with a family therapist. Given that the school counselor was male, he and Gerry (along with Gerry's mother and grandmother) decided they would continue their work together at school to support Gerry's development of a healthy relationship with a positive male role model.

Gerry, her mother, and grandmother began family therapy with some apprehension as the counseling process and being transparent with one another was new for them. The family therapist began by asking each to state, without comment from the others, what they saw as the issues in their family. After a pause, with Gerry looking down and her mother looking at her and shifting her gaze between the grandmother and therapist, Gerry's grandmother stated, "Gerry wants to be a boy and she's not a boy, she's a girl." Gerry rolled her eyes and her mother stated that she could see Gerry is not happy, but she does not know how to get her to talk. She began to cry, stating, "She does not trust me. She has shut me out." Gerry, visibly upset and on the verge of tears exclaimed, "They don't care about me; they just want me to do whatever will keep their little imperfect world from cracking apart."

Acknowledging the tension between the family members, the family therapist reflected "There's a lot that is said, but there seems to be even more that is unsaid." Aware of the depth of feeling and content that needed to be shared, the therapist continued by asking all three members of the family to share three things they hoped for their family. Gerry's grandmother began by stating that she'd like Gerry (1) to appreciate the fact that she is a girl growing into a woman and not be ashamed of her body, (2) to learn how to help Gerry be more proud of being a girl and help her to love herself, and (3) to see their family develop more closeness again. Gerry's mother followed by stating that she would like Gerry and her grandmother to be close again and talk as they had in the past. She would also like her relationship with Gerry to grow and to know her as she wants to be known rather than pressure Gerry to be someone she is not. Gerry shared one goal: to be accepted as she is.

Analysis and Commentary

Working with Gerry presents many challenges and opportunities to explore ways she can find support outside the home while her mother and grandmother develop their abilities to be supportive. It would be important for the clinician to consider Gerry's impressions of her sexuality and gender identity separate from the impositions of her mother and grandmother, while recognizing they will ultimately need to resolve the tension in their relationships. Gerry presents as a young woman who is frustrated because she is not being heard. Thus, therapy could foster empowerment and expanded alternatives (Guideline 7) through the use of the VCR model described earlier in this chapter (Hardy & Qureshi, 2012). Consistent with the VCR model, the clinician could validate Gerry by inviting her to use her self-definitions, if any, to guide their interactions. This could occur by inquiring how Gerry would like to be addressed, such as whether she has a preferred name and/or gender pronoun. The therapist might also work to understand Gerry's feelings about her mother and grandmother's attitudes and behaviors related to her gender (e.g., purchasing of clothes, forcing her not to play basketball with her friends, and insinuating sexual interaction with friends). Exploring Gerry's gender and sexual identities, providing her with language to describe what she might be feeling is a best fit, and relaxing the need for definition may prove to be particularly validating and respectful of her process. While the therapist may want to be sure to provide an LGBT-affirming therapeutic environment, it will be critical that he or she distinguish between the development of gender and sexual identity. Further, it should not be assumed that Gerry will ultimately identify as lesbian, bisexual, or transgender. Rather, work with her should center on exploration and processing questions without the necessity to commit to any identity.

It will be important for Gerry to know that she does not have to decide anything about her gender and sexual orientation at this time, that what she does decide may change, and that this possibility of change is fine. The therapist's demonstration of patient openness through this process will build Gerry's trust and communicate that she is respected. It is also possible that Gerry could feel validated by the therapist's recognition of how strong she has been to continue to affirm her more androgynous identity in spite of familial objections. Gerry could also be challenged about her behavior with regard to school and the fact that she has become disengaged and is spending time with a group that could reinforce risky behaviors (e.g., drug use, truancy).

Although Gerry displays gender nonconforming behaviors, her gender identity is likely to be unclear to her and is likely to evolve over time. She may eventually adopt a self-chosen label such as transgendered, lesbian, or bisexual, but for the present, some validation of the complexity of sexuality and sexual orientation issues is likely to be helpful. The use of social identity exploration tools, such as those discussed in Chapter 2, may assist Gerry to explore the meaning of her emerging sexuality, gender identity, and sexual orientation within the social context and in response to the various cultural expectations of others.

As part of this exploration, Gerry can be encouraged to consider how she wants to describe her gender identity to her family. For example, she might consider enlisting the help of an adult outside the home, perhaps a trusted family member or close family friend, school administrator, or someone from an LGBT youth advocacy organization. Coaching Gerry through the process of effectively communicating with her mother and grandmother could be of significant assistance as the family begins to understand and come to terms with Gerry's current gender identity expression. Finally, Gerry could be encouraged to consider ways she can reach out to get the support she needs. Consistent with Guideline 10, school-based programming like GLSEN (Gay, Lesbian, and Straight Education Network) or a GSA (Gay–Straight Alliance) might offer an age-appropriate prosocial way for Gerry to participate in an accepting community and at school, rather than spending time in the neighborhood with older males and using drugs.

As an aspect of the need for community and affinity, it might be useful for Gerry to be part of a sexual or gender identity questioning support group. Such a group would include a therapeutic focus that facilitates the processing of potential and/or experienced rejection by family and community due to one's perceived sexual orientation and/or gender identity. It is critical that as Gerry and her contemporaries process the negative and/or ambivalent reactions by family and friends, they have a safe space to develop healthy notions of identity that integrate their intersecting identities.

It would also be important that Gerry develop a sense of community outside of traditional therapy settings (Guideline 10). Referrals to resources like the Trevor Project (http://thetrevorproject.org) hotline would be appropriate to provide support in between sessions. It would also be critical for Gerry to have accurate information about sex and her health. Referral to an organization like the Advocates for Youth (http://www.advocatesforyouth.org) could be useful because it provides reliable information about making good decisions relative to one's health and body. Additionally, as Gerry learns to actively engage her right to self-determination and identification, work with youth-led activist organizations like Bay Area Youth Summit (BAYS; http://bayareayouthsummit.org) may serve to direct her rebellion toward supportive social change, rather than internalizing and manifesting depressive symptoms and using drugs as has been her approach to coping. Prosocial affiliation with youth-based groups has the potential to help Gerry more clearly define the contours of her identity alongside her peers. This type of involvement may be appropriate and could represent an indicator of healthy growth and identity integration.

It is important to understand that although initially committing to social action may be a bit overwhelming to Gerry, her decision to spend time with men and older boys in her community may be an attempt at social support outreach. Her decision to seek support outside of school or her family may be a reflection of the outsider status projected onto her for not confirming to traditional female gender role expectations. It is critical to consider the "why" of her choice. She has reported using drugs and skipping school to spend unsupervised time with this group, a choice that has been outside the knowledge of her mother and grandmother. Given the absence of her father, Gerry may be seeking connection and identification with the men/boys in her community. Further, some of what she has learned about her father has come through members of her community that knew him. While these may be reasons for her association, it is possible that Gerry is not mindful of the potential risks of unsupervised contact with men and older boys, especially if under the influence of controlled substances. Work with Gerry and her family will need to highlight the threats to her safety and provide other forms of affiliation, namely youth groups and other social organizations with which she can form supportive relational bonds.

Therapeutic work with Gerry's family system is also indicated, and a combination of both individual and family therapy would be appropriate.

Work with both the mother and grandmother would center on questioning and exploring the foundations of their gender roles and expectations. Although they may not think about it in the terms described in the literature, it will be important to examine the ways they were/are able to or were precluded from achieving the cult of true womanhood and how this model shapes their goals for Gerry. Additionally, the therapist might explore the absence of Gerry's father from her life and inquire about what she has been taught about him from her family and through his absence and their silence. Her mother and grandmother will need to examine Gerry's impressions of masculinity and femininity through ways gender has been "done" in their family. For example, the fact that she is socialized to conform to traditional gender roles, alongside the reality that both her mother and grandmother have obviously demonstrated a "functional androgyny" to carry out the operations of their home and lives, will need to be explored. This exploration may offer Gerry's mother and grandmother a pathway toward building empathy for Gerry who is also attempting to carve out her own sense of self in the face of external expectations.

As therapy unfolds and Gerry comes to terms with the intersectionality of her racial, sexual, and gender identities, it may be critical for her family to process their sense of loss about having a child who does not conform to their expectations. It is also important to discuss the positive goal of raising Gerry to be a happy, healthy adult. The clinician can also be very helpful in assisting this family with confronting the issue of acceptability in the eyes of their community. Gerry stated that she would like to be accepted for who she is in the face of her perception of her mother's and grandmother's wish to prevent their "little imperfect world from cracking apart." It may be helpful for them to speak with other families, perhaps of Black/African descent and/or with strong religious values, to find models for how they might grapple with this process in their family. Further, acquainting themselves with a family-based organization such as PFLAG (Parents, Family, & Friends of Gays and Lesbians) can be useful as they seek information about how to support a gender nonconforming youth. Should Gerry's identity development process reveal a lesbian orientation, support from an organization like PFLAG could further assist Gerry and her family as they work to offer effective guidance to her (Guideline 10).

Finally, work with Gerry's mother and grandmother should also focus on supporting their ability to integrate Gerry's sexuality and racial/gender identity into their faith discourse. Depending on the tenor and attitudes of their religious community, an attempt to facilitate a discussion with their spiritual/religious community could be an effective intervention. Sharing resources such as information about the Religious Institute, which offers gay affirmative materials, may serve to help reconcile some of their faith and sexuality conflicts (http://www.religiousinstitute.org/issue/lgbt-inclusion). Additionally, it may be helpful to connect them to organizations that provide education about current issues and concerns experienced by bisexual, lesbian, and transgendered Black/African persons, such as the National Black Lesbian and Gay Leadership Forum. Providing opportunities for Gerry's family to place Gerry's developing sexual and gender identities in a larger context holds potential to deepen their empathy and compassion for her. It is possible that Gerry's family will grow to accept and respect the unique intersection of racial, sexual, and gender identity journey; however, as they work through their resistance, the clinician can advocate for the importance of surrounding Gerry with a supportive community until her family can be fully responsive. Gerry can be encouraged to seek out the positive affirmations from her teachers, her peers, and women members of her church who respect her strong body and athletic skills. While Gerry's mother and grandmother work to build acceptance for her, it will be important to develop a network of supportive friends, community members, and professionals around her.

CONCLUSION

A review of the relevant literature suggests there are specific challenges to the health and well-being of Black/African women and girls that are tied to their gendered and racial standpoints. Psychologists and mental health practitioners seeking to competently support the concerns of Black/African women and girls will consider the implementation of interventions in well-informed and nuanced ways, responsive to the specific resources and limitations inherent to the varied experiences of each woman and girl. Larance (2012) warned there is not a one-size-fits-all approach to working with Black/African women victims of domestic violence and the same can be said for all Black/African women and girls. West's (2002) review of the violence literature related to Black/African women and girls acknowledged the dearth of work with women and girls that were not in the high-risk range. Whereas attention to risk groups is essential for appropriating resources for areas of significant need, the literature suggests that even apparently high functioning Black/African women and girls are overburdened by the intersection of their race and gender with daily life stressors and demands, amplifying the pressure and alienation they feel (Everett, Hall, & Hamilton-Mason, 2010). Thus, best practices and future research should consider a paradigmatic shift from deficit and deficiency hypotheses that pay attention to risk, to those that focus on the health and resilience of Black/African women and girls.

Along these lines, work related to Black/African women and girls seems to either focus on their unnatural strength, thus further perpetuating the strong Black woman ideology, or primarily on risk factors in the areas of sex, drug use/abuse, and violence. The literature review for this chapter also revealed that there is a virtual absence of health affirmative work about the lives of Black/African women and girls. The psychological community is left to wonder what a healthy Black/African woman or girl looks like. How would one know that a Black/African woman or girl is thriving? Similar to the development of the field of positive psychology, psychological theory, practice, and research need to turn toward exploring optimal health and well-being in order to identify pathways and outcomes for health that are culturally relevant and gender specific.

Finally, the role of gender in the lives of Black/African women and girls continues to be less frequently examined than that of race. The fields of legal studies and sociology have introduced intersectional analyses to psychology (Collins, 2000; Crenshaw, 1989), but continued inquiry about the ways systems of domination and intersecting identities shape experiences of women and girls of Black/African descent is needed. For example, Helms (2011) emphasized that although we know Black/African women cope with racial and gender-related discrimination and violence, limited attention is given by society and researchers to the mental and physical impacts of racism and ethnoviolence on Black women. It is imperative to extend the focus on these impacts to Black/African girls who are also traumatized by these experiences, likely for longer durations, and perhaps possess even fewer effective coping strategies than their adult counterparts.

The following recommendations are provided to guide continued work with Black/African women and girls and to establish more meaningful understandings and effective practices. Research and practice should focus on integrating the role of gender and other relevant identities in the lives of Black/African women and girls. Although an intersectionality analysis is being used more frequently, the complexity of identity and social experience that account for within group diversity among Black/African women and girls is not fully appreciated. Secondly, for the reasons stated above, a nuanced approach to intervention needs to be provided to ensure effective treatment of Black/African women and girls. As an appreciation for the varied identity and experiences within this subgroup is realized, it will be important to identify interventions that are most relevant and appropriate for subgroups within this population. Finally, as the literature indicates, it is important to be attentive to social and community networks of Black/African persons and to incorporate alternative approaches and community-based supports and advocacy to meet the needs of Black/African descent persons.

REFERENCES

American Psychological Association. (2007). Guidelines for the psychological practice with girls and women. *American Psychologist, 62*, 949–979. doi:10.1037/0003-066X.62.9.949

Binion, V. J. (1990). Psychological and androgyny: A black female perspective. *Sex Roles, 22*, 487–507. doi:10.1007/BF00288166

Bowleg, L., Huang, J., Brooks, K., Black, A., & Burkholder, G. (2003). Triple jeopardy and beyond: Multiple minority stress and resilience among Black lesbians. *Journal of Lesbian Studies, 7*, 87–108. doi:10.1300/J155v07n04_06

Boyd-Franklin, N. (1991). Recurrent themes in the treatment of African American women in group psychotherapy. *Women & Therapy, 11*(2), 25–40. doi:10.1300/J015V11N02_04

Brown, A. (2011). Descendants of "Ruth": Black girls coping through the "Black Male Crisis." *The Urban Review, 43*, 597–619. doi:10.1007/s11256-010-0162-x

Buckley, T. R., & Carter, R. T. (2005). Black adolescent girls: Do gender roles and racial identity impact their self-esteem? *Sex Roles, 53*, 647–661. doi:10.1007/s11199-005-7731-6

Cohen, C. (1999). *Boundaries of Blackness: AIDS and the breakdown of Black politics*. Chicago, IL: University of Chicago Press.

Cole, E. R., & Zucker, A. N. (2007). Black and White women's perspectives on femininity. *Cultural Diversity and Ethnic Minority Psychology, 13*(1), 1–9. doi:10.1037/1099-9809.13.1.1

Collins, P. H. (2000). *Black feminist thought*. New York, NY: Routledge.

Collins, P. H. (2005). *Black sexual politics: African Americans, gender, and the new racism*. New York, NY: Routledge.

Crenshaw, K. W. (1989). Demarginalizing the intersection of race and sex: A Black feminist critique of antidiscrimination doctrine, feminist theory, and antiracist politics. *University of Chicago Legal Forum, 89*, 139–167.

Dailey, D. E., Humphreys, J. C., Rankin, S. H., & Lee, K. A. (2011). An exploration of lifetime trauma exposure in pregnant low-income African American women. *Maternal and Child Health Journal, 15*, 410–418. doi:10.1007/s10995-008-0315-7

Degruy-Leary, J. (2005). *Post traumatic slave syndrome: America's legacy of enduring injury and healing*. Milwaukee, OR: Uptone Press.

Ehrlich, H. J. (2009). *Hate crimes and ethnoviolence: The history, current affairs and future of discrimination in America*. Boulder, CO: Westview Press.

Everett, J. E., Hall, J. C., & Hamilton-Mason, J. (2010). Everyday conflict and daily stressors: Coping responses of Black women. *Affilia: Journal of Women & Social Work, 25*(1), 30–42. doi:10.1177/0886109909354983

Ford, B. C. (2002). Violence and trauma: Predicting the impact on the well-being of African American women with severe mental illness. *Violence and Victims, 17*, 219–232. doi:10.1891/vivi.17.2.219.33646

Frame, M. W., Williams, C. B., & Green, E. L. (1999). Balm in Gilead: Spiritual dimensions in counseling African American women. *Journal of Multicultural Counseling and Development, 27,* 182–192. doi:10.1002/j.2161-1912.1999.tb00334.x

Froyum, C. M. (2010). Making 'good girls': Sexual agency in the sexuality education of low-income Black girls. *Culture, Health & Sexuality, 12*(1), 59–72. doi:10.1080/13691050903272583

Gay, C., & Tate, K. (1998). Doubly bound: The impact of gender and race on politics of Black women. *Political Psychology, 19,* 169–184. doi:10.1111/0162-895X.00098

Greene, B. (2000). African American lesbian and bisexual women. *Journal of Social Issues, 56,* 239–249. doi:10.1111/0022-4537.00163

Hardy, K. V., & Qureshi, M. E. (2012). Devaluation, loss, and rage: A postscript to urban African American youth with substance abuse. *Alcoholism Treatment Quarterly, 30,* 326–342. doi:10.1080/07347324.2012.690699

Harrell, S. P. (2000). A multidimensional conceptualization of racism-related stress: Implications for the well-being of people of color. *American Journal of Orthopsychiatry, 70*(1), 42–57. doi:10.1037/h0087722

Helms, J. E. (2011, October). *Ethnoviolence and Black Women.* Keynote address presented at the 11th Annual Diversity Challenge, sponsored by the Institute for the Study and Promotion of Race and Culture, Boston College, Chestnut Hill, MA.

Helms, J. E., Nicolas, G., & Green, C. (2012). Racism and ethnoviolence: Enhancing professional and research training. *Traumatology, 18,* 65–74. doi:10.1177/1534765610396728

Higginbotham, E. (1993). *Righteous discontent: The women's movement in the Black Baptist church, 1880–1920.* Cambridge, MA: Harvard University Press.

Jenkins, E. J. (2002). Black women and community violence: Trauma, grief and coping. *Women & Therapy, 25,* 29–44. doi:10.1300/J015v25n03_03

Jones, N. (2009). "I was aggressive for the streets, pretty for the pictures": Gender, difference, and the inner city girl. *Gender & Society, 23*(1), 89–93. doi:10.1177/0891243208326676

Josephs, L. L., & Abel, E. M. (2009). Investigating the relationship between intimate partner violence and HIV risk propensity in Black/African American women. *Journal of Family Violence, 24,* 221–229. doi:10.1007/s10896-009-9223-x

Kaslow, N. J., Jacobs, C. H., Young, S. L., & Cook, S. (2006). Suicidal behavior among low-income African American women: A comparison of first-time and repeat suicide attempters. *The Journal of Black Psychology, 32,* 349–365. doi:10.1177/0095798406290459

Larance, L. Y. (2012). Commentary on Wilson, Woods, Emerson, and Doneberg: The necessity for practitioner vigilance in assessing the full-context of an individual's life experiences. *Psychology of Violence, 2,* 208–210. doi:10.1037/a0027237

Littlefield, M. B. (2004). Gender role identity and stress in African American women. *Journal of Human Behavior in the Social Environment, 8,* 93–104. doi:10.1300/J137v08n04_06

Miller, J. (2008). *Getting played: African American girls, urban inequality and gendered violence.* New York: New York University Press.

Moore, M. R. (2006). Lipstick or Timberlands? Meanings of gender presentations in Black lesbian communities. *Signs: Journal of Women in Culture and Society, 32*(1), 113–139. doi:10.1086/505269

Musgrave, C. F., Allen, C. E., & Allen, G. J. (2002). Spirituality and health for women of color. *American Journal of Public Health, 92,* 557–560. doi:10.2105/AJPH.92.4.557

Nicolaidis, C., Timmons, V., Thomas, M. J., Waters, A. S., Wahab, S., Mejia, A., & Mitchell, S. R. (2010). "You don't go tell white people nothing": African American women's perspectives on the influence of violence and race on depression and depression care. *American Journal of Public Health, 100,* 1470–1476. doi:10.2105/AJPH.2009.161950

Noguera, P. A. (2008). *The trouble with Black boys: . . . And other reflections on race, equity, and the future of public education.* San Francisco, CA: Jossey-Bass.

Osunsami, S. (2012, January 18). Getting more people to care about missing Black women. *ABC News.* Retrieved from http://abcnews.go.com/blogs/headlines/2012/01/getting-more-to-care-about-missing-black-women/

Parks, S. (2010). *Fierce angels: The strong black woman in American life and culture.* New York, NY: One World, Ballantine Books.

Ponterotto, J. (2006). Understanding prejudice and racism. In J. G. Ponterotto, S. O. Utsey & P. B. Pedersen (Eds.), *Preventing prejudice: A guide for counselors, educators and parents* (2nd ed., pp. 3–25). Los Angeles, CA: Sage.

Root, M.P. (1992). Reconstructing the impact of trauma on personality. In M. Ballou (Ed.), *Personality and psychopathology: Feminist reappraisals* (pp. 229–266). New York, NY: Guilford Press.

Settles, I. H. (2006). Use of intersectional framework to understand Black women's racial and gender identities. *Sex Roles, 54,* 589–601. doi:10.1007/s11199-006-9029-8

Settles, I. H., Pratt-Hyatt, J. S., & Buchanan, N. T. (2008). Through the lens of race: Black and white women's perceptions of womanhood. *Psychology of Women Quarterly, 32,* 454–468. doi:10.1111/j.1471-6402.2008.00458.x

Shaw, A. (2005). The other side of the looking glass: The marginalization of fatness and Blackness in the construction of gender identity. *Social Semiotics, 15,* 143–152. doi:10.1080110350330500154725

Short, E. L., & Williams, W. S. (2013). From the inside out: Group work with women of color. *Journal for Specialists in Group Work, 12,* 1–21.

Stevens-Watkins, D., Brown-Wright, L., & Tyler, K. M. (2011). Brief report: The number of sexual partners and race-related stress in African-American adolescents:

Preliminary findings. *Journal of Adolescence, 34,* 191–194. doi:10.1016/j.adolescence.2010.02.003

Teitelman, A. M., Ratcliffe, S. J., Morales-Aleman, M. M., & Sullivan, C. M. (2008). Sexual relationship power, intimate partner violence and condom use among minority urban girls. *Journal of Interpersonal Violence, 23,* 1694–1712. doi:10.1177/0886260508314331

Thompson, M. P., Norris, F., & Runback, R. B. (1998). Comparative distress levels of inner-city family members of homicide victims. *Journal of Traumatic Stress, 11,* 223–242. doi:10.1023/A:1024494918952

Utsey, S. O., Giesbrecht, N., Hook, J., & Stanard, P. M. (2008). Cultural, socio-familial, and psychological resources that inhibit psychological distress in African American exposed to stressful life events and race-related stress. *Journal of Counseling Psychology, 55,* 49–62. doi:10.1037/0022-0167.55.1.49

Watlington, C. G., & Murphy, C. M. (2006). The role of religion and spirituality among African American survivors of domestic violence. *Journal of Clinical Psychology, 62,* 837–857. doi:10.1002/jclp.20268

Weekes, D. (2002). Get your freak on: How Black girls sexualize identity. *Sex Education, 2,* 251–262. doi:10.1080/1468181022000025802

Weekes, D. (2003). Keeping it in the community: Creating safe spaces for Black girlhood. *Community, Work and Family,* 6(1), 47–61. doi:1080/136688032000063897

Weisz, A. N. (2005). Reaching African American battered women: Increasing the effectiveness of advocacy. *Journal of Family Violence, 20,* 91–99. doi:10.1007/s10896-005-3172-9

Welter, B. (1966). The Cult of True Womanhood: 1820–1860. *American Quarterly, 18,* 151–174. doi:10.2307/2711179

West, C. M. (2002). Battered, black and blue. *Women & Therapy, 25,* 5–27. doi:10.1300/J015v25n03_02

White, A. (1999). Talking feminist, talking Black: Micromobilization processes in collective protest against rape. *Gender & Society, 13,* 77–100. doi:10.1177/089124399013001005

Williams, C. B. (2005). Counseling African American women: Multiple identities, multiple constraints. *Journal of Counseling & Development, 83,* 278–283. doi:10.1002/j.1556-6678.2005.tb00343.x

Williams, C. B., Frame, M. W., & Green, E. L. (1999). Counseling groups for African American women: A focus on spirituality. *Journal for Specialists in Group Work, 24,* 260–273. doi:10.1080/01933929908411435

Williams, W. S., Karlin, T., & Wallace, D. (in press). Project Sister Circle: Risk, intersectionality, and intervening in urban schools. *Journal of School Counseling.*

Wilson, H. W., Woods, B. A., Emerson, E., & Donenberg, G. R. (2012). Patterns of violence and sexual risk in low-income urban African American girls. *Psychology of Violence, 2,* 194–207. doi:10.1037/a0027265

Wing, A. K. (2003). *Critical race feminism: A reader*. New York: New York University Press.

Winkle-Wagner, R. (2008). Not feminist but strong: Black women's reflections of race and gender in college. *Negro Educational Review, 59,* 181–195.

Wright, C. V., Perez, S., & Johnson, D. M. (2010). The mediating role of empowerment for African American women experiencing intimate partner violence. *Psychological Trauma: Theory, Research, Practice, and Policy, 2,* 266–272. doi:10.1037/a0017470

Wyatt, G. E. (1997). *Stolen women: Reclaiming our sexuality, taking back our lives.* Hoboken, NJ: Wiley.

Wyatt, G. E., & Lyons-Rowe, S. (1990). African American women's sexual satisfaction as a dimension of their sexual roles. *Sex Roles, 22,* 509–524. doi:10.1007/BF00288167

Wyatt, G. E., Myers, H. F., Williams, J. K., Kitchen, C. R., Loeb, T., Carmona, J. V., . . . Presley, N. (2002). Does a history of trauma contribute to HIV risk for women of color? Implications for prevention and policy. *American Journal of Public Health, 92,* 660–665. doi:10.2105/AJPH.92.4.660

4

THE MOSAIC OF LATINAS IN THE UNITED STATES: PSYCHOLOGICAL PRACTICE WITH LATINA WOMEN AND GIRLS

DIANNA MARISOL GONZÁLEZ, CARRIE L. CASTAÑEDA-SOUND, AND RACHEL L. NAVARRO

Latinas are an ever-growing group with a rich history, influential present, and promising future. They comprise 15% of all women in the United States (U.S. Census Bureau, 2010), making them the largest female ethnic group of color. Whereas most Latinas share a common history of colonization and oppression, factors such as geography, sexual orientation, social class, and skin color intersect to create a diversity of experience, opportunity, and perspective. Consideration of how shared history and unique experiences contribute to complex identities is essential when providing Latinas psychological services. We begin by introducing the mosaic of Latinas in the United States.

http://dx.doi.org/10.1037/14460-004

Psychological Practice With Women: Guidelines, Diversity, Empowerment, C. Z. Enns, J. K. Rice, and R. L. Nutt (Editors)

Copyright © 2015 by the American Psychological Association. All rights reserved.

LATINAS IN THE UNITED STATES

Latinas represent a variety of racial, ethnic and national origins. Although the U.S. Census considers this group of individuals Hispanic (or of Spanish descent), Latinas most often identify themselves by country of origin (e.g., Guatemalan; Pew Hispanic Center [PHC], 2012). Consistent with patterns of immigration and the history of United States, six out of 10 Latinas in the United States have a Mexican background (Gonzales, 2008; Motel & Patten, 2012). Recent immigration from other Latin American countries and the Caribbean has shifted Latinas' demographics in that Central Americans, South Americans, and Caribbean Americans now represent 13%, 12%, and 13% of the immigrant Latina/o population in the United States, respectively (Motel & Patten).

Racial self-identification also differs among Latinas. According to the U.S. Census Bureau (2010), Latinas were more likely to identify as White. However, the PHC (2012) reported that Latinas identified themselves as "some other race" when given the option to identify as White, Black, or Asian. Generation status influences racial self-identification in that third-generation Latinas were more likely to identify as White than second-generation Latinas (PHC, 2012). Also, the history of Latinas in the Americas and the Caribbean contributes to diversity in Latinas' phenotypes. Often depicted as having brown skin, dark hair, and dark eyes (e.g., Dora the Explorer), Latinas can have stereotypical White-looking features (e.g., Jessica Perez, model), stereotypical African features (e.g., Zoe Saldana, actress), or stereotypical Asian features (e.g., Arlene Serna, Miss Teen Latina Global in 2012). Furthermore, some Latinas may appear racially ambiguous, often identifying as biracial or multiracial.

Further differences exist amongst Latinas. On average, U.S.-born Latinas are younger, report English as their dominant language, and have some college education compared with Latina immigrants (Gonzales, 2008). Although both U.S.-born Latinas and Latina immigrants are more likely to live in poverty compared with their non-Latina counterparts, U.S.-born Latinas tend to earn more than Latina immigrants (Gonzales, 2008). Additionally, U.S. Latinas who identify as lesbian or bisexual are at greater risk for poor general health outcomes and mental distress than their Latina heterosexual peers (Kim & Fredriksen-Goldsen, 2012). Such challenges and differences inevitably increase the diversity of experiences for U.S. women of Latina/o descent.

The aforementioned diversity of Latinas may be overlooked in an effort to highlight their historical and cultural commonalities. However, it is important to consider their intersecting identities in the provision of culturally competent and sensitive psychological services. The "Guidelines for Psychological Practice With Girls and Women" (APA, 2007, referred to as the Guidelines throughout this chapter) were created in part to inform the practice of professionals working with girls and women by contextualizing their experiences and promoting cultural competent practice. The Guidelines are applicable to the provision of psychological services to Latinas in that they highlight how multiple intersectionalities of identity along with historical and daily oppressions (e.g., racism, classism) and gender and cultural socialization (e.g., *marianismo*, language) impact Latinas' psychological well-being (e.g., economic stress, health disparities; González & Navarro, 2010). However, we argue that additional information is needed to enhance the application of the Guidelines with Latinas. To that end, this chapter discusses research and practice relevant to the major sections of the Guidelines and concludes with a case study.

DIVERSITY, SOCIAL CONTEXT, AND POWER (GUIDELINES 1–3)

Latinas' lived experiences occur within a multitude of social, historical, and cultural contexts that encompass aspects of oppression and privilege associated with their membership in at least two social groups— women and Latinas/os. According to the *Guidelines*, the impact of these experiences on Latinas' identities, socialization, and health must be taken into account when engaging in any type of psychological practice. Thus, psychologists must understand and address the diversity of Latinas' intersecting identities (Guideline 2), their experiences of gender socialization within the Latina/o culture (Guideline 1), and the impact of discrimination and bias on their physical and mental health (Guideline 3). Also, it is important to understand and promote Latinas' strengths and assets to prevent and intervene in the potentially detrimental effects of identity struggles, oppression, and discrimination. This section presents information and scholarship pertaining to these specific guidelines along with Latinas' strengths and assets.

Understanding and Addressing Latinas' Intersecting Identities

The mosaic of Latinas goes beyond simple demographics to a complexity of Latina identities wherein each Latina makes meaning from her differing sociocultural affiliations. Thus, Latinas' identities are embedded within their unique sociocultural contexts, contributing to intersections that result in great diversity of perception, thought, and behavior as well as access to resources and opportunities (Hurtado & Cervantez, 2009). Within this complexity, Latinas find themselves making sense of conflicting cultural group values, norms, and expectations.

Anzaldúa (1987) introduced the idea of *borderlands* to explain how Latinas embrace the ambiguity and contradictions inherent in holding multiple social perspectives and being able to do so without conflict or distress. Anzaldúa's concept of borderlands "denotes the space in which antithetical elements mix, not to obliterate each other nor to be subsumed by a larger whole but rather to combine in unique and unexpected ways" (Hurtado & Cervantez, 2009, p. 182). Thus, in the borderlands, Latinas make sense of their identities that may be associated with privilege (e.g., Whiteness, upper social class, being able-bodied, opposite-gender attraction) and those that may be associated with oppression (e.g., gender, indigenous descent, same-gender attraction, working class, being non-able-bodied). Borderlands afford Latinas the opportunity to find creative and politically progressive ways to manage the dialectic of identity that ultimately may result in social action (Hurtado & Cervantez, 2009), or what Anzaldúa called a *mestiza consciousness*.

Psychologists working with Latinas need to provide room for the exploration of complex identities and unique lived experiences and their influences on presenting concerns within the borderlands. Psychologists must resist the urge to homogenize Latinas into a singular sociocultural group while acknowledging the ways in which Latinas may be similar, particularly related to their expression of cultural values and their lived experiences as women and girls growing up within the Latina/o culture. While managing this dialectic, psychologists must attend to sociocultural mechanisms that influence Latinas' multiple identities, expression of cultural values, and lived experiences—namely acculturation, enculturation, and ethnic identity.

Latinas live within a context of intersecting cultures: the U.S. dominant culture, the general Latina/o culture, and their specific Latina/o culture. Whereas acculturation processes expose them to U.S. cultural norms, values, behaviors, and knowledge that may lead to their acquisition of a U.S. cultural identity, enculturation processes expose them to their culture of origin's norms, values, behaviors, and knowledge that may lead to their retention of a Latina/o cultural identity (Schwartz, Unger, Zamboanga, & Szapocznik, 2010). This process of socialization does not imply that Latinas must choose between the U.S. and Latina/o cultures; instead, each Latina consciously or unconsciously "chooses" aspects of each culture's norms, values, and behaviors to which she will adhere. It is important to acknowledge that Latinas' bidimensional experiences of acculturation and enculturation happen within varied contexts influenced by individual (e.g., sexual orientation, age, language fluency), familial (e.g., socioeconomic status [SES], resources) and environmental (e.g., geographic location, receptivity to other cultural groups) characteristics (Schwartz et al., 2010), resulting in myriad identities with differing levels of U.S. and Latina/o identity saliency. These different constellations of U.S. and Latina/o identity result in within-group variation in the expression of Latina/o cultural values, experiences of oppression and privilege, and ultimately the manifestation of physical and mental health concerns. Therefore, when working with Latinas, a comprehensive assessment of the different dimensions of their U.S. and Latina identities is crucial in providing culturally competent services.

Understanding the Role of Cultural Values in Latinas' Gender Socialization

Differential gender-role expectations are evident within the Latina/o culture (Arciniega, Anderson, Tovar-Blank, & Tracey, 2008; Castillo, Perez, Castillo, & Ghosheh, 2010). Traditional views of Latina/o culture have suggested that these expectations are rooted in a patriarchal system that ascribes positions of power and privilege to Latinos and positions of subordination to Latinas (Santiago-Rivera, Arredondo, & Gallardo-Cooper, 2002). Thus, Latinos are seen as the familial authority figures who have control over their wives, children, and property. However, more contemporary understandings of Latina/o culture suggest that Latinas hold a significant amount of power within the family based on their roles as cultural brokers, emotional nurturers, and interpersonal connectors (Santiago-Rivera et al., 2002). From this perspective, Latinas are seen as the "rock" of the family. Given that gendered behavior varies based on differing sociocultural affiliations and contexts, the reality of differential Latina/o gender socialization may lie somewhere between the traditional patriarchal and contemporary views of Latina/o culture. Thus, the complexity in understanding and addressing the impact of gender socialization in the lives of Latinas is profound.

Although gender-role expectations can vary greatly based on Latinas' multiple identities and contexts, a set of core cultural values may be relevant to the gender socialization of Latinas (Santiago-Rivera et al., 2002). These core cultural values include, but are not limited to, *marianismo*, *familismo*, *respeto*, and *simpatía*. In and of itself, *marianismo* is a set of norms that guides female gender role behavior (Castillo et al., 2010). This term was first coined by Stevens (1973) to highlight her observations of Latinas' ascribed subordinate position and their idealization as semidivine figures that counterbalance Latinos' carnal tendencies. Given the Latina/o culture's strong historical and current ties to Catholicism (68% of Latinas/os identify as Roman Catholic; Pew Hispanic Center, 2007a), Latinas are expected to model their behavior after the Virgin Mary (Stevens, 1973). Thus, Latinas are expected to be loyal, self-sacrificing, humble, passive, submissive, yielding, docile, chaste, and spiritually superior (Stevens, 1973). In traditional Latina/o families, adherence to *marianismo* may manifest itself in restrictions on Latinas' social activities and privileges (Raffaelli & Ontai, 2004), primarily to ensure they remain virginal until marriage (i.e., chaste). Indeed, Raffaelli and Ontai (2004) found that Latinas/os perceived their parents as instituting earlier curfews on school nights and weekends and restricting driving privileges, school activities, and workforce participation more for their daughters compared with their sons, essentially attempting to curb their daughters' dating behaviors.

Whereas traditional *marianista* beliefs manifest themselves in the gender socialization of Latinas, these beliefs only represent one dimension of Latina gender-role expectations. Contemporary scholarship of *marianismo* advocates for a multidimensional understanding of *marianista* beliefs (Castillo et al., 2010; Guzmán, 2011). For example, Guzmán's (2011) reconceptualization of *marianismo* takes into account aspects of traditional (e.g., self-sacrifice, passivity) *marianismo* along with more positive attributes of the Virgin Mary, namely, assertiveness, courage, and leadership. Thus, she argued that servant-leadership is an additional dimension of *marianismo* wherein servant-leaders take on the traditional qualities of a *marianista* for the betterment of others. According to Guzmán, Latina servant-leaders embrace advocacy and leadership roles within their families, schools, places of worship, and communities. Overall, the inclusion of servant-leadership in the understanding of *marianismo* takes into account the changing roles of Latinas within their families and society as a whole.

Castillo et al. (2010) and Guzmán (2011) also advocated for the inclusion of *familismo* in contemporary understandings of *marianismo*. *Familismo* is undeniably one of the most central Latina/o cultural values in that family is prioritized in day-to-day decisions and long-term goals (Raffaelli & Ontai, 2004; Santiago-Rivera et al., 2002). The Latina/o definition of family includes members of the immediate family, extended family members, godparents (*padrinas/os*), family friends, and religious leaders (Santiago-Rivera et al., 2002). *Familismo* reflects the importance of family unity, interdependence, loyalty, cooperation, affiliation, and responsibility (Santiago-Rivera et al., 2002). Whereas *familismo* is relevant for both Latinos and Latinas, Castillo et al. argued that the behavioral manifestation of *familismo* itself is gendered. Indeed, Latinos are expected to be family financial providers, protectors, and leaders (Arciniega et al., 2008). On the other hand, Latinas are expected to marry and honor their husbands, give birth and raise multiple children, attend to their family's physical and emotional health, and manage all household work (Santiago-Rivera et al., 2002). To honor and protect their families, Latinas may be active community members and leaders, particularly within their spiritual homes (Guzmán, 2011), and thus are seen as the family and spiritual pillar (Castillo et al., 2010).

Another cultural value that provides more dimensionality to Latina gender role expectations is that of *simpatía*. *Simpatía* is a cultural script for engaging in empathic, harmonious, smooth, and pleasant interpersonal interactions (Castillo et al., 2010). Behaviorally, this cultural norm may manifest itself in politeness and civility wherein conflict is completely avoided. Latinas who adhere to *simpatía* may not voice their personal thoughts or assert their needs, and they forgive others for transgressions as strategies for maintaining relationship harmony, particularly within their romantic partnerships (i.e., self-silencing to maintain harmony; Castillo et al., 2010).

For Latinas, *simpatía* is closely related to *respeto*—the value of being obedient, dutiful, and deferent to authority figures within and outside the family (Santiago-Rivera et al., 2002). *Respeto* functions to maintain the hierarchical structure within the Latina/o family structure, calling for Latinas to be obedient and subordinate to their husbands (Castillo et al., 2010) while also maintaining hierarchical structures within other societal institutions (e.g., schools, mental health and medical systems). Together, *simpatía* and *respeto* may reinforce traditional *marianista* beliefs and associated behaviors. At the same time, these cultural values may support Latinas' servant-leadership roles, particularly when they see conflict and disrespect within systems.

Adherence to both traditional and contemporary *marianista* beliefs and related socialization experiences may vary greatly based on Latina/o individual and familial contexts. Thus, it is imperative that psychologists assess differing levels of adherence to Latina gender role expectations and associated behaviors across multiple dimensions of cultural values and identities. For example, whereas a Latina may strongly adhere to *familismo* and servant-leadership, she may not adhere to the behavioral expectations of *simpatía* and *respeto* to the same degree. Moreover, Latinas in the United States are socialized within both their cultures of origin and the U.S. dominant culture, which emphasizes individualism, autonomy, and direct communication styles. Finally, Latinas who identify as lesbian or bisexual may find themselves under great pressure to conform to heterosexual Latina gender role norms (e.g., marrying a man and raising his children) and may be ostracized by their families if they do not. Understanding the complexity of Latinas' gender socialization experiences within their cultural context is essential in providing culturally appropriate and competent psychological services.

Impact of Discrimination and Bias on Latinas' Physical and Mental Health

As members of multiple socially oppressed groups, Latinas may experience discrimination that ultimately impacts their physical and mental health (Araújo & Borrell, 2006). Such discrimination includes (a) acute discriminatory stressors that occur intermittently but infrequently in Latinas' lives (e.g., negative hiring decisions, denial of housing or loans; Araújo & Borrell, 2006; Harrell, 2000), (b) chronic discriminatory stressors occurring daily (e.g., subtle or overt acts of exclusion, isolation, and degradations; unequal distribution of and access to economic and social resources; Araújo & Borrell, 2006; Harrell,

2000), and (c) vicarious discriminatory stressors (e.g., those acts experienced by others that are witnessed personally and/or via conversations or the media; Harrell, 2000). These aforementioned experiences are deemed stressful when they are perceived as discriminatory and result in physiological and psychological arousal (Williams, Neighbors, & Jackson, 2003).

Despite being a major concern for Latinas/os, there is little research examining the effects of perceived discrimination on Latinas' physical health. This limited research has focused on self-rated health quality, health symptoms, and/or physical limitations (Bermúdez-Millán et al., 2011; D'Anna, Ponce, & Siegel, 2010; Flores et al., 2008). Whether using qualitative (Bermúdez-Millán et al., 2011) or quantitative (D'Anna, Ponce, & Siegel, 2010; Flores et al., 2008) methodologies, this previous research has found that perceived discrimination (either chronic or related to health settings) negatively impacts Latinas' general physical health but to a lesser extent than for their Latino male peers. This previous research has also found that the negative effects of perceived discrimination on Latinas' general physical health are more pronounced at lower levels of social economic status. That is, perceived discrimination takes more of a toll on Latinas' physical health when their access to health care, health insurance, education, and work is restricted because of limited economic resources. This is true for Latinas in general (D'Anna et al., 2010), Mexican-origin women (Flores et al., 2008), and Puerto Rican women (Bermúdez-Millán et al., 2011).

Unlike the domain of physical health, there is a plethora of scholarship on the relation between perceived discrimination and Latinas' mental health. The majority of this research has focused on levels of depression (e.g., Bermúdez-Millán et al., 2011; Flores et al., 2008; Lorenzo-Blanco & Cortina, 2013; Ramos, Jaccard, & Guilamo-Ramos, 2003; Tillman & Weiss, 2009). Although researchers have concluded that perceived discrimination is positively associated with depression, this research also takes into account moderating factors in this relation, such as immigrant status and ethnicity (e.g., Tillman & Weiss, 2009), skin color (e.g., Ramos et al., 2003), acculturation (e.g., Lorenzo-Blanco & Cortina, 2013), and economic conditions (e.g., Bermúdez-Millán et al., 2011; Flores et al., 2008). For example, Tillman and Weiss (2009) argued that there is an immigrant advantage wherein foreign-born Latinas actually exhibited lower levels of lifetime stress, had fewer experiences of discrimination, and reported greater declines in depressive symptoms than their native-born female peers across a 2-year period. Levels of acculturation may explain nativity differences in the relation between discrimination and depression in that acculturation to the United States erodes family closeness and increases family conflict, leading to increased depressive symptoms for Latinas (Lorenzo-Blanco & Cortina, 2013).

Along with nativity and acculturation, ethnicity was also significantly related to depressive symptoms for Latinas (Tillman & Weiss, 2009). That is,

Nicaraguan and other Latinas were significantly less likely to report declines in depressive symptoms when compared with their Cuban peers. Cuban women often live in protective ethnic enclaves and thus may not experience overt discrimination as often. Therefore, when they do experience discrimination, it does have a greater negative impact initially, but the effects are not as long lasting (Tillman & Weiss, 2009). Furthermore, Nicaraguan women and other Latinas' (e.g., Puerto Rican, Dominican) experiences of discrimination may be tied to their skin color and phenotype, given that they may be phenotypically Indigenous or Black (Tillman & Weiss, 2009). Indeed, Ramos et al. (2003) found that Black Latinas reported increased levels of depression when compared with non-Black Latinas.

Like its impact on physical health, SES also appears to affect the relationship between perceived discrimination and mental health (Bermúdez-Millán et al., 2011; Flores et al., 2008). That is, negative effects of perceived discrimination on Latinas' mental health are stronger for those Latinas of lower SES than for their higher SES peers. This is true for Latinas in general (D'Anna et al., 2010), Mexican-origin women (Flores et al., 2008), and Puerto Rican women (Bermúdez-Millán et al., 2011).

Future research is needed to understand clearly the impact of perceived discrimination on physical and mental health across the multitude of Latina ethnic groups and across multiple Latina identities. For example, research speculates that the combination of antigay bias and ethnic discrimination may be linked to the finding that Latina lesbian/bisexual women are more likely to endorse struggling with depressive disorder than their heterosexual counterparts (Cochran, Mays, Alegria, Ortega, & Takeuchi, 2007); however, we were unable to locate research that directly tested this hypothesis. Such knowledge is necessary to inform culturally appropriate and sensitive psychological interventions for Latinas. It is essential to attend to Latinas' immigration status, ethnicity, acculturation, skin color/phenotype, sexual orientation, and SES when intervening in the link between perceived discrimination and health.

Understanding Latinas' Strengths and Assets

As Latinas struggle to redefine their femininity, they learn how to "speak up" (e.g., voice their beliefs, opinions, and observations) and use this skill to advocate for themselves and others in the face of discrimination and bias. For example, in a qualitative study of Mexican American early adolescent girls, Denner and Dunbar (2004) found that these girls challenged neighborhood boys to be better role models for the children who were watching their actions, protected their mothers when their nurturing roles were minimized within the family, explicitly pointed out sexist actions by their teachers, and acted as mediators in community rivalries by building relationships to prevent violence and promote peace. Similarly, Lopez (2006) found that Dominican high school girls resisted racial and gender oppression by voicing their dreams in class and attending to their academic pursuits. The more Latinas use their voices to advocate for themselves, their families, and their communities, the more empowered and confident they may become (Denner & Dunbar, 2004; Lopez, 2006), resulting in greater self-efficacy in various life domains.

Embracing traditional cultural values (e.g., *familismo, respeto*) and traditional gender roles (e.g., *marianismo*) may serve as protective factors for Latinas. In fact, *familismo* has been linked to less alcohol use and misuse for immigrant Latina adults living in predominately Spanish-speaking neighborhoods (Dillon, De La Rosa, Sastre, & Ibañez, 2012). Also, *familismo*, respect, and traditional gender roles have been linked to increased family cohesion, which was related to less depressive symptomatology for U.S.-born Latina adolescents (Lorenzo-Blanco, Unger, Baezconde-Garbanati, Ritt-Olson, & Soto, 2012). Furthermore, *familismo* was negatively related to risky sexual behaviors for Latina eighth graders (Guilamo-Ramos, Bouris, Jaccard, Lesesne, & Ballan, 2009). Taken together, previous research suggests that promoting the retention of traditional Latina/o culture values may protect Latinas against heavy alcohol use and misuse, depression, and risky sexual behaviors.

Along with *familismo* and *respeto*, Latinas' traditional gender roles tie them closely to their families. These close ties promote the retention of the Spanish language and propel Latinas into the role of language brokers (e.g., interpreting linguistic and cultural information, negotiating exchanges with outside agencies) for their families at a greater rate than their male peers (Buriel, Perez, De Ment, Chavez, & Moran, 1998). Although language brokering may seem like an added burden for Latinas, those who are language brokers in more places and have more familial responsibilities actually report fewer depressive symptoms (Love & Buriel, 2007). Retaining Spanish language competencies while simultaneously acquiring English language competencies also has academic benefits, with bilingual students being less likely to drop out of school than their monolingual Spanish or English-speaking peers (Feliciano, 2001). Building on Latinas' language competencies and family ties that provide language brokering opportunities and greater responsibility may be an important key in promoting their academic success and protecting them from depression.

Language brokering is also positively related to biculturalism (Buriel et al., 1998), another protective factor for Latinas. *Biculturalism* refers to acquiring proficiency and identification with both the traditional Latina/o culture of origin and the U.S. culture in terms of cultural values, practices, and behaviors (Schwartz & Unger, 2010), allowing Latinas to shift back and forth between these two cultures seamlessly. Benet-Martínez and Haritatos (2005) called this ability *cultural frame-switching*, arguing that it increases cognitive flexibility. In fact, previous research found that Latinas with higher levels of biculturalism were more likely to use a wider range of achieving styles within academic settings (Gomez & Fassinger, 1994) and have higher levels of academic achievement (Buriel et al., 1998). In general, bicultural Latinos exhibited high levels of social interest and lower levels of depression (A. O. Miranda & Umhoefer, 1998). Whereas increasing acculturation tends to erode strong family networks and cultural values, bicultural Latina/o families tend to display lower levels of conflict and display more commitment, help, and support for one another (A. O. Miranda, Estrada, & Firpo-Jimenez, 2000). By promoting biculturalism, psychologists are helping Latinas find their voices within two cultures, resulting in increased self-confidence. Overall, promoting Latinas' strengths and assets is a powerful way to prevent and reduce the harmful effects of identity struggles and discrimination.

PROFESSIONAL RESPONSIBILITY AND PRACTICE APPLICATIONS (GUIDELINES 4–9)

The Guidelines cite Worell and Johnson's (1997) definition of *psychological practice* as "clinical practice and supervision, pedagogy, research, scholarly writing, administration, leadership, social policy, and any of the other activities in which psychologists may engage" (p. 34). This section addresses the various ways that psychologists have a professional responsibility to be competent in their work with Latinas.

The Self of the Psychologist

Cultural competence with diverse clients has tremendous implications for professional practice and responsibility. Both Guidelines 4 and 5 (APA, 2007) and APA's (2003) *Guidelines on Multicultural Education, Training, Research, Practice, and Organizational Change for Psychologists* highlight self-awareness by acknowledging the fact that as cultural beings we hold worldviews that are informed by multiple identities in a sociopolitical context that "predispose individual psychologists to certain biases and assumptions about themselves and others" (p. 17). As a result, ongoing introspection about personal histories and worldviews is critical to culturally attuned practice. Particularly relevant to Latinas' experience are the social and political discourses about immigration, and the impact of these discourses on individuals, couples, and families. It is difficult to work with the Latina/o community without having some direct or indirect experience with immigration policies. Immigration issues include families and couples having members with different documentation statuses as well as the experience of microaggressions by Latinas who are not immigrants but are recipients of nativist comments. Preconceived notions of Latinas and the Latina/o community should be examined so that clients are not harmed. For example, supervisees may question whether they are mandated to report an undocumented client. Although this seems like an honest ethical and legal question, the question comes from a place of privilege and should be examined for underlying biases.

A psychologist also should be aware of the strengths and limitations of his or her own training and clinical experience with Latinas. Without a personal analysis of assumptions about Latinas regarding family obligations, identity, sexuality, SES, and cultural values, well-meaning interventions could perpetuate essentialist views of Latinas. Additionally, because of the diversity of Latinas, it would not be unusual for a Latina psychologist, who initially might seem to be a good match to work with a Latina client or supervisee, to hold internalized beliefs and assumptions that could be detrimental to the therapeutic or supervisory relationship. This could involve but is not limited to differences in the manifestation of cultural values, varying dialects and regional differences when speaking in Spanish, and religious and spiritual differences. Creating a cultural genogram is one training method to help supervisees examine their ethnic heritage as well as sources of pride, shame, resistance, and resilience (see Hardy and Laszloffy's, 1995, description of this exercise). Increasingly, graduate programs are responding to the call to train culturally and linguistically responsive clinicians and have developed culturally centered curricula to train bilingual therapists, such as Our Lady of the Lake's Psychological Services for Spanish-Speaking Populations certificate program (Biever, Gómez, González, & Patrizio, 2011).

Psychological Practice With Latinas

The past 20 years have seen shifts in the practice of psychotherapy toward a greater focus on evidence-based approaches. APA's (2006) Task Force on Evidence-Based Practice in Psychology defined *evidence-based practice* as "the integration of the best available research with clinical expertise in the context of patient characteristics, culture, and preferences" (p. 273). Whereas such a definition is broad enough to include a variety of evidence, some scholars, practitioners, and grant-funding agencies continue to equate evidence-based practice with empirically supported treatments. Brown (2006) provided a thoughtful analysis of this movement, particularly as it relates to feminist psychotherapy. Targeting the research that identifies the importance of therapeutic relationships for positive therapeutic outcomes (Norcross & Lambert, 2005), Brown explained that feminist therapists "have spent three decades thinking about how to make the therapeutic relationship more egalitarian, more empowering, and how to give the client more of a voice in therapy"

(p. 18). Clearly, feminist therapy is relevant to psychological practice with Latinas on the basis of the culturally congruent practice of developing the therapeutic alliance but also because of the focus on personal experiences that are tied to societal oppression. Feminist theory has traditionally disrupted dominant discourses that overpathologize women and girls by deconstructing the threads of patriarchy within the field of psychology (Brown, 1994). This is evident, for example, in the research about sexual objectification (Szymanski, Moffitt, & Carr, 2011) and intimate partner violence (Perilla, Serrata, Weinberg, & Lippy, 2012).

A gendered cultural lens is a perspective that is necessary to fully address the context of Latina women and girls in assessment and treatment. Important areas to consider during assessment are experiences of racism, xenophobia, classism, and linguistic prejudice, and how these experiences moderate the expression of psychological symptoms, as well as considering culturally bound diagnoses (e.g., *ataque de nervios* [nerve attack]; Hinton, Lewis-Fernández, & Pollack, 2009). Readers should be cautioned about the limited feminist scholarship examining the role of gender within these culture-bound syndromes.

Immigration brings many challenges to Latinas, and a careful assessment of Latina clients who have immigrated (voluntarily and involuntarily) to the United States is warranted to assess exposure to traumatic events, grief related to immigrating, minority stress and acculturation, and strategies for coping with stress (Falicov, 2012). Readers also are referred to the report by the APA Presidential Task Force on Immigration (2012) for a comprehensive review of the psychological process of immigration. In particular, the experience of immigration intersects with gender and mental health when women (a) experience higher rates of depression due to separation from their children and family who reside in the country of origin (J. Miranda, Siddique, Der-Martirosian, & Belin, 2005); (b) exhibit symptoms of posttraumatic stress disorder due to trauma exposure in the country of origin due to war, political violence, or community violence (Santa-Maria & Cornille, 2007); (c) experience increased marginality and victimization during the immigration if they are lesbian, bisexual, or transgendered (Morales, 2013); and (d) they are survivors of interpersonal violence (Vidales, 2010). As a result, clinicians should be mindful of culturally adapted approaches as well as clients' culturally informed resilience.

Díaz-Lázaro, Verdinelli, and Cohen (2012) argued for the use of empowerment feminist therapy (EFT) with immigrant Latinas. Their article applied the principles of EFT to a case example of a Latina immigrant. The critical components of their analysis reflected the four principles of feminist therapy identified by Worell and Remer (2003): "(a) Personal and social identities are interdependent, (b) the personal is political, (c) relationships are egalitarian, and (d) women's perspectives are valued" (as cited in Díaz-Lázaro et al., 2012, p. 84). This case analysis exemplified the blending of feminist and multicultural clinical approaches by centralizing the client's experience within a sociocultural and political context. Conceptualization of client problems within this context shifts the lens from solely intrapsychic explanations to a dynamic understanding of the client's positionality within multiple systems and processes (e.g., social inequality due to patriarchy, immigration status, language acquisition and maintenance, sexual orientation, and SES).

Cultural Adaptation and Culturally Centered Approaches

Cultural adaptation of existing psychotherapeutic approaches often involves adapting specific frameworks (see Bernal, Jiménez-Chafey, & Domenech Rodríguez, 2009). Researchers have found culturally adapted cognitive behavioral therapy to be efficacious with Latinas to address depression (J. Miranda et al., 2005), whereas others found both interpersonal psychotherapy and cognitive–behavioral therapy to be effective interventions with Puerto Rican adolescents experiencing depression (Rosselló, Bernal, & Rivera-Medina, 2008). Examples of cultural adaptation include conducting the treatment in Spanish, incorporating cultural values of *respeto* and *personalismo* in developing a strong therapeutic alliance and setting goals, including parents and extended family, and using culturally informed metaphors (*dichos*) and folktales from specific Latina/o cultures (*cuento* therapy; Domenech Rodríguez, Baumann, & Schwartz, 2011).

Comas-Díaz (2006) has written extensively about the cultural centering of mainstream psychotherapy with Latinas/os and has addressed the paradigmatic differences in Latina/o psychology, in particular, Latina/o notions of self, spiritual and cultural resilience, and *sabiduria* (wisdom) and empowerment. Comas-Díaz also reminded readers that the worldview of Latinas/os is one of social action and a "political consciousness, activism, and empowerment" (p. 437). This perspective ties to feminist and liberatory principles that the personal is political and that personal experiences of oppression and silencing often have social correlates. As a result, culturally responsive therapists will have knowledge of community resources for their Latina clients (e.g., workforce development training, culturally competent physicians, folk healers).

Role of Language

Language and cultural meaning are significant for bilingual Latinas. Research documents the role of language in psychotherapy through the use of cultural metaphors, or *dichos* (Comas-Díaz, 2006; Santiago-Rivera et al., 2002), as well as the use of the client's native language to facilitate emotion-focused therapy (Santiago-Rivera, Altarriba, Poll, Gonzalez-Miller, & Cragun, 2009). Bilingual Latinas may speak in English for a variety of reasons. For example, they may speak in the language in which memories are encoded (Santiago-Rivera et al., 2009) or they may speak in English when discussing highly charged topics (Espín, 2012). For example, bilingual lesbians "avoid equivalent words in their native tongue, probably because of the negative connotation of Spanish words that refer to their lesbian identity" (Espín, 2012, p. 51). Clearly, this is an area that warrants further research.

Language also is a factor in developing a therapeutic alliance (Comas-Díaz, 2006). During the initial meeting with a bilingual client, a therapist's use of Spanish may initiate a "linguistic handshake" (B. Perez, personal communication, August 1, 2012). However, the client may have questions about the therapist's country of origin when hearing his or her dialect and accent. Such questions may challenge therapists who balance professional ethics, therapeutic orientations, and cultural responsiveness when deciding to share personal information.

There are numerous considerations with regard to formal psychological assessment with Latinas. Although a thorough review is beyond the scope of this chapter, major issues involve (a) the continued training of the practitioner to provide culturally competent assessment, (b) the validity and reliability of the instrument with diverse communities (especially with regard to translation methods of the instrument and the formality of Spanish used), (c) knowledge and understanding of culturally relevant constructs and diagnoses, and (d) the skills required to provide results to clients in a culturally responsive manner (Acevedo-Polakovich et al., 2007). All intake procedures should include assessments of the client's social class, dominant language, and formal education in her preferred language. For instance, an indigenous dialect may be the Latina client's first language (e.g., Nahuatl, Mayan, Quechua), but she may have learned Spanish in a primary school in an underresourced area of a Spanish-speaking country. Notwithstanding the lack of cultural congruence, this will have implications for the validity of a psychological assessment measure translated into formal Spanish.

In addition to the aforementioned considerations, monolingual, bilingual, and multilingual clients may have complicated presentations of linguistic fluency and literacy. For example, although a client may be Spanish or English dominant, she may not be able to read and write in her dominant language. Likewise, a bilingual Latina client may not have the same degree of fluency or literacy in both languages. Because of this variability, assessment of verbal and literacy dominance is critical before choosing the language of the formal assessment.

COMMUNITY RESOURCES AND SOCIAL CHANGE/ACTIVISM (GUIDELINES 10 AND 11)

Guidelines 10 and 11 encourage the use of community resources and promote the therapist as a vehicle for social change and activism. In an effort to move in this direction, psychologists are encouraged to use a systemic and ecological framework when providing services to Latinas. Several scholars have encouraged psychological services outside the traditional individual approaches to therapy, including but not limited to services related to prevention, education, and social policy change (Adams, 2007; Lopez-Baez & Paylo, 2009; Vera et al., 2007).

Community Resources

Therapists may find that Latinas have more *confianza* in resources available in their community. Yosso (2005) noted that communities of color contain "cultural wealth," which includes familial, social, navigational, resistant, linguistic, aspirational, and cultural capital. Community cultural wealth helps marginalized communities overcome and oppose oppression. Any work with Latinas must consider and determine application of community cultural wealth in their treatment. For example, *familial capital* refers to spaces where cultural knowledges are nurtured and can include family, extended family members, and community circles (Yosso, 2005). Given the strong presence of spirituality for Latinas, this could include nonliving family members and places of worship. In addition, it would be important for helping professionals to be familiar with circles that could be of support to their client. *Social capital*, the "networks of people and community resources" available for Latinas, may include the use of community resources such as *promotoras*, also known as *community health workers. Promotoras* are community members with some sort of formalized and specialized training that is coupled with their own experiences and understandings of the community, who serve as advocates and educators for their communities (Torres & Cernada, 2003; U.S. Department of Health and Human Services, 2007). Social network groups, such as Wise Latina, could serve to empower clients outside of therapy. Providing psychological services for Latinas could also include navigational capital, an ability to navigate social institutions such as universities. Organizations such as the National Latina/o Psychological Association and Mujeres Activas en Letras and Cambios Social can provide Latinas with "skills to maneuver through social institutions" (Yosso, 2005, p. 80) and foster personal and professional development.

The Psychologist as Advocate

Psychologists are privileged with the ability to facilitate and advance social change within organizations and society (APA, 2007). Calls for action have been made to encourage psychologists to serve as agents of social change (Lopez-Baez & Paylo, 2009; Vera & Speight, 2003). Psychologists are urged to provide psychological services through prevention, education, and social policy interventions from local to national levels (APA, 2007). An example of a prevention intervention is the development of a *promotora de salud* group focused on the promotion of mental health and wellness in a rural and predominately monolingual Latino community (Côté & González, 2011). By partnering with the Women's Intercultural Center, an organization that aims to "provide a place for women to learn and work together to develop their social, spiritual, economic, and political potential" (Women's Intercultural Center, 2010), psychologists-in-training developed a *promotora* curriculum that integrated the lived experiences (Torres & Cernada, 2003) of the Latina participants and the psychological knowledge of the psychologists-in-training. As a result of their participation, several of the participants conducted presentations on mental health issues impacting their communities at a mental health conference. On a personal level the women reported an increase in their self-esteem.

Contributions at a policy level that address the mental health needs of Latinas are also important to consider. Melba Vasquez, the first Latina APA president, identified the topic of immigration as one of her presidential initiatives. As a result, *Crossroads: The Psychology of Immigration in the New Century*, a report by the APA Presidential Task Force on Immigration, was developed (APA Presidential Task Force on Immigration, 2011). This report served to inform culturally appropriate and sensitive psychological practices for Latinas/os with immigrant backgrounds.

CASE STUDY

The following case study illustrates ways in which the themes discussed in this chapter can be applied to the concerns of Daniela. This section provides information about the client, an analysis of the case, and culturally sensitive assessment and interventions for working with Daniela. The Guidelines inform the use of the biopsychosocial assessment and resulting interventions, and thus are highlighted throughout the case analysis.

Biopsychosocial Assessment

Daniela is a 20-year-old biethnic questioning Latina (Honduran, White) who was referred to counseling by her academic counselor as a result of being on academic probation. She is at risk of having her financial aid and admission revoked. She is in her junior year at a 4-year university and previously attended a community college. During intake she presents as anxious and sad as she reports that she is struggling to stay on top of her studies and makes the following statements: "I don't think I belong here," "Everyone is smarter than me," and "I don't have what it takes." With further exploration we learn that not only is she struggling in school, Daniela is also struggling to establish and maintain social relationships.

Daniela lives on campus and uses public transportation to go home on the weekends. Her family lives 3 hours away from her university. Her family includes her mother, siblings, and maternal grandmother. Daniela is the oldest of three siblings. She reported having significant responsibilities at home, such as helping her siblings with their homework, managing family finances, and caring for her ailing grandmother. In addition to helping her mother with her business, Daniela also has a part-time job on the weekends to contribute to the family income.

Her mother, Rosa, immigrated to the United States from Honduras when she was 24. Daniela's parents lived together until Daniela turned 4 years old. Although Daniela knows of her father, she has no relationship with him. Rosa later had a significant relationship with her younger siblings' father; the relationship ended after 10 years. At that point Daniela's grandmother moved to the United States to live with them permanently. Rosa sells food at a local community market and spends most of her time preparing and selling food. Because she is self-employed and struggles to make ends meet, she has been unable to afford health insurance for her family. This resulted in restrictions such that Daniela and her siblings could not play sports or engage in activities that could result in physical harm. Daniela and her siblings spent most of their free time helping their mother with her business and focusing on their academics. Daniela is the first in her family to go to college.

Daniela graduated in the top 1% in her high school and was valedictorian of her graduating class. Although she applied to and was accepted by prestigious universities, she was not guaranteed funding. With the encouragement of her mother and teachers she decided to attend a community college and transfer to the closest university. She received a full scholarship that covered tuition, room and board, and other educational expenses. Given her responsibilities at home, school, and work, Daniela has had little time to socialize after school. Her closest friends are her cousins and friends from high school who did not attend college. She has also been in a relationship for the past 4 years with a White male. Although she finds that he is supportive of her, she sometimes feels that he does not quite understand her responsibility to her family. He often tells her, "You have to worry about yourself and do your own thing." Furthermore, she has become increasingly aware of her attraction toward other females. She has begun to isolate herself from her partner and her family, fearing rejection, and has avoided meeting people as she grapples with understanding her identity.

Analysis of Case Study

As recommended by Guidelines 1, 2, 8, and 9, a comprehensive assessment of the different dimensions of U.S. and Latina identities is crucial. Through such an assessment the therapist learns that Daniela identifies and self-subscribes to the following labels: biethnic, questioning, first-generation college student, bicultural, bilingual, low income, and oldest daughter. As she enters her junior year in college, she is beginning to take more notice of her multiple identities. Although she has negotiated conflicting identities for most of her young life, the additive effect of the stressors associated with these identities (family, school, friends, and work) has made this borderland experience particularly distressing. In session, she discusses the differences she observes at home compared with school. For example, she notes the privilege of having a space of her own at school, whereas at home her family shares a one-bedroom apartment. In addition, she shares the guilt she feels about having health insurance while her mother and grandmother do not. Furthermore, she discloses both excitement and fear about being attracted to other women and the potential consequences this may have on her family. Throughout treatment, and consistent with Guidelines 1 and 2, the therapist works on identifying her multiple social affiliations and the significance they have for her and helps her address the contradictions in holding multiple social perspectives (Anzaldúa, 1987). In individual therapy, the therapist helps to validate and normalize her experience and begins to empower her to choose how and what aspects of each culture's norms, values, and behaviors she wishes to adhere to at the moment. Because Daniela is focusing on the differences between herself and others, given her multiple social affiliations, a useful intervention is to help Daniela identify the things she has in common with others, thus encouraging a more balanced and interpersonally connected perspective. The borderland experience could also be normalized by referring Daniela to a support group and/or sorority that might provide her with a community of women who could relate to and support her through her experience. Connecting her to professors and/or mentors who share a common experience could also be helpful in Daniela's treatment. The guiding approach is to empower Daniela to feel linked to the university community, her home, and her friends in a manner that is congruent and affirms her multiple identities.

Understanding the complexity of Daniela's gender socialization experiences and related behaviors within her cultural context, as suggested by Guidelines 1 and 9, is essential in providing her with culturally appropriate and competent psychological services that are consistent with the recommendations of Guidelines 4 and 6. Gender socialization for Daniela could be explored through the use of a family genogram (also see Chapter 2 in this volume for an example). Closer inspection of Daniela's genogram highlights the matriarchy of her family and the "power" innate to women in her family. Although her mother, Rosa, may not have a formal education, she has been able to model leadership and assertiveness for Daniela as a successful small business owner. This modeling provides Daniela with an opportunity to expand her view beyond the traditional roles displayed for Latinas. Daniela has also been socialized through a framework of *marianismo*. However, through her servant-leader roles she has been able to serve as an advocate for her siblings' educational needs. These experiences have helped her develop an ability to navigate the educational system and serve as an advocate for her own educational needs, thus capitalizing on her educational resiliency. These themes of resilience and empowerment are consistent with Guideline 7. Last, it is important to create a space that promotes dialogue around socialization. In particular, the therapist can address Daniela's self-reported thoughts of self-doubt and sense of belonging (at school, at home, and regarding her sexual orientation) by using interventions to explore what messages she might have received from different systems and inadvertently internalized.

When working with Daniela, it is important to consider her lived experiences of discrimination, as recommended by Guideline 3, and the impact it has on her and her family's mental and physical health. Although Daniela is documented, her mother and grandmother are not. The documentation status of the student and her family could be learned during the completion of a comprehensive assessment (Guideline 8). Although as a documented individual, Daniela herself may not struggle with access to certain privileges, she shares in the fear and anxiety that her mother and grandmother live with on a daily basis. Because of fear of deportation, Daniela may have learned that it was important not to bring attention to herself or her family. She may wonder whether academic probation might place unwanted attention on her by administrators. A useful intervention in this case would be to provide her with psychoeducation about academic probation. The therapist could also establish a treatment team and work closely with Daniela's academic advisor and financial aid officer to advocate on her behalf. Furthermore, given that her family members do not have access to health insurance and thus are more likely to experience diseases like diabetes, it is recommended that the treating provider be informed about community resources that might be available to family members, such as health fairs, free clinics, or *promotoras*. As a member of a mixed-documented family, Daniela may benefit from being connected to campus and community resources that create spaces for such circumstances. These efforts to provide linkages to community and campus resources are consistent with Guideline 10.

Attending to and promoting Daniela's strengths and assets can be powerful and important ways to prevent and diminish the potentially harmful effects of identity struggles and discrimination. As emphasized in Guidelines 6 and 7, her strengths should be identified and capitalized on throughout treatment.

Daniela's ability to code switch during session (i.e., between English and Spanish) provides a glimpse of her ability to shift between these two cultures seamlessly. Highlighting this language integration and fluidity of both languages in session could serve to provide her with an example of how she can integrate other aspects of her identity. The therapist can make process statements that highlight code switching in session in an effort to further explore its significance. In addition, the therapist can reference research that highlights the multiple benefits of bilingualism and the positive associations with academic confidence and performance (Buriel et al., 1998). This can extend to her bicultural and biethnic identities, thus further capitalizing on the skills fostered by experiencing duality. Furthermore, in line with Guideline 10, the therapist is encouraged to explore the cultural wealth available to Daniela in the community. This may include spiritual practices and organizations that foster faith and serenity when experiencing distress. Incorporating such cultural wealth in therapy would also encourage integration of Daniela's identities.

As an advocate, a role recommended by Guideline 11, the therapist can engage in multisystemic interventions that can address concerns of first-generation college students and/or students of color. Attending university town hall meetings and speaking with university administrators could serve to have Daniela's voice heard in spaces to which she might not have access. The therapist can serve as a consultant for campus organizations and encourage programs and outreach presentations that focus on the concerns expressed by Daniela. The therapist may even consider connecting with national organizations.

Lastly, a therapist can utilize an integrated approach of EFT (Díaz-Lázaro et al., 2012), *cuento* (folktale), and interpersonal therapy to facilitate exploration of Daniela's relationships with herself and others. An exploration of Latino cultural values, gender socialization, and sexual orientation will most likely occur in an effort to increase her awareness of her positionality within multiple relationships. The therapeutic alliance, which is emphasized in Guideline 7, could be utilized to understand where Daniela feels empowered or oppressed and silenced. Recommending books that are culture affirming and highlight common Latina experiences can add to her awareness (see Santiago-Rivera et al., 2002). A therapeutic intervention can include creating her narrative using a *cuento* therapy format.

CONCLUSIONS AND FUTURE DIRECTIONS

The Guidelines provide psychologists with a broad, overarching framework that can guide their work with girls and women from diverse cultural backgrounds. However, detailed cultural and contextual information is needed to make them fully applicable to specific diverse groups of women. Thus, this chapter provides more in-depth information and suggestions for providing culturally competent and sensitive psychological services to Latinas. As psychologists apply the Guidelines, it is essential that they attend to Latinas' multiple identities and the salience of these identities across context and time. Latinas are women from specific Latina/o ethnic subgroups who differ in their identification based on birthplace, geographic location, social class, sexual orientation, and ability among other dimensions of diversity. Also, psychologists must attend to Latinas' differing levels of acculturation, enculturation, and ethnic identity associated with both Latina/o and U.S. culture, particularly in understanding the effects of cultural socialization and experiences of discrimination and oppression on their physical and mental health outcomes.

We urge psychologists, when providing psychological services to Latinas, to use evidence-based practices that can be culturally adapted (Bernal et al., 2009), particularly feminist therapy (Brown, 2006). We also urge researchers and practitioners to collaborate in the validation of culturally adapted feminist approaches to therapy and other psychological services with Latinas. In adapting feminist therapy for work with Latinas, we suggest that psychologists attend to clients' community cultural wealth (Yosso, 2005) as a means of promoting individual and community strengths in the healing process. Ultimately, we urge psychologists to embrace various professional roles in their work with Latinas and to focus on needed changes on all ecological levels (e.g., individual, group, societal) to promote strength and healing. Psychologists truly have a role in advocating for social change that will positively impact the lived experiences of all Latinas.

REFERENCES

Acevedo-Polakovich, I., Reynaga-Abiko, G., Garriott, P. O., Derefinko, K. J., Wimsatt, M. K., Gudonis, L. C., & Brown, T. L. (2007). Beyond instrument selection: Cultural considerations in the psychological assessment of U.S. Latinas/os. *Professional Psychology: Research and Practice, 38,* 375–384. doi: 10.1037/0735-7028.38.4.375

Adams, E. (2007). Moving from contemplation to preparation: Is counseling psychology ready to embrace culturally responsive prevention? *The Counseling Psychologist, 35,* 840–849. doi:10.1177/0011000007304596

American Psychological Association. (2003). Guidelines on multicultural education, training, research, practice, and organizational change for psychologists. *American Psychologist, 58,* 377–402. doi:10.1037/0003-066X.58.5.377

American Psychological Association. (2006). Evidence-based practice in psychology. *American Psychologist, 61,* 271–285. doi:10.1037/0003-066X.61.4.271

American Psychological Association. (2007). Guidelines for psychological practice with girls and women. *American Psychologist, 62*, 949–979. doi:10.1037/0003-066X.62.9.949

American Psychological Association Presidential Task Force on Immigration. (2012). *Crossroads: The psychology of immigration in the new century.* Retrieved from http://www.apa.org/topics/immigration/report.aspx

Anzaldúa, G. (1987). *Borderlands/la frontera: The new Mestiza.* San Francisco, CA: Spinsters/Aunt Lute Book Company.

Araújo, B. Y., & Borrell, L. N. (2006). Understanding the link between discrimination, mental health outcomes, and life chances among Latinos. *Hispanic Journal of Behavioral Sciences, 28*, 245–266. doi:10.1177/0739986305285825

Arciniega, G. M., Anderson, T. C., Tovar-Blank, Z. G., & Tracey, T. J. G. (2008). Towards a fuller conception of *machismo*: Development of a traditional *machismo* and *caballerismo* scale. *Journal of Counseling Psychology, 55*, 19–33. doi:10.1037/0022-0167.55.1.19

Benet-Martínez, V., & Haritatos, J. (2005). Bicultural identity integration (BII): Components and psychosocial antecedents. *Journal of Personality, 73*, 1015–1049. doi:10.1111/j.1467-6494.2005.00337.x

Bermúdez-Millán, A., Damio, G., Cruz, J., D'Angelo, K., Segura-Pérez, S., Hromi-Fiedler, A., & Pérez-Escamilla, R. (2011). Stress and the social determinants of maternal health among Puerto Rican women: A CBPR approach. *Journal of Health Care for the Poor and Underserved, 22*, 1315–1330. doi:10.1353/hpu.2011.0108

Bernal, G., Jiménez-Chafey, M. I., & Domenech Rodríguez, M. M. (2009). Cultural adaptation of treatments: A resource for considering culture in evidence-based practice. *Professional Psychology: Research and Practice, 40*, 361–368. doi:10.1037/a0016401

Biever, J. L., Gómez, J. P., González, C. G., & Patrizio, N. (2011). Psychological services to Spanish-speaking populations: A model curriculum for training competent professionals. *Training and Education in Professional Psychology, 5*, 81–87. doi:10.1037/a0023535

Brown, L. S. (1994). *Subversive dialogues: Theory in feminist therapy.* New York, NY: Basic Books.

Brown, L. S. (2006). Still subversive after all these years: The relevance of feminist therapy in the age of evidence-based practice. *Psychology of Women Quarterly, 30*, 15–24. doi:10.1111/j.1471-6402.2006.00258.x

Buriel, R., Perez, W., De Ment, T. L., Chavez, D. V., & Moran, V. R. (1998). The relationship of language brokering to academic performance, biculturalism, and self-efficacy among Latino adolescents. *Hispanic Journal of Behavioral Sciences, 20*, 283–297. doi:10.1177/07399863980203001

Castillo, L. G., Perez, F. V., Castillo, R., & Ghosheh, M. R. (2010). Construction and initial validation of the Marianismo Beliefs Scale. *Counselling Psychology Quarterly, 23*, 163–175. doi:10.1080/09515070103776036

Cochran, S. D., Mays, V. M., Alegria, M., Ortega, A. N., & Takeuchi, D. (2007). Mental health and substance use disorders among Latino and Asian American lesbian, gay, and bisexual adults. *Journal of Consulting and Clinical Psychology*, *75*, 785–794. doi:10.1037/0022-006X.75.5.785

Comas-Díaz, L. (2006). Latino healing: The integration of ethnic psychology into psychotherapy. *Psychotherapy: Theory, Research, Practice, Training*, *43*, 436–453. doi:10.1037/0033-3204.43.4.436

Côté, L. M., & González, D. M. (2011, August). *Promotoras de salud mental: A strengths-based approach to community prevention and social justice efforts.* Poster presented at the 119th Annual Convention of the American Psychological Association, Washington, DC.

D'Anna, L. H., Ponce, N. A., & Siegel, J. M. (2010). Racial and ethnic health disparities: Evidence of discrimination's effects across the SEP spectrum. *Ethnicity & Health*, *15*, 121–143. doi:10.1080/13557850903490298

Denner, J., & Dunbar, N. (2004). Negotiating femininity: Power and strategies of Mexican American girls. *Sex Roles*, *50*, 301–314. doi:10.1023/B:SERS.0000018887.04206.d0

Díaz-Lázaro, C. M., Verdinelli, S., & Cohen, B. (2012). Empowerment feminist therapy with Latina immigrants: Honoring the complexity and socio-cultural contexts of clients' lives. *Women & Therapy*, *35*, 80–92. doi:10.1080/02703149.2012.634730

Dillon, F. R., De La Rosa, M., Sastre, F., & Ibañez, G. (2012). Alcohol misuse among recent Latino immigrants: The protective role of preimmigration *familismo*. *Psychology of Addictive Behaviors*. Advance online publication. doi:10.1037/a0031091

Domenech Rodríguez, M. M., Baumann, A. A., & Schwartz, A. L. (2011). Cultural adaptation of an evidence based intervention: From theory to practice in a Latino/a community context. *American Journal of Community Psychology*, *47*, 170–186. doi:10.1007/s10464-010-9371-4

Espín, O. M. (2012). "An illness we catch from American women"? The multiple identities of Latina lesbians. *Women & Therapy*, *35*, 45–56. doi:10.1080/02703149.2012.634720

Falicov, C. (2012). Immigrant family processes: A multidimensional framework. In F. Walsh (Ed.), *Normal family processes: Growing diversity and complexity* (4th ed., pp. 297–323). New York, NY: Guilford Press.

Feliciano, C. (2001). The benefits of biculturalism: Exposure to immigrant culture and dropping out of school among Asian and Latino youths. *Social Science Quarterly*, *82*, 865–879. doi:10.1111/0038-4941.00064

Flores, E., Tschann, J. M., Dimas, J. M., Bachen, E. A., Pasch, L. A., & de Groat, C. L. (2008). Perceived discrimination, perceived stress, and mental and physical health among Mexican-origin adults. *Hispanic Journal of Behavioral Sciences*, *30*, 401–424. doi:10.1177/0739986308323056

Gomez, M. J., & Fassinger, R. E. (1994). An initial model of Latina achievement: Acculturation, biculturalism, and achieving styles. *Journal of Counseling Psychology, 41,* 205–215. doi:10.1037/0022-0167.41.2.205

Gonzales, E. (2008). *Hispanic women in the United States, 2007.* Washington, DC: Pew Hispanic Center.

González, D. M., & Navarro, R. (2010, August). *Guidelines for psychological practice with Latina girls and women.* Paper presented at the 118th Annual Convention of the American Psychological Association, San Diego, CA.

Guilamo-Ramos, V., Bouris, A., Jaccard, J., Lesesne, C., & Ballan, M. (2009). Familial and cultural influences on sexual risk behaviors among Mexican, Puerto Rican, and Dominican youth. *AIDS Education and Prevention, 21*(Suppl. B), 61–79. doi:10.1521/aeap.2009.21.5_supp.61

Guzmán, C. E. (2011). *Toward a new conceptualization of* marianismo: *Validation of the Guzmán Marianismo Inventory* (Unpublished doctoral dissertation). New Mexico State University, Las Cruces.

Hardy, K. V., & Laszloffy, T. A. (1995). The cultural genogram: Key to training culturally competent family therapists. *Journal of Marital and Family Therapy, 21,* 227–237. doi:10.1111/j.1752-0606.1995.tb00158.x

Harrell, S. P. (2000). A multidimensional conceptualization of racism-related stress: Implications for the well-being of people of color. *American Journal of Orthopsychiatry, 70,* 42–57. doi:10.1037/h0087722

Hinton, D. E., Lewis-Fernández, R., & Pollack, M. H. (2009). A model of the generation of *ataque de nervios:* The role of fear of negative affect and fear of arousal symptoms. *CNS Neuroscience & Therapeutics, 15,* 264–275. doi:10.1111/j.1755-5949.2009.00101.x

Hurtado, A., & Cervantez, K. (2009). A view from within and from without: The development of Latina feminist psychology. In F. A. Villarruel, G. Carlo, J. M. Grau, M. Azmitia, N. J. Cabrera, & T. Chahin (Eds.), *Handbook of U.S. Latino psychology: Developmental and community-based perspectives* (pp. 171–190). Thousand Oaks, CA: Sage.

Kim, H. J., & Fredriksen-Goldsen, K. I. (2012). Hispanic lesbians and bisexual women at heightened risk or health disparities. *American Journal of Public Health, 102*(1), e9–e15. doi:10.2105/AJPH.2011.300378

Lopez, N. (2006). Resistance to race and gender oppression: Dominican high school girls in New York City. In J. Denner & B. L. Guzmán (Eds.), *Latina girls: Voices of adolescent strength in the United States* (pp. 79–92). New York, NY: New York University Press.

Lopez-Baez, S. I., & Paylo, M. J. (2009). Social justice advocacy: Community collaboration and systems advocacy. *Journal of Counseling & Development, 87,* 276–283. doi:10.1002/j.1556-6678.2009.tb00107.x

Lorenzo-Blanco, E. I., & Cortina, L. M. (2013). Latino/a depression and smoking: An analysis through the lenses of culture, gender, and ethnicity. *American Journal of Community Psychology, 51,* 332–346. doi:10.1007/s10464-012-9553-3

Lorenzo-Blanco, E. I., Unger, J. B., Baezconde-Garbanati, L., Ritt-Olson, A., & Soto, D. (2012). Acculturation, enculturation, and symptoms of depression in Hispanic youth: The roles of gender, Hispanic cultural values, and family functioning. *Journal of Youth and Adolescence, 41*, 1350–1365. doi:10.1007/s10964-012-9774-7

Love, J. A., & Buriel, R. (2007). Language brokering, autonomy, parent–child bonding, biculturalism, and depression: A study of Mexican American adolescents from immigrant families. *Hispanic Journal of Behavioral Sciences, 29*, 472–491. doi:10.1177/0739986307307229

Miranda, A. O., Estrada, D., & Firpo-Jimenez, M. (2000). Differences in family cohesion, adaptability, and environment among Latino families in dissimilar stages of acculturation. *The Family Journal, 8*, 341–350. doi:10.1177/1066480700084003

Miranda, A. O., & Umhoefer, D. L. (1998). Depression and social interest differences between Latinos in dissimilar acculturation stages. *Journal of Mental Health Counseling, 20*, 159–171.

Miranda, J., Siddique, J., Der-Martirosian, C., & Belin, T. R. (2005). Depression among Latina immigrant mothers separated from their children. *Psychiatric Services, 56*, 717–720. doi:10.1176/appi.ps.56.6.717

Morales, E. (2013). Latino lesbian, gay, bisexual, and transgender immigrants in the United States. *Journal of LGBT Issues in Counseling, 7*, 172–184. doi:10.1080/15538605.2013.785467

Motel, S., & Patten, E. (2012). *The 10 largest Hispanic origin groups: Characteristics, ranking, top counties*. Washington, DC: Pew Hispanic Center.

Norcross, J. C., & Lambert, M. J. (2005). The therapy relationship. In J. C. Norcross, L. E. Beutler, & R. F. Levant (Eds.). *Evidence-based practices in mental health: Debate and dialogue on the fundamental questions*. Washington, DC: American Psychological Association. doi:10.1037/11265-000

Perilla, J. L., Serrata, J., Weinberg, J., & Lippy, C. A. (2012). Integrating women's voices and theory: A comprehensive domestic violence intervention for Latinas. *Women & Therapy, 35*, 93–105. doi:10.1080/02703149.2012.634731

Pew Hispanic Center. (2007a). *Changing faiths: Latinos and the transformation of American religion*. Washington, DC: Pew Hispanic Center. Retrieved from http://www.pewhispanic.org/files/reports/75.pdf

Pew Hispanic Center. (2007b). *2007 national survey of Latinos: As illegal immigration issue heats up, Hispanics feel a chill*. Washington, DC: Author.

Pew Hispanic Center. (2012). *When labels don't fit: Hispanics and their views of identity*. Washington, DC: Author.

Raffaelli, M., & Ontai, L. L. (2004). Gender socialization in Latino/a families: Results from two retrospective studies. *Sex Roles, 50*, 287–299. doi:10.1023/B:SERS.0000018886.58945.06

Ramos, B., Jaccard, J., & Guilamo-Ramos, V. (2003). Dual ethnicity and depressive symptoms: Implications of being Black and Latino in the United States. *Hispanic Journal of Behavioral Sciences, 25*, 147–173. doi:10.1177/0739986303025002002

Rosselló, J., Bernal, G., & Rivera-Medina, C. (2008). Individual and group CBT and IPT for Puerto Rican adolescents with depressive symptoms. *Cultural Diversity and Ethnic Minority Psychology, 14*, 234–245. doi:10.1037/1099-9809. 14.3.234

Sabogal, F., Perez-Stable, E., & Otero-Sabogal, R. (1995). Gender, ethnic, and acculturation differences in sexual behaviors: Hispanic and non-Hispanic White adults. *Hispanic Journal of Behavioral Sciences, 17*, 139–159. doi:10.1177/ 07399863950172001

Santa-Maria, M. L., & Cornille, T. (2007). Traumatic stress, family separations, and attachment among Latin American immigrants. *Traumatology, 13*, 26–31. doi:10.1177/1534765607302278

Santiago-Rivera, A. L., Altarriba, J., Poll, N., Gonzalez-Miller, N., & Cragun, C. (2009). Therapists' views on working with bilingual Spanish–English speaking clients: A qualitative investigation. *Professional Psychology: Research and Practice, 40*, 436–443. doi:10.1037/a0015933

Santiago-Rivera, A. L., Arredondo, P., & Gallardo-Cooper, M. (2002). *Counseling Latinos and* la familia: *A practical guide.* Thousand Oaks, CA: Sage.

Schwartz, S. J., & Unger, J. B. (2010). Biculturalism and context: What is biculturalism, and when is it adaptive? *Human Development, 53*, 26–32. doi:10.1159/ 000268137

Schwartz, S. J., Unger, J. B., Zamboanga, B. L., & Szapocznik, J. (2010). Rethinking the concept of acculturation: Implications for theory and research. *American Psychologist, 65*, 237–251. doi:10.1037/a0019330

Stevens, E. P. (1973). *Marianismo:* The other face of *machismo* in Latin America. In A. Decastello (Ed.), *Female and male in Latin America* (pp. 88–109). Pittsburgh, PA: University of Pittsburgh Press.

Szymanski, D. M., Moffitt, L. B., & Carr, E. R. (2011). Sexual objectification of women: Advances to theory and research. *The Counseling Psychologist, 39*, 6–38. doi:10.1177/0011000010378402

Tillman, K. H., & Weiss, U. (2009). Nativity status and depressive symptoms among Hispanic young adults: The role of stress exposure. *Social Science Quarterly, 90*, 1228–1250. doi:10.1111/j.1540-6237.2009.00655.x

Torres, M., & Cernada, G. P. (2003). *Sexual and reproductive health promotion in Latino populations:* Parteras, promotoras y poetas: *Case studies across the Americas.* Amityville, NY: Baywood Publishing.

U.S. Census Bureau. (2010). *Current population survey. Annual social and economic supplement, 2010.* Retrieved from http://www.census.gov/population/age/data/ 2010comp.html

U.S. Department of Health and Human Services Health Resources and Services Administration, Bureau of Health Professions. (2007). *Community health worker national workforce study.* Retrieved from http://bhpr.hrsa.gov/healthworkforce/ reports/chwstudy2007.pdf

Vera, E. M., Caldwell, J., Clarke, M., Gonzales, R., Morgan, M., & West, M. (2007). The choices program: Multisystemic interventions for enhancing the personal and academic effectiveness of urban adolescents of color. *The Counseling Psychologist, 35*, 779–796. doi:10.1177/0011000007304590

Vera, E. M., & Speight, S. L. (2003). Multicultural competence, social justice, and counseling psychology: Expanding our roles. *The Counseling Psychologist, 31*, 253–272. doi:10.1177/0011000003031003001

Vidales, G. T. (2010). Arrested justice: The multifaceted plight of immigrant Latinas who faced domestic violence. *Journal of Family Violence, 25*, 533–544. doi:10.1007/s10896-010-9309-5

Williams, D. R., Neighbors, H. W., & Jackson, J. S. (2003). Racial/ethnic discrimination and health: Findings from community studies. *American Journal of Public Health, 93*, 200–208. doi:10.2105/AJPH.93.2.200

Women's Intercultural Center. (2010). *Mission, vision, and values*. Retrieved from http://www.womensinterculturalcenter.org/mission.html

Worell, J., & Johnson, N. G. (Eds.). (1997). *Shaping the future of feminist psychology: Education, research, and practice*. Washington, DC: American Psychological Association. doi:10.1037/10245-000

Worell, J., & Remer, P. (2003). *Feminist perspectives in therapy: Empowering diverse women* (2nd ed.). Hoboken, NJ: Wiley.

Yosso, T. (2005). Whose culture has capital? A critical race theory discussion of community cultural wealth. *Race, Ethnicity and Education, 8*(1), 69–91. doi:10.1080/1361332052000341006

5

LESBIAN, BISEXUAL, AND TRANSGENDER WOMEN

CONNIE R. MATTHEWS

The "Guidelines for Psychological Practice With Girls and Women" (hereinafter the Guidelines; American Psychological Association [APA], 2007) were developed with the intent of being applicable to all women. Thus, they inherently apply to work with lesbian, bisexual, and transgender women in their status as women. At the same time sexual minority women face unique challenges that go beyond the marginalization they might face in being women. This chapter identifies and describes some of those challenges as they specifically pertain to the recommendations put forth in the Guidelines. A case study follows this discussion, demonstrating how some of the concepts might appear in the context of therapy.

http://dx.doi.org/10.1037/14460-005
Psychological Practice With Women: Guidelines, Diversity, Empowerment, C. Z. Enns, J. K. Rice, and R. L. Nutt (Editors)
Copyright © 2015 by the American Psychological Association. All rights reserved.

WHY FOCUS ON LESBIAN, BISEXUAL, AND TRANSGENDER WOMEN?

Although studies are few in number, they have consistently shown that lesbians utilize counseling and therapy with some frequency. Two large representative studies (Bradford, Ryan, & Rothblum, 1994; Sorenson & Roberts, 1997) found that about 75% of lesbian respondents had worked with a mental health professional at least once, with many having done so more than once. Other studies (e.g., Cochran, Sullivan, & Mays, 2003; Morgan, 1992) have found similar results. In a study related to consumption and consequences of alcohol and other substances, Drabble and Trocki (2005) found that lesbians were 8 times more likely to have been in treatment than heterosexual women and bisexual women were 5 times more likely to have been in treatment, yet both groups were significantly less likely to report being satisfied with their treatment than heterosexual women. The World Professional Association for Transgender Health *Standards of Care* (2012) recommends that individuals undergoing hormone therapy or surgery related to gender identity have regular visits with a mental health or medical professional and requires documentation of persistent gender dysphoria. Thus, it is likely that psychologists will interact with lesbian, bisexual, and transgender women during their careers.

Despite the high therapy utilization rate by lesbians and likely substantial use by bisexual and transgender women, research has also found that mental health professionals are not always prepared to work with them. Phillips and Fischer (1998) surveyed doctoral students in clinical and counseling psychology training programs regarding the professional preparation they were receiving to work with lesbian, gay, and bisexual clients. The authors found that such training was inadequate and that "the vast majority of respondents did not feel adequately prepared by their graduate course work to work with [lesbian, gay, and bisexual] clients compared to heterosexual clients" (p. 725). They found that training to work with bisexual clients was even less adequate than training to work with lesbian and gay clients. This finding is consistent with another study in which the authors (Pilkington & Cantor, 1996) surveyed student affiliate members of the APA Division 44 (Society for the Psychological Study of Lesbian and Gay Issues) regarding their experiences of perceived heterosexist bias in their graduate training programs. Most of the participants were in the latter years of their training. More than half of the participants in the study reported bias in textbooks (53%), biased statements by instructors (58%), and/or other forms of bias (50%). Participants also reported very little coverage of gay or lesbian topics in the curriculum, with much of what was addressed pathologizing homosexuality. Although these studies are a bit dated, they nonetheless reflect the training of psychologists currently working in the field.

UNDERSTANDING SEXUAL ORIENTATION
AND GENDER IDENTITY

Before beginning a discussion of how the Guidelines might apply to working with lesbian, bisexual, and transgender women, it is important to have a basic understanding of some of the terms and concepts that come into such a discussion. First, it is necessary to distinguish between sexual orientation and gender identity. Because these two crucial areas of personal identity are often addressed together, they are sometimes confused as being part of the same overall construct. This confusion can be exacerbated by gender-role stereotypes that prescribe different ways of being in the world for men and women, including as they pertain to with whom one engages in intimate relationships (Fassinger & Arsenau, 2007).

Lev (2004) described four components of identity related to sex and gender.

Sex refers to biological sex. Is the person male or female? This is a purely physiological determination, although that determination involves multiple factors and can be rather complex because some individuals are born with physiological markers of both maleness and femaleness.

Gender identity refers to one's identification as man or woman. Typically, this identification corresponds with one's biological categorization as male or female, although not always. Some individuals experience incongruence between their sense of themselves as a person and their physical bodies. Thus, gender identity is how one defines oneself regardless of correspondence with physical maleness or femaleness.

Gender role represents an interface between individual characteristics and social constructions of sex and gender. Social prescriptions tend to define some attitudes, behaviors, and ways of being in the world as more appropriate for men and others as more appropriate for women. Associated terms are *masculine and feminine*. Thus, *masculine* is generally associated with men, whereas *feminine* is generally associated with women, although individual men and women might adhere to these expectations to greater or lesser degrees. Although Lev (2004) combined gender role and gender expression, the APA Task Force on Gender Identity and Gender Variance (2009) distinguished these constructs. They defined *gender expression* as "the way in which a person acts to communicate gender within a given culture; for example, in terms of clothing, communication patterns, and interests" (p. 28).

Sexual orientation describes one's physical and emotional attractions to one sex, either the same or different sex as the individual, both sexes, or neither sex. Savin-Williams (2007) further distinguished *sexual orientation* from *sexual behavior* and *sexual identity*. *Sexual behavior*, although seemingly self-explanatory, can be complicated as we debate which acts constitute sexual behavior. A sex scandal in 1998 involving President Clinton and a White House intern highlighted how complex such discussions can be when President Clinton seemed to question whether anything other than intercourse constituted sex. *Sexual identity* refers to the way in which one defines oneself. Sexual orientation, sexual behavior, and sexual identity are often consistent within individuals; however, sometimes they are not. For example, a woman might understand her sexual orientation to be heterosexual and identify as such yet engage in an intimate, even sexual, relationship with another woman while in prison. The implications of these definitions for assessing and working with lesbian, bisexual, and transgender women are discussed in the next section.

THE CONTEXT OF BEING A LESBIAN, BISEXUAL, OR TRANSGENDER WOMAN

One of the first things to keep in mind when working with lesbian, bisexual, or transgender women is that in many, if not most, instances their status is not immediately evident. This group represents a "hidden minority" (Fassinger, 1991). This invisibility comes as a result of what the poet Adrienne Rich referred to as "compulsory heterosexuality" (Rich, 1980). We are all raised to be heterosexual. Likewise, we are all raised with the assumption that the body into which we were born is consistent with an internal feeling of being a woman or man. The term *cisgender* is used to express this consistency. Neither is always the case. Not all people are heterosexual or cisgender. Women who identify as lesbian or gay have a same-sex sexual orientation; women who identify as bisexual have a same-sex and other-sex orientation. The broad term *transgender* refers to "an umbrella description for people whose gender identity, expression or behavior is different from those typically associated with their assigned sex at birth, including but not limited to transsexuals, cross-dressers, androgynous people, gender queers, and gender non-conforming people" (National Center for Transgender Equality, 2009). Thus, consistent with Guideline 1, it is important to go into every clinical situation with an open mind regarding clients' sexual orientation and gender identity rather than assuming heterosexuality and cisgender status unless and until the client reveals something different (Matthews, 2007). Indeed, it is important to assess the client's status in both of these areas early in the therapeutic process. Failure to do so can further marginalize clients who then must assume the burden and the risk of deciding if and when it is safe to reveal information that might subject them to harsh judgment or discrimination. Liddle (1996) found that gay and lesbian clients were twice as likely to terminate therapy after one session when their therapist assumed they were heterosexual. In conducting such assessment, it is important to avoid stereotyping clients based on immediate observable behavior.

Avoiding Stereotypes

All of the aspects of identity defined in the first section of this chapter are typically considered to be dichotomous and are generally assessed as such, to the degree that they are assessed at all (Lev, 2004). For example, intake forms generally ask clients to indicate their biological sex as male or female. Gender identity and gender role are rarely assessed; rather, they are assumed to correspond with a client's identified sex. Sexual orientation likewise is rarely assessed, although there is some indication that this is changing. When it is assessed, this usually occurs through discrete categories of heterosexual, homosexual, or bisexual. Lev (2004) argued that contrary to the popular practice of defining these four aspects of identity as discrete variables, all are continuous variables, or at least all have the capacity to be. Indeed, Bem (1974, 1975, 1977) has argued that masculinity and femininity are not one continuum but two, that both men and women exhibit characteristics of both masculinity and femininity, and that it is the way in which the two intersect that is informative. Contrary to the earlier belief that a high score on one dimension indicated a low score on the other, when measured separately, some individuals scored either high on both scales or low on both scales. More attention was given to those scoring high on both scales, which was termed *androgynous* (Bem, 1975, 1977). The concept of androgyny garnered substantial attention in the field at the time, although it has received less attention in recent years. Of note here is that as sexual orientation and gender identity have become more openly discussed, there are women and men who choose not to be constrained by a binary concept of gender and consciously adopt a more androgynous identity.

For example, although typically all of the biological markers that define one as male or female are consistent, sometimes they are not. Such physiological conditions are referred to as *intersex* (Lev, 2004) or, the more preferable term currently, *disorders of sexual development* (DSDs; APA Task Force on Gender Identity and Gender Variance, 2009). An example of DSD would be an infant born with both ovaries and testes and ambiguous external genitalia. It is beyond the scope of this chapter to provide extensive discussion of DSDs; however, it is worth noting that such situations provide complexities for the individuals involved and are worth knowing about when assessing clients. Often decisions about how to address such conditions are made by parents and/or medical professionals during infancy, with or without later informing the individual, which can provide a variety of challenges for individuals with DSDs. Thus, even the aspect of identity that might appear to be the most discrete is more complex than it appears.

Gender, gender role, and gender expression likewise often get subsumed under sex when assessing clients, yet such an approach often operates on assumptions and stereotypes. When we assume that all individuals who check "female" identify themselves as women and all individuals who check "male" identify themselves as men, we risk making critical mistakes. Furthermore, we put individuals who do not so identify in the position of having to confront us with our error or make decisions about whether it is worth taking such a risk of disclosure. As therapists, we also communicate, whether or not we so intend, that we lack knowledge and understanding of their life experience.

Likewise, making assumptions can be problematic when assessing the degree to which individuals appear to us to stray from socially prescribed gender roles. For example, the woman welder or firefighter or truck driver might simply be trying to provide a better standard of living for herself and her family than she could do working in occupations considered more feminine. This might be especially true for women who identify as lesbian and who lack access to the generally higher earning potential of a male partner. In addition, because gender, gender identity, gender role, sexual orientation, sexual behavior, and sexual identity are separate constructs, it is particularly important to remember that one's location on one continuum does not imply one's location on any of the other continua. Thus, women who identify as heterosexual are not necessarily more femininely and less masculinely inclined than women who identify as lesbian or bisexual. Heterosexual, bisexual, and lesbian women can fall anywhere on the femininity and masculinity continua.

Identity Development

Because of the assumption of heterosexuality, most people are raised as heterosexual. Thus, realizing that one is not, or might not be, heterosexual requires a process of rediscovering and redefining oneself. In a very real way, it represents a paradigm shift. Unlike members of some other marginalized groups, who grow up in families whose members serve as models, protectors, and educators, most sexual minority women are raised by heterosexual parents who not only have no understanding of the process but who often fight or resist the process. Therefore, many women and girls going through the process of developing an identity as lesbian or bisexual or transgender need to turn to other sources for guidance in navigating the process. Some will seek counseling. Thus, consistent with Guideline 2, it is vital that counselors have a working knowledge of lesbian, bisexual, and transgender identity development. Because identity development is an evolving area of the field of lesbian, gay, bisexual, and transgender (LGBT) psychology, such understanding will likely require periodic revisiting and continuing education.

In the area of identity development, far more scholarship has been done with lesbian women than with other sexual or gender minority women. Early models were stage models that grew out of work done on identity development in gay men. Cass's (1979, 1984) sexual identity development model is the most notable. Gramick (1984), Chapman and Brannock (1987), and Sophie (1986) built on those models to develop ones specific to lesbians. There are some differences in the models, including differences in the number of stages incorporated as well as in the degree to which lesbian identity development is attributed to essentialist versus social constructionist perspectives. Szymanski and Hilton (2013) synthesized these and other models into four common dimensions. They identified the first dimension as *feeling different*. This might involve a sense that one is not like other girls or women; it might include wondering whether one might be lesbian or bisexual. The second dimension is *coming out to self*. This process represents a clearer acknowledgement of oneself as lesbian or bisexual. It might also include learning to negotiate one's way through the stigma and heterosexism that accompany a nonheterosexual identity. The third dimension is *coming out to others*, which means making continuous choices about whether and when to acknowledge one's nonheterosexual orientation to others, knowing that such revelations might bring consequences. The fourth dimension is *identity synthesis*, which includes a positive framework for one's nonheterosexual orientation as well as an integration of one's sexuality into other aspects of one's life. Sexual orientation and sexual identity become less a focus of identification and more a part of one's larger identity.

More recent scholarship has contributed to the recognition that sexual identity development is more complex than these stage models fully accommodate. For instance, Fassinger and her colleagues (Fassinger & Arseneau, 2007; McCarn & Fassinger, 1996) have developed models that incorporate not only individual identity but group identity as well. Originally, this included group identity associated with being part of the LGBT community (McCarn & Fassinger, 1996). Fassinger and Arseneau (2007) incorporated the recognition that an individual's other group identities, such as those related to gender, race, ethnicity, faith tradition, socioeconomic status, and other cultural groups, are also influenced by one's identification as lesbian or bisexual. Five of the 20 (Numbers 11, 12, 13, 14, 15) *Guidelines for Psychological Practice With Lesbian, Gay, and Bisexual Clients* (APA, 2011b) directly address the importance of considering the ways in which racial and ethnic group status, religion and spirituality, cohort and age differences, youth status, and disability might influence being gay, lesbian, or bisexual. In addition, other APA guidelines such as the *Guidelines on Multicultural Education, Training, Research, Practice, and Organizational Change for Psychologists* (APA, 2003), and the *Guidelines for Assessment of and Intervention With Persons With Disabilities* (APA, 2011a) can be used as companion documents.

Diamond (2005, 2006, 2008, 2013) has added additional breadth and depth to the literature on lesbian identity development with recent research showing that sexual identity in women might be more fluid than earlier models projected. A full review of her work is beyond the scope of this chapter; however, several things are worth noting. Whereas some women do present rather stable identifications over time, some women do not. In one study, Diamond (2005) referred to stable lesbians, stable nonlesbians, and nonstable lesbians. Furthermore, changes over time represent not only fluidity in physical and/or emotional attractions and behaviors but also fluidity in labeling or resistance to labeling at all. Thus, the nonstable lesbian group did not necessarily identify as bisexual, either over time or at specific times, although some women in this category do eventually adopt a bisexual identity. The implication of this new area of lesbian identity research is that there might not always be end points to identity development. Thus, in assessing sexual orientation, identity, and behavior, it is important to assess not only an individual's current status but also the path she has taken to her current status as well as what she anticipates in the future. Individual differences might distinguish a person not only from other persons but also from herself at different points in time. Thus, we need to consider within- as well as between-individual differences in assessment. It is likely that this line of research will continue to refine our understanding of lesbian identity development.

This discussion has focused on lesbian identity development because to date there has been very little research done on bisexual identity development or transgender identity development. One of the challenges facing bisexual women is that there has been a tendency to discount bisexuality as either a transition between a heterosexual identity and a gay or lesbian identity or a reluctance to fully relinquish heterosexual privilege (Dworkin, 2001). As a result, bisexual women can be as likely to experience marginalization from the lesbian community as from society in general. This reality adds complexity to bisexual identity development that has yet to be fully explored. Likewise, work in the area of transgender identity development is still evolving. These are two areas in which it will be critical for psychologists to follow the scholarship over time.

Something to keep in mind when considering identity development is that as women move toward or between identities as lesbian or bisexual, they move away from a heterosexual identity. As discussed earlier in the chapter, most women are raised as heterosexual. Thus, to adopt an identity as lesbian or bisexual means to give up a heterosexual identity. Indeed, even women who are resistant to labeling of any sort also resist a heterosexual label. Although there are a number of implications of this, perhaps none is greater than moving from a privileged identity to a marginalized identity. Matthews and Bieschke (2001) likened this process to the enculturation process immigrants experience leaving a homeland in which they are part of the majority to join a new culture in which they are not. They suggested that several factors might influence this process, including the family culture around sexual orientation that the individual has had to negotiate, the individual's own internal processes, coming out initially and over time, and the nature of involvement with the LGBT community. In addition, any experiences of bias, discrimination, prejudice, or violence related to sexual orientation should be considered. They suggested that these factors and others have the potential to influence an individual's transition between identities.

Minority Stress

Over the past couple of decades, theoretical and empirical work has applied minority stress theory to the gay, lesbian, and bisexual population. Brooks (1981) defined *minority stress* as "a state intervening between the sequential antecedent stressors of culturally sanctioned, categorically ascribed inferior status, resultant prejudice and discrimination, the impact of these forces on the cognitive structure of the individual, and consequent readjustment or adaptational failure" (p. 84). Meyer (2003) extended Brooks's work with lesbians to use minority stress theory as a framework for describing and exploring the ways in which lesbians and gay men experience stress-related mental health consequences due to their marginalized status.

Stigmatization and oppression, including violence, toward people who identify as lesbian, gay, or bisexual are well established (e.g., Herek, Gillis, Cogan, & Glunt, 1997; Marzullo & Libman, 2009). Discrimination and victimization occur in employment, housing, child custody, assaults of every type, harassment, and even murder. They also occur in the form of daily hassles (Swim, Johnston, & Pearson, 2009); microaggressions (Nadal, Rivera, & Corpus, 2010); and other acts that stigmatize people who identify as lesbian, gay, or bisexual as "other" in a world that values conformity (Garnets, Herek, & Levy, 2003).

The physical and mental health consequences of such oppression are also well documented. For example, in a pair of national population-based studies, Cochran and Mays (Cochran et al., 2003; Mays & Cochran, 2001) examined the relationship of psychological distress, the prevalence of mental disorders, and the use of mental health services to perceived discrimination among lesbian, gay, and bisexual adults. Cochran et al. (2003) found that lesbian and bisexual women were almost four times more likely than heterosexual women to meet the criteria for generalized anxiety disorder and were more likely to meet the criteria for two or more disorders. Almost 24% of lesbian and bisexual women met the criteria for two or more psychiatric disorders. In a companion study, Mays and Cochran (2001) found that gay, lesbian, and bisexual participants were more likely to report discrimination than their heterosexual counterparts and that the discrimination made life harder for them. Such experiences were also associated with negative mental health status.

Research has also found that lesbian, gay, and bisexual people can experience minority stress through actions that do not target them individually. In a survey of lesbian, gay, and bisexual people living in Colorado, following the passage of a 1992 amendment that essentially legalized discrimination against them within the state, Russell (2000) found significant increases in measures of depression, posttraumatic stress disorder, and anxiety in participants after the election. Qualitative data provided further description of the psychological effects of passage of the amendment. Rostosky, Riggle, Horne, and Miller (2009) likewise found that lesbian, gay, and bisexual participants living in states that passed amendments in 2006 limiting marriage to one man and one woman showed increased levels of minority stress and psychological distress.

It is difficult to know what the future will hold with respect to such legislation. Currently there seems to be a wave of legislation that shows movement toward greater equity for LGBT people. As this chapter is being written, several additional states have legalized same-sex marriage, U.S. Supreme Court rulings on two cases extended recognition of same-sex marriage and essentially struck down the Defense of Marriage Act, and additional lower level court rulings have struck down some state laws limiting marriage to unions between a man and a woman. Several federal agency policy decisions have extended the reach of these rulings by establishing that legally performed same-sex marriages will be recognized at the federal level, regardless of whether the couple currently lives in a state that legally recognizes same-sex marriage. It seems likely that these rulings and other cases that are currently in the courts in several states will have a serious impact on the lives of lesbian and bisexual women. Still, even favorable rulings can feel precarious, as women see current challenges to access to birth control and abortion that had seemed settled decades ago. There is currently no federal protection from employment discrimination for LGBT people and none on the horizon. Thus, this is a very fluid time with respect to the rights of LGBT people, which in itself has the potential to be stressful. It will be important for therapists to stay abreast of the rapidly changing landscape and be prepared to address the impact of such changes with their lesbian, bisexual, and transgender clients. For example, as same-sex marriage becomes more accessible and more accepted, women in same-sex relationships might face relationship decisions that previously did not need to be addressed.

Given the level of exposure that sexual minority women have to marginalization and oppression and the effects such exposure has on mental health, it is important that psychologists working with sexual minority women are prepared to address such experiences. It is also important to recognize that for most sexual minority women, minority stress related to sexual orientation or gender identity might represent only part of the overall minority stress they experience. Thus, it is important to be able to address the interactions of stresses related to such additional statuses as race, ethnicity, disability, socio-economic status, faith tradition, and other statuses with sexual orientation and gender identity.

PROFESSIONAL RESPONSIBILITY AND PRACTICE WITH LESBIAN, BISEXUAL, AND TRANSGENDER WOMEN

As noted earlier in this chapter, most psychologists are likely to work with lesbian, bisexual, or transgender women at some point during their careers, whether they know it or not. Because it might not be immediately evident which clients identify as lesbian, bisexual, or transgender, it is important to practice with all clients in ways that are positively affirming with respect to sexual orientation, behavior, and identity (Matthews, 2007), as well as with respect to gender orientation, identity, and expression. Although assessing all clients as described above might help some clients feel safe enough to immediately reveal this information, others might be reluctant to offer such information, even if asked, until they have had the opportunity to assess the person with whom they are working.

Asking the relevant questions can help to establish some level of credibility with the client; however, clients will have different thresholds regarding what they need from therapists before feeling safe enough to be fully open. This might especially be the case if the client has previously had negative experiences related to coming out or has been the victim of discrimination, harassment, or bias related to sexual orientation or gender orientation. It might also be the case if the client's presenting concern is not directly related to sexual orientation or gender identity. Some clients might reveal this information only on a need-to-know basis. Still, being open and affirming with all clients with respect to sexual orientation and gender orientation can help to empower clients and can begin to challenge internalized homophobia, whereas failure to be affirming can fuel internalized homophobia or enhance caution about revealing nonheterosexual or non-gender-normative feelings and behaviors.

Whereas affirmative practice with lesbian, bisexual, and transgender women is fundamental to Guideline 4, it might also pose challenges for some psychologists, whose own cultural background and traditions might promote different perspectives on sexual identity and gender identity. Thus, consistent with Guideline 5 of these guidelines, as well as with the *Guidelines for Psychological Practice With Lesbian, Gay, and Bisexual Clients* (APA, 2011b) and the *Guidelines on Multicultural Education, Training, Research, Practice, and Organizational Change for Psychologists* (APA, 2003), conscious self-awareness of one's own beliefs, attitudes, and values around sexual identity and gender identity, as well as the ways in which these statuses interact with each other and other cultural statuses, is essential. Because heterosexism is such an endemic part of our social fabric, such awareness must involve deep self-exploration that goes beyond general proclamations of being unbiased or believing that any nonheterosexual orientation is morally wrong.

Attitudinal nuances can interfere with affirmative practice if left unchecked. For example, tolerating a same-sex or bisexual orientation or perceiving it as an acceptable though somehow less preferable alternative to a heterosexual orientation is less than affirmative. Consciously or unconsciously encouraging a woman who identifies as bisexual to act only on her attractions to men is likewise less than affirmative, as is encouraging her to decide whether she is "really" lesbian or "really" heterosexual (APA, 2011b). It is also not appropriate to assume that because a client is lesbian, bisexual, or transgender that her presenting problem is related to that.

A practice receiving a lot of attention from the media at the time this chapter is being written involves efforts to change sexual orientation or sexual identity. Such efforts are not considered affirmative (APA, 2011b; APA Task Force on Appropriate Therapeutic Responses to Sexual Orientation, 2009). APA has published a *Report of the Task Force on Appropriate Therapeutic Responses to Sexual Orientation* (APA Task Force on Appropriate Therapeutic Responses to Sexual Orientation, 2009), which includes a major review of research on efforts to change sexual orientation. The task force concluded that, overall, most of the research lacked scientific rigor and that the recent research was least rigorous. What they were able to glean from existing research that could be considered credible is that there is no evidence to support the effectiveness of trying to change sexual orientation, and that in some cases there was indication of harm. It is also worth noting that almost all of the research was exclusively with men, with very little of the research involving girls or women. The task force also concluded that because homosexuality and bisexuality are normal variants of human behavior and do not constitute mental illness or psychopathology, they do not need to be changed. The report acknowledges the distress that some people experience due to social attitudes, stigma, and discrimination and recommends an affirmative approach in therapy that includes "acceptance and support, comprehensive assessment, active coping, social support, and identity exploration and development" (p. 86).

This position might present a dilemma for psychologists whose own cultural traditions, particularly faith traditions, might be in conflict with an affirmative approach toward sexual orientation. Although we in the field recognize the reality, and at times intensity, of the dilemma, it is important to address some of the ethical considerations related to potential responses. Discussions show up periodically in professional e-mail lists that involve issues of competence and referral. Standard 2: Competence of the APA's "Ethical Principles of Psychologists and Code of Conduct" (APA, 2010) is invoked, citing responsibility not to practice outside of the boundaries of one's competence. Well-intended psychologists recognize that if affirmative practice is required, they lack the competence to work with clients whose sexual orientation, identity, or particularly behavior is inconsistent with their own value systems. They recognize that referral is preferable to attempting to change the client's orientation, identity, or behavior or to consciously or unconsciously impose their own values on the client. This is addressed in the Application section of Guideline 10.

Although on the surface this appears to be a reasonable argument, it nonetheless fails to take into account other elements of the Ethical Principles (APA, 2010). For example, Standard 3.01, Unfair Discrimination admonishes unfair discrimination based on a variety of statuses, including sexual orientation and gender identity. To categorically refuse to work with clients solely on the basis of cultural status is tantamount to discrimination, which can exacerbate the effects of the discrimination the client might have experienced in other areas of her life. Furthermore, several standards within Standard 2: Competence offer provisions that address situations in which it might be appropriate for psychologists to practice in areas that might otherwise be considered outside of their scope of practice. These include Standard 2.01(d), Providing Services When Services Might Not Otherwise Be Available, and Standard 2.02, Providing Services in Emergencies. Thus, even within the realm of working within the boundaries of one's competence, there is an expectation that psychologists must be competent enough to work with clients they might otherwise refer elsewhere. There is also an implication in Standard 2.01 (b) that psychologists develop competence to work with culturally diverse clients, including those whose sexual orientation and/or gender identity might differ from the larger population. Although this standard does mention referral, when taken together with Standard 3.01 and Principle E, Respect for People's Rights and Dignity, there is the implication that such instances might be temporary while one acquires the competence. Thus, whereas Guideline 10 recommends referral when appropriate for the client, this is not intended to be a substitute for gaining the competence necessary to work with diverse clients, including those whose value systems might differ from the psychologist's. Categorical refusal to work with lesbian, bisexual, or transgender women is not endorsed or implied by this guideline. Working collaboratively with local resources might be as or more appropriate than referral in most instances.

In addition, there might be pragmatic concerns related to referral. These situations might include cases in which the psychologist has a specialization that might be limited in her or his locale, such as work with victims of trauma, veterans, co-occurring disorders, or any area of expertise to which a client might otherwise have limited access. In addition, public and private third-party payers might place limits on service providers available to clients. Psychologists working in schools, prisons, hospitals, and other venues in which clients have few, if any, options for choosing service providers often have few, if any, options for referral. The same can be true for psychologists working in rural areas or other underserved communities.

Perhaps most important is the effect on clients who experience marginalization in many aspects of their lives, including sometimes from their own families and friends. Even without meeting a client, sending a message that an individual would not be welcome or could not be helped due to sexual orientation or gender identity reinforces other messages the individual has received, personally or through the larger social system, which adds to any internalized stigma or shame the individual might be experiencing related to sexual orientation or gender identity. Although the influence of this message might vary depending on a woman's prior experiences, as well as her level of identity development, the potential is there to contribute to rather than alleviate the effects of marginalization.

In addition, because sexual orientation and gender identity are not always immediately known, challenges arise when a client discloses a lesbian, bisexual, or transgender identity well into the therapeutic relationship. Sometimes it is only within the safety of the therapeutic relationship that a client feels safe enough or empowered enough to reveal this information. She has generally taken a risk in revealing her status. Should the psychologist respond in a manner that suggests that there is something problematic about this revelation, and especially if such a revelation leads to the need for referral, the message the client receives is far from affirming.

Working with transgender clients during transition is a specialized No area of practice, so this is a situation in which referral might be appropriate; however, that does not relieve psychologists from the responsibility of being aware of and knowledgeable about transgender issues and concerns. For example, although a client might see a psychologist specializing in work with transgender clients as she or he moves closer to transition, that same client might do earlier self-exploration with a psychologist with whom she or he has become comfortable in the context of other work. In addition, all of the pragmatic issues described previously might apply in this situation as well. The psychologist and the client might have few options beyond working together.

RESOURCES AND ADVOCACY

Because sexual orientation and gender identity represent hidden minority statuses, resources available to support lesbian, bisexual, and transgender women can sometimes be hard to find. Thus, consistent with Guideline 10, it is important for psychologists to be familiar with resources in their local communities so that they can help connect clients with such support systems. This involves not just the obvious LGBT community centers but also being familiar with the knowledgeable and affirmative service providers in a variety of areas. For example, if a client is experiencing discrimination on the job or in a child custody case, it is important to be able to refer her to an attorney who is knowledgeable about working with issues related to sexual orientation and/or gender identity. Likewise, it is important to be able to refer clients struggling with spirituality to local churches and faith communities that have open and affirming commitments to LGBT people. In short, any service or service provider to whom a psychologist might refer clients should be screened for their awareness, knowledge, and skills in working affirmatively with lesbian, bisexual, and transgender clients. It is also important not to assume that providers who are strong in one area are strong in all areas. For example, service providers who are strong on lesbian issues might be less knowledgeable or affirmative about bisexual or transgender issues.

Larger, more urban communities are likely to have more options for supporting lesbian, bisexual, and transgender women. Resources are likely to be easier to find. This makes it even more critical for psychologists working in smaller communities to be knowledgeable of resources available locally or nearby. It is also important to be familiar with national organizations that might have resources available online or that might have lists of resources available in the states. Such national organizations might also be resources for information for psychologists to educate themselves on issues relevant to sexual minority women. The *Guidelines for Psychological Practice With Lesbian, Gay, and Bisexual Clients* (APA, 2011b) includes appendices of Internet resources and advocacy and affinity organizations within a broad range of religious and spiritual denominations. This might be a good place to start building a resource file. The APA LGBT Concerns Office (http://www.apa.org/pi/lgbt/) is another valuable resource.

In addition to being able to connect lesbian, bisexual, and transgender women with resources, it is also important for psychologists to serve as advocates at both the individual and systems levels, consistent with Guideline 11. Matthews and Adams (2009) described a variety of ways in which psychologists can serve as advocates in their local communities, including working with local chapters of parents and friends of lesbians and gays, helping local school districts to create environments that are affirmative for all students, or working in the public policy arena to defeat discriminatory legislation or to advocate for protective legislation.

The following section addresses the case of Joan, which is designed to demonstrate how the concepts addressed in this chapter and the Guidelines with which they are associated might apply in practice with clients. The section begins with a description of Joan's situation, followed by application of the Guidelines and concepts addressed in the chapter.

THE CASE OF JOAN

Joan in Context

Joan is a 45-year-old White woman who was referred by a psychologist who is working with her daughter, Ashley. Ashley is in the eighth grade, and she had been referred to the psychologist by her school counselor, who had noticed that her grades had steadily dropped over the past 2 years. The school counselor also noticed that Ashley had gone from being a fairly outgoing student to someone who seemed withdrawn and distracted. During the course of Ashley's work with the psychologist, she revealed that although her mother tried to hide it from her, there was a lot of tension, including some physical violence, between her mother and her mother's partner, and Ashley was very concerned about her mother. Ashley did not offer a name for the partner and did not correct the psychologist when she referred to the partner as "he." Without revealing details of their sessions, with Ashley's permission, the psychologist suggested that Ashley was struggling with some family concerns and that it might be helpful if Joan also saw a psychologist. Joan was somewhat apprehensive about seeing a psychologist herself, but was—reluctantly—willing to try it if it would help Ashley.

Joan is very slow to open up, but over the course of the first few sessions she reveals that her partner's name is Judy and that they have been together for 5 years. She says that Ashley does not know they are partners; she thinks they are friends. They live together but do not share a bedroom when Ashley is in the house. She acknowledges that there is tension and that there have been some physical altercations; however, she is quick to point out that Judy is a very loving person who is devoted to Ashley and that things are not always tense. She later indicates that things have been getting worse.

Joan describes herself as bisexual; however, she adds that she does not really like labels and does not understand why they are so important to some people. She dated boys in high school. None of them excited her, but she did not question her sexuality at that time; she had no reason to do so because she really had no exposure to anything except the traditional heterosexual norm. When she went away to college, she had intimate relationships with several women over the course of the 4 years she was there. They were exciting relationships, although none of them lasted more than a few months. She decided then that the reason her high school dating had been so tepid was because she was lesbian. Throughout college she had a close friendship with a gay man, and the two of them would sometimes go out together as a cover. She is quick to emphasize that they have never been romantically involved, nor has either of them ever wanted that.

After college, she dated both men and women and gradually came to realize that she might have been too quick to rule out attraction to men, although her attraction to women never waned. After a birth control slip-up, she became pregnant with Ashley, and because she and Ashley's father were in a somewhat serious relationship at the time, they married. Both expected it to be "'til death do us part." Nonetheless, they grew apart, and divorced when Ashley was 6. They live in the same community, and although Joan has primary custody of Ashley, Ashley's dad is actively involved in her life. Most communication between Joan and her ex-husband pertains to Ashley and is not always cordial. Although he does not know that Joan and Judy are a couple, and indeed knows nothing of Joan's involvement with women, he is aware that Judy is lesbian and has raised concerns about Joan exposing Ashley to "that kind of environment." Joan's response that more child support would enable them to live on their own has thus far quieted those complaints, but Joan stresses that she does not trust him or what he would do if he learned that she and Judy were romantically involved.

Joan and Judy dated for a year before moving in together. They rent a house in a middle-class neighborhood and share expenses equally; neither could afford the house on her own. Joan is a teacher in a school district that is nearby, but not the district where Ashley attends school. Judy works as a computer technician. Both are occasionally involved with the lesbian community in a small city about 20 miles away. They met through activities with that community, and Judy insists that they continue to attend events when they can. Joan has always been a bit apprehensive because of her teaching position, although she does not object.

Joan reports that things were wonderful at first. Judy was very attentive to Joan, and she and Ashley took an immediate liking to each other. Over time, though, Judy began complaining that Joan identifies as bisexual rather than lesbian. This began as what seemed like playful teasing, but

Joan began to realize that this really bothered Judy. Joan has tried to discuss the matter with Judy; however, Judy's responses have gotten increasingly cutting. She seems alternately hurt because she thinks that Joan is not fully satisfied with her and angry that Joan is "copping out," unwilling to let go of the remnants of heterosexual privilege that fully identifying as lesbian would entail. Judy frequently suggests that Joan is only with her because she could not make a relationship with a man work and argues that she is not so good at being with a woman either. More recently, Judy has gone into a jealous rage whenever Joan even responds in a friendly way to men. She is also jealous of Joan's friendships with women, to the point that Joan almost never socializes without Judy.

Joan explains that Judy has always been somewhat moody, but lately her dark moods have become more prominent and more frequent. Although she used to have sporadic outbursts followed by sincere apologies and efforts to make up, she now seems spiteful all the time. Judy has even threatened to tell Ashley, Ashley's dad, and Joan's principal about the true nature of their relationship. Joan indicates that things are often worse when Judy drinks, which seems to be more often. Joan also mentions that Judy's outbursts have become physical. At first these outbursts were not directed at anybody and consisted of slamming doors and occasionally throwing or breaking things. Over the past 6 or 8 months, Joan has become the target of Judy's physical aggression. These acts have included pushing and shoving, slapping, throwing things at Joan, and, a few weeks ago, threatening her with a knife. Joan admits that she has started to become afraid of Judy.

When asked if she has contacted the police or a domestic violence center, Joan replies that she has not and seems surprised by the question. She stresses that she only came to counseling herself because she hoped it would help Ashley. She says that she does fear that some of Ashley's struggles might be related to the tension in the house. Joan says that she would never consider calling the police or doing anything that might draw attention to the fact that she is in a relationship with a woman. She is really not comfortable talking about it now.

Working With Joan

Safety issues are an important aspect of Joan's case. Therefore, it is important for the psychologist working with Joan to be able to quickly get a sense of the situation. This includes recognizing first that domestic abuse is occurring and, second, that for Joan her sexual orientation and the domestic abuse are related but separate issues. Judy is exploiting the vulnerability Joan feels regarding their same-sex relationship; however, this is not the cause of the abuse. Feminist theories of domestic violence, which have contributed much in terms of bringing attention to the problem and highlighting the cultural factors that foster it, fall short when it comes to same-sex domestic violence (Kanuha, 2005). The focus on men battering women creates confusion in cases where women perpetrate violence, especially against other women (Pitt & Dolan-Soto, 2001; Seelau & Seelau, 2005). Such confusion can make it difficult for either the parties involved or mental health professionals to recognize what is occurring as domestic violence.

To some extent, the Guidelines mirror this. Intimate partner violence is discussed in the introductory Purpose and Scope section of the Guidelines; however, aside from a passing reference to the fact that domestic violence can occur in same-sex relationships, the focus is on male violence against women. Although this reflects the statistical prevalence of such violence, it can contribute to overlooking such violence when it occurs in same-sex relationships, especially when the perpetrator is a woman. It can also contribute to the assumption that if intimate partner violence is present, the relationship must be heterosexual. Note that all of the mental health professionals involved in this case, including Ashley's school counselor, her psychologist, and Joan's psychologist, assumed that Joan's partner was a man. Joan's therapist put her in the position of having to take the risk of revealing the true nature of the relationship when she was already experiencing vulnerability around Judy threatening to expose her.

Joan's case highlights some of the issues that are similar to heterosexual domestic violence and some of the areas that are unique to same-sex domestic violence, especially when one of the partners identifies as bisexual. As with heterosexual domestic violence, same-sex partner abuse can include emotional abuse, physical abuse, sexual abuse, and financial abuse. Although she does not identify it as such, Joan clearly describes emotional abuse and physical abuse. Because other forms of abuse can also be present, it is important to explore whether sexual abuse and/or financial abuse is also occurring. Is Judy forcing or coercing Joan to be sexual when she does not want to be, perhaps under threat of exposing their relationship? Is she pressuring Joan to engage in sexual practices Joan is not comfortable with or to be sexually involved when Ashley is in the house, contrary to their agreement? Is Judy threatening to move out and leave Joan with a home that she cannot afford?

In the process of assessing for the extent of the abuse, the psychologist can begin helping Joan to understand power and control. The therapist can help her learn how to do power analyses so that she can assess for herself the role that power and control play in her relationship with Judy. Although power analysis is a common approach in feminist therapy (e.g., Worell & Remer, 2003), such analysis is often done in the context of dominant groups' power over marginalized groups. In this case, both Joan and Judy are part of marginalized groups; however, Judy is exploiting the vulnerability that Joan experiences in her marginalization. Thus, in following Guidelines 4, 5, and 6, it is important that psychologists are aware that working with lesbian, bisexual, and transgender women might require creative application of feminist principles. For example, feminist therapists might need to look beyond the typical power dynamics involving dominant and marginalized populations to recognize power imbalances within marginalized populations. In Joan's case, this means recognizing the potential for a woman to be abusive toward another woman. Also common to heterosexual and same-sex domestic violence, the abuse, both verbal and physical, has escalated over time. Given that Joan has reported that Judy threatened her with a knife and that Joan is now afraid of Judy, it would be important to help Joan develop a safety plan. This, too, will require some creativity because both Joan and Judy are part of the same marginalized community. For example, it might be important to help Joan to consider potential allies and support systems outside of the lesbian community. This will likely feel threatening for her, at least initially, so sensitivity is needed to recognize her vulnerability while gently encouraging her to move beyond it.

Isolation is common for victims of domestic violence, whether they are in heterosexual or same-sex relationships. It is one way that perpetrators of abuse maintain power and control. It has additional implications in same-sex situations. Because of homophobia and the associated stigma, isolation can be a concern for many LGBT people, even when domestic violence is not an issue. Especially for somebody like Joan, who fears the ramifications of key people in her life discovering her secret, it can be hard to find others with whom she can be herself. Joan does have a community, but it is also Judy's community, and it is one in which they are known as a couple. This is one of the struggles the LGBT community has had in addressing domestic violence—finding ways to respond when all parties are members of the same community without cutting off anybody from support in dealing with the minority stress that comes with living in a heterosexist society. Speaking with a psychologist in itself helps to break down Joan's isolation. Helping her to find ways to build a support system apart from Judy will be critical not only in response to the abuse but also in helping to address external and internal homophobia and biphobia. Thus, the psychologist's familiarity with local resources for lesbian and bisexual women is critical to helping Joan find options. This taps into Guidelines 10 and 11, addressed earlier in the chapter. Joan's psychologist will have to help Joan find resources in the community where she can be safe from Judy as well as safe from discrimination and bias related to her status as a bisexual woman. Her psychologist might also have to be an advocate in helping the local domestic violence program, police department, and other local resources for victims of violence become more informed and responsive to same-sex domestic violence.

biphobia

There are indications that both external and internal homophobia and biphobia are issues for Joan that Judy is using to manipulate her, so it is important to assess for this. That LGBT people face challenges and threats due to social intolerance is well documented, as are the stress and other assaults on their mental health that can result (see earlier discussion). Women who are bisexual often experience additional stresses because they can face attacks from both society at large for being too lesbian and from the lesbian community for not being lesbian enough. Joan is experiencing this in her fear of the ramifications should her ex-husband and her school district learn of her relationship with Judy as well as in Judy's attacks that her self-definition as bisexual is a cop-out. These factors add layers of complexity to same-sex domestic violence that are not present in cross-sex domestic violence. Rather than having one's intimate relationship be a respite from the minority stress created by external forces, these forces are used as further ammunition for establishing power and control in the relationship. Joan indicates that Judy is doing this with her threats to expose their relationship to people who could use this knowledge to harm Joan and perhaps Ashley as well. Likewise, Judy's constant criticism regarding Joan's identification as bisexual fuels any internal shame or discomfort Joan may be harboring regarding her sexuality. Balsam and Szymanski (2005) found that the bisexual women in their study reported more "LGB-specific psychological aggression" (p. 266) than lesbian women. Consistent with Guideline 3, psychologists can educate themselves on the effects that bias and discrimination can have on bisexual women and be prepared to help clients like Joan address it within her relationship and within her larger social environment.

Although Joan has considered herself bisexual for most of her adult life, it appears that she has never been out to any great extent. In college she made a point of dating a male friend to protect herself from discovery. She never told her husband about her previous relationships with women. She is not out to her daughter despite the fact that the two of them share a home with her partner. Although there might be real and rational reasons for Joan's caution, it is also very possible that internalized homophobia and biphobia might be a factor. It is important to explore with Joan the messages she has learned about being bisexual, where she has learned them, and the degree to which she has internalized them. The psychologist must be knowledgeable enough to help her to separate myth from reality and to begin to consider alternative narratives. What is also important to keep in mind is that the external and internal homophobia and biphobia that Joan experiences represents a vulnerability that Judy manipulates to exert power and control over Joan. Thus, addressing the abuse means also addressing this.

We help Joan to articulate the safety concerns that are present for her and to develop plans for responding to them, both proactively and reactively.

To the extent that there are factors that make her more vulnerable, we help her to identify them and to find resources to minimize the vulnerability. One of the ways that we help to reduce vulnerabilities for Joan and others like her is to reduce the systemic vulnerabilities that exist in the community. Consistent with Guideline 11, it is important to work to encourage local jurisdictions to enact nondiscrimination laws that protect LGBT individuals from being fired on the basis of sexual orientation or gender identity. If that seems like too distant a goal, working with individual employers, especially those that might be particularly troublesome, might be a place to start. Likewise, working with local family court systems to educate them about the research on parenting can help to reduce the possibility of lesbian, bisexual, and transgender women losing custody of their children. In this case, working with the local police department and domestic violence program to help them to recognize, understand, and better respond to same-sex domestic violence is also important. Although Judy might find other ways to be abusive, removing some of the systemic threats to Joan's well-being help her to be less vulnerable.

CONCLUSION AND FUTURE DIRECTIONS

In considering the Guidelines, it is important to recognize the unique experiences of lesbian, bisexual, and transgender women. Although the Guidelines are the same for heterosexual and lesbian, bisexual, and transgender women, there are contextual factors that influence the ways in which the Guidelines are applied when working with these populations. This chapter has offered a starting place for understanding some of these unique applications. When applying the Guidelines to work with lesbian, bisexual, and transgender women, it is important to remember that they are women as well as sexual minorities. Some will identify themselves first as women and then as sexual minorities; others will identify most strongly with their sexual minority status. For many, the salience of each status might change over time. Lesbian, bisexual, and transgender women are also often women with other identities, some of which might have more salience for them than either their status as women or their status as sexual or gender minority women. Thus, all of the chapters in this book apply to lesbian, bisexual, and transgender women, and this chapter applies to heterosexual women as well. Indeed, the focus for the future will be on learning more about the ways in which different aspects of identity intersect. Research is beginning to emerge that addresses some of the complexity of multiple minority identities (e.g., Nettles & Balter, 2012). It will be essential that psychologists stay current with this research to ensure that they are fully knowledgeable of the influences and implications of the intersections of sexual orientation and gender identity with other aspects of identity.

REFERENCES

American Psychological Association. (2003). Guidelines on multicultural education, training, research, practice, and organizational change for psychologists. *American Psychologist, 58*, 377–402. doi:10.1037/0003-066X.58.5.377

American Psychological Association. (2007). Guidelines for psychological practice with girls and women. *American Psychologist, 62*, 949–979. doi:10.1037/0003-066X.62.9.949

American Psychological Association. (2010). *Ethical principles of psychologists and code of conduct (amended June 1, 2010).* Washington, DC: Author. Retrieved from http://www.apa.org/ethics/code/principles.pdf

American Psychological Association. (2011a). *Guidelines for assessment of and intervention with persons with disabilities.* Washington, DC: Author. Retrieved from http://www.apa.org/pi/disability/resources/assessment-disabilities.aspx?item=1

American Psychological Association. (2011b). *Guidelines for psychological practice with lesbian, gay, and bisexual clients.* Washington, DC: Author.

American Psychological Association Task Force on Appropriate Therapeutic Responses to Sexual Orientation. (2009). *Report of the Task Force on Appropriate Therapeutic Responses to Sexual Orientation.* Washington, DC: American Psychological Association. Retrieved from http://www.apa.org/pi/lgbt/resources/therapeutic-response.pdf

American Psychological Association Task Force on Gender Identity and Gender Variance. (2009). *Report of the Task Force on Gender Identity and Gender Variance.* Washington, DC: Author. Retrieved from http://www.apa.org/pi/lgbt/resources/policy/gender-identity-report.pdf

Balsam, K. F., & Szymanski, D. M. (2005). Relationship quality and domestic violence in women's same-sex relationships: The role of minority stress. *Psychology of Women Quarterly, 29*, 258–269. doi:10.1111/j.1471-6402.2005.00220.x

Bem, S. L. (1974). The measurement of psychological androgyny. *Journal of Consulting and Clinical Psychology, 42*, 155–162. doi:10.1037/h0036215

Bem, S. L. (1975). Sex role adaptability: One consequence of psychological androgyny. *Journal of Personality and Social Psychology, 31*, 634–643. doi:10.1037/h0077098

Bem, S. L. (1977). On the utility of alternative procedures for the assessing of psychological androgyny. *Journal of Consulting and Clinical Psychology, 45*, 196–205. doi:10.1037/0022-006X.45.2.196

Bradford, J., Ryan, C., & Rothblum, E. D. (1994). National lesbian health care survey: Implications for mental health care. *Journal of Consulting and Clinical Psychology, 62*, 228–242.

Brooks, V. R. (1981). *Minority stress and lesbian women.* Lexington, MA: Lexington Books.

Cass, V. C. (1979). Homosexual identity formation: A theoretical model. *Journal of Homosexuality, 4*, 219–235. doi:10.1300/J082v04n03_01

Cass, V. C. (1984). Homosexual identity formation: Testing a theoretical model. *Journal of Sex Research, 20*, 143–167. doi:10.1080/00224498409551214

Chapman, B. E., & Brannock, J. C. (1987). Proposed model of lesbian identity development: An empirical examination. *Journal of Homosexuality, 14*(3–4), 69–80. doi:10.1300/J082v14n03_05

Cochran, S. D., Sullivan, J. G., & Mays, V. M. (2003). Prevalence of mental disorders, psychological distress, and mental health service use among lesbian, gay, and bisexual adults in the United States. *Journal of Consulting and Clinical Psychology, 71*, 53–61. doi:10.1037/0022-006X.71.1.53

Diamond, L. M. (2005). A new view of lesbian subtypes: Stable versus fluid identity trajectories over an 8-year period. *Psychology of Women Quarterly, 29*, 119–128. doi:10.1111/j.1471-6402.2005.00174.x

Diamond, L. M. (2006). What we got wrong about sexual identity development: Unexpected findings from a longitudinal study of young women. In A. M. Omoto & H. S. Kurtzman (Eds.), *Sexual orientation and mental health: Examining identity and development in lesbian, gay, and bisexual people* (pp. 73–94). Washington, DC: American Psychological Association. doi:10.1037/11261-004

Diamond, L. M. (2008). *Sexual fluidity: Understanding women's love and desire.* Cambridge, MA: Harvard University Press.

Diamond, L. M. (2013). Concepts of female sexual orientation. In C. J. Patterson & A. R. D'Augelli (Eds.), *Handbook of psychology and sexual orientation.* New York, NY: Oxford University Press.

Drabble, L., & Trocki, K. (2005). Alcohol consumption, alcohol-related problems, and other substance use among lesbian and bisexual women. In E. Ettore (Ed.), *Making lesbians visible in the substance use field* (pp. 19–30). New York, NY: Harrington Park Press. doi:10.1300/J155v09n03_03

Dworkin, S. H. (2001). Treating the bisexual client. *Journal of Clinical Psychology, 57*, 671–680. doi:10.1002/jclp.1036

Fassinger, R. E. (1991). The hidden minority: Issues and challenges in working with lesbian women and gay men. *The Counseling Psychologist, 19*, 157–176. doi:10.1177/0011000091192003

Fassinger, R. E., & Arseneau, J. R. (2007). "I'd rather get wet than be under that umbrella": Differentiating the experiences and identities of lesbian, gay, bisexual, and transgender people. In K. J. Bieschke, R. M. Perez, & K. A. DeBord (Eds.), *Handbook of counseling and psychotherapy with lesbian, gay, bisexual, and transgender clients* (2nd ed., pp. 19–49). Washington, DC: American Psychological Association. doi:10.1037/11482-001

Garnets, L. D., Herek, G. M., & Levy, B. (2003). Violence and victimization of lesbians and gay men: Mental health consequences. In L. D. Garnets & D. C. Kimmel (Eds.), *Psychological perspectives on lesbian, gay, and bisexual experiences* (pp. 188–206). New York, NY: Columbia University Press.

Gramick, J. (1984). Developing a lesbian identity. In T. Darty & S. Potter (Eds.), *Women-identified women* (pp. 31–44). Palo Alto, CA: Mayfield.

Herek, G. M., Gillis, J. R., Cogan, J. C., & Glunt, E. K. (1997). Hate crime victimization among lesbian, gay, and bisexual adults: Prevalence, psychological correlates, and methodological issues. *Journal of Interpersonal Violence, 12,* 195–215. doi:10.1177/088626097012002003

Kanuha, V. K. (2005). Compounding the triple jeopardy: Battering in lesbian of color relationships. In N. J. Sokoloff & C. Pratt (Eds.), *Domestic violence at the margins: Readings on race, class, gender, and culture* (pp. 71–82). New Brunswick, NJ: Rutgers University Press.

Lev, A. I. (2004). *Transgender emergence: Therapeutic Guidelines for working with gender-variant people and their families.* New York, NY: Routledge.

Liddle, B. J. (1996). Therapist sexual orientation, gender, and counseling practices as they relate to ratings of helpfulness by gay and lesbian clients. *Journal of Counseling Psychology, 43,* 394–401. doi:10.1037/0022-0167.43.4.394

Marzullo, M. A., & Libman, A. J. (2009). *Hate crimes and violence against lesbian, gay, bisexual, and transgender people.* Washington, DC: Human Rights Campaign. Retrieved from http://www.hrc.org/resources/entry/hate-crimes-and-violence-against-lgbt-people

Matthews, C. R. (2007). Affirmative lesbian, gay, and bisexual counseling with all clients. In K. J. Bieschke, R. M. Perez, & K. A. DeBord (Eds.), *Handbook of counseling and psychotherapy with lesbian, gay, bisexual, and transgender clients* (2nd ed., pp. 201–219). Washington, DC: American Psychological Association. doi:10.1037/11482-008

Matthews, C. R., & Adams, E. (2009). Using a social justice approach to prevent the mental health consequences of heterosexism. *The Journal of Primary Prevention, 30,* 11–26. doi:10.1007/s10935-008-0166-4

Matthews, C. R., & Bieschke, K. J. (2001). Adapting the Ethnocultural Assessment to gay and lesbian clients: The Sexual Orientation Enculturation Assessment. *The Journal of Humanistic Education and Development, 40,* 58–73. doi:10.1002/j.2164-490X.2001.tb00102.x

Mays, V. M., & Cochran, S. D. (2001). Mental health correlates of perceived discrimination among lesbian, gay, and bisexual adults in the United States. *American Journal of Public Health, 91,* 1869–1876. doi:10.2105/AJPH.91.11.1869

McCarn, S. R., & Fassinger, R. E. (1996). Revisioning sexual minority identity formation: A new model of lesbian identity and its implications for counseling and research. *The Counseling Psychologist, 24,* 508–534.

Meyer, I. H. (2003). Prejudice, social stress, and mental health in lesbian, gay, and bisexual populations. *Psychological Bulletin, 129,* 674–697. doi:10.1037/0033-2909.129.5.674

Morgan, K. S. (1992). Caucasian lesbians' use of psychotherapy: A matter of attitude? *Psychology of Women Quarterly, 16,* 127–130.

Nadal, K. L., Rivera, D. P., & Corpus, M. J. H. (2010). Sexual orientation and transgender microaggressions: Implications for mental health and counseling. In D. W. Sue (Ed.), *Microaggressions and marginality: Manifestation, dynamics, and impact* (pp. 217–240). Hoboken, NJ: Wiley.

National Center for Transgender Equity. (2009). *Teaching transgender: A resource from the National Center for Transgender Equity*. Washington, DC: Author. Retrieved from http://transequality.org/Resources/NCTE_Teaching_Transgender.pdf

Nettles, R., & Balter, R. (Eds.). (2012). *Multiple minority identities: Applications for practice, research, and training*. New York, NY: Springer.

Phillips, J. C., & Fischer, A. R. (1998). Graduate students' training experiences with lesbian, gay, and bisexual issues. *The Counseling Psychologist, 26*, 712–734. doi:10.1177/0011000098265002

Pilkington, N. W., & Cantor, J. M. (1996). Perceptions of heterosexual bias in professional psychology programs: A survey of graduate students. *Professional Psychology: Research and Practice, 27*, 604–612. doi:10.1037/0735-7028.27.6.604

Pitt, E., & Dolan-Soto, D. (2001). Clinical considerations in working with victims of same-sex domestic violence. *Journal of the Gay and Lesbian Medical Association, 5*, 163–169. doi:10.1023/A:1014266212280

Rich, A. (1980). Compulsory heterosexuality and lesbian existence. *Signs: Journal of Women in Culture and Society, 5*, 631–660.

Rostosky, S. S., Riggle, E. D. B., Horne, S. G., & Miller, A. D. (2009). Marriage amendments and psychological distress in lesbian, gay, and bisexual (LGB) adults. *Journal of Counseling Psychology, 56*, 56–66. doi:10.1037/a0013609

Russell, G. M. (2000). *Voted out: The psychological consequences of anti-gay politics*. New York, NY: New York University Press.

Savin-Williams, R. C. (2007). *The new gay teenager*. Cambridge, MA: Harvard University Press.

Seelau, S. M., & Seelau, E. P. (2005). Gender-role stereotypes and perceptions of heterosexual, gay, and lesbian domestic violence. *Journal of Family Violence, 20*, 363–371. doi:10.1007/s10896-005-7798-4

Sophie, J. (1986). A critical examination of lesbian identity development. *Journal of Homosexuality, 12*, 39–51.

Sorensen, L., & Roberts S. J. (1997). Lesbian uses of and satisfaction with mental health services: Results from Boston Lesbian Health Project. *Journal of Homosexuality, 33*, 35–49.

Swim, J. K., Johnston, K., & Pearson, N. (2009). Daily experiences with heterosexism: Relations between heterosexist hassles and psychological well being. *Journal of Social and Clinical Psychology, 28*, 597–629. doi:10.1521/jscp.2009.28.5.597

Szymanski, D. M., & Hilton, A. N. (2013). Feminist counseling psychology and lesbians, bisexual women, and transgender persons. In C. Z. Enns & E. N. Williams (Eds.), *The Oxford handbook of feminist multicultural counseling psychology* (pp. 131–154). New York, NY: Oxford University Press.

Worell, J., & Remer, P. (2003). *Feminist perspectives in therapy: Empowering diverse women* (2nd ed.). Hoboken, NJ: Wiley.

World Professional Association for Transgender Health. (2012). *Standards of care for the health of transsexual, transgender, and gender nonconforming people*. Minneapolis, MN: Author. Retrieved from http://www.wpath.org/site_page.cfm?pk_association_webpage_menu=1351

6

THE INTERSECTION OF GENDER AND ETHNICITY: ASIAN–PACIFIC ISLANDER AMERICAN WOMEN

PHI LOAN LE AND KHANH T. DINH

I fought my war every night in bed with men. Who talks about my war? Who asks me if I'm hurt or wounded? Nobody asks. Not even the closest person to me, my mother, knows or asks. No one knows, it's just a silent war that I have inside of me. . . . I know a lot of Vietnamese women in this country who are ex-prostitutes, they have the same feeling, but we are still in the closet, we are ashamed, embarrassed. We aren't just criticized by American society but the Vietnamese society too. Even my own people the Vietnamese community here in the United States, they look down on me because I did something that brought shame to our ancestors.
—Nguyen Ngoc Xuan (cited in Travis-Robyns, 2004)

The "Guidelines for Psychological Practice With Girls and Women" (American Psychological Association [APA], 2007; hereinafter referred to as Guidelines) use multicultural, nonsexist, and feminist lenses to guide psychological practice with women and girls from all social, racial, and ethnic groups; sexual orientations; and levels of ability or disability in the United States. Although the Guidelines represent an important first step in encouraging psychologists to integrate the diverse and intersecting social identities of women and girls in practice, also needed are concrete suggestions and recommendations for their implementation with specific populations. The quote at the beginning of this chapter demonstrates the complex life experiences of Asian–Pacific Islander American (APIA) women, including those who are coping with past traumas and cultural and identity disconnects in finding a home in the United States. This chapter offers relevant information about psychological practice with APIA women. Furthermore, the inclusion

http://dx.doi.org/10.1037/14460-006
Psychological Practice With Women: Guidelines, Diversity, Empowerment, C. Z. Enns, J. K. Rice, and R. L. Nutt (Editors)
Copyright © 2015 by the American Psychological Association. All rights reserved.

of case studies provides examples of specific applications of the Guidelines for working with APIA women. The first case study highlights the themes and issues related to Guidelines sections on diversity and social context and on professional responsibility and practice. The second case study integrates a description and an analysis of the topics relevant to the chapter as a whole.

NOT EASILY DEFINED: INTRODUCTION TO APIA WOMEN

The demographics of APIAs include a broad array of more than 40 cultural–ethnic groups, with distinct and unique historical and immigration experiences. The U.S. Census Bureau (2010) separated APIA populations into two separate categories: Asians (Chinese, Filipino, Indian, Vietnamese, Korean, Japanese, Pakistani, Cambodian, Hmong, Thai, Laotian, Taiwanese, Bangladeshi, and Burmese) and Native Hawaiians and other Pacific Islanders. D. W. Sue and Sue (2013) further classified APIAs into three broad categories: Asian Americans (Asian Indians, Chinese, Filipinos, Japanese, and Koreans), Southeast Asians (Cambodians, Laotians, and Vietnamese), and Pacific Islanders (Hawaiian, Guamanians, and Samoans). In addition to the many diverse languages spoken by APIA groups, there is substantial variability within these groups regarding customs, values, beliefs, religions, and worldviews. For example, there are more than 100 dialects within the Filipino culture. In addition to their diverse cultural backgrounds, APIAs immigrated to the United States at different times and for different reasons. For instance, the first wave of Chinese laborers arrived in the 1840s, whereas the first wave of Southeast Asian refugees arrived in the 1970s (Takaki, 1989).

Given the tremendous diversity among APIAs, blending all the distinct Asian ethnic groups under one category is troublesome. It is difficult, if not impossible, to make generalizations about APIA women as a group. At least three different chapters would be necessary to address the distinct cultural groups described by D. W. Sue and Sue (2013). In addition, issues impacting APIA women with intersecting identities as lesbian, bisexual, and transgendered (LBT) persons have only begun to receive attention in the literature (Y. B. Chung & Singh, 2009). Within many APIA communities, LBT women face invisibility and silence because their sexual identity is often perceived as a "Western disease" or a sign of being "Americanized." The struggles of Asian LBT women as gender and sexual minorities are often isolated from their struggles as racial minorities. To increase understanding of the experience of APIA LBT women, researchers and clinicians need to attend not only to their status as racial, gender, and sexual minorities but also the intersection of their identities (Y. B. Chung & Singh, 2009).

The need for clinicians to consider clients' cultural identities as well as their immigration history cannot be stressed enough because of the diverse immigration history within and between APIA groups. For APIA women, the impact of immigration and resettlement on gender role expectations and identities further reflects the complexity and challenges of their multiple identities. Dion and Dion (2001) encouraged a thorough examination of the likely tensions experienced by daughters of immigrant families in negotiating parental expectations and behaviors toward their daughters and how a deeper understanding of gender can contribute to a clearer picture of the experiences of APIA women immigrants. Clearly, the diverse experiences of APIA women cannot be captured in one chapter. However, as a beginning step, our discussion explores some relevant issues for APIA women in general, and case studies are used to demonstrate a few essential considerations necessary for clinicians working with this group. In the future, we urge a more focused, less broad approach to applying the guidelines to specific groups of APIA women.

DIVERSITY, SOCIAL CONTEXT, AND POWER

Consistent with Guidelines 1, 2, and 3, clinicians working with APIA women need to be aware of and recognize the impact of stereotypes, bias, and oppression. This section expands on these themes by addressing myths and stereotypes applied to APIA women, invisibility issues, and mental health barriers. A case study illustrates these themes at the conclusion of this section.

Myths and Stereotypes

APIAs, often portrayed as the "model minority," represent a complex and diverse group with problems and barriers that are usually hidden. The term *model minority* originated in the racially charged 1960s and referred to the relative economic success of Japanese and Chinese Americans. National median household income data used to uphold APIAs as a model minority is a poor indicator of the economic well-being of APIAs and racial progress. It hides the reality that many APIAs are living in poverty (DeNavas-Walt, Proctor, & Smith, 2012). Furthermore, census data reveal that in general, APIA households are larger than the average U.S. household and have more people working and contributing to the household income. The model minority myth portrays Asians as the American success story, protected from conflicts, difficulties, and discrimination because of their cultural emphasis on education and hard work. Although APIAs as a group have higher household and personal income in comparison with other racial minority groups, the poverty rate for Asians continues to be higher than that for non-Hispanic Whites (DeNavas-Walt et al., 2012). Among the Southeast Asian Cambodian and Hmong American groups, poverty rates are twice as high as the national level (U.S. Census Bureau, 2011–2013).

APIAs often are excluded from national discourse about racism and race relations. Most recently, as the debates about undocumented immigrants in the United States have raged on, issues impacting the 1 million undocumented Asian immigrants (Passel, Capps, & Fix, 2004) remain hidden in the media. The model minority myth discounts the effects of bias and discrimination on the lives of APIAs and renders their experiences invisible. Similar to other marginalized groups in the United States, APIAs are often pigeonholed and have no choice but to deal with racism and discrimination. For example, research has revealed that 98% to 99% of Filipino Americans have confronted daily and lifetime racism (Alvarez, Juang, & Liang, 2006). Furthermore, misperceptions and stereotypes can negatively affect the self-identity, racial identity, psychological well-being, and intergroup relations of APIAs (D. W. Sue & Sue, 2013).

Attaining a thorough understanding of the varied needs of APIA communities is challenging when the successes of specific APIA groups are overgeneralized (Chao, Chiu, Chan, Mendoza-Denton, & Kwok, 2012). APIA women have to confront not only additional harmful stereotypes from Western culture but also gender oppression in traditional Asian cultures, which tend to emphasize Confucian patriarchal influences and the valuing of gendered virtues—for example, the three obediences of women to their fathers, their husbands, and their sons. When issues of bias and discrimination are examined, dichotomous stereotypes are common. On the one hand, APIA women are often portrayed as passive, weak, quiet, sexually exotic, excessively submissive, and dutiful, an image that is consistent with the hypersexual, subservient "China Doll," but on the other hand, other images portray them as the treacherous, untrustworthy "Dragon Lady" (Espiritu, 1997). When combined with the model minority myth, traditional Asian cultural values of endurance and yielding to others make it even more difficult for APIA women to voice their marginalized experiences, which can be detrimental to recognizing and validating their needs (Chan, 1987). The many acculturation challenges faced by APIA women due to economic struggles and racism cannot be taken lightly, and a deeper understanding of their experiences requires the deconstruction of the model minority myth and other harmful images.

Invisibility

Stereotypical perceptions, as described in the previous section, impose unrealistic and one-dimensional images on APIA women and negatively impact their struggles for visibility and recognition of the diversity that exists among them. It is possible that APIA women receiving conflicting cultural messages about their identities may experience conflict about their sense of control over life decisions. For many traditional Asian cultures grounded in Buddhism and Confucian philosophies, the concepts of acceptance of suffering and personal sacrifice can further intensify APIA women's struggle to voice their experiences and identities (True, 1997). Unrealistic standards set by the mainstream's stereotypes and by the traditional Asian cultural values of their families and communities contribute to stressors affecting APIA women's sense of well-being (Suzuki, Ahluwalia, & Alimchandani, 2012).

Given that little research has examined the specific aspects of APIA women's needs and experience, it is not surprising that APIA women remain invisible in a number of ways. The objectified, passive, quiet images of APIA women, coupled with "invisibility" oppression, present a challenge for researchers and clinicians searching for a deeper, more nuanced understanding of APIA women's issues. When steps are taken to explore their experiences more deeply, what emerges is a more complex picture. For example, Pyke and Johnson (2003) examined the effects intersecting racial and gender hierarchies have on everyday gender identity construction for daughters of Korean and Vietnamese immigrant women. The study's participants constructed White American women's identity traits as independent, powerful, outspoken, and self-assured. In contrast, Asian women were perceived as quiet, passive, and submissive. Their findings underscored the challenges facing APIA women, whose search for the path to gender equality and empowerment might include painful denial of "their ethnicity and connections to other APIA women through the adoption and replication" of harmful stereotypical images of Asian women (Pyke & Johnson, 2003, p. 50).

Although APIA women often share Confucian or Buddhist influences, these traditions are experienced differently as they are combined with indigenous cultural traditions and sociopolitical factors. For example, the history of Chinese women garment workers in New York underscores how the transnational shifting of gender norms and Chinese culture presented multiple gender relation challenges within the Chinese American family (Bao, 2001). At the same time, in-depth, focused exploration serves to highlight the complex life experiences of this particular group of Chinese American women and how shifting gender norms served to galvanized them to defy traditional cultural expectations and to stand up for themselves. To fully understand APIA women's experiences, researchers must continue to venture deeply into their specific communities and examine the multiple factors that impact their lives.

Mental Health Barriers

Research on APIAs has been growing in recent years as scholars and activists call for more awareness of and sensitivity to the needs of this group. Although this is important progress, the majority of focus in the literature has been on APIAs as a general group (Iwamoto & Liu, 2010; B. S. Kim et al., 2003; Suzuki & Greenfield, 2002; Yeh & Hwang, 2000; Yoo & Lee, 2008). Over the past decades, despite the growth in the literature from the multicultural and feminist movements, research on Asian American women, their mental health concerns, and their help-seeking behaviors has proceeded at a much slower pace (C. I. Hall, 2009); particularly lacking is an understanding of APIA LBT individuals, who face multiple layers of oppression due to their triple minority status.

Existing data demonstrate that APIAs underutilize mental health treatment, an alarming trend given that Asian American women between the ages of 15 and 24 and over 65 have the highest suicide rates of all racial–ethnic groups (National Center for Health Statistics, 2011). For APIA women, the silence surrounding depression and suicide is partly the result of the inadequate mental health system and their ambivalent or negative feelings about therapy. Other barriers here include the cultural value of "saving face," in which socially approved traits function as a means to maintain group cohesion (Zane & Yeh, 2002) and a collectivistic orientation. In contrast, bringing attention to individual needs is often considered a selfish act. In exploring the narratives of APIA women who attempted suicide, Noh (2007) stressed the importance of considering sociopolitical causes, including racial and gender oppression, in order to provide more effective healing.

The remarkable scarcity in the literature about mental health issues specific to APIA women also presents additional barriers for clinicians seeking to work with this population. More specifically, little is known about their sexual behaviors, identities, and experience of sexual abuse. Where there are existing data, APIA women often report that the topic of sexuality is taboo and uncomfortable. In addition, APIA girls and women often receive negative and restrictive messages from parents about their sexuality (J. L. Kim, 2009). Even less information exists with regard to sexual abuse within the APIA community. A review of the literature highlighted the problems that arise for APIA women because most state and national agencies failed to separate data for APIA victims, who were shown to be overwhelmingly reluctant to disclose or report sexual abuse (Okazaki, 2002).

It is vital to address existing barriers to effective mental health interventions for APIAs. In general, APIA clients question the credibility of therapy as a way for resolving their life problems (S. Sue & Zane, 2009). Mistrust of Western values and approaches, combined with APIAs' historical experiences of oppression by Euro Americans, contribute to the continued underutilization of mental health services (David, 2010). The fields of multicultural and feminist psychology need to further explore the barriers experienced by discrete APIA ethnic groups, taking into account their historical, cultural, and sociopolitical experiences. This deliberation is essential in order to reduce the current disparity between levels of distress and the utilization of mental health services.

The following brief case study illustrates themes relevant to Guidelines 1, 2, and 3 and emphasizes the impact of a therapist's understanding and recognition of bias and oppression on a client's trauma experience and healing.

CASE STUDY: IN-DEPTH ILLUSTRATION AND APPLICATION OF THE GUIDELINES

In the following case study, information has been modified to protect confidentiality. Tina, a 26-year-old Filipina American junior majoring in dance, came to therapy to seek help for feelings of depression after the death of her aunt. Tina shared with the intake therapist that she did not know what else to do. She did not remember ever feeling this way before. Her aunt, who was "like a mother" to Tina, died suddenly from a heart attack. Tina stated that she could not stop crying since she found out about her aunt's death. She had not been to her classes for 2 weeks, and although she did not seem to care about her classes, she did not want to repeat them. Tina was seen for six sessions to help her deal with her grief and complete her classes for the semester. At the end of the first set of six sessions, Tina stated that she wanted to continue in therapy to deal with "other issues" she had been unable to bring up. After a summer break, Tina came back to the counseling center in the fall, met with a different therapist for an intake, and requested to see an APIA female therapist for therapy, stating that she hoped an APIA female therapist could understand more about the cultural values she needed to explore.

Tina was born in the Philippines. Her maternal grandparents raised her until she was 4 years old. Her mother was working and was not home much, and Tina's grandmother cared for Tina and her younger brother during that time. The client never met her father or his family. When she was about 4 years old, her mother remarried. Tina was not sure how her mother met her stepfather, whom she called her "American" stepfather. He told her mother to pick one child to raise. Her mother chose Tina over her younger brother, who stayed with their maternal grandparents. Tina lived with her mother and stepfather in Hong Kong until she was about 9 years old. Tina remembered that once they left the Philippines, her stepfather told her "you are White now" and that she should only speak English. At 6 years of age, a man Tina described as a "Chinese" waiter in a gambling club molested her while her mother gambled nearby. In addition, her stepfather started to molest Tina when she was around 7 years old. When her stepfather moved the family to the United States, Tina was able to spend a lot of time with her maternal aunt, who lived nearby. However, her aunt's Euro American husband and father-in-law also molested Tina. During the time of the abuse, Tina's mother was addicted to gambling and was "not around much."

During therapy, Tina was able to share her childhood traumas and her feelings of being "invisible" in her family, with her stepfather, and with regard to her new identity as a Filipina American woman. The Filipina American identity was a new one for her because she had not considered herself an American previously. Her Euro American stepfather's message that she had to discard her identity as a Filipina to be accepted by him stood out to her, and she never felt that she could ever be "White enough." In trying to forge her own identity, she felt "lost" after the sudden death of her maternal aunt, who was her main connection to her identity as a Filipina. As have other survivors of childhood sexual abuse, Tina blamed herself for what happened. Her pains surrounding these multiple traumas were exacerbated and intensified by her confusion about her identity as a Filipina and the perpetrators' identities as non-Filipino. Tina wondered whether she had been abused because she was "too Filipina" and not "White enough." The therapist's identity as a 1.5-generation (individuals who migrated to a new country before or during their early teens) Vietnamese American feminist psychologist was "good enough" for Tina because during the first session, the therapist initiated explorations about Tina's multiple identities as a Filipina American survivor and integrated historical and sociocultural context into her presenting concerns (Guidelines 1, 2, and 3).

Later, as therapy was ending, Tina shared with the therapist that she had walked away from the first session with a sense of relief that she had been "seen." Tina believed that although the therapist was from a different ethnic background, the connection and understanding of their similar experiences as APIA women made the process "safer" for her to share her pain and anger toward "White people" as a result of the abuse and oppression she had endured.

This case study highlights a number of themes relevant to Guidelines 1, 2, and 3. The therapist's intentional integration and validation of the client's painful experience with racism and sexism and her struggles in being "seen" by herself and others in the first session provided a foundation for her healing process. The clear affirmation of the impact of cultural values in the first session created a trusting therapeutic relationship in which bias and oppression could be safely explored and deconstructed. The steps taken to have a holistic understanding of the cultural influences and immigration traumas facilitated the client's search to ground her complex intersecting and multiple identities as a Filipina American survivor.

PROFESSIONAL RESPONSIBILITY AND PRACTICE APPLICATIONS

As Guideline 4 advises, psychological practice that has originated from Western worldviews and concepts increases the challenge of applying culturally sensitive approaches. The growing work from multicultural psychology and feminist psychology has moved therapists toward understanding the importance of integrating cultural and sociopolitical factors in interventions with diverse populations (e.g., Brown & Root, 1990; Reid, 2002). In addition, the work of Jean Baker Miller on relational–cultural theory (RCT) offers a complementary framework for clinicians to explore how sociocultural challenges such as power, marginalization, and socialization impact the mental health and relational development of individuals (Miller, 2008). Clinicians applying RCT engage their clients through mutual empathy to move them out of isolation and toward healing connections. The RCT basic tenets of authenticity, connections, and growth through and toward relationship can be particularly applicable to APIA women's collectivistic and relational cultures. Additionally, G. C. N. Hall, Hong, Zane, and Meyer (2011) proposed adapting certain components of mindfulness and acceptance psychotherapies to provide a culturally syntonic approach to treatment that is more consistent with Asian American cultural values. Iwamoto and Liu's (2010) research on the relationship between racial identity, ethnic identity, Asian cultural values, and race-related stress in predicting the psychological well-being of APIA and Asian international college students also provides some useful information for culturally affirming practice. On discovering that a majority of the research participants reported experiencing stress due to racism, the authors recommended exploring how clients' encounters with racism may have impacted their racial–ethnic identity (Iwamoto & Liu, 2010).

Culturally competent mental health services for APIA women also require a foundation of assessment and intervention tools that honor each client's multiple and intersecting identities, including an understanding of the client's unique socio–political–cultural experience in the United States (Guidelines 4, 6, 8). Bauer, Rodriguez, Quiroga, and Flores-Ortiz (2000) identified significant social, cultural, and political barriers that impede abused Latinas and Asian immigrant women from seeking help and communicating effectively with providers. In addition to language barriers, immigrant women face social isolation, discrimination, and fear of deportation, as well as the cultural barriers of shame and stigma related to abuse. Addressing these barriers at various levels (individual, family, community, societal) is integral to improving culturally responsive treatment and services for APIA women.

The need for clinicians working with women and girls to apply interventions that are found to be effective, as stated in Guideline 6, requires consideration of the unique and complex postimmigration experiences because approximately 62% of APIA females are foreign born (U.S. Census Bureau, n.d.). In addition to having been subjected to historical acculturation stresses of discrimination, poverty, and psychological problems, APIA women have faced traditional patriarchal traditions and strict gender discrimination from their own families and communities. For many APIA women, their refugee experiences might be fraught with traumas that need to be understood within the context of acculturation, racism, and sexism in the United States. In examining ethnic and gender differences, R. C. Chung and Bemak (2002) indicated that Vietnamese, Cambodian, and Laotian women reported a significantly higher level of psychological distress than their male counterparts. Aside from dealing with the traumas stemming from their forced migration and loss of family, community, and country, the psychological well-being of these women was further compromised by the lack of social support networks and the economic struggles they experienced as they settled in their new country. These findings demonstrate the need for clinicians to have an understanding of both pre- and postmigration experiences in order to provide competent health care services to APIA women of immigrant and refugee backgrounds.

Consistent with Guideline 9, clinicians working with APIA women under the guiding principle of valuing women's perspectives need to be attentive to the multiplicity and complexity of their clients' racialized gendered experiences (Pyke & Johnson, 2003). In their comprehensive reviews of domestic violence literature using a race, class, gender, and sexual orientation intersectional analysis, Sokoloff and Dupont (2005) proposed that although culture remains crucial to understanding and combating issues such as domestic violence, the impact of structural forms of oppression such as racism, colonialism, economic exploitation, and heterosexism must also be considered. For many APIA women, traditional Asian family structure and gender role expectations may contribute to conflicting emotional experiences. As racial minorities who have suffered from discrimination by the dominant culture, the traditional family structure functions as both a source of oppression as well as protection against racism (Espiritu, 2001). Effective psychological practice with APIA women through a multicultural feminist lens must include a thorough exploration of intersecting and multiple identities of APIA women.

Finally, much of what exists in the multicultural literature focuses on increasing awareness, sensitivity, and understanding of the client's multiple identities. Guideline 5 emphasizes the importance of psychologists' self-awareness and how their backgrounds may influence their practices. Clinicians working with APIA women need to consider fully the concerns of APIA women in their socio–cultural–political contexts and engage in self-education about these areas. Because APIA women are likely to have experienced multiple forms of discrimination and insensitivity from mental health service providers, clinicians are urged to be intentional in building trust as a therapeutic foundation in their work with APIA women. Interventions that are culturally aware, gender focused, and integrate the client's complex experience as an APIA woman go a long way toward building trust. For example, some appropriate self-disclosure by the therapist can facilitate cultural alliance building with an APIA client who values a "heart-oriented" philosophy as part of her cultural identity. A multicultural feminist approach with APIA women needs to explore how the clinician's personal and professional cultural identities impact the therapeutic relationship, as emphasized in Guidelines 4, 5, and 8. The following questions present opportunities for therapists to apply the guidelines in working with APIA women.

- How are assessment and intervention strategies shaped by the therapist's own identities, experiences, and training?
- How do the similarities and differences between the therapist's and client's worldviews, identities, and values affect assumptions and expectations of therapy and the therapeutic relationship?
- How can the practice of psychotherapy, originated from Western values, be applied to empower APIA women *and* honor their multiple and intersecting identities?

CASE STUDY: IN-DEPTH ILLUSTRATION AND APPLICATION OF THE GUIDELINES

The second case study of the chapter highlights a number of ways psychologists can apply the Guidelines in working with the complexities of culture, values, and beliefs in therapy with Asian American women. The detailed descriptions bring to life the integration of the Guidelines into culturally nuanced feminist therapy. More specifically, this case illustrates the centrality of the therapeutic relationship in the gender and culturally affirming approach of a feminist psychologist working with a Vietnamese female client. Case information has been modified to protect confidentiality.

The Client

Van, a 38-year-old Vietnamese American woman, was enrolled in a pharmacy technical program at an urban community college. During the intake session, she reported some confusion about being referred to the counseling center by her professor. Apparently, the professor had become concerned about Van after she started failing her quizzes at the beginning of the semester. Van had taken another class with this professor and had done very well during the previous semester. She requested a Vietnamese-speaking "doctor," even though she spoke fluent English.

Van completed high school in Vietnam but had to work to support herself and family after she emigrated to the United States. Van shared that the reason for her falling grades had been her inability to focus this semester. She had always loved school and was excited about getting good grades during her first year in college. However, this semester, her "brain has not worked." She had been trying but "just could not do it." Over the summer, Van and her 43-year-old husband of 7 years had separated and she had moved to her mother's house with their 5-year-old daughter while he moved in with his parents. According to their custody agreement, he had their daughter on every other weekend.

The Therapist and the Psychotherapy Process

The therapist was a Vietnamese American psychologist in her 40s. Sessions were conducted in a mixture of Vietnamese and English at the client's request, though there were times when the therapist, as a 1.5-generation Vietnamese American and trained in Western psychology, struggled to translate English words and Western psychological concepts into their equivalent meanings in Vietnamese. The therapist's difficulties in finding Vietnamese words to explain Western psychology presented an opportunity for symbolic and literal collaboration between therapist and client. The therapist acknowledged her limitations while recognizing that it was an opportunity to invite the client to claim her voice and power as she engaged in a process that was culturally unfamiliar to her. During these moments, the client worked to help the therapist search for "close enough" translations.

Consistent with Guidelines 4 and 7, which emphasize the importance of culturally sensitive practices and an empowering therapeutic relationship, the therapist worked to help normalize how Western psychotherapy might feel for Van because of her cultural values about "not airing one's dirty laundry" and not "talking badly" about one's family. Van talked about feeling "*nhẹ hơn*" or "lighter" after having a chance to share her story with someone. In addition, Van decided to address the therapist as *chị* (meaning "older sister") instead of *bác sĩ* (meaning "doctor"), when cultural issues were explored during the first session. She stated that because she had shared so much with her therapist, *chị* would make her feel *"gần gũi hơn"* (closer), and feeling closer to her therapist would make the therapy process feel less foreign. To further empower the client in defining a therapeutic relationship that resonated more with her cultural values and comfort level, the therapist shifted from the typical six-to-10-session short-term model to fully support the client's initial decision to commit to therapy on a weekly basis, should she need to *nói chuyện* (talk) with the therapist.

The therapist's identity as a feminist psychologist required a balanced approach when clarifying her feminist values and exploring the intersection of gender and culture in the work with this particular client (Guidelines 4 and 5). During one session, the therapist became aware of her own feelings of frustration when Van appeared to make choices that were disempowering to her. The client had shared that she tried to give her husband another chance and ended up with the same result of feeling humiliated. In the following dialogue, therapist and client come to a deeper understanding of how race and gender affect Van's struggles as she risks bringing up a culturally taboo topic:

Van: [*in describing her relationship with her husband*] He was my first sexual partner. I gave him so much of myself. I can't see myself doing that with any other man . . . [*client looked embarrassed*].

Therapist: And it's really hard to let go. You feel bad when he's in your life but that fear . . .

Van: The future without him, I see nothing . . .

Therapist: It's hard seeing yourself without him and the thought of being alone and lonely for the rest of your life is scary. You mentioned that he was your first sexual partner . . . I can see that it was hard to bring up . . . how would it feel for us to talk about sex here?

Van: [*after long pause during which eye contact was averted*] Well, I've never mentioned anything like that with anyone else, not even my best friend . . . I want to tell you . . . maybe you can help me understand . . . the things that he got me to do sexually . . . I've never even heard of it. I did it for him. [*Van started to cry for the first time in session*]

Therapist: I can see you've been carrying a lot with this. . . . In Vietnam, women don't go around talking about sex. I want you to know that anything that's important for you to bring up, including sex, I am comfortable with us talking about it. Though it might feel *kỳ`* [odd] initially.

The client went on to talk about her feelings of shame about allowing her husband to coerce her into different "abnormal" sexual positions that did not feel comfortable for her and how, in her eyes, she could never imagine any "normal" man would accept her in the future. Once she felt that she was able to talk about sex with the therapist, Van became more willing to explore more deeply how the gender power dynamics and cultural context influenced her decision-making process about the sexual relationship with her husband. Consistent with the cultural message of being a "good wife," Van felt that she had to accommodate herself to her husband's sexual needs and silenced her discomfort. She realized that in that process, she ended up feeling bad about herself, typical of many interactions with her husband throughout their relationship. As culture and gender were integrated into the therapeutic process, Van began to uncover layers of confusing messages that had impacted her feelings of distress and her identity as a Vietnamese American woman (Guidelines 6, 7, 9).

Over the few months prior to coming to treatment, Van had been preoccupied with thoughts about what she could do to save her marriage. She had initiated divorce papers because she knew her husband wanted a divorce and she wanted to make him happy. He had been "distant" with her for more than a year prior to the separation. Her husband had accused her of being "jealous and insecure" when she confronted him about his "chatting" with a woman on the Internet. He believed she did not "have the character to be a mother" to their daughter because of her lack of education and "low self-esteem."

From the beginning of their courtship, he had claimed to be "superior" to her in many ways, including his education and profession (an engineer), his English fluency due to his arrival in the United States 10 years before her, and his experience in relationships. Because of her belief that she needed to be a better wife, Van "endured" through challenging times, such as when her husband would leave for a week at a time without telling her where he went or would stay out late with his friends. Her husband was her first sexual partner, and she was unable to see herself being with anyone else. Van's mother and her in-laws blamed her for the separation because she was the one who filed the papers. Her mother had a hard time at first supporting the separation due to her strong Catholic identity.

> Van: My mother has started to see how mean he is to me. How badly he talked about me to other people. He blames me for the ending of our marriage even when it's him who does not want to be married anymore. She sees how he does not come around to see his daughter. She told me recently that if I am unable to endure the marriage, then I can go ahead and divorce him and stay single for the rest of my life to take care of my daughter.

Therapist: Her message to you sounded like "You can end your marriage but don't get involved in any other relationship for the rest of your life." How do you make sense of that message?

Van: I told you my dad died when I was only 8 years old. It was really hard for my mom. She stayed single and raised me. She was so young. She did not date . . . she didn't get married again . . . she worked and took care of me. . . . She was living in Đà Nẵng [a city in the South Central coast of Vietnam]. . . . She had to be a *mẹ hiền* . . . *làm guöng* [a good mother, an example] for me . . . she needed to focus on her role of being a mother and nothing else.

Therapist: I remember you sharing with me that you grew up with aunts and uncles caring for you when your mother worked. They were there for her and for you. How are things different for you now?

Van: I don't have any siblings. My close cousins are in Vietnam. I have my mother but she is getting older and her health is weak. It was less lonely in Vietnam. Here, all my friends are busy with their lives.

Therapist: Yeah, it was very different for your mom in Vietnam. It must be hard for her to adjust to being here in the U.S. In her time in Vietnam, to be a "good woman" after your dad died, she had to stay single. . . . Now here in the U.S., the roles for women. . . . Your role as a woman, as a mother, in the U.S., it's a different culture, different time . . .

Van: But being a good Vietnamese American woman . . . my mother told me she did not want me to be Mỹ trắng [Euro American] . . . and I'm not!

Therapist: Let's talk about what it means for you to be a "good Vietnamese American" woman . . . how will you *làm guöng* [be an example] for your daughter here in the U.S. . . . as a woman who is Vietnamese American.

In conceptualizing Van's concerns, the therapist integrated cultural values through a feminist lens, using a relational–cultural approach (Jordan, 2010) to create a safe and empowering environment where Van could openly give voice to her feelings and needs. The relational–cultural approach was consistent with the therapist and client's shared "heart-oriented" cultural traditions in which interconnectedness and authenticity facilitated a healing and therapeutic relationship. As the therapy progressed and cultural values were brought into the room, Van became more trusting and began to open up about her pain. She and the therapist discussed the cultural constraints that might be harmful to women as well as the strengths that might arise from certain cultural values. Van acknowledged her ability to care genuinely for others. In addition, the interdependent orientation of her culture enabled her to develop a healing and supportive relationship with others. In discussing therapy progress and the therapeutic relationship, Van was able to share with the therapist her initial doubts and fear about therapy; however, once she saw that the therapist could understand the cultural nuances impacting her life without making judgments, she started to believe that therapy could be helpful.

In the process of therapy, Van became aware that she had been "paralyzed" in the relationship with her husband and had "sacrificed" much of her "self" and her own values and identity. Initially, although she was able to talk openly about her feelings of sadness, confusion, grief, and humiliation, Van worked hard to contain her feelings in the room. She often presented with stoicism in sharing painful feelings. She talked about the cultural concept of *chịu đựng* (to endure) for Vietnamese women and how her mother had brought up this value to question her about divorcing her husband. When the therapist affirmed and validated her feelings of sadness, Van often responded with "maybe this is my karma." At times, given her feminist identity, the therapist was aware of her feelings of sadness and frustration with the "sacrifices" Van was making in her life and how elusive the concept of self-care was as a treatment goal. During these moments, the therapist worked to ensure that the therapy process would continue to be receptive to Van's values and identities as a Vietnamese American woman. The therapist needed to communicate support and acceptance while working to empower Van as she came to terms with the ending of her marriage (Guidelines 5, 6, 7). As therapy progressed, Van made more connections between her pain and struggles and her almost knee-jerk tendency to put herself and her feelings last. Self-care made sense to her when it was discussed in the context of her collectivistic culture. For example, in doing the work needed to build her strengths, she would be able to take care of her daughter and mother in ways that were less draining and help increase her confidence about being a "good Vietnamese American woman" (Guidelines 1, 2, 4).

This case study reflects the integration of applying the Guidelines in using the RCT approach with an APIA client. Even as the client struggled with issues of grief and loss (in particular, the impending ending of her marriage), themes of cultural and sociopolitical impacts on her perspectives and expectations of therapy and her identity development as a Vietnamese American woman and as a mother were integral to the therapy process. In addition to the application of Guidelines 1 through 4 in exploring issues of power and oppression as impacting the client's intersecting and multiple identities, the therapist's deliberate examination and transparency in disclosing her own values and assumptions as they might influence the client provided a foundation for the therapeutic relationship (Guidelines 5–9). Despite her initial mistrust of the therapy process, the client was able to take the risk of being vulnerable in therapy as she began to trust that the therapist was attentive to and respected the complexity of her multiple identities.

IMPLICATIONS FOR PRACTICE

The cases presented in this chapter highlight the importance of contextualizing clinical interventions with APIA women through multicultural, feminist lenses. The Guidelines provide a framework for psychologists to create a safe, therapeutic, gender-fair culture in which APIA women can give voice to their stories and bring to consciousness their coping strengths and resiliency. Whereas silence is interpreted as weak and passive in the Western White feminist movement, in many Asian cultures, silence is a reflection of patience, power, and the intelligence needed to overcome challenges. Other cultural strengths include the strong emphasis on interpersonal relationships with family, friends, and community as sources of support system for APIA women. Lived experiences of APIA women throughout U.S. history—from Chinese women in the mid-1800s surviving on nothing but hope, to Japanese American women keeping their families together under the inhospitable conditions of internment camps, to Vietnamese and Cambodian refugee women coping with traumas in their search for freedom—evoke the spirit and strengths of APIA women often obscured by harmful stereotypes. The experiences of APIA women are complex, and to gain a complete understanding of APIA women, psychologists must move away from stereotypes and caricatures, be mindful of the biases of their Western perspectives and training, and consider specific sociopolitical and cultural legacies (Root, 1995). The intentional use of the Guidelines in psychological practice with APIA women facilitates the full integration of the uniqueness of each client's racial and gender experiences and their impact on the therapeutic process. We propose that clinicians working with APIA women within the multicultural feminist empowerment model consider the following questions to explore with their APIA clients:

- What does it mean for you to identify as an APIA woman? What are the cultural values that impact your current and past experience?
- What strengths and barriers do you face as an APIA woman living in the United States?

- How are you connected with your family, community, and work? What types of support do you get from these connections? How do these connections add more tension to your life?
- What do you do with conflicting messages between traditional Asian values and Western expectations? What do you need to find your balance when confronted with incompatible views of how you "should" be as a woman?
- As an Asian–Pacific Islander, a woman [include all other salient aspects of identities such as race, class, sexual identities, education, etc., that are meaningful to clients], how do you define who you are? What kind of support do you need in that process?
- Given the values that are salient to you, what are your thoughts, feelings, and expectations about therapy? How do you imagine these values might impact our therapeutic relationships?

CONCLUSIONS AND FUTURE DIRECTIONS

Historically, the work of feminists, although vital to bringing attention to gender issues impacting the lives of women and girls, has not resonated with women of color in the United States (Brown, 1995). The Guidelines are based on more than 40 years of work by nonsexist and feminist psychologists who are committed to deepening our understanding and integration of the "complex" work in psychological practice with women. APIA women have been largely invisible in the history of the feminist movement in the United States. The multicultural movement in psychology, instrumental in broadening psychology and psychotherapy to include diverse cultures, needs to continue to focus on including gender perspectives within specific cultural groups.

For APIA women, mental health and therapy are complicated by factors such as cultural and immigration experience, language barriers, socioeconomic stress, racism, sexism, and homophobia. Issues of underutilization of mental health services are often linked with inadequate resources to address culturally responsive treatment. These barriers include lack of access to care, language challenges, and lack of culturally and linguistic responsive providers. Psychological practice with APIA women needs to be contextualized with the unique concerns of APIA women's multiple identities and diverse experiences. An integral aspect of this effort includes reaching out to clients' communities and resources to empower APIA women as they access support that is culture and gender relevant. For example, various resources that offer services and information for survivors of domestic violence and sexual assault in many different Asian language and dialects (The Center for the Pacific

Asian Family, 2013) can serve as a bridge for APIA women seeking mental health services that are rooted in Western ideologies.

The diversity that exists within and between different ethnic groups deepens the complexity for clinicians seeking to provide effective mental health services for APIA women. It is outside the scope of this chapter to present a lengthy, comprehensive analysis of clinical considerations for working with diverse APIA women. As previously discussed, the assumptions of homogeneity among APIA women are problematic given the differences in their experiences, such as migration, ethnicity, socioeconomic status, sexuality, and so forth. For example, the forced migration and cultural adjustment of Southeast Asian refugees differs vastly from the immigration experiences of many other APIA groups. Clinicians working with Cambodian, Hmong, Laotian, and Vietnamese clients need to be sensitive to stressors associated with pre- and postmigration traumas (Dinh, 2009). Similarly, APIA women's varied perspectives on mental health treatment reflect their acculturation modes as well as other intersecting identities. C. I. Hall (2009) emphasized that some APIA women may prefer traditional indigenous healing methods, such as their faith or spirituality, whereas others may opt for a blend of both Western and traditional methods, or Western methods only.

The two cases presented in this chapter, a Filipina American and a Vietnamese American, reflect the diversity of APIA women. Although both clients were immigrants and had to struggle against oppression, racism, and sexism, their life narratives differed significantly, as depicted in the respective case studies. In work with U.S.-born APIA women and women from other Asian ethnic groups, the therapeutic process and outcomes may highlight other differences or salient sociocultural issues, such as the effects of intergenerational conflict and acculturation gaps on mental health in families with foreign-born parents but U.S.-born children (Dinh & Nguyen, 2006). In addition, it is expected that acculturation to Western culture for U.S.-born APIA women would more likely result in familiarity and comfort with psychotherapy and other aspects of Western culture. Furthermore, significant differences exist not only between but also within specific ethnic groups when clinicians take into considerations intersecting and multiple identities of APIA women. For instance, the experience of a lesbian Filipina or Vietnamese American may be very different from that of a heterosexual Filipina or Vietnamese American woman because the former may have to confront another complex dynamic of oppression, homophobia, both within and outside her family, in addition to racism and sexism. In general, we strongly stress that clinicians attend to both etic and emic characteristics and life circumstances in order to tailor the most appropriate treatment in their work with APIA women and girls.

On the systemic intervention level, psychological practice with APIA women should benefit from expanding the roles of psychologists to include advocacy and social justice work. There is a need for continued work by psychologists to further illuminate cultural protective factors and the role of historical trauma, colonization, poverty, racism, sexism, language, and anti-immigrant sentiment in APIA women's mental health issues and utilization of services. The Guidelines recommend tailoring assessment and intervention to foster positive relationships and empowerment. Clinicians' awareness and understanding of complex factors and dynamics, including but not limited to multiple and intersecting cultural identities, immigration history and experience, and sociopolitical forces, are most critical. These initiatives would represent an important first step for clinicians to play a significant role in meeting the mental health needs of APIA women and girls.

REFERENCES

Alvarez, A. N., Juang, L., & Liang, C. T. H. (2006). Asian Americans and racism: When bad things happen to "model minorities." *Cultural Diversity and Ethnic Minority Psychology, 12*, 477–492. doi:10.1037/1099-9809.12.3.477

American Psychological Association. (2007). Guidelines for psychological practice with girls and women. *American Psychologist, 62*, 949–979. doi:10.1037/0003-066X.62.9.949

Bao, X. (2001). *Holding up more than half the sky: Chinese women garment workers in New York City, 1948–92*. Urbana: University of Illinois Press.

Bauer, H. M., Rodriguez, M. A., Quiroga, S. S., & Flores-Ortiz, Y. (2000). Barriers to health care for abused Latina and Asian immigrant women. *Journal of Health Care for the Poor and Underserved, 11*, 33–44. doi:10.1353/hpu.2010.0590

Brown, L. S. (1995). Cultural diversity in feminist therapy: Theory and practice. In H. Landrine (Ed.), *Bringing cultural diversity to feminist psychology: Theory, research, and practice* (pp. 143–161). Washington, DC: American Psychological Association. doi:10.1037/10501-007

Brown, L. S., & Root, M. (1990). *Diversity and complexity in feminist therapy*. New York, NY: Harrington Park Press.

The Center for the Pacific Asian Family. (2013). *Prevention and community education*. Retrieved from http://www.nurturingchange.org/get-involved/prevention-and-community-education

Chan, C. S. (1988). Asian-American women: Psychological responses to sexual exploitation and cultural stereotypes. *Women & Therapy, 6*(4), 33–38. doi:10.1300/J015V06N04_05

Chao, M. M., Chiu, C. Y., Chan, W., Mendoza-Denton, R., & Kwok, C. (2012). The model minority as a shared reality and its implication for interracial perceptions.

Asian American Journal of Psychology. Advance online publication. doi:10.1037/a0028769

Chung, R. C., & Bemak, F. (2002). Revisiting the California Southeast Asian mental health needs assessment data: An examination of refugee ethnic and gender differences. *Journal of Counseling & Development*, 80, 111–119. doi:10.1002/j.1556-6678.2002.tb00173.x

Chung, Y. B., & Singh, A. A. (2009). Lesbian, gay, bisexual, and transgender Asian Americans. In A. Alvarez & N. Tewari (Eds.), *Asian American psychologies: Current perspectives* (pp. 233–246). New York, NY: Taylor & Francis.

David, E. J. R. (2010). Cultural mistrust and mental health help-seeking attitudes among Filipino Americans. *Asian American Journal of Psychology*, 1, 57–66. doi:10.1037/a0018814

DeNavas-Walt, C., Proctor, B. D., & Smith, J. C. (2012, September). *Income, poverty, and health insurance coverage in the United States: 2011* (U.S. Census Bureau, Current Population Report P60-243). Washington, DC: U.S. Government Printing Office.

Dinh, K. T. (2009). The A-B-C in clinical practice with Southeast Asians: Basic understanding of immigration and resettlement history. In N. T. Trinh, Y. Rho, K. Sanders, & F. Lu (Eds.), *Handbook of mental health and acculturation in Asian American families* (pp. 123–141). Totowa, NJ: Humana Press. doi:10.1007/978-1-60327-437-1_7

Dinh, K. T., & Nguyen, H. H. (2006). The effects of acculturative variables on Asian American parent–child relationships. *Journal of Social and Personal Relationships*, 23, 407–426. doi:10.1177/0265407506064207

Dion, K. K., & Dion, K. L. (2001). Gender and cultural adaptation in immigrant families. *Journal of Social Issues*, 57, 511–521. doi:10.1111/0022-4537.00226

Espiritu, Y. L. (1997). *Asian American men and women*. Thousand Oaks, CA: Sage.

Espiritu, Y. L. (2001). "We don't sleep around like white girls do": Family, culture, and gender in Filipina American life. *Signs: Journal of Women in Culture and Society*, 26, 415–440. doi:10.1086/495599

Hall, C. I. (2009). Asian American women: The nail that sticks out gets hammered down. In A. Alvarez & N. Tewari (Eds.), *Asian American psychologies: Current perspectives* (pp. 193–209). New York, NY: Taylor & Francis.

Hall, G. C. N., Hong, J. J., Zane, N., & Meyer, O. L. (2011). Culturally competent treatments for Asian Americans: The relevance of mindfulness and acceptance-based psychotherapies. *Clinical Psychology: Science and Practice*, 18, 215–231. doi:10.1111/j.1468-2850.2011.01253.x

Iwamoto, D. K., & Liu, W. M. (2010). The impact of racial identity, ethnic identity, Asian values, and race-related stress on Asian Americans and Asian international college students' psychological well-being. *Journal of Counseling Psychology*, 57, 79–91. doi:10.1037/a0017393

Jordan, J. (2010). *Relational–cultural therapy*. Washington, DC: American Psychological Association.

Kim, B. S., Hill, C. E., Gelso, C. K., Goates, M. K., Asay, P. A., & Harbin, J. M. (2003). Counselor self-disclosure: East Asian American client adherence to Asian cultural values, and counseling practice. *Journal of Counseling Psychology*, *50*, 324–332. doi:10.1037/0022-0167.50.3.324

Kim, J. L. (2009). Asian American women's retrospective reports of their sexual socialization. *Psychology of Women Quarterly*, *33*, 334–350. doi:10.1111/j.1471-6402.2009.01505.x

Miller, J. B. (2008). Telling the truth about power. *Women & Therapy*, *31*, 145–161. doi:10.1080/02703140802146282

National Center for Health Statistics. (2011). *Health, United States, 2011: With special feature on socioeconomic status and health*. Hyattsville, MD: Author.

Noh, E. (2007). Asian American women and suicide: Problems of responsibility and healing. *Women & Therapy*, *30*(3/4), 87–107. doi:10.1300/J015v30n03_08

Okazaki, S. (2002). Influences of culture on Asian Americans' sexuality. *Journal of Sex Research*, *39*, 34–41. doi:10.1080/00224490209552117

Passel, J. S., Capps, R., & Fix, M. (2004). *Undocumented immigrants: Facts and figures*. Washington, DC: Urban Institute Immigration Studies Program.

Pyke, K. D., & Johnson, D. L. (2003). Asian American women and racialized femininities: "Doing" gender across cultural worlds. *Gender & Society*, *17*, 33–53. doi:10.1177/0891243202238977

Reid, P. T. (2002). Multicultural psychology: Bringing together gender and ethnicity. *Cultural Diversity and Ethnic Minority Psychology*, *8*, 103–114. doi:10.1037/1099-9809.8.2.103

Root, M. P. P. (1995). The psychology of Asian American women. In H. Landrine (Ed.), *Bringing cultural diversity to feminist psychology: Theory, research, and practice* (pp. 265–301). Washington, DC: American Psychological Association. doi:10.1037/10501-012

Sokoloff, N. J., & Dupont, I. (2005). Domestic violence at the intersections of race, class, and gender: Challenges and contributions to understanding violence against marginalized women in diverse communities. *Violence Against Women*, *11*, 38–64. doi:10.1177/1077801204271476

Sue, D. W., & Sue, D. (2013). *Counseling the culturally diverse: Theory and practice* (6th ed.). Hoboken, NJ: Wiley.

Sue, S., & Zane, N. (2009). The role of culture and cultural techniques in psychotherapy: A critique and reformulation. *Asian American Journal of Psychology*, *S*(1), 3–14. doi:10.1037/1948-1985.S.1.3

Suzuki, L. A., Ahluwalia, M. K., & Alimchandani, A. (2012). Asian American women's feminism: Sociopolitical history and clinical considerations. In C. Z. Enns & E. N. Williams (Eds.), *The Oxford handbook of feminist multicultural counseling psychology* (pp. 183–198). New York, NY: Oxford University Press.

Suzuki, L. K., & Greenfield, P. M. (2002). The construction of everyday sacrifices in Asian Americans and European American: The roles of ethnicity and acculturation. *Cross-Cultural Research*, *36*, 200–228. doi:10.1177/10697102036003002

Takaki, R. (1989). *Strangers from a different shore: A history of Asian Americans*. New York, NY: Penguin Books.

Travis-Robyns, S. R. (2004). What is winning anyway? Redefining veteran: A Vietnamese American woman's experiences in war and peace. In L. T. Vo, M. Sciachitano, S. H. Armitage, P. Hart, & K. Weathermon (Eds.), *Asian American women: The frontiers reader* (pp. 125–149). Lincoln: University of Nebraska Press.

True, R. H. (1997). Asian American women. In E. Lee (Ed.), *Working with Asian Americans* (pp. 420–427). New York, NY: Guilford Press.

U.S. Census Bureau. (2010). *The Asian population: Allegany County, N.Y.* Retrieved from http://www.census.gov/prod/cen2010/briefs/c2010br-11.pdf

U.S. Census Bureau. (2011–2013). *American Community Survey: 2010 data release*. Retrieved from http://www.census.gov/acs/www/data_documentation/2010_release

U.S. Census Bureau. (n.d.). *Selected population profile in the United States: 2009-2011 American Community Survey 3-year estimates*. Retrieved from http://factfinder2.census.gov/faces/tableservices/jsf/pages/productview.xhtml?pid=ACS_11_3YR_S0201&prodType=table

Yeh, C., & Hwang, M. Y. (2000). Interdependence in ethnic identity and self: Implications for theory and practice. *Journal of Counseling & Development, 78*, 420–429. doi:10.1002/j.1556-6676.2000.tb01925.x

Yoo, H. C., & Lee, R. M. (2008). Does ethnic identity buffer or exacerbate the effects of frequent racial discrimination or situational well-being of Asian American? *Journal of Counseling Psychology, 55*, 63–74. doi:10.1037/0022-0167.55.1.63

Zane, N., & Yeh, M. (2002). The use of culturally-based variables in assessment: Studies on loss of face. In K. S. Kurasaki, S. Okazaki, & S. Sue (Eds.), *Asian American mental health: Assessment theories and methods* (pp. 123–138). New York, NY: Kluwer Academic/Plenum Publishers. doi:10.1007/978-1-4615-0735-2_9

7

WOMEN WITH DISABILITIES: AFFIRMATIVE PRACTICE AND ASSESSMENT

MARTHA E. BANKS, KATHLEEN S. BROWN, LINDA R. MONA, AND ROSALIE J. ACKERMAN

Psychology has come to recognize that the effects of biases related to disabilities have been detrimental to the increasingly complex needs of women with disabilities (WWD). Currently, about 27 million women in the United States have disabilities, and the number is growing (Centers for Disease Control and Prevention [CDC], 2013a). Definitions of *disability* have evolved and broadened over time and may include medical, legal, social, or political factors. For the purposes of this chapter, *disability* is defined broadly as a condition that creates impairments, activity limitations, and participation restrictions, independent of whether the condition is congenital, acquired, acute, or chronic in nature. Disability reflects the interaction between features of a person's body and features of the society in which he or she lives. The National Institute on Disability and Rehabilitation Research's (NIDRR) "New Paradigm of Disability" emphasizes the interactions among a variety of factors in order to better illuminate the experience of people with disabilities (PWD; Pledger,

http://dx.doi.org/10.1037/14460-007
Psychological Practice With Women: Guidelines, Diversity, Empowerment, C. Z. Enns, J. K. Rice, and R. L. Nutt (Editors)
Copyright © 2015 by the American Psychological Association. All rights reserved.

2003). This interactionist paradigm affords providers insights and strategies for enhancing resiliency, empowerment, and well-being among clients with disabilities and invites creative and sophisticated research on the efficacy of currently available psychotherapeutic approaches for people with disabilities in a variety of clinical settings (Olkin, 1999).

WWD need the same general health care as women without disabilities, but they may also need additional care to address their specific needs. WWD are more likely than women without disabilities and men with disabilities to report not having seen a physician because of cost (CDC, 2013a). WWD experience a narrower margin of health, both because of poverty and social exclusion and also because they may be vulnerable to secondary conditions, such as pressure sores or urinary tract infections (World Health Organization [WHO], 2013). Regular screenings and follow-up in women's health is the current standard of care for the prevention and treatment of certain diseases, such as breast and cervical cancer. WWD, however, are less likely to be screened within the recommended guidelines (CDC, 2013b). WWD may not have learned about reproductive health and thus may be unaware of reproductive health care (Center for Research on Women With Disabilities, 2013).

Given these data, psychologists must be aware of the unique challenges experienced by WWD in their greater vulnerability related to secondary conditions, comorbid conditions, age-related conditions, participation in health risk behaviors, and higher rates of premature death and tailor their practice accordingly. Psychologists are encouraged to strengthen alliances with advocacy groups for WWD, address questions about how WWD are considered within a framework of affirming feminist psychology (Nosek, 2010), and examine the relevance of existing American Psychological Association (APA) practice guidelines within such a perspective. When clinical providers collaborate consistently and plan and provide care within the context of a comprehensive lens of disability, the patient's experience as a whole person rather than a collection of ailments becomes salient. This shift in conceptualization and approach sets the foundation for disability culturally competent healthcare, and the resulting benefits are both immediately practical and potentially transformative for the client (Clemency Cordes, Cameron, Mona, Syme, Coble-Temple, in press).

This chapter presents perspectives based on the clinical practices of the authors and relevant information from books specifically addressing psychological practice with WWD and girls with disabilities (e.g., Banks & Kaschak, 2003; Marshall, Kendall, Banks, & Gover, 2009) in order to further highlight the diverse life experiences of living with disability and to suggest feminist practices that will decrease health disparities. This task is accomplished by highlighting the APA's "Guidelines for Psychological Practice With Girls and Women" (hereinafter the Guidelines; APA, 2007) as supplemented by the APA "Guidelines for Assessment of and Intervention With Persons With Disabilities" (APA, 2012) and discussing how the Guidelines apply to feminist thinking about WWD and girls with disabilities. A case study that illustrates the application of the Guidelines is also offered. Exploring culture-specific issues faced by WWD, the multiple roles of WWD, the importance of "informal" support systems, and the intersection between feminism and disability assist in framing the discussion on the intersectionality of disability and gender as related to the Guidelines.

DIVERSITY, SOCIAL CONTEXT, AND POWER (GUIDELINES 1–3)

The Guidelines emphasize the importance of understanding the life experiences, issues, biases, forms of discrimination, and intersections among women's multiple identities. It is imperative that psychologists and other clinicians understand the life experiences of WWD and incorporate the Guidelines into their practices. Approximately 12.4% of women in the United States have disabilities. Rates of disability reflect ethnic health disparities: 14.5% of Black–African American women, 16.3% of Native American or Alaskan Native women, 6.8% of Asian American women, 8.7% of Latinas, and 13.4% of European American women have disabilities (Erickson, Lee, & von Schrader, 2013). Traditional feminist psychology has seldom considered the influence and impact of disability on women's lives. *Ableism* continues to be a covert but still detectable and powerful force in feminist psychology (Campbell, 2009). Banks and Mona (2007) noted that feminism has primarily addressed the strengths of women and focused away from women's weaknesses, including those resulting in disabling conditions.

Disabilities may be acquired or experienced across the life span. Salley (2009) described the possible contrasting ways in which society can respond to the acquisition of a disabling condition by presenting the example of a woman who was suddenly unable to perform her assigned duties as she had done for many years. Problematic responses to the woman's disability included blaming, misattribution of her sick leave as "vacation," and attempted comparative "diagnosis" (impact of sprain vs. broken bones) by people with no health care training. These responses came while the woman was exposed, for the first time, to other PWD and was struggling with the implications for her own and her family's identity.

An important part of practice with WWD involves understanding the experience of disability in the context of discrimination. Feminist practice involves integrating the psychologist's expertise with the client's knowledge of her own experience. Campbell (2009) wrote,

From the moment a child is born, he or she emerges into a world where he or she receives messages that to be disabled is to be *less than*, a world where disability may be tolerated but in the final instance, is inherently negative. We are all, regardless of our status, shaped and formed by the politics of ableism. (pp. 19–20)

Campbell defined *ableism* as "attitudes and barriers contributing to the subordination of people with disabilities in liberal society" (p. 21), underlying the implementation of *disableism*, which is the actual discrimination manifested as "the differential or unequal treatment of people because of actual or presumed disabilities" (p. 21). She added, "Ableism can be associated with the production of ableness, the perfect body and, by default, the implication that disability is the loss of ableness" (p. 21). In contrast, "disableism relates to the production of disability and fits well into a socially constructed understanding of disability" (p. 21).

Thus, ableism becomes, like racism and sexism, a system by which mainstream society devalues those with disabilities while privileging those without disabilities. Worth and intelligence are equated to being able-bodied or able-minded, whereas disability is conflated with stupidity and worthlessness. The social model of disability, in contrast, is based on a distinction between the terms *impairment* and *disability*. *Impairment* refers to the actual attributes (or loss of attributes) of a person, whether in terms of limbs, organs, or psychologically, whereas the term *disability* is used to refer to restrictions caused by society when it does not give equivalent accommodation to the needs of individuals with impairments (Pledger, 2003). Thus, attempts to change PWD, often derived from a medical model, can be both discriminatory and prejudiced (Pledger, 2003).

Olkin (1999) described the social model of disability in terms of individuals with disabilities being understood to have a minority cultural experience within an ableist cultural milieu. Such an affirming understanding can in turn can lead to the development of cohesion, mutual support, and empowerment for individuals who identify as PWD. Furthermore, the social model of disability has also been described in terms of the socioeconomic effects of disability that are experienced when people are disabled by a lack of resources to meet their needs. The potential of people to contribute to society and add economic value to society is often underestimated in PWD unless they are given equal rights and equally suitable facilities and opportunities as others. Campbell (2009) noted that because of ableism, there is little attention to "suicide, drug and alcohol use, and additional mental health stressors among 'successful' disabled people" (p. 23), which has led to an uncritical acceptance and awareness of internalized ableism. Psychologists and other clinicians need to be mindful of Campbell's warning that "the pathologization of disability has meant that therapy predominantly concentrates on normalization and is not necessarily directed to attending to the harms of ableism ([that is] living with prejudice)" (pp. 23–24).

Guideline 3 addresses the importance of understanding the impact of bias and discrimination in areas such as health systems, education, workplace, religious institutions, legal system, families and couples, and research methods and language. These are all areas of concern for WWD. The third guideline is consistent with the NIDRR New Paradigm, which shifts conceptualization of disability from a solely medical model to a socioecological approach that includes the context or contexts in which disablement occurs (Pledger, 2003). In this model of disability, enabling a WWD lies within the interaction of the person and several dimensions of the environment. Therefore, the concepts of power and privilege within the therapeutic relationship itself can take on different context and meanings for the psychologist working with a WWD than in psychological practice with women without disabilities.

Health Systems

WWD face substantial barriers that limit their access to health care services. Such barriers include physical, attitudinal, and policy barriers; lack of information about how disability affects their health; limited finances; and insufficient personal assistance (Thierry, Turk, Panko-Reis, & Dennis, 2004). WWD seldom receive comprehensive health evaluations (Iezzoni, 2011). Health care providers, including psychologists, need to be better educated and trained to address the full complement of health care needs of WWD. Awareness of the impact of environmental and access barriers within their practice, noncompliant transportation barriers, or attitudinal barriers to sexual health need to become part of the conversation in providing healthcare to WWD. Psychologists in their advocacy role are urged to also focus on socioeconomic factors such as education, employment, and training to increase income and improve access to health plans that provide access to physician services (Mwachofi & Broyles, 2008).

When conceptualizing WWD, there is often a focus on the disability while the rest of the woman is ignored (Rohmer & Louvet, 2009). Women who are members of multiple marginalized groups are likely to find that health conditions linked to stereotypes are more likely to be assumed, such as the presumption that body size is tied to level of physical activity. In contrast, other health issues might be ignored, such as sexually transmitted infections (Fredriksen-Goldsen, Kim, Muraco, & Mincer, 2009). In other circumstances, there might be overinclusion, such as conflating lesbians with bisexual women (Kim & Fredriksen-Goldsen, 2012) or ignoring cultural variations (e.g., country of origin or descent, socioeconomic status, educational background) within broad ethnic categories (Banks, 2012, 2013b).

In psychology, there tends to be an overreliance on stage theories to explain how a WWD responds to her disability psychologically (Anderson & Whitfield, 2013). For WWD, variations in manifestations of disability (visible or invisible; dormant, part-time, or situational; congenital or acquired; or any combination of these) dictate that individual women and their specific circumstances must be considered during assessment and treatment (Banks, 2013b). Nonstandardized administration of test assessment for people with sensory impairments, adapting psychoeducational handouts in alternative formats for people with sensory and mobility limitations, and having WWD identify the ways in which disability has impacted the presenting problem for which they seek therapy are all examples of disability-affirming services. Many people with physical disabilities experience a triad of symptoms of fatigue, pain, and muscle weakness that may require scheduling a comprehensive assessment over several days or therapy sessions for morning appointments. The experience of anger by WWD tied to their perception of others' blindness to their restrictions (e.g., grocery store carts in aisles impeding wheelchair access) needs to be fully assessed to determine appropriate treatment interventions in the context of righteous anger, appropriate assertiveness versus aggressiveness, and narcissism. Regulation of affect becomes part of the disability experience in a nuanced way different for WWD than for women without disabilities.

When WWD are referred for specialty care, they encounter additional problems (Lagu et al., 2013). Some health care facilities and providers are not prepared to assess or treat WWD. Facilities might not be environmentally accessible and/or the assessment equipment might not be adaptable, such as some mammography machines and pelvic exam tables. Such inaccessibility is illegal, and the U.S. Department of Justice (2010) provides specific guidance for health care providers to comply with the Americans With Disabilities Act (ADA; 1990) and the ADA Amendments Act (2008). Despite this, a recent survey of 256 medical practices in four U.S. urban cities found alarming results related to attempts to schedule an appointment for a fictional patient who was of larger size and hemiparetic, used a wheelchair, and could not self-transfer from chair to examination table (Lagu et al., 2013). Fifty-six practices (22%) reported that they could not accommodate the patient, nine (4%) reported that the building was inaccessible, 47 (18%) reported inability to transfer a patient from a wheelchair to an examination table, and only 22 (9%) reported use of height-adjustable tables or a lift for transfer. Gynecology was the subspecialty with the highest rate of inaccessible practices (44%). Much work needs to be done to ensure that health care specialists provide education to WWD about their illness or disabling condition, inform them about clients' legal rights, connect clients with a social worker or health care advocate, make referrals to allied practitioners or legal services, and assist clients in assertively communicating with their health care providers as components of their standard treatment plans.

A major challenge is to determine how psychology can best contribute to the health of women of color with disabilities (WoCWD) within the context of their cultural identification. In addition to the Guidelines (APA, 2007) on diversity, social context, and power, Guidelines 7 and 8 of the APA "Guidelines for Assessment of and Intervention With Persons With Disabilities" (APA, 2012) call for psychologists to be aware of the common experiences shared by PWD while "recogniz[ing] social and cultural diversity in the lives of persons with disabilities" (p. 49). The 13th "Guideline for Assessment of and Intervention With Persons With Disabilities" calls for "consider[ation of] disability as a dimension of diversity together with other individual and contextual dimensions" (p. 52). Many psychologists hold the mistaken belief that because they "accept" all people, further training around disability and other cultural factors is unnecessary (Pedersen, Crethar, & Carlson, 2008). Psychologists need to advocate and acquire the skills needed for competency-based educational curricula to change attitudes, knowledge, and skills of health care providers in meeting the unique health care needs and diverse presentations of WWD. Such curricula need to be based on evidence-based research. For example, in many hospital systems, disability simulation exercises continue to be used to attempt to increase clinical providers' understanding of the social experience of disability. Data on simulation exercises indicate that using these types of exercises reduces disability to merely a physical experience when it is more an interpersonal and psychosocial experience (Olkin, 1999).

WoCWD have to cope not only with issues directly related to their disabilities but also with social, economic, and cultural factors that can harm their health. For example, lower wages and higher unemployment rates found among PWD are barriers to affordable, high-quality health care. WoCWD also may have to deal with health care professionals who lack knowledge about their "race"-related medical conditions (Comas-Díaz, 2013; Jacobsen, 2013; Smedley, Stith, & Nelson, 2003). Gover (2009) described the life-threatening circumstances under which she was diagnosed with diabetes. She had been rushed to a hospital with a blood sugar above 500 milligrams/deciliter. This range is not unusual for Native Americans with adult-onset diabetes but is generally associated with life-threatening diabetic ketoacidosis, which "is the most common cause of death in children and adolescents with type 1 diabetes and accounts for half of all deaths in diabetic patients younger than 24 years of age" (Kitabchi, Umpierrez, Miles, & Fisher, 2009, p. 1335). Health staff were unfamiliar with her strain of diabetes and were "almost in hysterics over [her] condition" (Gover, 2009, p. 124), thus delaying treatment until consultation with the Indian Health Service.

Historically, perceptions of PWD have been permeated with ignorance, fear, neglect, and superstition, and these social factors ultimately will affect the care they receive (Munyi, 2012). Wright (1960) described the phenomenon that takes place when a person with a disability is seen as disabled not only with respect to the specific area of disability but also with regard to other characteristics, such as personality and adjustment. Within the health care arena, such biased reactions can affect providers' ability to listen; understand; and provide empathic, respectful care to empower WWD in understanding and preventatively addressing their health care needs. These societal reactions in turn can also have potential negative consequences on the development of the personal, social, and psychological needs of WWD.

Implicit models of disability that affect our therapeutic effectiveness with PWD need to be explored as a means of self-assessment and as the first step towards embracing disability cultural competence (Clemency Cordes et al., in press). Personal awareness of the ways in which disability is conceptualized can assist with challenging our own personal frameworks. In addition, being aware of disability in our interactions with clients and challenging our own ableist values will increase our effectiveness in assessment and treatment (Clemency Cordes et al., in press). Physician surveys have revealed negative responding by physicians to individuals with diagnoses such as drug addiction, alcoholism, mental illness, and obesity (Klein, Najman, Kohrman, & Munro, 1982). Physicians in this study associated obesity and other negatively perceived conditions with poor hygiene, noncompliance, hostility, and dishonesty. Similar findings were revealed in a survey of mental health workers who attributed more negative symptoms and rated more severely an obese patient compared with overweight and average weight clients on a variety of dimensions of psychological functioning (Young & Powell, 1985). Discriminatory behaviors and "antifat" attitudes among health care providers continue toward individuals with obesity (Puhl & Brownell, 2001). Fear of addiction by pain management specialists can also negatively impact judgments and practices of health care professionals, especially in light of the frequency of comorbidities of obesity, pain, and addiction in the lifetime experience of many with disability (McCaffery & Ferrell, 1997).

Education

The lack of cross-cultural norms for various assessment measures used for health-related conditions may disproportionately affect WWD more than women without disabilities. This lack of cross-cultural knowledge can have an especially negative impact on other areas of their lives, such as education. Mukherjee, Reis, and Heller (2003) described various problematic issues in therapy with an Asian American woman and full-time college student who was hit by a truck. After the traumatic injury, she had difficulty continuing in school and dropped to half time. She denied the difficulties she was facing and did not accept support services. She did not begin treatment with a feminist neuropsychologist for nearly a year and a half. Assessment of her problems was impeded by a lack of research on Asian Americans. It was difficult to determine if her language difficulties were due to the fact that English was not her first language or were a consequence of the traumatic brain injury (TBI). Finally, her psychologist struggled with the conflict between a supervisor's desire to focus on stereotypic shame and the psychologist's concern that "the feelings of hopelessness, self-blame and regret were intertwined with [the client's] brain injury" (p. 14).

Workplace

WWD also face discrimination when they pursue employment. Whether their disabilities are considered severe or not, only 31.1% of these women are likely to be employed compared with 35.9% employment among men with disabilities (Erickson et al., 2013). In 2010, 15.1% of WWD were living in poverty compared with a poverty rate of 11.8% among men with disabilities (Nazarov & Lee, 2012). With regard to legal protection in the workplace, laws in many countries do address the employment rights of PWD. The focus of laws includes percentages of workforces reserved for PWD, prohibition of discrimination against PWD, mandatory accessibility of buildings, fiscal and tax exemptions, and governmental provision of health care for PWD (and sometimes their families). The laws vary in content and enforcement (Gharaibeh, 2009). In the United States, the ADA and the ADA Amendments Act of 2008 specifically outlawed discrimination against PWD in "employment, housing, public accommodations, education, transportation, and communication, recreation, institutionalization, health services, voting, and access to public services" (Section 12101(a)(3)).

Many WWD need workplace accommodations in order to succeed in employment. These needs require negotiation with a potential employer, or in the case of disability acquired while employed, with the current employer. Negotiation necessitates revealing disability. Despite legal requirements, anecdotal reports (Bouton, 2013) indicate that some employers do not provide accommodations and do not hire or continue employment of WWD when disability is revealed. This reality impedes women's willingness to pursue accommodations and is clearly an issue of both gender and disability. Psychologists and other clinicians who treat WWD are encouraged to be aware of employment needs for WWD and current rates of discrimination. Olkin (2002) noted that many WWD are susceptible to mental and physical fatigue and muscle pain, making it important that negotiating accommodations not be skipped or delayed. As health care providers, psychologists can also assist women in determining appropriate break time and space.

Religious Institutions

The assessment and incorporation of an individual's spiritual and religious beliefs into a treatment plan is integral to a comprehensive bio-psychosocial evaluation in health care. Thus, religion and spirituality need to be assessed in the lives of WWD (Boswell, Hamer, Knight, Glacoff, & McChesney, 2007; Bryant-Davis, Ellis, & Perez, 2013). Contrary to their espoused beliefs, religious settings are not always supportive. Many religious buildings are physically inaccessible to women with mobility limitations; such buildings are, unfortunately, exempt from compliance with ADA accessibility.

Often in religious services, there is a focus on health. Some religious leaders proclaim, "I woke up this morning, clothed in my right mind" without consideration for the implications for people with psychiatric disabilities. In organized religions, there are few positive images of WWD. In some religions, women or their ancestors are blamed for their disabilities. On the other hand, in the Christian Gospel, there are instances of a paradigm shift away from blaming ancestral sin for disability, as shown in this passage:

> As he [Jesus] went along, he saw a man blind from birth. His disciples asked him, "Rabbi, who sinned, this man or his parents, that he was born blind?" "Neither this man nor his parents sinned, but this happened so that the works of God might be displayed in him." (John 9:1–3 [New International Version])

In spite of the potential barriers posed by organized religion, coping research supports the value of encouragement of faith and spirituality and related benefits for adjustment to both developmental and acquired disabilities (McNulty, Livneh, & Wilson, 2004; Poston & Turnbull, 2004). Focus groups with parents of children with developmental disabilities found that having faith or believing in something greater than oneself, using prayer, and attributing meaning to the child's disability provided resources to enable them to meet the challenges the disability posed for their family quality of life (Poston & Turnbull, 2004).

McNulty et al. (2004) discussed the difficulties in operationalizing and measuring spirituality and religiousness in rehabilitation research because of the complex multidimensional character of the constructs. In researching the association between spirituality and religion and physical and emotional outcomes in adjustment to disability, various physiological (e.g., neuroendocrine), psychological (e.g., belief systems), social (e.g., family, social groups), and behavioral (e.g., lifestyle practices) pathways that link the two must also be considered

(Fetzer Institute, 1999). However, there is also no single assessment instrument to measure the multifaceted domains of spirituality and religiousness identified by the Fetzer Institute (1999). Despite these obstacles, it is critical to determine the roles of religion and spirituality in affirming psychological assessment and treatment for women. In addition, psychologists and other practitioners are encouraged to maintain awareness of religious and spiritual resources that are accessible to and supportive of WWD.

Legal System

"The shortage of women in the justice system and government decreases their opportunities to design and influence legislation that may protect them and children from violence and ensure their basic human rights" (APA, 2007, p. 962). This shortage is even starker for WWD, who are often stereotypically assumed to be incompetent (Bell, Henthorne, Hill, Turnbull-Humphries, & Zito, 2009; Corrigan et al., 2005). It is important that such stereotypes are recognized and confronted. The assumption of incompetence interferes with the opportunities for WWD to obtain and maintain education and employment and to fulfill family roles without harassment (Akram & Hollins, 2010; Lightfoot, Hill, & LaLiberte, 2010). Mukherjee et al. (2003), for example, described a woman who had sustained a devastating TBI and her struggle as she married and considered pregnancy; nonetheless, she was able to deal successfully with multiple challenges of parenting despite her physical limitations.

Families and Couples

WWD are members of families in all constellations (Fredriksen-Goldsen & Erera, 2003) and fulfill all of the roles that women hold. However, WWD, including mothers, are sometimes considered to be incompetent and childlike. Such attributions of incompetence are increased exponentially on the basis of each additional marginalization a woman experiences (Banks, 2012; McDonald, Keys, & Balcazar, 2009). Lesbians with acquired disabilities encounter inappropriate interference by families of origin and health professionals when they attempt to maintain desired family roles. Although there is literature about discrimination experienced by lesbians seeking to care for partners with disabilities (Riggle, Rostosky, Prather, & Hamrin, 2005; see also Chapter 5, this volume), less attention has been given to lesbians with disabilities (Fredriksen-Goldsen, Kim, & Barkan, 2012; Fredriksen-Goldsen et al., 2009; Kim & Fredriksen-Goldsen, 2012).

Psychological treatment that is affirmative and embodies a woman-centered perspective can empower WWD to fulfill desired family roles.

Consider a client's situation that exemplifies the complexity of roles faced by WWD (Nabors & Pettee, 2003). The client is an African American woman who sustained a TBI in a motor vehicle accident. She was admitted for inpatient rehabilitation for 1 month after the accident. During that time, her brother had a stroke. The family was very supportive during her hospitalization, visiting often and encouraging her, but when she returned home, she was expected to provide care for her brother, put her own rehabilitation on hold, and resume all of her previous familial activities as if she were "all well" as soon as she was discharged from the hospital. The family ignored her symptoms and fatigue (Nabors & Pettee, 2003) and assumed that she would continue in her usual family roles that she had held before she became disabled.

Banks (2003) also described the familial context of disability across the life span, examining an international understanding of disability. Families are generally unprepared to deal with disability. Their responses can range from attempts to remove disability, denial of members' needs, and overprotectiveness to gaining knowledge regarding a specific disability, healthy advocacy for members with disabilities, and activism in the larger community. In many instances, family members are caregivers without training or adequate support to provide appropriate care. There is a high risk of abuse if the family circumstances include significant levels of stress (Banks, 2007). Psychological treatment must attend to the intersection of culture and disability with other social situations of families experiencing disability (Leung, 2013). Such treatment can enable families to support WWD. Through their attitudes or actions, family members might be discouraging toward members with disabilities. Some WWD do not strive beyond arbitrary limits set or implied by families, whereas others perceive the discouragement as a challenge (McDonald et al., 2009). Affirmative treatment practices focused on strength-based care can enable WWD to achieve despite negative messages from their families. Psychologists and other clinicians must also integrate families, no matter what the configuration, into psychological treatment (Evans-Campbell, Fredriksen-Goldsen, Walters, & Stately, 2005; Fredriksen-Goldsen & Farwell, 2005; Fredriksen-Goldsen & Hooyman, 2005; Muraco & Fredriksen-Goldsen, 2011).

Research Methods

Caution should be exercised when using research methods that have not been developed or normed with WWD in mind. Banks (2012) addressed the lack of empirically based treatments for people who are members of multiple marginalized groups, such as WWD. The APA (2005) *Policy Statement on Evidence-Based Practice in Psychology* suggests incorporating the best research evidence; clinical expertise; "patient's specific problems, strengths, personality, sociocultural context, and preferences" (p. 2); and clinical implications:

> Clinical decisions should be made in collaboration with the patient, based on the best clinically relevant evidence, and with consideration for the probable costs, benefits, and available resources and options. It is the treating psychologist who makes the ultimate judgment regarding a particular intervention or treatment plan. The involvement of an active, informed patient is generally crucial to the success of psychological services. (p. 3)

With respect to research involving WWD, as Artman and Daniels (2010) noted, "The key stakeholders (PWD) are rarely directing, or significantly included in, research that is about them" (p. 443). It is important, then, for WWD themselves to be researchers and to participate in research. A participatory action research model, in which WWD are included in all phases of research, from development of research questions through the interpretation of findings, better educates and informs the public and professionals rather than having other people define their experiences (Marshall, Kendall, Catalano, & Barnett, 2008). Guideline 3 of the "Guidelines for Assessment of and Intervention With Persons With Disabilities" (APA, 2012) includes examples of psychology and other journals that publish research on practice for and by PWD and suggests that psychologists read the surgeon general's statement (U.S. Department of Health and Human Services, 2005) that disability issues are a priority for research.

Researchers, educators, and clinicians need to consider ways to promote the International Classification of Function, Health, and Disability (ICF) model in research with and involvement of WWD (WHO, 2001), which attempts to measure the interactional model of disability espoused by NIDRR. The ICF focuses on the components of health rather than on the consequences of disease. The ICF approach encompasses all aspects of health with the inclusion of physical, social, and environmental factors that interact with an individual's health conditions to produce outcomes in terms of activities and participation. It is intended to be a universal classification system, meaning that it covers all people, not just PWD. The model "gives permission" to address people's self-determined goals very broadly, which mirrors the call for disability-affirming practices with WWD.

Therefore, research with WWD needs to include dimensions of activity and participation, as well as environmental factors, to capture the complex interactional nature of the life experiences of WWD and their families. Health care providers can use the ICF model to guide the selection of measurement tools both to inform goal setting and decision making processes and to determine meaningful outcomes. Outcome measures need to be developed to provide tools needed to evaluate the effectiveness of interventions for WWD related to quality of life and life satisfaction. Research-based knowledge on WWD in the rehabilitation process is also needed not only at the client and practitioner levels, but also within training programs to target prospective professionals who intend to enter the field (Lewis, Brubaker, & Armstrong, 2009).

Language

Terminology that is inclusive of the ways in which WWD identify themselves needs to be better understood. The APA (2010), in its *Publication Manual*, encourages the use of person-first language when referring to PWD. The goal was to place the disability as a secondary classification with the focus being on the person first. Person-first language has been specifically recommended in Guideline 6 of the APA "Guidelines for Assessment of and Intervention With Persons With Disabilities" as a way to "use appropriate language and respectful behavior toward individuals with disabilities" (APA, 2012, p. 48). This practice is probably most appropriate for women whose disabilities have been experienced in relative isolation. Such women have not had the experience of being with other PWD and do not consider themselves to be part of a group whom others have defined.

The use of disability-first language, however, is not acceptable to all people and can be a reflection of culture. Some people who identify with disability culture prefer that the term *disability* be used first when writing or speaking about the disability community. In addition, not all members of the disability community conceptualize defining language in a similar fashion. For example, the Deaf community consider themselves to be a linguistic minority—not disabled (Corbett, 2003). Given different perspectives in the use of person-first versus disability-first identification and language, it is recommended that psychologists query the individual WWD to ascertain how she self-identifies and determine her preference in the therapist's use of language.

PROFESSIONAL RESPONSIBILITY AND PRACTICE (GUIDELINES 4–6 AND 9)

These guidelines speak of the importance of psychological self-awareness, and the use of psychological practices that foster positive relationships and empowerment. In an era in which there is emphasis on empirically based practice, it is difficult to determine which treatments are effective for WWD because of the lack of research, limited inclusion of WWD in clinical trials, and the aforementioned wide variations in manifestations of disability (Banks, 2012). Artman and Daniels (2010) therefore concluded that psychologists are generally poorly prepared to practice with PWD and are at high risk for experiencing counterproductive countertransference. The social model of disability (Gill, 1987) reframed disability by taking the focus away from the person's disability, shifting the focus toward society in its failure to provide people with access and treat them with the same respect afforded persons without disabilities. Psychologists' understanding of the implications of this model is critical to inform their practice in working with WWD.

Schriempf (2001) argued that both feminist theory and the social model of disability fail to take into account the importance of the body in subjective and sexual experiences of women with disabilities. Integration of the body and disability into feminism and the importance of attention to the body and gender are critical for practice and policies regarding disability (Garland-Thompson, 2002; Watson, McKie, Hughes, Hopkins, & Gregory, 2004). Western culture defines ideal femininity in terms of physical attractiveness, the desire to love and be loved, and the ability to mother. WWD often experience negative consequences in those instances in which there is an inability to meet or choice not to meet these cultural expectations. Psychologists can prepare themselves to engage in appropriately accommodating practice and advocacy by using the previously discussed NIDRR interactionist model of disability as a foundation before other evidenced-based interventions are employed. This model emphasizes components of health rather than consequences of disability.

Self-Awareness

Self-awareness of one's attitudes is central to working with WWD. People bring a mixture of personal beliefs, attitudes, and/or fears to the idea of the disability experience. Thinking about and working with WWD may threaten concepts a psychologist has held about who she is. Concepts of strength and deficits, independence and dependence, and other attitudinal beliefs need to be explored in the process of working with WWD. Gibson (2009) wrote,

> Unlike cultural encapsulation where there is no challenge to one's cultural affiliation, clients with disabilities may not only represent a fear of the unknown, but also bring about a sense of vulnerability for the clinician. Such vulnerability may include gaining a sudden awareness that disability is an equal opportunity life experience. Thus, perhaps for the first time in their lives, clinicians are being exposed to the concept that they or a loved one could acquire a disability. Similar to how many fear death and dying to avoid thoughts of one's own mortality, working with clients with disabilities may trigger fear and avoidance of disability. (p. 146)

Dunn and Burcaw (2013) addressed how exploring the disability identity of individuals by listening to the content of their disability narrative and recognizing the psychosocial influence of identity themes can help therapists combat unconscious biases and stereotypes unknowingly held by the provider. Knowledge of clients' disability identity can help therapists guide WWD in formulating treatment goals consistent with their values and actions in circumstances in which their disability is a salient factor. Olkin (1999) suggested that disability identities exist on a continuum and can be shaped by the following inquiry: When do people consider themselves to be persons with disabilities? This question clarifies the extent to which a woman who may possess a disability identifies herself as someone with a disability.

Further, it is important for psychologists not to assume that a visible disability is a client's presenting problem but to pay attention to the concerns that brought her to therapy (Iezzoni, 2006). Clinicians must avoid making disability a scapegoat for issues that might very well appear in the lives of any woman, just as it is imperative for nondisabled psychologists not to imagine the experience of a form of disability to be more negative than it actually is because stigma and bias can manifest in opposite extremes. By the same token, it is critical not to minimize an invisible or relatively unknown disability. Williams and Upadhyay (2003) described the difficulty Williams had with a therapist who was unable to stay on topic when she wanted to discuss her disability identity development and adjustment to a learning disorder. When Williams began to date a man who was blind and wanted to work on the impact of his blindness on their relationship, the therapist tried to focus on the *therapist's* preconceived notions about the boyfriend's blindness and ignored the relationship issues and the client's other concerns.

Williams described an inappropriate comment by her therapist and the ensuing discussion:

> Approximately halfway into one particular session, my therapist asked me a question: "Let me see if I understand this right. If you had a miracle pill that could take away your disability, you wouldn't take it?" Without hesitating I said, "No." Then I tried to explain that I wouldn't take a miracle pill because I feel that my disability is a major part of my self identity and if I took that away I would lose a major part of who I am as a person. Not feeling heard, I continued by mentioning that if my boyfriend had an option for such a miracle pill, he also would refuse it for the same reasons. That my therapist appeared shocked would be an understatement. He then launched into a mini-dissertation about how he could not understand why I wouldn't take such a pill. (Williams & Upadhyay, 2003, p. 151)

All psychologists have a responsibility to develop awareness of their own biases in order to avoid making the same kind of remarks to WWD who seek psychological services. This awareness building is crucial for disability culturally competent services. Olkin's disability-affirmative therapy (DAT; Olkin, 2009), which calls for cultural knowledge and affirmation, assists providers with facilitating treatment. DAT is a metatheoretical perspective that provides a disability-positive context wherein specific treatment interventions can be applied. The DAT model encompasses several components: (a) empowerment and acknowledgment of social marginalization and environmental barriers; (b) appreciation of the dynamic nature of disability; (c) consideration of the medical realities of PWD and recognition of personal coping strategies; and (d) provision of a therapeutic environment that provides affirmative goal-setting, an integrated view of the self, and encapsulates the values of flexibility and creativity that are prized in the disability community. Embedding established therapeutic practices (e.g., cognitive–behavioral therapy, behavioral therapy, relaxation techniques) into a disability-affirmative framework will allow for a truly integrated approach that includes addressing the individual's symptoms (e.g., physical discomfort, emotional distress) as well as the facilitating social and political factors (e.g., inadequate health care; Mona, Syme, & Cameron, 2014).

Practice Applications

One consideration in working with WWD is attentiveness to the whole person. Feldman and Tegart (2003) described a peer group of African American women with arthritis, a disabling condition experienced by nearly 27% of African American women (Leigh & Huff, 2006). The women were primarily concerned with their weight, caregiving, and work. When considering weight in relation to health faced by African American women, the clinician needs to examine genetics, diet, and slave history (Banks, 2010, 2012). Slaves of African descent in the American colonies and the United States were generally given the least healthy foods. This food disparity continued through the Jim Crow era. Today, the most affordable foods are the least healthy, containing a lot of saturated fat and sugar; such unhealthy food continues to be the most available food for African Americans, many of whom live in impoverished conditions.

Many of the women in Feldman and Tegart's (2003) arthritis group were gainfully employed and raising or providing care for young children. Psychologists need to consider these multiple work and family roles when conducting assessments and developing treatment plans. At the same time, we need to honor and appreciate the perceptions of clients with respect to conditions that are considered by others to be disabling. The women dealing with arthritis, for the most part, did not consider arthritis to be a disability, yet were quite worried that they might become disabled (Feldman & Tegart, 2003). A disabled identity acknowledges that one's membership in an oppressed group includes healthy and positive attitudes about oneself and other members of the same oppressed group. The benefit is healthful self-perception, not accommodation or access to support services. Campbell (2009) wrote,

> Internalized ableism can mean the disabled person is caught between a rock and a hard place. To attain the benefit of a disabled identity, one must constantly participate in the processes of disability disavowal, aspire toward the norm, reach a state of near-ablebodiedness, or at the very least to effect a state of passing. (p. 27)

Passing is a concept that is probably most often discussed in the context of racism, and the attempt by some members of marginalized racial and ethnic groups to adopt the cultural behaviors of dominant groups in order to avoid being perceived as members of the marginalized group. The same concept has been used to address some sexual minorities' responses to heterosexism. We do need to acknowledge that "for some marginalized groups, *passing* as 'normal' is a protection strategy against discrimination and maltreatment" (Poulin & Gouliquer, 2003, p. 95). Passing within the context of disability was best exemplified by the successful hiding by Franklin D. Roosevelt of his profound disability from the world during his presidency. This passing as nondisabled not only denied the physical restrictions of Roosevelt's disability but also reinforced the affective deception imposed on the disabled to always be cheerful (Post, 1995; Post & Robins, 1990; Pressman, 2013). As psychologists work with WWD, they are challenged with determining the difference between adaptive passing and detrimental passing. Poulin and Gouliquer (2003) described one lesbian's experience of an invisible disability, debilitating irritable bowel syndrome symptoms during menses. The combination of heterosexism and ableism by health care professionals interfered with and delayed appropriate treatment. By using makeup and careful scheduling of activities, that woman was described as "pass[ing] for a straight, healthy person" (Poulin & Gouliquer, 2003, pp. 96–97).

Passing, however, is not necessarily benign. Murray Nettles (2001) wrote eloquently about the perils of passing that can lead to avoidable worsening of health or the death of a WWD, if passing serves to hide symptoms in need of treatment, such as an undiagnosed brain tumor interfering with intellectual, emotional, and physical function. Despite memory problems, fatigue, speech problems, and seizures misattributed to menopause and the hectic schedule of a successful academic, Murray Nettles continued to teach and manage her multiple family roles. Passing as "normal" for many years reinforced habits and roles, which ultimately deceived the client's family and physicians from noticing the process of memory and cognitive changes and prolonged receipt of appropriate health care.

In contrast to passing, Gibson (2009), using a multicultural model similar to those of Cross (1971) and Helms (1990), identified a positive disability identity development model that leads to a healthy incorporation of disability into one's self-perception. The three stages are as follows:

- Stage 1: Passive awareness: Begins during the first part of life and can continue into adulthood. During this stage, self-perception is influenced by dominant medical models.
- Stage 2: Realization: Often occurs in adolescence and early adulthood. During this stage, which accompanied by negative emotions, the individual identifies herself or himself as having a disability.
- Stage 3: Acceptance: Adulthood. This phase is marked by embracing oneself as valuable, and making commitments to advocacy and activism.

Understanding the evolving responses of WWD to societal stigma, pressures, and discrimination, while attending to the strengths and weaknesses of individual WWD, is the bedrock of affirmative and feminist psychological practice with this group of women. The multiple roles these women hold, the impact of current and historic attitudes about disability and other personal characteristics, and the wide variance in identities are considered in the ongoing assessment throughout psychological treatment.

COMMUNITY RESOURCES AND SOCIAL CHANGE–ACTIVISM

Community Resources

In working with WWD, psychologists keep themselves apprised of resources for their clients. In doing so, they consider Guideline 10 (psychologists strive to recognize that families of individuals with disabilities have strengths and challenges) and Guideline 12 (psychologists strive to learn about the opportunities and challenges presented by assistive technology) of the APA "Guidelines for Assessment of and Intervention With Persons With Disabilities." Healthy families of WWD and girls with disabilities can serve as advocates and exhibit resilience (APA, 2012); they can often share information about the quality of health, education, technological, and community resources.

It is critical to determine the actual accessibility of resources, including the availability of transportation. As Banks (2010) noted,

> For women with mobility disabilities, in urban areas there are specialized transportation services, but those services can be inconsistent. There is usually limited availability, advanced appointments are necessary, and

there are minimal options for activities. For example, transportation services are sometimes only available for health care appointments, but not for shopping, hairdressing, or entertainment venues. (p. 438)

Community resources, in the age of the Internet, include websites with information on resources around the world. Disabled Women on the Web (http://www.disabilityhistory.org/dwa/library_h.html) is a resource site developed by and for WWD. Psychologists and other clinicians will find this resource quite valuable. Another valuable resource is the Women With Disabilities Center at the Rehabilitation Institute of Chicago (http://www.ric.org/conditions/womens-health/).

Social Change–Activism: Abuse of WWD

WWD are at higher risk for physical abuse and psychological abuse than women without disabilities. Abuse is 5 to 8 times more likely among WWD than men with disabilities and more likely among women with than without disabilities (Nosek & Hughes, 2003). The risk is further increased if the women need to rely on others for assistance. These individuals include family members and health professionals (Banks, 2007). Psychologists have a responsibility to determine whether a WWD is in danger of being abused and should explore the nature and extent of any discovered or suspected abuse. Psychologists then need to be trained in how to assess and respond to the specific nuances of abuse in WWD.

WWD experience many types of abuse. These include isolation; withholding of medications, food, clothes, bathing, or other services; talking without interpretation, teasing, or bullying; making fun of a woman's disability; hitting; beating; and sexual abuse. Abuse is an ongoing problem for WWD, as noted by Banks (2007): "Women with disabilities, on average, endure domestic violence for longer periods than women without disabilities and are at high risk for being abused by multiple perpetrators" (p. 5). Abuse can lead to early death; unchecked intimate partner violence has been shown to end with the death of the victim. Therefore, proactive psychological treatment must address safety issues for WWD with the realization that safety planning is complicated for WWD, in part because of a lack of accessible service (Banks, 2013a; Powers et al., 2009). When WWD wish to leave their partners, Olkin (2002) discussed various obstacles they may encounter that include physical needs, financial needs, custody concerns, and relationship issues unique to their circumstances. The combined effects of gender and disability in the face of abuse pose unique challenges for WWD.

The following concluding section presents a case study of a woman who struggled with adapting to disability and discusses how her treatment incorporated many of the issues and considerations presented in the first part of this chapter with attention to each of the Guidelines (APA, 2007).

CASE STUDY: TRAUMATIC BRAIN INJURY AND POSTTRAUMATIC STRESS DISORDER

In order to maintain confidentiality, this example represents a combination of three clients from the fourth author's practice. The client, Roxanne, is a 37-year-old European American self-identified lesbian, partnered with Margie, a 48-year-old European American self-identified bisexual woman, who was raising a 4-year-old grandson in their home. Roxanne and Margie had been partners for several years before Roxanne joined the navy and was deployed to both Iraq and Afghanistan. While Roxanne was overseas, Margie became guardian of her grandson because his parents were unable to care for him. Roxanne served as a military nurse (Guideline 1: unique life events) and was raped while in military service (Guideline 2: oppression). She was assaulted during the rape and sustained a TBI.

Roxanne experienced several difficulties when she returned home. After discharge from the military, she tried to gain employment as a home health care registered nurse, but she had trouble following directions to the homes of clients and got lost while driving. She was extremely uncomfortable sleeping in the same bed with Margie and resuming a sexual relationship with her. Roxanne was unable to get along with Margie's grandson. The impact of her changed behavior on Margie included embarrassment in public, loss of assistance with household tasks, and inability to calm Roxanne when she became agitated. Margie perceived herself as having to take care of two 4-year-olds.

Roxanne sought treatment unsuccessfully from several health professionals. She felt uncomfortable with all of them, particularly with men. Roxanne was referred to a feminist neuropsychologist for assessment and treatment. When she entered treatment, Roxanne had explosive anger and temper tantrums. She was embarrassed by her explosiveness but was unable to control it. One result of that embarrassment was that Roxanne isolated herself from other people. Of particular concern were her depression, pain, memory problems, and relationship stress with Margie. Roxanne also complained of constipation and diarrhea, nightmares, racing heart, panic attacks, headaches, sweat reactions, fear of living alone, fear of sexual advances and relations, mismanagement of money, inability to drive, fear of men, and fear of socializing in the community. Such symptoms are often observed in women who have experienced TBI under circumstances that also result in posttraumatic stress disorder (PTSD).

It was difficult to obtain a history from Roxanne. When asked about the cause of known brain injury, she was unable to tell the neuropsychologist how she had been assaulted, and Margie needed to provide brief details. Eventually, Roxanne was able to reveal that she had been a victim of childhood sexual assault and adulthood intimate partner violence. As a result, it is not clear how many TBIs she had sustained (Guideline 3). Neuropsychological assessment was conducted using the *Ackerman–Banks Neuropsychological Rehabilitation Battery* (*A-BNRB*; Ackerman & Banks, 2006), which includes an affirming, woman-centered approach to determining strengths that can be recruited to address weaknesses in rehabilitation (Guidelines 8 and 9). Interviews and the formal testing were conducted across 3 weeks because of Roxanne's pain and difficulty tolerating the testing environment for more than about half an hour at a time. Neuropsychological assessment revealed difficulty with attention and concentration, poor short-term memory, third-grade-level mathematics skills, and left–right confusion. Her driving skills were also compromised by her inability to accurately perceive directions. Test results also indicated confabulation in speech and writing. She experienced severe anxiety, depression, and impulsivity—symptoms consistent with TBI. The *A-BNRB* also assesses client awareness of poor performance, reactions to the stress of testing, and frustration tolerance. Roxanne was seldom aware of her poor performance. When she was aware, she had strong negative reactions, crying and being upset about her inability to do tasks that had previously been very easy. Roxanne had minimal ability to self-correct and very low frustration tolerance, a frequent clinical complaint with brain injury.

Following initial assessment and feedback, the treatment planning and ensuing therapy were handled collaboratively with Roxanne. She was invited to become her own "clinical scientist" to evaluate her progress in therapy. The therapist's understanding of the importance of addressing neuropsychological issues combined with women's concerns, such as the combination of PTSD and TBIs as consequences of assault, including sexual assault and intimate partner violence, were critical to treatment planning (Guideline 4). At the same time, the therapist recognized and sought consultation to address her limited experience in treating members of sexual minorities (Guideline 5).

Neuropsychological treatments occurred biweekly, then weekly, for the next 36 months. Treatment involved a combination of family psychology, hypnotherapy, cognitive rehabilitation, and biofeedback in conjunction with computerized tasks to increase attention time (Guidelines 6 and 7). Relaxation techniques, primarily involving diaphragmatic breathing, were used for pain reduction. Hypnotherapy was employed to assist in dealing with the assaultive incidents. Cognitive–behavioral psychotherapy was used to improve community functioning; decrease confabulation; and address Roxanne's anxiety, depression, and impulsivity (Ackerman, 2004). The goal of cognitive–visual therapy was improvement in perception of left and right directions and a decrease in arithmetic, writing, and copying errors. Family therapy, which included family members of her choice (Guideline 4), was used to work on the sexual relationship between the partners, financial concerns, employment and disability issues, social phobia emanating from her fear of men postrape, and family stress. The therapist also assisted Roxanne in finding a sexual assault victims' support group (Guideline 10).

Because of Roxanne's pain and low frustration tolerance, the therapy sessions were scheduled for 2 hours each. The format was half an hour working with the computer, half an hour of cognitive tasks, and about 20 minutes of family psychotherapy. Roxanne was given time to rest between portions of sessions. Before continuing to the next task, she was guided through relaxation exercises. As therapy progressed, she was able to handle relaxation without guidance from the psychologist.

Subsequently, Roxanne's physiological responses to stress were monitored through computerized biofeedback with attention to muscles signaling pain (Basmajian, 1989). As her stress increased, her heart rate increased to dangerous levels, putting her at risk for stroke. A focus of cognitive–behavioral psychotherapy was used to assist Roxanne in understanding the need for controlling her heart rate. This approach was conducted in conjunction with psychotherapy to address daily arguments with Margie and her grandson, the strained sexual relationship, and holiday stress. A seizure disorder was diagnosed, and Roxanne was placed on a low dose of antiseizure medication. Anxiety was monitored to determine if it was a manifestation of and/or immediate postictal reaction to subclinical seizures. Margie was able to assist Roxanne in recognizing that she needed to relax, and they were able to collaborate in calming Roxanne when she was upset.

Because Roxanne was unable to work, the family experienced financial difficulties. Margie's sole income was funding provided for the care of her grandson. The psychologist assisted the family in pursuing disability for Roxanne and testified on Roxanne's behalf to pursue support for disability compensation. With the disability pension and child support, there was enough money for the family, which reduced stress for the couple.

Therapy came to an end when the psychologist moved away from the area where Roxanne lived. Although worried about how she would be able to manage, Roxanne did not want to work with another therapist. The psychologist arranged for Roxanne to begin further rehabilitation therapies to continue the progress made in the combination therapy that had taken place over 3 years. Roxanne recognized the need for continued therapy, demonstrating improvement from her lack of understanding when therapy had started. At the end of the 3 years, the couple had not resumed sexual relations but were able to sleep through the night together. They had identified a lesbian-focused sex therapy program in another city that they planned to pursue.

This case study is presented in the hopes of contributing not only to understanding of the complexity of assessment and treatment of WWD but also to the clinical literature on underdiagnosis and treatment of TBI sustained by women (Guideline 11). It is intended to exemplify the need for comprehensive assessment, followed by treatment of the whole woman, attending to her social network and the quality of support she receives for life satisfaction.

CONCLUSION

WWD live at the intersection of the identities of disability and gender, experiencing unique forms of sexism endemic to that intersection. Psychologists and clinicians are challenged to recognize their own and society's misconceptions about WWD (Nosek, 2010). This chapter gives voice to WWD who describe their own experiences, addresses a wide spectrum of issues faced by WWD, and concludes with a case study with an example of comprehensive and multifaceted therapy. We thank our colleagues who have worked diligently on the development of the APA "Guidelines for Psychological Practice With Girls and Women." The integration of these guidelines with the APA "Guidelines for Assessment of and Intervention With Persons With Disabilities" will continue to positively advance our knowledge, understanding and practice with WWD.

REFERENCES

Ackerman, R. J. (2004). Applied psychophysiology, clinical biofeedback, and rehabilitation neuropsychology: A case study—Mild traumatic brain injury and post-traumatic stress disorder. *Physical Medicine and Rehabilitation Clinics of North America, 15*, 919–931. doi:10.1016/j.pmr.2004.04.001

Ackerman, R. J., & Banks, M. E. (2006). *Ackerman–Banks Neuropsychological Rehabilitation Battery professional manual* (4th ed.). Akron, OH: ABackans Diversified Computer Processing.

Akram, A., & Hollins, S. (2010). Being a parent with a disability. In S. Tyano, M. Keren, H. Herrman, & J. Cox (Eds.), *Parenthood and mental health: A bridge between infant and adult psychiatry* (pp. 311–323). Chichester, England: Wiley. doi:10.1002/9780470660683.ch28

American Psychological Association. (2005). *Policy statement on evidence-based practice in psychology.* Retrieved from http://www.apapracticecentral.org/ce/courses/ebpstatement.pdf

American Psychological Association. (2007). Guidelines for psychological practice with girls and women. *American Psychologist, 62*, 949–979. doi:10.1037/0003-066X.62.9.949

American Psychological Association. (2010). *Publication manual of the American Psychological Association* (6th ed.). Washington, DC: Author.

American Psychological Association. (2012). Guidelines for assessment of and intervention with persons with disabilities. *American Psychologist, 67*, 43–62. doi:10.1037/a0025892

Americans With Disabilities Act of 1990. Pub. L. No. 101–336, 42 U.S.C., § 12111, 12112.

Americans With Disabilities Act (ADA) Amendments Act of 2008, Pub. L. No. 110–325, 42 U.S.C.A. § 12101.

Anderson, S., & Whitfield, K. (2013). Social identity and stroke: "They don't make me feel like, there's something wrong with me." *Scandinavian Journal of Caring Sciences, 27*, 820–830. doi:10.1111/j.1471-6712.2012.01086.x

Artman, L. K., & Daniels, J. A. (2010). Disability and psychotherapy practice: Cultural competence and practical tips. *Professional Psychology: Research and Practice, 41*, 442–448. doi:10.1037/a0020864

Banks, M. E. (2003). Disability in the family: A life span perspective. *Cultural Diversity and Ethnic Minority Psychology, 9*, 367–384. doi:10.1037/1099-9809.9.4.367

Banks, M. E. (2007). Women with disabilities, domestic violence against. In N. A. Jackson (Ed.), *Encyclopedia of domestic violence* (pp. 723–728). New York, NY: Taylor & Francis.

Banks, M. E. (2010). 2009 Division 35 Presidential Address: Feminist psychology and women with disabilities: An emerging alliance. *Psychology of Women Quarterly, 34*, 431–442. doi:10.1111/j.1471-6402.2010.01593.x

Banks, M. E. (2012). Multiple minority identities and mental health: Social and research implications of diversity within and between groups. In R. Nettles & R. Balter (Eds.), *Multiple minority identities: Applications for practice, research, and training* (pp. 35–58). New York, NY: Springer.

Banks, M. E. (2013a). Ideal recovery for women who receive traumatic brain injury from intimate partner violence. In H. Muenchberger, E. Kendall, & S. Prout (Eds.), *Traumatic brain injury: Systems of support for healing and health* (pp. 153–167). Santa Barbara, CA: Praeger.

Banks, M. E. (2013b). Women of color with disabilities. In L. Comas-Díaz & B. Greene (Eds.), *Psychological health of women of color: Intersections, challenges, and opportunities* (pp. 219–231). Westport, CT: Praeger.

Banks, M. E., & Kaschak, E. (Eds.). (2003). *Women with visible and invisible disabilities: Multiple intersections, multiple issues, multiple therapies.* New York, NY: Haworth Press.

Banks, M. E., & Mona, L. R. (2007). Leadership and collaboration among women with disabilities. In J. L. Chin, B. Lott, J. K. Rice, & J. Sanchez-Hucles (Eds.), *Women and leadership: Transforming visions and diverse voices* (pp. 330–340). Boston, MA: Blackwell. doi:10.1002/9780470692332.ch16

Basmajian, J. V. (Ed.). (1989). *Biofeedback: Principles and practice for clinicians* (3rd ed.). Baltimore, MD: Williams & Wilkins.

Bell, B., Jr., Henthorne, S. R., Hill, D. A., Turnbull-Humphries, J. W., & Zito, S. T. (2009). Autonomy and disability: A quest for quality of life. In C. A. Marshall, E. Kendall, M. E. Banks, & R. M. S. Gover (Eds.), *Disabilities: Insights from across fields and around the world: Vol. 2. The context: Environmental, social, and cultural considerations* (pp. 17–38). Santa Barbara, CA: Praeger/ABC-CLIO.

Borneman, T. (2009). Foreword. In C. A. Marshall, E. Kendall, M. E. Banks, & R. M. S. Gover (Eds.), *Disabilities: Insights from across fields and around the world: Vol. 1. The experience: Definitions, causes, and consequences.* (pp. ix–xi). Westport, CT: Praeger.

Boswell, B., Hamer, M., Knight, S., Glacoff, M., & McChesney, J. (2007). Dance of disability and spirituality. *Journal of Rehabilitation, 73*(4), 33–40.

Bouton, K. (2013, September 21). Quandary of hidden disabilities: Conceal or reveal? *New York Times.* Retrieved from http://www.nytimes.com/2013/09/22/business/quandary-of-hidden-disabilities-conceal-or-reveal.html

Bryant-Davis, T., Ellis, M. U., & Perez, B. (2013). Women of color and spirituality: Faith to move mountains. In L. Comas-Díaz & B. Greene (Eds.), *Psychological health of women of color: Intersections, challenges, and opportunities* (pp. 167–183). Santa Barbara, CA: Praeger.

Campbell, F. K. (2009). Disability harms: Exploring internalized ableism. In C. A. Marshall, E. Kendall, M. E. Banks, & R. M. S. Gover (Eds.) *Disabilities: Insights from across fields and around the world: Vol. 1: The experience: Definitions, causes, and consequences.* (pp. 19–33). Westport, CT: Praeger.

Center for Research on Women With Disabilities. (2013). *Reproductive health information for women with disabilities.* Retrieved from https://www.bcm.edu/research/centers/research-on-women-with-disabilities/index.cfm?PMID=0

Centers for Disease Control and Prevention. (2013a). *Women with disabilities.* Retrieved from http://www.cdc.gov/ncbddd/disabilityandhealth/women.html

Centers for Disease Control and Prevention. (2013b). *Women with disabilities and breast cancer screening.* Retrieved from http://www.cdc.gov/features/breast cancer screening/

Clemency Cordes, C., Cameron, R. P., Mona, L. R., Syme, M. L., & Coble-Temple, A. (in press). Perspectives on disability within integrated healthcare. In L. A. Suzuki, M. Casas, C. Alexander, & M. Jackson (Eds.). *Handbook of multicultural counseling* (4th ed.). Thousand Oaks, CA: Sage.

Comas-Díaz, L. (2013). Culturally competent psychological interventions with women of color. In L. Comas-Díaz & B. Greene (Eds.), *Psychological health of women of color: Intersections, challenges, and opportunities* (pp. 373–407). Santa Barbara, CA: Praeger.

Corbett, C. A. (2003). Special issues in psychotherapy for minority Deaf women. In M. E. Banks & E. Kaschak (Eds.), *Women with visible and invisible disabilities: Multiple intersections, multiple issues, multiple therapies* (pp. 311–329). New York, NY: Haworth Press. doi:10.1300/J015v26n03_09

Corrigan, P. W., Watson, A. C., Heyrman, M. L., Warpinski, A., Gracia, G., Slopen, N., & Hall, L. L. (2005). Structural stigma in state legislation. *Psychiatric Services, 56,* 557–563. doi:10.1176/appi.ps.56.5.557

Cross, W. E. (1971). The Negro-to-Black conversion experience: Towards a psychology of Black liberation. *Black World, 20,* 13–27.

Dunn, D. S., & Burcaw, S. (2013). Disability identity: Exploring narrative accounts of disability. *Rehabilitation Psychology, 58,* 148–157. doi:10.1037/a0031691

Erickson, W., Lee, C., & von Schrader, S. (2013). *Disability statistics from the 2011 American Community Survey.* Ithaca, NY: Cornell University Employment and Disability Institute. Retrieved from http://www.disabilitystatistics.org

Evans-Campbell, T., Fredriksen-Goldsen, K. I., Walters, K. L., & Stately, A. (2005). Caregiving experiences among American Indian two-spirit men and women: Contemporary and historical roles. *Journal of Gay & Lesbian Social Services: Issues in Practice, Policy & Research, 18*(3–4), 75–92.

Feldman, S. I., & Tegart, G. (2003). Keep moving: Conceptions of illness and disability of middle-aged African-American women with arthritis. In M. E. Banks & E. Kaschak (Eds.), *Women with visible and invisible disabilities: Multiple intersections, multiple issues, multiple therapies* (pp. 127–143). New York, NY: Haworth Press. doi:10.1300/J015v26n01_08

Fetzer Institute. (1999). *Multidimensional measurement of religiousness/spirituality for use in health research.* Kalamazoo, MI: Author.

Fredriksen-Goldsen, K. I., & Erera, P. I. (2003). Lesbian-headed stepfamilies. *Journal of Human Behavior in the Social Environment, 8,* 171–187. doi:10.1300/J137v08n02_11

Fredriksen-Goldsen, K. I., & Farwell, N. (2005). Dual responsibilities among Black, Hispanic, Asian, and White employed caregivers. *Journal of Gerontological Social Work, 43,* 25–44. doi:10.1300/J083v43n04_03

Fredriksen-Goldsen, K. I., & Hooyman, N. R. (2005). Caregiving research, services, and policies in historically marginalized communities: Where do we go from here? *Journal of Gay & Lesbian Social Services: Issues in Practice, Policy & Research, 18*(3–4), 129–145. doi:10.1300/J041v18n03_08

Fredriksen-Goldsen, K. I., Kim, H.-J., & Barkan, S. E. (2012). Disability among lesbian, gay, and bisexual adults: Disparities in prevalence and risk. *American Journal of Public Health, 102,* e16–e21. doi:10.2105/AJPH.2011.300379

Fredriksen-Goldsen, K. I., Kim, H.-J., Muraco, A., & Mincer, S. (2009). Chronically ill midlife and older lesbians, gay men, and bisexuals and their informal caregivers: The impact of the social context. *Sexuality Research & Social Policy, 6*(4), 52–64. doi:10.1525/srsp.2009.6.4.52

Garland-Thompson, R. (2002). Integrating disability, transforming Feminist theory. *National Women's Studies Association Journal, 14*(H), 1–32.

Gharaibeh, N. (2009). Disability in Arab societies. In C. A. Marshall, E. Kendall, M. E. Banks, & R. M. S. Gover (Eds.), *Disabilities: Insights from across fields and around the world: Vol. 1. The experience: Definitions, causes, and consequences* (pp. 63–79). Westport, CT: Praeger.

Gibson, J. (2009). Navigating societal norms: The psychological implications of living in the United States with a disability. In C. A. Marshall, E. Kendall, M. E. Banks, & R. M. S. Gover (Eds.), *Disabilities: Insights from across fields and around the world: Vol. 2. The context: Environmental, social, and cultural considerations* (pp. 139–150). Westport, CT: Praeger.

Gill, C. J. (1987). A social perspective on disability and its implications for rehabilitation. *Occupational Therapy in Health Care, 4,* 49–55.

Gover, R. M. S. (2009). "I thought I was going to live forever." In C. A. Marshall, E. Kendall, M. E. Banks, & R. M. S. Gover (Eds.), *Disabilities: Insights from across fields and around the world: Vol. 1. The experience: Definitions, causes, and consequences* (pp. 123–128). Westport, CT: Praeger.

Helms, J. E. (Ed.). (1990). *Black and White racial identity: Theory, research, and practice.* New York, NY: Greenwood Press.

Iezzoni, L. I. (2006). Make no assumptions: Communication between persons with disabilities and clinicians. *Assistive Technology, 18,* 212–219. doi:10.1080/10400435.2006.10131920

Iezzoni, L. I. (2011). Eliminating health and health care disparities among the growing population of people with disabilities. *Health Affairs, 30,* 1947–1954. doi:10.1377/hlthaff.2011.0613

Jacobsen, F. M. (2013). Psychopharmacological treatment and women of color. In L. Comas-Díaz & B. Greene (Eds.), *Psychological health of women of color: Intersections, challenges, and opportunities* (pp. 167–183). Santa Barbara, CA: Praeger.

Kim, H.-J., & Fredriksen-Goldsen, K. I. (2012). Hispanic lesbians and bisexual women at heightened risk for health disparities. *American Journal of Public Health, 102,* e9–e15. doi:10.2105/AJPH.2011.300378

Kitabchi, A. E., Umpierrez, G. E., Miles, J. M., & Fisher, J. N. (2009). Hyperglycemic crises in adult patients with diabetes. *Diabetes Care, 32,* 1335–1343. doi:10.2337/dc09-9032

Klein, D., Najman, J., Kohrman, A. F., & Munro, C. (1982). Patient characteristics that elicit negative responses from family physicians. *The Journal of Family Practice, 14,* 881–888.

Lagu, T., Hannon, N. S., Rothberg, M. B., Wells, A. S., Green, K. L., Windom, M. O., . . . Lindenauer, P. K. (2013). Access to subspecialty care for patients with mobility impairment: A survey. *Annals of Internal Medicine, 158,* 441–446. doi:10.7326/0003-4819-158-6-201303190-00003

Leigh, W. A., & Huff, D. (2006). *Women of color health data book: Adolescents to seniors* (3rd ed., NIH Publication No. 06-4247). Bethesda, MD: Office of Research on Women's Health, National Institutes of Health.

Leung, P. (2013). Culture, disability, and caregiving for people with traumatic brain injury. In H. Muenchberger, E. Kendall, & J. Wright (Eds.), *Health and healing after traumatic brain injury: Understanding the power of family, friends, community, and other support systems* (pp. 217–226). Santa Barbara, CA: Praeger.

Lewis, A. N., Brubaker, S. J., & Armstrong, A. J. (2009). Gender and disability: A first look at rehabilitation syllabi and a call to action. *Review of Disability Studies, 5*(2), 3–14.

Lightfoot, E., Hill, K., & LaLiberte, T. (2010). The inclusion of disability as a condition for termination of parental rights. *Child Abuse & Neglect, 34,* 927–934. doi:10.1016/j.chiabu.2010.07.001

Marshall, C. A., Kendall, E., Banks, M. E., & Gover, R. M. S. (Eds.). (2009). *Disability: Insights from across fields and around the world* (Vols. 1–3). Westport, CT: Praeger.

Marshall, C. A., Kendall, E., Catalano, T., & Barnett, L. (2008). The spaces between: Partnerships between women researchers and indigenous women with disabilities. *Disability and Rehabilitation, 30,* 191–201. doi:10.1080/09638280701532276

McCaffery, M. & Ferrell, B. R. (1997). Nurses' knowledge of pain assessment and management: How much progress have we made? *Journal of Pain Symptom Management, 14,* 175–188.

McDonald, K. E., Keys, C. B., & Balcazar, F. E. (2009). Living with a learning disability and other marginalized statuses: A multilevel analysis. In C. A. Marshall, E. Kendall, M. E. Banks, & R. M. S. Gover (Eds.), *Disabilities: Insights from across fields and around the world: Vol. 1. The experience: Definitions, causes, and consequences* (pp. 177–192). Westport, CT: Praeger.

McNulty, K., Livneh, H., & Wilson, L. M. (2004). Perceived uncertainty, spiritual well-being, and psychosocial adaptation in individuals with multiple sclerosis. *Rehabilitation Psychology, 49,* 91–99. doi:10.1037/0090-5550.49.2.91

Mona, L. R., Syme, M. L., & Cameron, R. P. (2014). Sexuality and disability: A disability–affirmative approach to sex therapy. In Y. Binik & K. Hall (Eds.), *Principles and practice of sex therapy* (pp. 457–481). New York, NY: Guilford Press.

Mukherjee, D., Reis, J. P., & Heller, W. (2003). Women living with traumatic brain injury: Social isolation, emotional functioning and implications for psychotherapy. In M. E. Banks & E. Kaschak (Eds.), *Women with visible and invisible disabilities: Multiple intersections, multiple issues, multiple therapies* (pp. 3–26). New York. NY: Haworth Press. doi:10.1300/J015v26n01_01

Munyi, C. W. (2012). Past and present perceptions towards disability: A historical perspective. *Disability Studies Quarterly, 32*(2), 16.

Muraco, A., & Fredriksen-Goldsen, K. (2011). "That's what friends do": Informal caregiving for chronically ill midlife and older lesbian, gay, and bisexual adults. *Journal of Social and Personal Relationships, 28,* 1073–1092. doi:10.1177/0265407511402419

Murray Nettles, S. (2001). *Crazy visitation: A chronicle of illness and recovery.* Athens: University of Georgia Press.

Mwachofi, A. K., & Broyles, R. (2008). Is minority status a more consistent predictor of disability than socioeconomic status? *Journal of Disability Policy Studies, 19,* 34–43. doi:10.1177/1044207308315275

Nabors, N. A., & Pettee, M. F. (2003). Womanist therapy with African American women with disabilities. In M. E. Banks & E. Kaschak (Eds.), *Women with visible and invisible disabilities: Multiple intersections, multiple issues, multiple therapies* (pp. 331–341). New York, NY: Haworth. doi:10.1300/J015v26n03_10

Nazarov, Z., & Lee, C. G. (2012). *Disability statistics from the Current Population Survey.* Ithaca, NY: Cornell University Rehabilitation Research and Training Center on Disability Demographics and Statistics. Retrieved from http://www.disabilitystatistics.org

Nosek, M. A. (2010). Feminism and disability: Synchronous agendas in conflict. In H. Landrine & N. F. Russo (Eds.), *Handbook of diversity in feminist psychology* (pp. 501–533). New York, NY: Springer.

Nosek, M. A., & Hughes, R. B. (2003). Psychosocial issues of women with physical disabilities: The continuing gender debate. *Rehabilitation Counseling Bulletin, 46,* 224–233. doi:10.1177/003435520304600403

Olkin, R. (1999). *What psychotherapists should know about disability.* New York, NY: Guilford Press.

Olkin, R. (2002). Could you hold the door for me? Including disability in diversity. *Cultural Diversity and Ethnic Minority Psychology, 8,* 130–137. doi:10.1037/1099-9809.8.2.130

Olkin, R. (2009). Disability-affirmative therapy. In I. Marini & M. A. Stebnicki (Eds.), *The professional counselor's desk reference* (pp. 355–369). New York, NY: Springer.

Pedersen, P. B., Crethar, H. C., & Carlson, J. (2008). *Inclusive cultural empathy: Making relationships central in counseling and psychotherapy.* doi:10.1037/11707-005

Pledger, C. (2003). Discourse on disability and rehabilitation issues: Opportunities for psychology. *American Psychologist, 58,* 279–284. doi:10.1037/0003-066X.58.4.279

Post, J. M. (1995). *When illness strikes the leader: The dilemma of the captive king.* New Haven, CT: Yale University Press.

Post, J. M., & Robins, R. S. (1990). The captive king and his captive court: The psychopolitical dynamics of the disabled leader and his inner circle. *Political Psychology, 11,* 331–351. doi:10.2307/3791693

Poston, D. J., & Turnbull, A. P. (2004). Role of spirituality and religion in family quality of life for families of children with disabilities. *Education and Training in Developmental Disabilities, 39,* 95–108.

Poulin, C., & Gouliquer, L. (2003). Part-time disabled lesbian passing on roller blades or PMS, Prozac, and essentializing women's ailments. In M. E. Banks & E. Kaschak (Eds.), *Women with visible and invisible disabilities: Multiple intersections, multiple issues, multiple therapies* (pp. 95–108). New York, NY: Haworth Press.

Powers, L. E., Renker, P., Robinson-Whelen, S., Oschwald, M., Hughes, R., Swank, P., & Curry, M. A. (2009). Interpersonal violence and women with disabilities: Analysis of safety promoting behaviors. *Violence Against Women, 15*, 1040–1069. doi:10.1177/1077801209340309

Pressman, M. (2013, July 12). The myth of FDR's secret disability. *Time*. Retrieved from http://ideas.time.com/2013/07/12/the-myth-of-fdrs-secret-disability/

Puhl, R., & Brownell, K. D. (2001). Bias, discrimination, and obesity. *Obesity Research, 9*, 788–805. doi:10.1038/oby.2001.108

Riggle, E. D. B., Rostosky, S. S., Prather, R. A., & Hamrin, R. (2005). The execution of legal documents by sexual minority individuals. *Psychology, Public Policy, and Law, 11*, 138–163. doi:10.1037/1076-8971.11.1.138

Rohmer, O., & Louvet, E. (2009). Describing persons with disability: Salience of disability, gender, and ethnicity. *Rehabilitation Psychology, 54*, 76–82. doi:10.1037/a0014445

Salley, B. B. (2009). Excerpts From *Meditations of the heart on the workings (or not) of the hand*. In C. A. Marshall, E. Kendall, M. E. Banks, & R. M. S. Gover (Eds.), *Disabilities: Insights from across fields and around the world: Vol. 1. The experience: Definitions, causes, and consequences* (pp. 243–248). Westport, CT: Praeger.

Schriempf, A. (2001). (Re)fusing the amputated body: An interactionist bridge for feminism and disability. *Hypatia, 16*, 53–79. doi:10.1111/j.1527-2001.2001.tb00753.x

Smedley, B. D., Stith, A. Y., & Nelson, A. R. (Eds.). (2003). *Unequal treatment: Confronting racial and ethnic disparities in health care*. Washington, DC: National Academies Press.

Thierry, J. A., Turk, M., Panko-Reis, J., & Dennis, S. W. (2004). Framing the issues: What do we know? In *Breaking down barriers to health care for women with disabilities: A white paper from a national summit* (pp. 6–12). Washington, DC: National Center for Policy Research for Women and Families for the Office on Disability, U.S. Department of Health and Human Services.

U.S. Department of Health and Human Services. (2005). *The surgeon general's call to action to improve the health and wellness of persons with disabilities*. Retrieved from http://www.surgeongeneral.gov/library/disabilities/

U.S. Department of Justice. (2010). *Americans with Disabilities Act: Access to medical care for individuals with mobility disabilities*. Retrieved from http://www.hhs.gov/ocr/civilrights/understanding/disability/adamobilityimpairmentsgudiance.pdf

Watson, N., McKie, L., Hughes, B., Hopkins, D., & Gregory, S. (2004). (Inter) dependence, needs and care: The potential for disability and feminist theorists to develop an emancipatory model. *Sociology, 38*, 331–350. doi:10.1177/0038038504040867

Williams, M., & Upadhyay, W. S. (2003). To be or not be disabled. In M. E. Banks & E. Kaschak (Eds.), *Women with visible and invisible disabilities: Multiple intersections, multiple issues, multiple therapies* (pp. 145–154). New York, NY: Haworth Press.

World Health Organization. (2001). *International classification of functioning, disability and health*. Geneva, Switzerland: Author.

World Health Organization. (2013). *Disability and health* (Fact Sheet No. 352). Retrieved from http://www.who.int/mediacentre/factsheets/fs352/en/

Wright, B. (1960). *Physical disability: A psychological approach*. New York, NY: Harper & Row. doi:10.1037/10038-000

Young, L. M., & Powell, B. (1985). The effects of obesity on the clinical judgments of mental health professionals. *Journal of Health and Social Behavior, 26*, 233–246. doi:10.2307/2136755

8

PSYCHOLOGICAL PRACTICE WITH NATIVE WOMEN

WENDY M. K. PETERS, KEE J. E. STRAITS, AND PILAR E. GAUTHIER

Stay strong as I know you can. We native women are strong the elders tell us so; we have to be, to help not only the children, but the men who are busy getting food and protecting our homes and of course, we need to be strong for the next generation.

—Ojibwa Elder

Throughout North America, Native communities have historically experienced economic adversity, social dysfunction, and disparities in health and wellness when compared with most other majority populations. Moreover, the marginalization of Native peoples as a populace, the underappreciation of the significance of culture in psychological practice, and the dearth of Natives in research and wellness professions have too often resulted in misunderstanding, misdiagnoses, and mistreatment of Native persons. Consequently, to engage in appropriate psychological practice and increase the efficacy of treatment of Native women and girls, accurate depictions of lived experience are of critical importance.

For the purposes of this discussion, we clarify that our use of the terms *Indigenous*, *Natives*, *Native peoples*, and *Native Americans* predominantly refer to people who identify as American Indian (AI), Alaska Native (AN), or Native Hawaiian (NH). However, the broad blanket implied by the use of

http://dx.doi.org/10.1037/14460-008
Psychological Practice With Women: Guidelines, Diversity, Empowerment, C. Z. Enns, J. K. Rice, and R. L. Nutt (Editors)
Copyright © 2015 by the American Psychological Association. All rights reserved.

any one term does not imply notions of homogeneity among Native peoples. With well over 500 legally recognized tribal entities in the United States alone, and many more peoples both in the United States and its neighboring countries who ethnically identify as Native or Indigenous, we stress our assertion that they are as culturally distinctive from one another as they are numerous. Yet, AI, AN, and NH do share common threads within their worldviews. Some of these common beliefs include a sacred view of children, regard and esteem toward elder epistemology, a reverence for the place and environment, and a cosmological understanding for the natural order of things (King, 2009). Furthermore, because Native peoples do have differing histories, circumstances of acculturation, relations with the U.S. government, and core values that comprise their distinct worldviews, we are, at times, forced to make generalizations for the sake of brevity. This reality means that psychologists should use caution with regard to the ensuing characterizations of Native people.

The authors of this chapter, who are ourselves Native women representing different tribes, bring our lived experiences and our culturally authentic knowledge to bear on the American Psychological Association's (APA's) "Guidelines for Psychological Practice With Girls and Women" (2007), hereinafter referred to as the Guidelines. Our intercultural approach is representative of the many intersections present among different Native peoples. Throughout this chapter, we attempt to underscore the complexities introduced through ethnic diversity and to dispel the unrealistic assumption that any professional, even one of Native ethnicity, can be knowledgeable about every possible nuance of Native female psychology. Last, we note that in order to present a realistic portrayal of the many permutations and issues that are commonly seen in Indian Country, and to arrive at a better understanding of how Native cultures can influence the mental health of Native women and girls, we also include illustrative case studies.

For the vast majority of Native women and girls, whether they realize it or not, their lives are tied to particular historical realities. This chapter first provides an overview of this context, including the Native worldview and the sociocultural history of Native peoples. Particular aspects of note herein, such as historical trauma and colonization, spirituality, cultural diversity, tribal sovereignty, and violence, are mentioned because they have had a significant impact on the lives and well-being of Native peoples. We then provide specific recommendations for the application of the Guidelines with Native women and girls. We illustrate and discuss the many challenges that Native women or girls might typically experience, and we introduce the concepts of resilience and retraditionalization. These views demonstrate how the inherent strengths of Native women and the sustainable lifeways and ancient traditions of Native people, which are currently being rediscovered and revitalized among Native cultures, may provide a path for healing future generations.

CONTEXT AND UNDERPINNINGS OF A NATIVE WORLDVIEW

In order to conceptualize a Native worldview, it helps to start at the beginning. Tradition and history tell us that Native knowledge was conferred through ancient and sacred stories of origin, rich with pedagogy and archetypal personages. These Native myths were not fictitious but rather were the existents of collective memories that were cosmological, ontological, epistemological, and metaphysical in nature and indicative of the consciousness from which they came (Allen, 1992; Mohawk, 2006). Gregory Cajete (2000) stated that "worldviews are conveyed via mythology in informal, formal, unconscious, and conscious ways" (p. 62). Furthermore, the Native worldview is a construct of social and cultural mores that predate Western civilization and is divergent from Western ways of thinking (Deloria, 1993).

Throughout the Western hemisphere, there have long been imperialistic assumptions that interpret the Native worldview as primitive (Deloria, 1993), less developed, or not as complex as contemporary Western worldviews. The Native worldview is actually far more complex and developed than that of many Western and Eurocentric cultures (Peters, 2011). Beck (2006) asserted how the Native worldview is, in accordance with what has been termed *spiral dynamics*, an integral theory of human development that describes the constant flux and adaptation of one's worldview in relation to the context of one's environment. Founded on earth-based wisdoms, Native ways of knowing were conceived from the interconnected relationships with natural elements, cycles, and processes. Native epistemologies were also keenly attuned to the mystical and spiritual, perceptions that were achieved via nonordinary states of consciousness. Actions such as telepathic communication with entities that were other than human (e.g., spirits, animals, natural elements, inanimate objects such as rocks) and superhuman feats such as shape shifting or transmutation were considered commonplace in ancient times and all things that Native peoples integrated into their teaching (Arrows, Cajete, & Lee, 2010). This kind of deeper awareness into otherworldly realms was inherent, instinctual, and intuitive and reflected abilities that came only with a considerable insight and an intimate understanding of self and surroundings (Mohawk, 2006).

Culture, a somewhat broader concept, enacts a people's cosmological worldview and includes their notions of self-identity, beliefs, lifestyle, etiquette, history, language, and connection with their place or geography (Abrams & Primack, 2001; Hay, 1998). Also very relevant is an understanding of the ontological perspectives of Native people. *Monism*, a concept fundamental to most Native cultures, is the ontological philosophy that all things emanate from a single source and are thus connected. Considering this connection foundational to every relationship, *monism* underscores the values, beliefs, and behaviors characteristic of Native cultures and encompasses the sacred. As such, Native people seek to approach relationships in a positive way and tend to revere and honor relationships with family, ancestors, community, and the natural environment (Abrams & Primack, 2001; Hay, 1998). Belief in monism also fosters more spiritual, holistic, and ecological worldviews. Appreciating the significance with which these core values shape and inform the Native worldview helps psychologists and practitioners to foster the sense of cultural attunement necessary for effective and respectful interactions with Native people.

Cultural and Historical Background

Under the guise of good intentions, *manifest destiny* was a widely held belief of European settlers with imperialist ambitions that subsequently became the primary impetus for Western expansionism across America in the 1800s (Prucha, 1973). Based on the notion that the U.S. was destined to expand its democratic institutions, it assumed a superior moral right to govern others who were considered impediments to that end. The movement resulted in the annexation of many Western lands and territories, including Alaska and Hawaii. The Americans had followed the lead of their European predecessors, forging into the West, seizing preoccupied lands, and assimilating Native peoples, often by force (Segal & Stineback, 1977). The homelands, languages, and sovereignty of Native peoples were intentionally targeted for eradication in an effort to nullify Native culture (Lyons & Mohawk, 1998; Niezen, 2000).

Consequently, many historical and literary depictions, including those in today's popular media, still interpret Native peoples as they did on first Western contact hundreds of years ago. Less stereotypic and biased attitudes have evolved through the years, yet the reality is that the majority of information disseminated to the general public is often inaccurate, misleading, and largely based on demographic speculation or cultural misinterpretations about their current struggles. When Westerners first encountered Native peoples, they interpreted what they observed through a lens biased by their own cultural values and beliefs. As a result, early settlers operated under the assumption that Native peoples were primitive and barbaric (Wasson, 1973), and the newcomers set out to supplant Native culture with their own.

What ensued were widespread hegemonic policies and the forced assimilation of Native peoples. These oppressive practices completely disregarded the long-standing social and cultural structures that Native peoples had established over many generations and, in some cases, even millennia (Campbell & Evans-Campbell, 2011). Not only did these actions severely disrupt the continuity of Native cultures, but as the colonizers became the

dominant culture, so too did their beliefs and attitudes. Likewise, their inter-
pretations about the behaviors and beliefs of peoples who were entirely foreign to their scope of understanding became the prototypical examples and
the basis for the stereotypes and ideals about Native peoples that prevail to
this day (Campbell & Evans-Campbell, 2011).

The Western values imposed on Native peoples were detrimental and
often irreparably changed the sexual landscape for Native peoples by altering
many of the traditional male–female interactions, gender roles, and expectations that were inextricably tied to their culture and identity as individuals,
communities, and societies (Evans-Campbell, Fredriksen-Goldsen, Walters,
& Stately, 2005). Prior to colonization, individual tribes had histories of
matriarchal or patriarchal societal structures. Irrespective of those established
societal structures, Ella Deloria (Yankton Dakota) contended that traditionally, work among men and women was divided equally despite the difference
or nature of the work (Fitzgerald & Fitzgerald, 2005). The balance of power
between men and women was also relatively equal. In other words, regardless of
political structure, Native women were not disadvantaged in comparison with
men. However, Native women today may experience a wide range of differences in their status that can change depending on kinship, tribal enrollment–
membership rules, socioeconomics, and the prevailing gender ideology relative
to men (Fiske, 1995; Lawrence, 2003).

For Native peoples, differences in gender were really more about cultural forms and function. For example, women were considered sacred in
their capacity for generativity and childbirth. Transgendered individuals
were recognized and appreciated as being with two spirits, a gender role more
centered in spirituality than sexuality (Wilson, 1996). Gender incongruence,
as in third- or fourth-gender persons, was not judged as anomalous behavior.
Instead, Two-Spirit people were often revered as sacred within a given community, combined elements of male and female behavior, and fulfilled specific
spiritual roles within their respective cultures (Woodsum, 1995). However,
with changing times have also come changes in attitudes. Today, the acceptance and tolerance of Two-Spirit people can vary widely among Natives.
No longer cloistered among their communities, Native gays and lesbians
will often blend traditional concepts of Indian identity with contemporary
definitions of gay/lesbian identity and can be found on reservations, in urban
settings, and everywhere in between (Walters, Evans-Campbell, Simoni,
Ronquillo, & Bhuyan, 2006). Thus although some of the advice in this chapter may apply to psychological practice with Two-Spirit people, there is little
in the scholarly literature on contemporary Native gays and lesbians, and it
is a topic significant enough for a separate discussion.

Subsequently, in the cultural upheaval brought about by colonization,
White males assumed dominance while Native females forfeited all rights

and heritability to leadership and were forcibly moved into passive roles of servitude (Wasson, 1973). Additionally, the near eradication of the traditional family systems espoused by Native peoples brought about a loss of purpose to members within those familial compositions (Baldridge, 2001; Campbell & Evans-Campbell, 2011). The communal-family-centric systems that had permitted Native peoples to thrive and sustain themselves within their natural environments ceased to function and were supplanted with Western approaches to "proper" child-rearing, "civilized" culture, and Christian missionary teachings (Unger, 1977; Wasson, 1973).

The usurpation of cultural practice, traditional values, and family structures soon gave way to the forced removal of children from their families throughout the early 1800s to mid-1900s (Baldridge, 2001). Native children were literally roped and dragged, like cattle, to Christian boarding schools and missions (Unger, 1977). Many Native children were forced to accept foreign methods of teaching, language, and concepts (Szasz, 2003). Isolated from their families and seldom permitted contact, thousands of Native children died under horrifying conditions that spawned physical illness, brutality, and heartbreak (Baldridge, 2001; Unger, 1977). These actions would also have dire consequences for the future, such as the many disparities in health, education, and economic prosperity that now exist among Native peoples, which are discussed in greater detail later in this chapter.

With the loss of their children, the cycle of imperialism was ensconced. Weeping mothers and grandmothers were left without purpose. The fear, hopelessness, and helplessness among the men, once warriors and protectors, rendered them powerless against the sheer numbers and weaponry of the U.S. government (White, Godfrey, & Iron Moccasin, 2006). The intergenerational family system that had once fostered relationships and cultivated sustainable societies had suffered a trauma of such magnitude that it wounded Native peoples to the depth of their souls, broke their spirits, and annihilated their respective indigenous nations (Duran, 2006).

Historical Trauma, Intergenerational Trauma, and Soul Wounding

Although many societies throughout history have experienced hegemony, conquest, and even genocide, the wake of the trauma and the aftermath for Native peoples have been similar despite the heterogeneity among their cultures. Having previously noted spirituality and connectedness as fundamental values within the Native worldview, Peters (2011) asserted that the similarities in outcomes for AI, AN, and NH peoples are due to the attempted extermination of those people's most vital core value, monism, or what can be interpreted as the potential severance from their source of Spirit. Given a belief in connectedness that has been culturally engrained and embodied over countless generations, the progeny of AI, AN, and NH peoples are still bereft with the same deep spiritual wounding. As a consequence, this intergenerational phenomenon has not only pervaded all of their relations but also must be factored into present day outcomes (Peters, 2011).

Now recognized as one of the most dominant narratives throughout Indian Country, historical trauma (HT), also known as intergenerational trauma (IT), is considered a major etiological agent in relation to the social determinants of health and well-being among Native populations (Walters et al., 2011). Yet, others view HT/IT as an outcome of societal oppression and marginalization, and this perspective is consistent with the emphasis of Guidelines 2 and 3 with regard to recognizing how oppression and bias affect women and girls. Regardless of etiology or outcome, the symptoms of HT/IT are too often mistaken for individual pathologies or incorrectly interpreted as something more acute such as posttraumatic stress disorder, which is both insufficient and inappropriate for addressing all the attendant complexities introduced by this intergenerational constellation of features.

Prior to Western integration, the societal conditions that now plague Native communities were almost nonexistent (Brave Heart & DeBruyn, 1998). The fact is that all across the Western hemisphere, the process of colonization impacted Native peoples by instigating a scenario of assimilation that has since had disastrous consequences for the biopsychosocial outcomes of Native descendants. Today, most Native communities subsist within ecologies that have spawned alarming rates of health disparities and a dearth of prosperity that rivals most third-world countries. Yet, in order to appreciate just how pervasive HT/IT is among Native peoples and their communities, a recounting of historical events from a Native perspective is imperative.

Among the first to identify this phenomenon among Native peoples, Duran (2006; Duran & Duran, 1995) coined the term *indigenous soul wound*, a wound long recognized by Native American elders as "spiritual injury, soul sickness, soul wounding, and ancestral hurt" (Duran, 2006, p. 15). Duran and Duran (1995) initially characterized the indigenous soul wound as a "common thread . . . that weaves across much of the pain and suffering found in the Native American community across the United States and perhaps the entire Western Hemisphere" (p. 24). Similarly, Brave Heart's research (2003; Brave Heart-Jordan, 1995) compared the outcomes of Jewish holocaust survivors and their descendants with the widespread impaired grief associated with the historic, cumulative, massive group traumas perpetrated against her tribe, the Lakota Sioux.

Whereas Duran (2006; Duran & Duran, 1995) recognized that the Native soul wounding prevailed in epidemic proportions, Brave Heart's groundbreaking research evidenced something far more complex. Introducing a new dimension and deeper insights into a long-standing systemic issue,

Brave Heart (1995, 2003), in collaboration with DeBruyn (Brave Heart & DeBruyn, 1998), asserted that unresolved grief and its associated attendants are intergenerational in nature and, if left unresolved, will be transmitted epigenetically and memetically, even to those without direct exposure to the original trauma. HT/IT may also pervade whole communities and even entire societies (Brave Heart, 2003).

More than anecdotal, the intergenerational aspects of trauma have been evidenced by recent scientific findings and new understandings in relation to epigenetics. Defined as heritable changes in gene expression caused by functionally relevant modifications to the genome that do not involve altering the underlying DNA sequence, epigenetics offers conclusive evidence of how biophysiological mechanisms can enable the effects of parents' experiences to be passed down to subsequent generations, potentially lasting for multiple generations (González-Pardo & Pérez Álvarez, 2013; Jablonka & Lamb, 2002). This argument is based on the fact that gene expressions are passed from one generation to the next via pathways that involve the same kinds of modifications in gene expression that are seen in tissue differentiation (Harper, 2005). Further, Harvell and Tollrian (1999) identified specific prerequisites for the development of what they called *inducible defenses*, which can also be characterized as adaptive behavior. In the case of Native peoples, long-term oppression (a well-documented aspect of colonization) is a prerequisite that meets the criteria for epigenetic transmission (Harper, 2005).

Similarly, social scientists reference *memes*, or cultural items transmitted by repetition in a manner analogous to the biological transmission of genes (Dawkins, 1976). *Memetics*, the study of memes, demonstrates how cultural elements are passed on from generation to generation. Spiral dynamics integral theory asserts that a particular set of values and entire belief systems are relayed via memetic transmission. These concepts also explain how an entire society can be affected by events and circumstances that occurred in its past (Beck, 2006). Propagated and transmitted across the ecologies of the mind, the memes and epigenetic character of their ancestry may still be present within Native culture and genetics. Despite alterations in appearance over time and changes in Native ways and experiences, the legacy of antiquity persists and is literally embodied by the descendants of AI, AN, and NH.

CONSIDERATIONS AND SPECIFIC CONCERNS REGARDING NATIVE PEOPLE

Because of the considerable diversity across tribes and the small proportion of Native women compared with the general U.S. population, accurate epidemiological data on Native peoples is lacking. This omission undermines the general visibility and awareness of the severity of public health issues affecting this group. Likewise, there is a serious paucity of statistically significant outcome studies on appropriate treatments and interventions that can help practitioners to understand fully and apply to Native populations (Gone & Trimble, 2012). Without large-scale outcome studies and with only a few evidence-based programs that even address and treat health disorders among Native populations, there is also very little comprehensive data available on violence against women who fall under tribal jurisdiction (U.S. Department of Health and Human Services, 2005).

For most Native people, a majority of the salient issues impacting their well-being can be traced back to the introduction of unnatural lifeways brought about through colonization (Allen, 1985). Many scholars also suggest that violence against AI/AN women directly relates to their historical victimization, in that the domination and oppression of Native peoples makes them even more susceptible to internalized oppression and victimization (Bubar & Thurman, 2004). These dynamics also serve to increase economic deprivation and dependency while at the same time eroding tribal rights and sovereignty (Gone & Trimble, 2012).

Considered as having *sovereign status*, Native persons associated with federally recognized tribes potentially fall under a different set of legal rights than most other Americans. This confusing division of authority among tribal, federal, and state governments presents a nightmare of jurisdictional complexity that further limits any tribal court criminal jurisdiction over non-Natives. Many of the laws enacted to protect sovereign Natives do not apply to non-Natives who commit acts of domestic violence on Indian reservations and render non-Natives virtually immune from prosecution because they are not sovereign subjects. As a result, in 1994, the Federal Crime Control Bill supported the development of the Violence Against Women Act to strengthen the reach and prosecution strategies and options for law enforcement in combating violence against AI women and children, as well as to enhance victim services involving violent crimes against women (Perry, 2004). It should be noted that NHs were disenfranchised of their sovereign status. Thus, under U.S. law, they are afforded the same rights and protections as any American citizen and are not recognized as a protected class, leaving them vulnerable to exploitation.

Subsequently, data have emerged regarding the effectiveness of local, state, and federal responses to violence against AI women, indicating that it still occurs and affects a devastating proportion of women. A 2004 U.S. Department of Justice report estimated that AI women residing on reservations suffer domestic violence and physical assault at rates as much as 50% higher than the next most victimized demographic, far exceeding women of other ethnicities and locations (Perry, 2004). According to the Centers for

Disease Control and Prevention (CDC), 39% of Native women surveyed self-identified as victims of intimate partner violence (Black & Breiding, 2008). Similarly, another CDC study found that AI/AN women ($N = 8,000$) were from the racial group most likely to report a physical assault by an intimate partner (Tjaden & Thoennes, 2000).

At least 70% of the violent victimizations experienced by AIs are committed by persons not of the same race, a rate 5 times that of interracial violence involving other racial groups. According to the U.S. Department of Justice, AI/ANs experience interracial violence at a substantially higher rate than White or Black victims (Greenfield & Smith, 1999). Additionally, AI/AN women are more than 2.5 times (5 vs. 2 per 1,000) more likely to be raped or sexually assaulted than other women in the United States (Perry, 2004). Spanning a spectrum of violence that ranges between verbal abuse and murder, most AI women do not even report incidents of violent crimes because they believe nothing will be done (Amnesty International, 2007). Even fewer data are available about the incidence of violence occurring among the NH population. Their small numbers are often combined with data from much larger ethnic groups such as Asians or other Pacific Islanders. Nonetheless, the few agencies that do report statistical data relating to NH persons indicate that NH victimization is similar to that of AI or AN victimization (Yoshihama & Dabby, 2009).

Cultural Considerations for Existing Guidelines

The current Guidelines (APA, 2007) are aspirational, ethical, and helpful for the professional development of psychologists who practice within contemporary Western culture and who engage with clients who can also appreciate those perspectives. However, in applying the specific practice guidelines to treating individuals who may not espouse or appreciate the inherent values of Western society, a process of interpretation and adaptation needs to occur. Thus, a few notes and comments follow about the cultural adaptation or interpretation of some of the guidelines.

Guidelines 1 to 3 pertain to diversity, social context, and power. Guideline 1 may be interpreted as developing an awareness and understanding of the considerable history and background that impact Native people, as well as the specific culture of the individual client. Despite an individual's level of acculturation or knowledge of her or his own heritage, especially for Native individuals, it is often just a matter of time before the cultural traits and behavioral expressions passed on through epigenetic and memetic transmission become evident in personality and within the social context of community. Guideline 2 emphasizes recognizing and utilizing information about oppression, privilege, and identity development. Guideline 3 relates to the impact of bias and discrimination on physical and mental health, and here psychologists should be mindful that Native peoples, at present, represent the most impoverished demographics anywhere in the United States.

Guidelines 4 and 5 make reference to professional responsibility. Cultural sensitivity, with consideration and respect for local norms and mores, is the key to Guideline 4. Psychologists should keep in mind that some cultural values and traditions may be incongruent with Western style values or traditions. For example, many Native communities regard children as sacred beings, and families consider them to be a gift. This is not to say young mothers are encouraged to bear children thoughtlessly; however, when a child is born, even an unplanned child, women from Native cultures have traditionally been prepared for and embrace motherhood. Take the case of a young woman who recently lost her younger sister to an alcohol overdose and whose parents were battling lifelong heroin addictions. When she became pregnant, psychologists applying Western values and perspectives were concerned about the well-being of the baby. The reality was that the baby actually motivated the family toward stabilization. They believed the baby was a gift meant to replace the sister who had passed, and the new mother was adamant about honoring that gift through pursuing her general equivalency diploma (GED) and continuing her sobriety.

Guideline 5, recognizing how one's own socialization, attitudes, and knowledge about gender may affect one's practice, should serve to remind psychologists that their way may not always be the best way or the right way to approach or resolve an issue. The perception associated with a woman's menstrual cycle provides an excellent example relevant to Guideline 5. In Western cultures, the female menstrual cycle has often carried a negative connotation. Westerners who are socialized to regard menses as anything but sacred have historically interpreted Native cultural practices and beliefs around menses in a similar way. Noting that Native women are often excluded from participation or even being present at certain sacred ceremonies and rituals, Western ethnographers have posited it was because menstruating women were unclean or contaminated. Yet, the reality is quite the opposite. A woman's ability to regularly experience considerable blood loss and recovery is understood as a generative, transformative, spiritual power. It is also seen as a time when feminine power is highly amplified. Likewise, possessing a power so great as to birth new life, it follows that such great powers may potentially weaken another's power (e.g., those attending the ceremonies and rituals). In some cases, such power could even bring harm, or worse, take life rather than give it (Allen, 1992; Fitzgerald & Fitzgerald, 2005; Kameeleihiwa, 1999).

The remaining six guidelines relate to practice applications. Guideline 6, which encourages employing interventions and approaches found to be effective with women and girls, should definitely involve incorporating traditional alternatives into the mix of treatments when possible, such as how to engage a girl during her first menstrual cycle. Further, cultural treatment alternatives should not be immediately disregarded. When it comes to Native people, there is a dearth of evidence-based treatments (EBTs) that have been tested specifically with Native individuals. The call for EBTs initially brought responses that questioned their validity for ethnic minorities (Bernal & Scharron-del-Rio, 2001; Nagayama Hall, 2001). As research has evolved, there is growing evidence to suggest that some EBTs (e.g., for depression) are generalizable to African American and Latino communities (Huey & Polo, 2008; Miranda et al., 2005), yet there remains a gap in our understanding of EBTs for Native Americans. To date, only two treatments, one for older Native Americans with depression and one targeting Native youth suicide, have met the requirements to be considered EBTs (Gone & Alcántara, 2007). A few others, such as Project Venture, which targets substance use among Native youth, have not made it into the research literature, although they are listed on the Substance Abuse and Mental Health Services Administration National Registry of Evidence-Based Programs and Practices. The scant literature then makes it challenging to apply Guideline 6 for Native women and girls.

As Gone and Alcántara (2007) pointed out, an additional challenge in considering EBTs for Native populations arises from the historical context of colonization. Some contend that EBTs simply perpetuate colonizing practices in the therapy room, whereas others argue for the importance of accountability when practitioners provide treatment to Native populations. Proponents of EBTs for Natives emphasize the importance of culturally adapted treatments. There is also evidence pointing to the greater effectiveness of culturally adapted treatments for racial–ethnic groups over standard EBTs (Griner & Smith, 2006), and the handful of EBTs for Natives share this characteristic. Although most treatment for Natives is not empirically supported, the argument for cultural relevance holds strong. For example, Hazel and Mohatt (2001) found that a number of programs involving cultural and spiritual processes had a positive impact on AN sobriety as well as being key to the prevention of AN alcohol abuse and addiction. Similarly, cognitive–behavioral interventions, in combination with spiritual and sociocultural components, create more cultural congruency, such as the AI adaptation for trauma-focused care (BigFoot & Schmidt, 2010). Thus, we recommend seeking culturally specific consultation in conjunction with the application of an EBT to increase the likelihood of effective treatment with Native women and girls. Additionally, we propose that therapists reconsider how therapy (and the therapist) may be viewed by the Native client within a history of domination and cultural loss. Opening oneself to community-centered approaches to wellness for women and girls rather than fixating on individual treatments may better address the larger sociocultural processes that maintain illness despite the lack of evidence.

Suggestions for interpreting Guidelines 7, 8, and 9 are similar to those offered for Guidelines 4 and 5. For issues relating to initiative, empowerment, unbiased assessments, diagnoses, and the problems presented through sociopolitical context, local norms and mores must be taken into consideration. Often, simply understanding the Native American experience and how it relates to contemporary Native American families will provide a fresh perspective and context for their struggles in therapy. Likewise, because some cultural values and traditions may be incongruent with Western style values or traditions, emphasis should be on the best interest and benefit of clients and their community.

A case making recent headlines aptly illustrates both sides of a difficult situation and pertains to issues such as those denoted by Guidelines 7, 8, and 9. The "Baby Veronica" case references the adoption of a Native child (Cherokee). After years and a series of reversals and appeals, the case has yet to come to an end. However, the U.S. Supreme Court did finally award custody of Baby Veronica to her adoptive parents, who prevailed over the child's biological father and against the jurisdiction of the Cherokee Nation. Contesting the validity of the case, which was brought under the Indian Child Welfare Act (ICWA), one of the most important AI laws ever enacted, were more than 20,000 well-intentioned people who signed the "Save Veronica" petition calling for an amendment to ICWA that would prevent the return of children like Veronica (Zug, 2012). Likewise, given the biased media coverage in favor of the adoptive parents and the impassioned public response, it is fair to assume that a culturally uninformed psychological professional consulting for a case such as this might empathize with public sentiment and jump to a similar conclusion. In fact, many psychologists did just that and were among those who signed the petition and sent letters to the court in favor of the adoptive parents.

Yet, despite the court's decision, the biological father's plea as well as the tribe's interest held considerable merit of their own and involved a number of issues relating to Guidelines 7, 8 and 9—initiative, empowerment, unbiased assessments, diagnoses, and problematic sociopolitical context. Support for the biological father was expressed by many major Indian and child welfare organizations that were in opposition to upholding the adoption—including four ethnic minority psychological associations. Moreover, the Cherokee tribe's enforcement of ICWA was intended expressly for situations such as this. Enacted in 1978 "to protect the best interests of Indian children and promote the stability and security of Indian tribes and families," it also recognizes and attempts to rectify the history of forced removal of AI children from their families and tribes.

Given that many Natives continue to struggle and recover from the egregious history that systematically removed countless AI children from their homes, families, and tribes, and placed them for adoption, never to return, neither healing nor amelioration can occur as long as the majority culture prevails and Natives continue to lose their children. Thus, to ensure a tribe's control over its children and its future, ICWA must also apply to voluntary adoptions as well (Zug, 2012). The preceding example indeed poses a dilemma for anyone's ethics, but it also serves to underscore the dire necessity of being fully informed as well as being aware of and limiting personal bias when working across cultures.

Guidelines 10 and 11 are similar in that they relate to client advocacy. Relevant education, community resources, and social change of institutional and systemic bias are all worthy pursuits and much needed when working with Native communities. The important thing to keep in mind regarding these guidelines and Native people is that much help is needed, while too few resources are available. Quite recently, community-based participatory programs for service, advocacy, research, and social change have begun to spring up throughout Native enclaves. Founded on principles of self-determination and healing, these programs need allies, advocates, and supporters. As professionals in caregiving, psychologists can help by getting informed, and involved and by collaborating with Native programs and communities to aid in the efforts of self-determination and healing.

Where Guidelines and Theory Meet Practice

Although fictitious, the depictions that follow are composites of individuals who are representative of the many issues and the complexity frequently encountered when working with Native women. They are examples that are intended to inform practitioners and help dispel potential misconceptions that may occur as a result of cultural misinterpretations or miscommunication. Embedded within the narratives, one can also see where values, beliefs, and customs can and do intersect among Native cultures.

The case scenarios that follow are of two different Native women, each demonstrating the challenges described in this chapter. The first case study is designed to illustrate the complexity and intergenerational nature of issues that a psychologist may encounter when working with women from Native communities. The second case study provides more in-depth information and is based on a real-life example of lived Native experience. Further, it is an example of some of the challenges that a non-Native or a less experienced therapist may come up against in the course of everyday practice with Natives. The case is followed by a discussion of some of the mistakes or therapeutic choices that could be problematic, as well as considerations on how the Guidelines might be applied to support more effective treatment.

Case Scenario One: Carla

Carla is a 30-year-old Native American woman who referred herself for family therapy after discovering that her only daughter, Melissa, had been molested by a family member on her husband Joe's side. Concerned with understanding the effects of the molestation on her daughter, Carla sought counsel in an effort to help her support her daughter in healing and to learn how to protect her from further harm. She also hoped to find support for herself in processing her anger and feelings of betrayal directed towards Joe's family.

When the incident of molestation first came to light, Carla confided in Joe and then in his sister. However, neither responded to the situation as she had assumed they should. Joe was reticent. Unlike Carla, he did not want to "make waves" with his family or confront his relative. He also felt they should just leave the issue alone and allow it to subside. Joe's sister, although sympathetic about the incident, also echoed Joe's sentiments. Joe's family were members of Tribe A and had a very traditional background. Joe's tribal community, although small, maintained its language and traditional cultural and spiritual practices. The community's success in maintaining a strong culture was enabled by a cohesive communal bond that protected it from destructive external influences. Yet, that same communal characteristic also left Joe's tribe vulnerable to internal conflicts that had been suppressed for the sake of preserving tradition. They viewed themselves as a quiet, simple, demure people who seldom reacted strongly or got too excited about the happenings surrounding them, whether positive or negative.

Originally from the South, Carla's family were members of Tribe B, otherwise said to be "tribally enrolled." However, the Indian Relocation Act moved Carla's parents to an urban area where there were more job opportunities. Her family's subsequent detachment from Tribe B's community, relatives, and cultural roots led to a less traditional upbringing. Raised in the city, Carla could be considered an "urban Indian" because she had become fully acculturated to a mainstream American lifestyle. Carla's daughter was not Joe's biological child. Pregnant at 15, Carla was a child who had given birth to a child. She had been married to Joe for 12 years, and her daughter, now 14, had been raised by Joe since she was 2 years old, making him the only father figure she had ever known.

When Carla learned about what had happened to her daughter, she immediately questioned her own feelings and reactions. Joe's muted reaction also cast doubt on her sense of judgment, reasoning, and her relationship with him. As a child, Carla had been abused by a relative, and she was very aware of her own unresolved issues. In fact, although sexually active during her teens with boys of similar age, Carla actually suspected her daughter might have been conceived when Carla was molested by the relative who had abused her while she was growing up. Realizing that the cycle she had lived through was playing out all over again in her daughter's life, Carla was struggling to find resolution for herself and her daughter.

Therapeutic Considerations in the Case of Carla

The complexities in Carla's situation first require the considerable clinical expertise necessary for addressing sexual abuse. Furthermore, trauma, parental guilt, and an appreciation for the entangled web of family relationships necessitate a depth of cultural understanding (Guideline 9) that is unbiased (Guideline 8) and, most important, recognizes the psychologist's own socialization, attitudes, and knowledge about gender (Guideline 5) so as not to unwittingly further oppression and perpetuate historical traumas. The therapist who does an initial intake and assessment will want to consider the Guidelines (APA, 2007) in light of the information specific to Native communities, including tribal diversity, cultural values, historical trauma, and violence, in order to formulate a treatment plan.

Tribal Diversity

A traditional intake and assessment does not often include detailed information about the ethnocultural backgrounds of clients beyond a checked box. Additionally, if the therapist only went so far as to accept the checked box stating that all family members identified as "American Indian," she would neglect to discover tribal affiliations, enrollment status, levels of acculturation, cultural traditions and values, and involvement of each family member, and how the diversity among Native peoples may be relevant to a more accurate, nuanced assessment.

The astute therapist knew that Carla's Tribe B had historically been matriarchal. On the other hand, Joe's Tribe A, after an extended history of influence with the Spanish, was patriarchal. In keeping with Guideline 5, the therapist could appreciate how important it was to understand Carla's cultural identity and values, and how they might influence her perceptions and role as a mother and wife. Similarly, the therapist wondered whether the different tribal values, histories, and levels of acculturation influenced both parents in their responses, the limits they felt, and the solutions they envisioned. For example, several barriers may be present given the family's differing tribal affiliations and enrollment status.

In Tribe A, men are generally the ones in positions of leadership and acknowledged as the decision-makers. The direct confrontation of males in positions of authority or leadership is considered culturally inappropriate. In Tribe A, men also have ownership of property. Thus, if Carla were to separate from or divorce Joe, she and her daughter would lose both their home and right to live with Tribe A. Roles and expectations for women in Tribe A are distinct from those in Tribe B and will also need to be explored.

Tribal enrollment is significant in that it regulates social access to support resources and greatly influences the cultural identity development of Native people. For example, some tribes will not allow nonenrolled members to engage in forms of spiritual support because of taboos around some religious and ceremonial aspects of life. As a consequence, Carla's position as an outsider to her husband's tribe limits her ability to find allies within Tribe A and to access their community support systems. Melissa is even more limited, having no tribal affiliation. It is likely that her identity as a Native woman and her relationship with both Tribe A and Tribe B add more levels of complexity to understanding her experience of molestation at an age at which identity takes center stage in psychosocial development.

Understanding the extent of diversity among tribal cultures and how that may affect each person's perspective, range of choices, and consequences for future actions is critical for effective counseling or in forming a plan for treatment. Likewise, taking the family's diverse heritage into account should also include the strengths present within the situation. For example, Joe is well respected and deeply involved in Tribe A's religious ceremonies. Carla is a well-spoken professional woman who has managed to blend into her husband's community very well for many years. Melissa has been raised in a stable, two-parent, loving household that has successfully integrated traditional and acculturated Native lifeways.

Cultural Views, Values, and Spirituality

In keeping with Guideline 8, it is especially important when working with Native peoples to explore the underlying cultural values that may be influencing individual actions and perceptions of events. A psychologist lacking insight into her or his own socialization and biases (Guideline 5) might immediately empathize with Carla, an individual with values more reflective of dominant culture. On the other hand, Joe might be perceived as resistant, enabling, uncaring, or promoting oppression against girls and women. In Carla's case, one value that may impact Carla's or Joe's view of their daughter's molestation is the differing emphasis on and experience of community and cohesion in familial relationships. Tribes and Native individuals might demonstrate these core values in different ways depending on their individual and tribal histories, as well as their current positioning within the greater society. For instance, with 850 members currently living on the reservation, Joe's community demonstrates its emphasis on community and relationships in ways such as participating in frequent public dances in which all members of the tribe are in some way involved, or more privately, such as through the understanding that one does not speak of events that could cause deep disruption among families when the tribe's very existence is dependent on the cohesion of the group.

Already detached from her own tribe's culture through urban relocation, Carla had often found herself in conflict when having to make decisions such as keeping her daughter in school for an important exam or taking her out to participate in the tribe's ceremonial day. In this case, understanding the value of community and cohesion in protecting tribal existence would be important in being able to appreciate Joe's perspective. Another important consideration is that Melissa's experience may not override that of family cohesion or family members' instincts to protect themselves. Instead, the situation has the potential to spark a conflict for Carla and her daughter with Joe's family, further alienating both mother and daughter from tribal support. Carla's direct approach to talking about her daughter's molestation may be perceived as a threat to the perpetrator and his family, and perhaps even the tribe. However, if the therapist can understand how important cohesion has been to sustaining an entire community against external threats, she is more likely to be successful in drawing out common values and uniting the parents in action.

Historical Trauma and Violence Against Women

Joe's tribe was previously characterized as "demure" and seldom impassioned about the happenings surrounding them. In fact, the psychologist is aware that sexual abuse is more prevalent among the smaller, close-knit Tribe A communities, although it is rarely spoken about. The psychologist makes use of Guideline 2 by seeking information about the oppression or privilege that different group memberships carry. Particularly where Native people are concerned, grasping the history behind current oppression is essential. The astute psychologist is aware that some of the history of sexual abuse began with the influx of Spanish colonizers who were known to rape Native women and force their subservience. Native men, having been decimated by disease and battle, and often subject to other unimaginable abuses and torture, were often unable to prevent the abuse of their women.

Additionally, tribal tradition and protocol prior to colonization might have addressed the situation very differently. However, after generations of subjugation and abuses by Spanish colonizers and subsequent Anglo-European attempts at ethnic and cultural annihilation, European gender norms, roles, and stereotypes, such as the belief that women are property and subservient to men, have supplanted many Native perspectives and traditions. Consequently, as something that might be easily overlooked or misinterpreted by a non-Native behavioral health professional, or worse, interpreted as passivity on the part of Joe, the collective behavior exhibited by the tribe may be more indicative of the loss of hope and disempowerment that many Native people have come to accept as existential. Yet, the therapist can never assume that these general histories are known or accepted by the client and must always begin with the client's perspective and the histories passed down within each specific tribal community and family.

Stereotypes of Native women continue to be found in and perpetuated by the dominant culture even today. Notions of "Indian princesses," such as Pocahontas, who purportedly aided White settler John Smith to the detriment of her own people, and whose role was sexualized at a young age (she met John Smith at roughly age 12 and never had a romantic relationship with him), promote the objectification of Native women and girls and usurp Native culture. Thus, in accordance with Guideline 3, the psychologist assessing this client may want to better understand the current types of bias and discrimination that Carla and her daughter face and help to build empowerment (Guideline 7).

Treatment Planning and Interventions

In cases such as Carla's, there are multiple considerations in treatment planning and intervention. First and foremost, as in any similar case, mandated reporting and safety planning would be at issue. Sovereign status can also pose a peculiar issue that often arises when working with tribal communities. A tribe's laws and justice system may be different from that of the state. Some tribes do not have a children's code or equivalent legislation to outline steps to be taken in child abuse cases. Many even have their own tribal social services that deal with reports of child abuse. In Carla's case, knowing where to report abuse given the child's tribal affiliations could be even more complicated. Consequently, just finding out the appropriate steps to reporting for the tribe is essential. Reviewing the history of Native children who were forcibly removed from their homes and the current reputation of social services, consulting with individuals knowledgeable in working with that specific tribe, assessing the family's perspectives on reporting, as well as weighing the current risk status of the child for further abuse, are all relevant aspects that would have considerable bearing on the outcomes of the situation. At times, responses that may be clear-cut with non-Native families are not as simple to interpret with Native families, and solutions that serve to protect Carla and her daughter while also seeking justice in the most culturally sensitive way possible are best.

Once initial safety issues and reporting requirements are addressed, effective treatment may include evidence-based approaches with respect to Guideline 4. Despite the fact that only a few treatments have been specifically validated with Native populations, trauma-focused cognitive–behavioral therapy (TF-CBT) may be an appropriate treatment option for both the parents and the child. TF-CBT addresses distorted beliefs and attributions related to the abuse while providing support for the child to talk about traumatic experiences. It also reduces the negative emotional and behavioral responses following traumatic events, including child sexual abuse, domestic violence, and other traumatic losses. TF-CBT is also effective with nonabusive parents as they cope with their own responses to their child's distress. TF-CBT may be especially advantageous in such programs as the culturally adapted one developed by BigFoot and Schmidt (2010), called Mending the Circle, for Native children. Other forms of therapy targeting trauma and sexual abuse may also be appropriate or effective, depending on how receptive the family is and the therapist's ability to adapt the therapy to reflect the family's values and unique complexities with respect to Guideline 9.

Beyond evidence-based or Western treatments (e.g., CBT, medication management), it would be important for a therapist to explore with Carla whether interventions that utilize community resources (Guideline 10) and traditional approaches to healing are appropriate for her family situation. For example, certain ceremonies may be more culturally congruent and possibly hold greater effectiveness for Carla's status as a Native mother. However, because a majority of Native women are in cross-cultural relationships (whether across racial groups or tribal–ethnic groups), there may be cultural implications regarding a women's role that can impact religious or spiritual approaches to healing. In some tribes, regalia and certain garments represent "medicine powers" and are only to be worn by certain women who are also enrolled tribal members. Some tribes may allow Native women from outside their tribe to participate in ceremonies, such as sweat lodge or Sun Dance, with the permission of certain elders. In Carla's case, we know that access to her husband's tribal ceremonies for healing is not permissible. However, daunting as it may seem, given that Carla has never been affiliated with her own tribe, an exploration of its ceremonies might help Carla and her daughter to reconnect with that culture in ways that ultimately facilitate healing.

In this case, the psychologist is also aware that Carla's daughter, Melissa, has an affiliation (although not enrolled) with a tribe that maintains strong puberty rites for its young women, and Melissa is of an appropriate age to engage in such a ceremony. Participation in a ceremony could also be a potential avenue to explore with the family to help heal some of the trauma she has been subject to in relation to sexual maturation. It may also help Melissa by giving her a cultural context for her transition into womanhood in which she can reclaim her power. The non-Native psychologist, however, must take caution in even suggesting or exploring some aspects of traditional ceremonies. The best practice would be to always allow the clients to lead where cultural alternatives are concerned. Perhaps a more judicious path would be to connect the family with appropriate cultural mentors or healers from their own communities, then maintain open communication with these essential collaborators for treatment.

As depicted in the case study, a therapist working from a non-Native healing paradigm must constantly reflect on the components as outlined within the Guidelines and seek out cultural specialists from within the communities. Doing so may not necessarily result in immediate and effective answers, but may in fact provide more insight into ways that healing can be initiated and best understood. In therapy, it would be helpful for the therapist to understand how her or his role can positively impact Carla and her daughter through collaborative goal setting, appropriate advocacy, and interventions that are suited to their cultural needs. Hopefully it is clear to the reader that to take on a case such as Carla's is to appreciate that it would mean encountering much more than one individual client. Instead, the therapist may need to encounter the entire family, maybe the extended family, and potentially, even the tribal communities from which family members come. Caution should always be taken to prevent the unwitting harm of an already vulnerable population due to a therapist's uninformed knowledge of localized cultural mores.

Case Scenario 2: Cindy

Cindy is a Native woman in her early 20s. She was self-referred to therapy services for a mental health screening, required for the special GED program that enabled young adults to complete high school and attain a diploma. During her assessment, Cindy shared openly about struggling with depression and suicidality. She spoke about the loss of her mother to alcoholism when she was in high school and about not knowing her father, who had committed suicide when she was 2 years old.

Cindy had played a primary role in the care of her three younger siblings during the later years of her mother's alcoholism. Living with her grandparents while attending high school on the reservation, Cindy eventually dropped out of school after having missed too many classes as a result of taking care of her siblings when her mother was ill. When her mother passed away, Cindy's aging grandparents, who were in their late 70s, had been given custody of Cindy and her siblings. Not long after that, Cindy moved out of her grandparents' house to live with her boyfriend and his parents, also on the reservation. Despite the move, Cindy continued to take responsibility for the care of her siblings. She later decided to leave the reservation and finish high school in a specialized GED program that would fast-track her to getting a diploma so she could support and care for her siblings once again. Her future goal was to complete a vocational program for business administration.

The mental health assessor determined that Cindy had some indicators of anxiety, which were deemed normal for a new adult in her current situation. Likewise, in response to further inquiry during intake, Cindy denied any current suicidality or depression, stating that she had learned to manage by reading, getting support from friends, and focusing on her education. She also stated that she had returned to school because she knew it was what her mother would have wanted for her. Because Cindy appeared (a) stable, (b) oriented to the future, (c) had clearly identified educational goals, (d) was able to list a few resources and supports, (e) had stated reasons to live and denied being suicidal, and (f) had not displayed any symptoms that would signal other mental health issues during the past year, she was accepted into the program without requiring further mental health services.

On admission to the GED program, all students receive academic counseling support as a part of the curriculum, including attending group meetings to check in with students and assess educational progress and barriers. Cindy commenced with the program, and no reports about her were brought to the attention of the mental health services staff that would indicate she needed further assessment in any areas related to her mental health. She appeared to have a plan in place for achieving the academic milestones set forth for successful completion of the program. Cindy was not seen by a mental health provider again until a few months later, just past the Christmas break, when she was brought in after having a panic attack during one of her classes.

In this session, Cindy stated that she had taken on too many courses. She now believed she would not be able to complete the semester for fear of failing her classes. She also had several past due papers that were as yet incomplete. Exploring more deeply, her therapist learned that Cindy would not complete an assignment unless she thought she would receive an A. Further, Cindy had also taken on a larger course load than most students. In their session, the therapist reevaluated her depressive symptoms. She stated that she had been having sleep difficulties, which resulted in trouble making it to classes, and she feared it was severely hindering her ability to keep up with the workload. Cindy had also begun eating more and had gained a considerable amount of weight in a short period of time, which caused her added anxiety and frustration.

A suicide assessment found that Cindy only experienced fleeting thoughts of suicide but had no current plan or intent. She did indicate she had been experiencing social difficulties with peers whom she had once considered friends. She claimed they tried to draw her into substance use and spoke badly about her when she was not around. As a result, she decided to stop spending time with them. Cindy also believed that if she could lessen the course load, it would relieve her stress and help her do better overall.

The therapist determined that anxiety was the primary concern to be addressed and asked to have Cindy come in for weekly sessions to receive CBT to help decrease her anxiety symptoms. On the basis of Cindy's life changes and future goals, the therapist felt Cindy's concerns related to the successful completion of her program and her impending transition into adulthood. The therapist provided her with a few exercises to help her anxiety and asked her to come back the following week. Cindy failed to show up for her next two scheduled appointments but did call her counselor to request help with decreasing her course load to part time, stating she had had another panic attack and did not think she could complete the program.

A week after the phone call, Cindy returned to see her counselor. She appeared to be upset and crying and expressed that she did not want to be a failure or return to her reservation, where there were no jobs and nothing to do. She stated that her family did not support her decision to move to the city to complete the program and that they believed she would fail. It should be noted that until this point, the therapist had been providing psychotherapy that was consistent with mainstream practice as an academic counselor. Likewise, although the therapist was certainly not incompetent, this juncture serves to highlight the fact that too many behavioral health professionals involved in working with Native people fail to understand the scope and gravity of the lived Native experience and how very different it can be from mainstream society, especially for those Natives who live on or in proximity of a reservation.

Subsequently, on realizing she might be dealing with something more complex and serious, the therapist shifted her approach and sought deeper insight into the situation to understand better the dynamics and more effectively be of help to Cindy. Thereafter, both Cindy and her therapist worked together to explore her family's dynamics and Cindy's own perceptions regarding her choice to leave the reservation to get an education. They discussed Cindy's absence from home, her choice to pursue education, and what it meant for her to have left the reservation.

Cindy stated that she was the first in her family to leave the reservation willingly. Her family believed that once she left, she would not return. Cindy reported that no one in her family had ever gone to college. Her grandfather, who was a well-respected traditional healer, had only completed the fifth grade and had never left the reservation. Her grandmother had been sent to boarding school off the reservation but had never spoken about her experience in boarding school and had not left the reservation since she returned. Cindy also reported that her mother had graduated from high school and completed some vocational school but quit once she had entered into multiple abusive relationships. When her mother began drinking, Cindy was 6 years old. Cindy also has two older brothers who have been in and out of prison since high school. Both are alcoholic and unemployed. Yet, when sharing her family's values, Cindy spoke affectionately about the importance of her family and the ways in which she often helped them (e.g., taking care of siblings; helping with hauling water, cooking, and cleaning; giving money, clothing, or other personal material items whenever another family member was in need). She also reported that her only father figure, an elder gentleman she had known since childhood on the reservation, had passed away a year ago. It was the memory of their last conversation and of him telling her "go to school" that had prompted her to apply for the program in the first place, despite feeling conflicted about turning her back on her family.

Cindy returned as scheduled for the next three sessions. The therapist learned more about Cindy's family and her role within it. They discussed the many conflicts between the differing values of her family's expectations of her and how they seemed to compete with her school requirements. In addition, there were numerous traumatic events that had occurred in her family. Some of Cindy's most salient experiences included an abusive and controlling relationship with her former boyfriend, a rape that went unreported because of fear of repercussions, the reality of having depressed caregivers such as her mom and grandparents, and her belief in being at fault for her father's suicide.

Therapeutic Considerations

Cindy had a childhood filled with adversity: She witnessed parental substance abuse, rape, incarceration of family members, the loss of her primary caretaker in high school, unstable living arrangements between different relatives and her boyfriend's homes, as well as the knowledge of her father's suicide. As an adult, she has been assessed as experiencing depression, anxiety, suicidal ideation, and obesity. In addition, Cindy felt the pressures of being the only family member to have left her reservation willingly to finish high school.

Despite the fact that neither the assessment nor initial intake session captured a full understanding of her struggles, Cindy did seek counseling support. Subsequently, her therapist employed Guidelines 1, 2, and 3, moving away from her initial conceptualization of Cindy and placing Cindy's experiences in ecological context by relating her anxiety to her strong family ties and her unconventional role as a Native woman and coparent to her siblings. Likewise, realizing that Cindy's anxiety was something more than typical education-specific anxiety, the therapist also employed Guidelines 4 and 5 by looking more deeply at Cindy's background and exploring the motivation behind Cindy's choices and behavior. That knowledge clarified how Cindy, unlike her peers similar in age, was not necessarily seeking an education to fulfill her own personal goals but rather to satisfy the obligation she felt was necessary to help care for her family. Cindy also discovered that the geographical separation from her family compounded the pressure she was already experiencing. Feeling increasingly isolated, she needed the support of the therapist because she was not able to get it from her relatives, given they themselves were incapable of relating to her struggles.

An important note here is that most clients, no matter their worldview, have a difficult time perceiving their problems objectively and relating or contrasting their own values and beliefs for the purposes of deeper processing. Often, when a person holds a different worldview, as Cindy did, it may not be readily apparent until it clashes up against the dominant worldview. This can often result in the inability to cope. For Cindy, the extreme distress, compounded by cultural barriers in therapy, are what resulted in her breakdown.

Finally, it is unclear in the treatment plan how the therapist arrived at her conclusions about the anxiety diagnosis, the focus of the sessions, or the CBT exercises issued for decreasing her symptoms. What does appear evident is that the therapist did not obtain specific information regarding Cindy's tribal affiliations, her role as the oldest woman in her family, or the potential consequences of her life choices, all of which should have been addressed if following Guidelines 1 through 7. It was not until Cindy broke down that the therapist realized that a change was needed in the focus of the sessions. Additionally, the therapist's role as an academic counselor was limited, leaving Cindy no choice but seek out alternative resolutions to her situation. Engaging Cindy in a culturally competent way would have prompted her therapist to seek consultation with appropriate community resources and might have also led to obtaining support that would have included Cindy's family. Examples of such resources are described and noted throughout this chapter.

Possible Alternatives in Therapy

In the case of Cindy, despite making seemingly significant progress into her underlying issues, the therapist was unable to help her move beyond the academic setting and enter into more pragmatic next steps of therapy. Appropriate intervention for Cindy would mean helping her to reconcile the loss she had experienced in moving away from home as well as possibly including her family in her therapy sessions. Although these may be less conventional interventions, especially for an academic counseling setting, they are more culturally attuned and might have encouraged Cindy to have greater confidence in navigating the unknown and more comfort in her choices and decisions and might have facilitated her adaptation to more conventional therapies and treatments over time by fostering a relationship of trust for Cindy and her therapist. Cindy's role as a female in her tribe may well have been a driving factor in her leadership and sense of responsibility for the welfare of her family.

Assessing for a client's cultural understanding, including how her past and current experiences and goals for therapy relate to her cultural context, can help therapists in creating a more complete case conceptualization and intervention strategy that is not dominated by a CBT approach and focused only on current symptomatology. Furthermore, CBT models encourage an integration of coping mechanisms that may need to be tailored for a Native student attempting to overcome trauma that has been embedded over several generations and which is different than behavior that reflects current life events and conditions. For further reading about gender and culturally sensitive assessment and conceptualization, readers are encouraged to consult Chapter 2 of this volume. In addition, tribally based interventions and approaches linked to retraditionalization (discussed briefly in the next section) expand the range of interventions available to therapists.

The pathology of symptoms and behavior seen in Native people is not necessarily unique in terms of behavioral health, as seen in Cindy's case. However, working with Native persons, especially those who may live on a reservation, does come with its own unique set of challenges. In this regard, the multitude of issues and barriers to accessing appropriate types of care may well exacerbate the situation versus helping it. Therefore, when it comes to care and treatment of Native people, the greatest impact on professional practice is a compassionate and flexible understanding of the complexities related to culture and intercultural adaptation. Cindy's story underscores the necessity for the practice applications that are outlined in Guidelines 6 through 11. The individual therapist or counselor or the educational organization sponsoring the GED program all could be more effective by having a greater awareness of the sociopolitical context and showing cultural sensitivity for the ethnic populations under their purview. Such awareness enables them to increase accuracy in assessment and diagnoses; support more culturally appropriate interventions and approaches; foster initiative and empowerment to supplant apathy and oppression; offer or develop more relevant mental health, education, and community resources; and finally, promote change in institutional and systemic bias.

BUILDING A FUTURE FOR NATIVE WOMEN AND CHILDREN

Although the preceding case scenarios may seem somewhat dire or overwhelming, portraying the everyday lived experiences commonly occurring in Indian Country also serves to underscore the notion of resiliency throughout Native communities. In this regard, Native women have steadily risen into positions of leadership since the 1960s. This has also been an important step in reclaiming their rightful roles among tribal leadership. Culturally attuned approaches to healing, community collaboration, and self-determined initiatives are also making inroads toward achieving much-needed social change, and reviving and revitalizing Native cultures.

In response to historically high dropout rates for Native clients in therapy, Native American professionals have been committed to creating more culturally congruent therapy services (Sue, 1977). Practices such as the use of a historical trauma scale may provide more insight into an indigenous worldview (Whitbeck, Adams, Hoyt, & Chen, 2004). Community-based participatory research focused on public health and case consultations highlights the role of the tribe as their own cultural experts and supports community well-being. Tribally based intervention strategies contribute to creating collaborative and trusting relationships in counseling (Gone & Trimble, 2012; King, 2009).

Another positive endeavor is the concept of *retraditionalization*, which refers to the return to traditional cultural forms (Edwards, 2002; Menzies, 2005). Native peoples throughout North America and Hawaii have shifted toward more culturally informed alternatives. Recent community-based education initiatives that are founded on traditional values, orientations, and principles but also incorporate modern technologies have begun to yield positive results (Goodyear-Kaopua, 2013; Ole-Henrik, 2005). Some Native communities have even initiated culturally appropriate interventions for violence against women both within and outside the criminal justice system. These family or community forums emphasize restorative and reparative approaches to justice over existing punitive models (Bachman, Zaykowski, Kallmyer, Poteyeva, & Lanier, 2008).

The welfare and future of Native children are especially important. A key feature of many community-based interventions is identifying children at risk for child abuse and neglect. Using tools and assessments that are culturally appropriate and integrating best practices in child welfare are also critical for protecting this at-risk population. Agencies such as the National Indian Child Welfare Association are helping to implement initiatives that are culturally competent, community-based, and focused on the strengths and assets of families. Likewise, Native children and adolescents who receive mental health care services are more likely to receive these services through a juvenile justice system or an inpatient facility than are non-Native children (Bigfoot & Schmidt, 2010).

The approaches for addressing prevention and safety related to violence against Native women are also being reconsidered. Mending the Sacred Hoop (http://mshoop.org/), an organization that provides technical assistance in addressing domestic violence, recommends longer term temporary housing and affordable permanent housing that would offer more viable alternatives for battered women leaving abusive relationships. An instrumental partner in the development of the Violence Against Women Act, Futures Without Violence is another nongovernmental agency focused on education programs, national policy development, professional training programs, and public actions designed to end violence against women, children, and families on a global level.

In conclusion, we must return the beginning, to the Native stories of origin. As the foundation for their ancient cultures, the lore of Native peoples represents much more than myths or stories. As archetypes, the personages, or ancestors as considered by Natives, have served to model personality, behavior, morality, values, and other natural or human characteristics. They are also credited with having provided their progeny with the knowledge of how to live in harmony and balance with nature itself, the very keys to survival and sustainability (Allen, 1992; Mohawk, 2006). For NH, it is told that Haumea, their goddess of earth, nature, and sustenance, is reborn in each succeeding generation of her descendants. As such, Haumea lives in every Hawaiian woman and made this promise to all her daughters: "All Haumea has done, I too can do" (Kameeleihiwa, 1999, p. 7). Hawaiian history remembers the strength and wisdom of its women as rulers, queens, healers, and skillful experts of many arts (Jensen, 2005; Kameeleihiwa, 1999).

When Native women such as Pocahontas were caught in crucial moments of oppressive contact, they often demonstrated deep perceptiveness and valiant leadership in their decisions and managed to retain their cultural pasts while forging new relationships that would ensure a future for their children. Even today, charismatic leaders like Cecilia Fire Thunder, former president of the Oglala Sioux in South Dakota, or Joyce Dugan, the former chief of the Eastern Band of Cherokee Indians, or Caleen Sisk, chief of the Winnemem Wintu tribe, are but a few of many eminent contemporary Native women. Yet, the courage, strength, and resilience of Native women, however, are not limited only to their leaders or chieftains.

Native women have forged a new identity as warriors of Spirit as they continue spurring change and adaptations in traditions and culture while also maintaining a cohesive history. For those undaunted by hegemony and oppression, they recognize their responsibility to embrace life-affirming behaviors in the face of the tremendous losses experienced through policies such as genocide, assimilation, relocation, and current ongoing traumas such as violence and substance use disorders. They have gathered in their circles, worked to reclaim and revitalize what was left of their traditions, and turned their attentions to their children and the next generations of women warriors. Unbeknownst to the women, they have intuitively incorporated a strength-based approach and applied principles of positive psychology (GreyWolf, 2013). Exhibiting character strengths and virtues that look at what is good, right, and working within their cultures and communities, Native women have established culturally based charter schools, community revitalization projects, mentoring programs, and more. Native women can also take credit for much of the healing that is taking place and spreading throughout Native communities. Just like their foremothers, Native women are living up to their inherent capacity to endure and transform their current hardships. Consequently, it is imperative for professionals in practice, both Native and non-Native alike, to foster the self-empowerment of Native women by honoring their sovereignty, not just from a legal perspective but also from a cultural one that at the very least acknowledges a worldview with systems and dynamics that may be different from their own.

REFERENCES

Abrams, N. E., & Primack, J. R. (2001). Cosmology and 21st-century culture. *Science, 293,* 1769–1770. doi:10.1126/science.1063090

Allen, P. (1985, April) *Violence and the American Indian woman: Working to prevent sexual and domestic violence* (Vol. 1, No. 4). Seattle, WA: Center for the Prevention of Sexual and Domestic Violence.

Allen, P. (1992). *The sacred hoop: recovering the feminine in American Indian traditions.* Boston, MA: Beacon Press.

American Psychological Association. (2007). Guidelines for psychological practice with girls and women. *American Psychologist, 62,* 949–979. doi:10.1037/0003-066X.62.9.949

Amnesty International. (2007). *Maze of injustice: The failure to protect indigenous women from sexual violence in the USA.* New York, NY: Author.

Bachman, R., Zaykowski, H., Kallmyer, R., Poteyeva, M., & Lanier, C. (2008). *Violence against American Indian and Alaska Native women and the criminal justice response: What is known* (NCJ 223691). Washington, DC: U.S. Department of Justice, Office of Justice Programs. Retrieved from https://www.ncjrs.gov/pdffiles1/nij/grants/223691.pdf

Baldridge, D. (2001). Indian elders: Family traditions in crisis. *American Behavioral Scientist, 44,* 1515–1527. doi:10.1177/00027640121956953

Beck, D. (2006). *Spiral dynamics: Mastering values, leadership and change: Exploring the new science of memetics.* Oxford, England: Blackwell.

Bernal, G., & Scharron-del-Rio, M. R. (2001). Are empirically supported treatments valid for ethnic minorities? An alternative approach for treatment research. *Cultural Diversity and Ethnic Minority Psychology, 7,* 328–342. doi:10.1037/1099-9809.7.4.328

BigFoot, D. S., & Schmidt, S. R. (2010). Honoring children, mending the circle: Cultural adaptation of trauma-focused cognitive–behavioral therapy for American Indian and Alaska Native children. *Journal of Clinical Psychology, 66*, 847–856. doi:10.1002/jclp.20707

Black, M. C., & Breiding, M. J. (2008). Adverse health conditions and health risk behaviors associated with intimate partner violence—United States, 2005. *Morbidity and Mortality Weekly Report, 57*, 113–117. Retrieved from http://www.cdc.gov/mmwr/preview/mmwrhtml/mm5705a1.htm

Brave Heart, M. Y. H. (1998). The return to the sacred path: Healing the historical trauma and historical unresolved grief response among the Lakota through a psychoeducational group intervention. *Smith College Studies in Social Work, 68*, 287–305. doi:10.1080/00377319809517532

Brave Heart, M. Y. H. (2003). The historical trauma response among natives and its relationship with substance abuse: A Lakota illustration. *Journal of Psychoactive Drugs, 35*, 7–13. doi:10.1080/02791072.2003.10399988

Brave Heart, M. Y. H., & DeBruyn, L. M. (1998). The American Indian holocaust: Healing historical unresolved grief. *American Indian and Alaska Native Mental Health Research, 8*, 56–78.

Brave Heart-Jordan, M. Y. H. (1995). *The return to the sacred path: Healing from historical trauma and historical unresolved grief among the Lakota* (Doctoral dissertation). Retrieved from ProQuest Dissertations and Theses (Order No. 42453443)

Bubar, R., & Thurman, P. J. (2004). Violence against Native women. *Social Justice, 31*(4), 70–86.

Cajete, G. (2000). *Nativescience: Natural laws of interdependence.* Santa Fe, NM: Clear Light Books.

Campbell, C. D., & Evans-Campbell, T. (2011). Historical trauma and Native American child development and mental health: An overview. In M. C. Sarche, P. Spicer, P. Farrell, & H. E. Fitzgerald (Eds.), *American Indian and Alaska Native children and mental health: Development, context, prevention, and treatment* (pp. 1–26). Santa Barbara, CA: Praeger/ABC-CLIO.

Dawkins, R. (1976). *The selfish gene.* New York, NY: Oxford University Press.

Deloria, V. (1993). If you think about it you will see it is true. *Noetic Science Review, 27*, 62–71.

Duran, E. (2006). *Healing the soul wound: Counseling with American Indians and other native peoples.* New York, NY: Teachers College Press.

Duran, E., & Duran, B. (1995). *Native American postcolonial psychology.* Albany: State University of New York Press.

Edwards, Y. J. (2002). *Healing the soul wound: The retraditionalization of Native Americans in substance abuse treatment* (Doctoral dissertation). Retrieved from ProQuest Dissertations and Theses. (Order No. 3042866)

Evans-Campbell, T., Fredriksen-Goldsen, K. I., Walters, K. L., & Stately, A. (2005). Caregiving experiences among American Indian two-spirit men and women: Contemporary and historical roles. *Journal of Gay & Lesbian Social Services*, 18(3/4), 75–92. doi:10.1300/J041v18n03_05

Fiske, J. (1995). Political status of Native Indian women: Contradictory implications of Canadian state policy. *American Indian Culture and Research Journal*, 19(2), 1–30. Available at http://www.law-lib.utoronto.ca/Diana/fulltext/fisk.pdf

Fitzgerald, J., & Fitzgerald, M. O. (Eds.). (2005). *The spirit of Indian women*. Bloomington, IN: World Wisdom.

Four Arrows, D., Cajete, G., & Lee, J. (2010). *Critical neurophilosophy & indigenous wisdom*. Rotterdam, the Netherlands: Sense.

Gone, J. P., & Alcántara, C. (2007). Identifying effective mental health interventions for American Indians and Alaska Natives: A review of the literature. *Cultural Diversity and Ethnic Minority Psychology*, 13, 356–363. doi:10.1037/1099-9809.13.4.356

Gone, J. P., & Trimble, J. E. (2012). American Indian and Alaska Native mental health: Diverse perspectives on enduring disparities. *Annual Review of Clinical Psychology*, 8, 131–160. doi:10.1146/annurev-clinpsy-032511-143127

González-Pardo, H., & Pérez Álvarez, M. (2013). Epigenetics and its implications for psychology. *Psicothema*, 25, 3–12. doi:10.7334/psicothema2012.327

Goodyear-Kaopua, N. (2013). *The seeds we planted: Portraits of a native Hawaiian charter school*. Minneapolis: University of Minnesota Press.

Greenfield, L. A., & Smith, S. K. (1999). *American Indians and crime* (NCJ 173386). Retrieved from http://www.bjs.gov/content/pub/pdf/aic.pdf

GreyWolf. I. (2013, August). Indigenous women: Reframing native history, heritage, and cultural distinctions. In D. Willis (Chair). *Women warriors of spirit*. Symposium conducted at the Annual Convention of the American Psychological Association, Honolulu, HI.

Griner, D., & Smith, T. B. (2006). Culturally adapted mental health interventions: A meta-analytic review. *Psychotherapy: Theory, Research, Practice, Training, 43*, 531–548. doi:10.1037/0033-3204.43.4.531

Harper, L. V. (2005). Epigenetic inheritance and the intergenerational transfer of experience. *Psychological Bulletin, 131*, 340–360. doi:10.1037/0033-2909.131.3.340

Harvell, C. D., & Tollrian, R. (1999). Why inducible defenses? In R. Tollrian & C. D. Harvell (Eds.), *The ecology and evolution of inducible defenses* (pp. 3–9). Princeton, NJ: Princeton University Press.

Hay, R. (1998, Fall). A rooted sense of place in cross-cultural perspective. *The Canadian Geographer/Le Géographe canadien, 42*, 245–266. doi:10.1111/j.1541-0064.1998.tb01894.x

Hazel, K. L., & Mohatt, G. V. (2001). Cultural and spiritual coping in sobriety: Informing substance abuse prevention for Alaska Native communities. *Journal of Community Psychology, 29*, 541–562. doi:10.1002/jcop.1035

Huey, S. J., & Polo, A. J. (2008). Evidence-based psychosocial treatments for ethnic minority youth: A review and meta-analysis. *Journal of Clinical Child and Adolescent Psychology, 37*, 262–301. doi:10.1080/15374410701820174

Jablonka, E., & Lamb, M. J. (2002). The changing concept of epigenetics. *Annals of the New York Academy of Sciences, 981*, 82–96. doi:10.1111/j.1749-6632.2002.tb04913.x

Jensen, L. (2005). *Daughters of Haumea = Nā kaikamahine`o Haumea: Women of ancient Hawai`i.* San Francisco, CA: Pueo Press.

Kameeleihiwa, L. (1999). *Nā wahine kapu = Divine Hawaiian women.* Honolulu, HI: Ai Pōhaku Press.

King, J. (2009). Psychotherapy within an American Indian perspective. In M. E. Gallardo & B. W. McNeill (Eds.), *Intersections of multiple identities: A casebook of evidence-based practices with diverse populations* (pp. 113–136). New York, NY: Routledge/Taylor & Francis Group.

Lawrence, B. (2003). Gender, race, and the regulation of native identity in Canada and the United States: An overview. *Hypatia, 18*(2), 3–31. doi:10.1111/j.1527-2001.2003.tb00799.x

Lyons, O., & Mohawk, J. (Eds.). (1998). *Exiled in the land of the free: Democracy, Indian nations & the U.S. constitution.* Santa Fe, NM: Clear Light Books.

Menzies, P. M. (2005). *Orphans within our family: Intergenerational trauma and homeless aboriginal men* (Doctoral dissertation). Retrieved from ProQuest Dissertations and Theses. (Order No. 305364858)

Miranda, J., Bernal, G., Lau, A., Kohn, L., Hwang, W. C., & LaFromboise, T. (2005). State of the science on psychosocial interventions for ethnic minorities. *Annual Review of Clinical Psychology, 1*, 113–142. doi:10.1146/annurev.clinpsy.1.102803.143822

Mohawk, J. (2006, May 9). *Surviving hard times: It's not for sissies.* Retrieved from http://www.yesmagazine.org/issues/5000-years-of-empire/surviving-hard-times-its-not-for-sissies

Nagayama Hall, G. C. (2001). Psychotherapy research with ethnic minorities: Empirical, ethical, and conceptual issues. *Journal of Consulting and Clinical Psychology, 69*, 502–510. doi:10.1037/0022-006X.69.3.502

Niezen, R. (2000). *Spirit wars: Native North American religions in the age of nation building.* Berkeley: University of California Press.

Ole-Henrik, M. (2005). Indigenous education. *Childhood Education, 81*, 319–320. doi:10.1080/00094056.2005.10521319

Perry, S. W. (2004). *A BJS statistical profile, 1992–2002: American Indians and crime* (NCJ 203097). Washington, DC: U.S. Department of Justice, Office of Justice Programs. Retrieved from http://www.bjs.gov/content/pub/pdf/aic02.pdf

Peters, W. M. K. (2011). *The indigenous soul wound: Exploring culture, memetics, complexity and emergence* (Doctoral dissertation). Retrieved from ProQuest Dissertations and Theses. (Order No. 3474460)

Prucha, F. P. (Ed.). (1973). *Americanizing the Indians: Writings by "Friends of the Indians" 1880–1900.* Lincoln: University of Nebraska Press.

Segal, C. M., & Stineback, D. C. (1977). *Puritans, Indians, and manifest destiny.* New York, NY: Putnam.

Sue, S. (1977). Community mental health services to minority groups. Some optimism, some pessimism. *American Psychologist, 32,* 616–624. doi:10.1037//0003-066X.32.8.616

Szasz, M. C. (2003). *Education and the American Indian: The road to self-determination since 1928.* Albuquerque: University of New Mexico Press.

Tjaden, P., & Thoennes, N. (2000). *Full report of the prevalence, incidence, and consequences of violence against women* (NCJ 183781). Washington, DC: U.S. Department of Justice, Office of Justice Programs. Retrieved from https://www.ncjrs.gov/pdffiles1/nij/183781.pdf

Unger, S. (Ed.). (1977). *The destruction of American Indian families.* New York, NY: Association on American Indian Affairs.

U.S. Department of Health and Human Services, Substance Abuse and Mental Health Services Administration. (2005). *Suicide among American Indians/Alaska Natives.* Retrieved from http://www.sprc.org/sites/sprc.org/files/library/ai.an.facts.pdf

Walters, K. L., Evans-Campbell, T., Simoni, J. M., Ronquillo, T., & Bhuyan, R. (2006). "My spirit in my heart": Identity experiences and challenges among American Indian two-spirit women. *Journal of Lesbian Studies, 10*(1–2), 125–149. doi:10.1300/J155v10n01_07

Walters, K. L., Mohammed, S. A., Evans-Campbell, T., Beltran, R. E., Chae, D. H., & Duran, B. (2011). Bodies don't just tell stories, they tell histories: Embodiment of historical trauma among American Indians and Alaska natives. *Du Bois Review: Social Science Research on Race, 8*(1), 179–189. doi:10.1017/S1742058X1100018X

Wasson, W. C. (1973). *Philosophical differences between Europeans and Native Americans as an explanation of the alienation of Native American students from the educational system* (Doctoral dissertation). Retrieved from ProQuest Dissertations and Theses. (Order No. 7328641)

Whitbeck, L. B., Adams, G. W., Hoyt, D. R., & Chen, X. (2004). Conceptualizing and measuring historical trauma among American Indian people. *American Journal of Community Psychology, 33*(3–4), 119–130. doi:10.1023/B:AJCP.0000027000.77357.31

White, J. M., Godfrey, J., & Iron Moccasin, B. (2006). American Indian fathering in the Dakota nation: Use of Akicita as a fatherhood standard. *Fathering, 4*(1), 49–69. doi:10.3149/fth.0401.49

Wilson, A. (1996). How we find ourselves: Identity development and two-spirit people. *Harvard Educational Review*, 66, 303–308.

Woodsum, J. A. (1995). Gender & sexuality in Native American societies: A bibliography. *American Indian Quarterly*, 19, 527–554.

Yoshihama, M., & Dabby, C. (2009). *Facts and stats: Domestic violence in Asian, Native Hawaiian and Pacific Islander homes*. San Francisco, CA: Asian and Pacific Islander Institute on Domestic Violence.

Zug, M. (2012, August 23). Doing what's best for the tribe. *Slate*. Retrieved from http://www.slate.com/articles/double_x/doublex/2012/08/baby_veronica_returns_to_her_biological_father_affirming_icwa_south_carolina_s_supreme_court_made_the_right_decision_.html

9

TRANSNATIONAL PSYCHOLOGICAL PRACTICE WITH WOMEN: PERSPECTIVES FROM EAST ASIA AND JAPAN

SAYAKA MACHIZAWA AND CAROLYN ZERBE ENNS

The phrases *transnational practice* and *transnational feminism* highlight interactions among nation, gender, sexuality, race, and other identities and convey the reality that boundaries marked by place and nation are often fluid and changing (Mohanty, 2003). Addressing human needs requires collaboration, networking, and acts of solidarity across national borders. Transnational practice also encompasses the diasporic experiences of immigrant and refugee populations as well as notions of cultural hybridity and "third culture" identities (Horne & Arora, 2012). In addition, it supports efforts to understand the interrelatedness of a wide range of human rights and structures, such as basic economic, health, education, political, and peace needs, which often have a broad impact within societies and across national boundaries. Thus, transnational practice may occur within one's culture of origin, a culture in which one is displaced, or a setting in which one is residing as a temporary sojourner. Transnational perspectives can also enrich multicultural perspectives and are

http://dx.doi.org/10.1037/14460-009
Psychological Practice With Women: Guidelines, Diversity, Empowerment, C. Z. Enns, J. K. Rice, and R. L. Nutt (Editors)
Copyright © 2015 by the American Psychological Association. All rights reserved.

relevant to practice with many immigrant populations or with persons who are attempting to integrate multiple cultural identities.

The diversity of women within North America is the primary focus of the "Guidelines for Psychological Practice With Girls and Women" (American Psychological Association [APA], 2007; hereafter referred to as the Guidelines). Rather than defining their purview too broadly and risking the possibility of addressing complex transnational women's issues inadequately or superficially, contributors to the Guidelines called on future groups to consider their broader relevance to cultures beyond North America. In keeping with that charge, a major goal of this chapter is to begin to explore implications, modifications, and extensions of the Guidelines for working with women in transnational contexts. Recognizing the impossibility of doing justice to the broad range of issues facing women around the world as well as their movement across borders, we introduce general themes related to transnational practice but limit our discussion of specific examples to East Asia and women of Japanese descent, especially first-generation immigrants.

In addition to the Guidelines, five major themes that inform the APA (2004) *Resolution on Culture and Gender Awareness in International Psychology* are useful for guiding transnational practice (Rice & Ballou, 2002). First, psychologists benefit from exploring and understanding how standpoints and perspectives vary across cultures and how valued sources of authority may differ. Deep understanding of cultural dimensions is supported by recognizing and appreciating how individuals from diverse cultural contexts have adapted to and coped with the realities of their circumstances. Second, productive transnational work is built on a respect for pluralism and differences. Respect for pluralism supports efforts to investigate multiple views and methods for dealing with human issues and carefully weighing the strengths, weaknesses, advantages, and disadvantages of various points of view. Respect for difference, however, does not imply that all perspectives are equally valid, nor does it require the acceptance of all relativistic views, such as the position that the acceptance of interpersonal violence is embedded in some cultural contexts and thus should not be questioned or challenged (Espín, 2005).

Third, psychologists are encouraged to work toward building awareness of power dynamics in diverse cultural contexts, committing themselves to reducing power asymmetries, and supporting egalitarian relationships with working partners and clients around the world (Rice & Ballou, 2002). This principle includes considering how knowledge is often reinforced by dynamics of power and privilege, including what we may call "North American privilege." The fourth theme recommends the critical analysis of Western perspectives, including Western perspectives on feminism and gender issues. Such analysis calls for critical thinking about the analysis of oppression and privilege found in dominant psychological theories. A final theme encourages psychologists to explore the extensive and profound influence that external factors and macrosystemic variables have on individuals. Geopolitical forces and systemic arrangements that privilege some and disadvantage others may be overlooked or discounted within dominant, individualistically oriented North American psychologies. The challenge of understanding the complexity of oppression and privilege is magnified when working across cultural contexts. To summarize, four central assumptions are embedded in both the Guidelines and the themes just described, including the importance of (a) recognizing and valuing diversity and multiple identities, (b) exploring the unique privileges and oppressions experienced by diverse groups of women, (c) attending to power dynamics across cultures and contexts, and (d) addressing institutional and systemic variables as well as working toward social change.

POSITIONALITY, SELF-KNOWLEDGE, AND CULTURAL CONTEXT

We turn now to a discussion of concepts, worldviews, values, and self-knowledge that facilitate transnational work. *Positionality* is especially relevant to this chapter and refers to self-awareness about one's multiple social identities and positions with regard to sources of power and privilege. Western privilege and power typically include access to economic power, class status, cultural capital, neocolonial power, power that comes from access to English, and the power to "orientalize, exoticize, ethnicize, racialize or sexualize members of other nations or groups" (Mackie, 2001, p. 182). To create a truly egalitarian psychology of women that does not treat practices and experiences of privileged groups as the norm, it is necessary to "shift the axis" or "pivot the center" (Mohanty, 1991) by placing women from diverse regions of the world at the center of inquiry. By centralizing the experiences of women with nondominant social identities, "we raise our awareness and understanding of the experiences of all women either implicitly or directly" (Butler, 2000, p. 177) and facilitate alliance building.

Understanding one's positionality in transnational context is facilitated by "world traveling" self-awareness activities (Lugones, 1987). First, self-awareness is facilitated by efforts to understand the cultural practices that have created "us," such as by exploring how systems of oppression have influenced Western women and clarifying how these oppressions may parallel or differ from experiences of women across the globe. Second, awareness of positionality is fostered by looking at "what it is to be ourselves in their eyes" (p. 18), such as by considering one's country's role in colonizing other groups as well as how well-intentioned actions may inadvertently perpetuate colonizing attitudes. Finally, efforts designed to see women in various parts of the world as they see themselves support an attitude of humility and a willingness to accept the expertise of women as they speak in their own voices.

To conceptualize how positionality is related to the Guidelines, a working group considered the international and transnational implications of the Guidelines and concluded that the general themes and 11 statements are applicable to global contexts (Enns & Machizawa, 2008). Participants also proposed, however, that the Guidelines could be enhanced by redefining some concepts more inclusively as well as exploring and integrating research and theory from contexts beyond the North America. For example, terms such as *consciousness raising*, *identity development*, and *assertiveness* are embedded in Western indigenous frameworks. Deconstructing, translating, and transforming these concepts, as well as generating useful culture-specific counterparts, are likely to increase the usefulness of the Guidelines. Furthermore, although many gender issues, such as interpersonal violence, have international, global, and transnational relevance, the use of specific cultural lenses is important for developing culturally sensitive applications.

Working group participants also expressed concern about the subtle, implicit ways in which Western modes of thought and language gain primacy or are accepted uncritically (Enns & Machizawa, 2008). For example, English is typically used as a medium for intercultural communication, and Western psychological writings are often translated into other languages with only limited consideration of the cultural relevance of concepts or approaches. Even when psychological concepts hold similar meaning across cultures, there may be subtle differences in the connotations of words. Furthermore, many international graduate students who experience North American–based psychological training tend to become socialized and assimilated into a Western-based psychological community (Duan et al., 2011). On returning to their countries of origin as psychologists, they may inadvertently disseminate and reproduce Western models uncritically, which can sometimes resemble a kind of internalized neocolonialism. The uncritical dissemination of Western approaches can contribute to a psychology that is less than optimal or relevant to the cultural context.

The findings of a qualitative study of eight Southeast Asian counseling psychologists who received their doctoral degrees in the United States (Duan et al., 2011) addressed the individualistic focus of counseling practice in the United States and the higher value placed on individual than community well-being. Interviewees acknowledged the usefulness of North American counseling theories in theory but emphasized the need to adapt or develop techniques and methods for use in varying cultural contexts. Several participants identified differences in counselor-patient relationships in the United States and their home cultures. For example, the strict boundaries and time-limited focus of counseling is inconsistent with the types of life-long mentoring and support networks found in some cultures. Other participants noted the limitations of North American ethical codes when used in other cultures, especially ethical statements related to therapeutic relationships. As an illustration, gift giving is a part of everyday social life in some Asian cultures, and declining a gift may be perceived as rude or offensive. In contrast to the individualistic belief that multiple relationships can decrease objectivity, some non-Western participants whose life experiences are embedded in cultures of interdependence may have difficulty trusting a stranger with whom they have no preexisting connection (Duan et al., 2011). To summarize, integrating U.S.-based knowledge with indigenous practice is challenging but important for empowering transnational practice.

EGALITARIAN TRANSNATIONAL COLLABORATION

Effective transnational practice is often facilitated by cross-national mentoring and collaborative partnerships that allow psychologists from other countries to learn from each other. In this section, we share brief observations based on our own and others' professional collaborations (e.g., Horne & Arora, 2012; Horne & Mathews, 2006; Horne, Matthews, Brown, & Degroff, 2009; Norsworthy & Khuankaew, 2004). Collaborative relationships may begin as teacher–student relationships, mentoring relationships, or professional relationships and may be solidified through reading, international travel and study, conversations at conferences, and participation in professional organizations (Enns, Kasai, & Machizawa, 2006). This chapter represents one outcome of a transnational collaboration. The first author of this chapter (Sayaka Machizawa) was an undergraduate student of the second author (Carolyn Zerbe Enns). Our shared interest and background in Japan contributed to our work together (Sayaka came from her native Japan to the United States to complete her college degree, and Carolyn was born in Japan and lived in Japan as a child and adolescent). As our relationship has changed and developed over a 15-year period, we have enjoyed multiple opportunities to learn from each other by serving as guest speakers in each other's classes, interacting in multiple contexts (Japan and North America), copresenting at conferences, cowriting papers, and coparticipating in committees that focus on women's issues around the world (e.g., APA Division 52, International Committee for Women). The observations in this section are especially relevant to our ongoing partnership.

For Western psychologists, enriching collaborative partnerships are supported by humility, a desire to learn, and recognition of the expertise of collaborating partners. Interacting in multiple cultural contexts, including the "home" contexts of each individual, can deepen both persons' understanding of the challenges and rewards of transnational work and can facilitate bidirectional comentoring. In addition, much can be gained through personal sharing among colleagues about how they approach intercultural interactions, balance personal and professional roles, and respond to difficulties or biases they encounter.

For the North American partner who wishes to develop collaboration skills, longer term immersion in another culture allows for a deeper and richer understanding of the challenges and benefits of intercultural learning and practice. Intercultural development and competence tend to proceed along a predictable path, with early phases marked by a tendency to exaggerate or minimize cultural differences and later phases marked by greater awareness of complexity, curiosity, empathic understanding of self and others, and the ability to integrate multiple frames of reference (Bennett, 2004). Observing and monitoring one's personal development over time helps provide an "emotional passport" that consists of skills for quieting the mind when facing cultural challenges and the ability to tolerate ambiguity when facing unexpected circumstances (Abarbanel, 2009). Cultural immersion in an unfamiliar context also promotes greater awareness of one's own cultural patterns, hidden meanings, and "taken for granted" assumptions.

Knowledge of cultural similarities and differences in how mentoring and collaborative relationships are structured is invaluable. In Japan, for example, senior members of an organization (*sempai*) often serve as coaches or guides to their junior peers (*kohai*). Mentees typically practice respect and use formal language, and mentors often reciprocate by committing themselves to long-term bonds that foster a level of closeness and significance that is less typical in North American contexts. Thus, a collaborating partner from Asia may initially appear less assertive than might be the case in mentor–mentee interactions within North America. As a result of different cultural norms, it is useful to spend time sharing and clarifying cultural values and their role in collaborative relationships.

Western psychologists often rely heavily on partners from other countries to communicate in English rather than attempting to learn the language of their international colleagues. Deep respect for collaborators is embedded in efforts to learn the language of the persons with whom we work. Although language learning is complex, and proficiency may not be feasible, efforts to develop basic language skills can not only enhance communication but also reinforce working alliances and build trust.

DIVERSITY, SOCIAL CONTEXT, AND POWER (GUIDELINES 1–3)

Arnett (2008) noted that most psychological research is based on studies of approximately 5% of the world's population. Similarly, Henrich, Heine, and Norenzayan (2010) suggested that most psychology research is typically based on WEIRD people, that is, individuals from Western, Educated, Industrialized, Rich, and Democratic contexts. Forming a solid knowledge base for working in transnational contexts requires substantial expansion of this foundation.

In this section, our goal is to articulate knowledge domains that are central to gaining culturally sensitive and ecologically sound analyses of gender-related issues for psychological practice. The areas we discuss are based on a framework developed by Norsworthy and Khuankaew (2004). The domains are illustrative rather than exhaustive and include (a) values and cultural dimensions; (b) philosophical and religious belief systems; (c) social and family system structures; (d) economics (including social class), work, and educational opportunities; (e) government, legal systems, and law enforcement; (f) social justice movements and feminisms; and (g) discrimination, oppression, and class–ethnic conflict.

The life experiences and needs of women around the world vary substantially, and it is impossible in this short chapter to provide information that is relevant across complex contexts and diverse social and national identities. To avoid superficial coverage, we briefly define the dimensions and provide examples of specific knowledge that are most relevant to Japanese women. At the end of each section, we provide brief commentary about the relevance of these dimensions to Japanese American women. However, our coverage provides only a glimpse of the diversity that is found among Asian American women's lives (see Tewari & Alvarez, 2009, for additional information).

As noted earlier, a transnational approach can be useful for working with women within their culture of origin or who emigrate from their nation of origin, are living in a second country as short-term sojourners, or are making a transition to another country as immigrants. A transnational perspective may less useful when working with a woman whose family history includes several generations within North America. For example, by the second generation after immigrating to the United States, a majority (six of 10) of adult children of Asian immigrants tend to think of themselves as "typical Americans," which points to the rapid pace at which self-perceptions may change and the importance of being cautious about drawing generalizations about the ways in which Japanese American and Asian American women may internalize so-called "Asian values" (Pew Research Center, 2013b).

The time period, circumstances, and consequences of immigration are important factors when considering the realities of women's lives (Suzuki, Ahluwalia, & Alimchandani, 2012). Although the most rapid period of Asian immigration began after 1960 and continues to the present, a majority of Japanese Americans trace their family's migration to the late 1880s and early 1900s, when Japanese American men sought economic opportunities in North America. After a brief period, however, the Gentlemen's Agreement of 1907 was adopted, and Japanese men were no longer permitted to enter the United States. Further immigration was typically limited to women, often coming to the United States as "picture brides," or women who were matched to Japanese immigrant men on the basis of the photographs and family recommendations (Sakamoto, 2007). Japanese immigrants faced substantial discrimination (e.g., denial of citizenship or land ownership opportunities, being barred from many professions) but sought to make a better life for their children, who were able to seek citizenship as members of the second generation. During World War II, 120,000 persons of Japanese descent were sent to internment or concentration camps, which contributed to the dismantling of the Japanese American family structure and community (Spickard, 2009). These historical events as well as acculturation and assimilation practices contribute to generational differences in cultural values, behaviors, and attitudes among Japanese Americans. In fact, each generational cohort is given a distinct Japanese name (e.g., Issei, Nisei, Sansei) to reflect these differences (Hikoyeda, Mukoyama, Liou, & Masterson, 2006). Familiarity with the unique immigration and migration histories of individuals and their related experiences of acculturation (Kim, 2009) is important for competent practice.

Values and Cultural Dimensions

In this brief overview, we focus on four of the cultural dimensions described by Hofstede (Hofstede, Hofstede, & Minkov, 2010). *Individualism versus collectivism* focuses on the degree to which a culture encourages individual self-reliance and personal achievement (individualism) or values embedded in cohesive, interdependent, and lifelong in-groups that provide extensive care and identity for its members in exchange for group loyalty (collectivism). Second, *femininity versus masculinity* refers to the degree to which gender-differentiated roles are present and valued within a culture as well as the degree to which a culture emphasizes caring and quality of life (more "feminine" dimensions) or traditional forms of success, competition, and materialism (more "masculine" dimensions). Third, *power distance* involves the extent to which power differences are accepted within a society, especially the degree to unequal power dynamics are tolerated or valued by less powerful members of a culture. Fourth, *uncertainty avoidance* refers to the extent to which cultures develop clear beliefs, rituals, guidance, or institutions for dealing with potentially ambiguous or anxiety-provoking situations. These cultural dimensions interact in unique ways within cultures, leading to substantial diversity. For those who prefer other alternatives to this model, which was developed in cross-cultural comparisons of organizational environments, a variety of other useful options are also available for conceptualizing cultural variations in values and worldviews (e.g., social axioms of Leung & Bond, 2004; basic values of Schwartz, 2012).

When applying the Hofstede dimensions (Hofstede et al., 2010), Japan ranks very high on uncertainty avoidance and masculinity (see http://www. geert-hofstede.com). Uncertainty is avoided through an intricate web of cradle-to-grave social training and rituals, including rules about gender appropriate behavior. Social rules are reinforced by a complex set of "double codes" that dictate specific behaviors for outside (*soto*) spheres requiring polite behavior (*tatemae*) and inner circle (*uchi*) contexts that allow for authentic expression (*honne*; Sugimoto, 2010). Japan is also identified as one of the most "masculine" countries in the world, in part because of a variety of gender-differentiated roles that are described later in this chapter. It is important to note, however, that gender differentiation is not necessarily synonymous with gender inequality (see the section Feminism and Social Justice Movements later in this chapter).

On other dimensions, collectivism is endorsed at a modest level, and Japanese social structures as enacted within the family, education, and work worlds tend to be oriented toward a respect for seniority and hierarchy (an aspect of power distance), as shown by the ways in which social behaviors are negotiated according to one's interactions with persons of *sempai* (senior) status or *kohai* (junior) status. Compared with its Asian neighbors, Japan is generally described as less collectivist than China or Korea, but it ranks as more "masculine" than its neighbors. The indigenous emotion of *amae* is related to Japanese forms of collectivism and is defined as the ability to presume, depend on, and enjoy the benevolence and unconditional acceptance of another person (Doi, 1973). It is expressed nonverbally and reinforces closeness and warmth between persons in intimate relationships. In their relationship roles, women often bear the burden of expressing *amae* toward others but may have few opportunities to receive *amae*, which can contribute to challenges to well-being (Enns & Kasai, 2003; Kawanishi, 2009).

Knowledge of these cultural dimensions can support meaningful comparisons as well as awareness of diversity within regions such as Asia. Substantial within-culture variations also exist, and the manner in which these dimensions are manifested is often shaped or modified by various social institutions such as religion, family structures, or government. Although the values of sojourners and first-generation immigrants to North America are most likely to resemble those endorsed by persons from their countries of origin, second-generation immigrants are more likely to subscribe to attitudes that resemble "typical American" perspectives (Pew Research Center, 2013b). In order to practice competently, it is important for psychologists to clarify the degree to which an individual's personal values conform to typical North American worldviews, values associated with a specific country or ethnic group, or a mixture of values from multiple sources.

Philosophical and Religious Belief Systems

Patriarchal belief systems and methods of solidifying male authority vary across cultures and may focus on beliefs about intellectual competence, physical or emotional characteristics, family roles, and many other social domains. Within East Asia (e.g., China, Taiwan, Korea, Vietnam, Hong Kong, Japan), Buddhism and Confucianism represent belief systems that are often associated with traditional gender beliefs or hierarchical social arrangements (Gross, 1993; Shimamoto, 2006). Confucius described a virtuous woman as one who was subordinate to her father before marriage, to her husband after marriage, and to her son after her husband died (Vohra, 1999). Because of the gender inequality embedded in traditional Confucianism, Asian women who accept or live according to the Confucian tradition might be viewed by Western feminists as victims of "false consciousness" or as "antifeminist" (Kitagawa, 2007). However, many Asian women who live in societies that value self-effacement, harmony, and connectedness may experience Western feminisms as alienating or incomplete because of their emphasis on autonomy and independence. Collectivist versions of gender equality and Confucian or Buddhist feminism can be integrated with a Confucian or a Buddhist understanding of human nature (Clark & Wang, 2004; Gross, 1993). Compared with most Western feminisms, these alternatives place less emphasis on individual rights and short-term gains and greater priority on interconnectedness among women in a web of relationships as well as a willingness to work within existing family, community, and political systems to achieve long-term goals that benefit all (Enns, 2004).

Buddhism, an important foundation for religious and spiritual coping in Asia, calls on individuals to accept the reality of discomfort and suffering in the world and to cope through awareness, acceptance, and transcendence (Gross, 1993). Although identified as a potential source of misogyny, Buddhism also holds the potential for productive coping and mindfulness. In addition, Buddhist practice is also associated with beliefs about abortion that are less divisive than those found within North America. Buddhist beliefs about the fluidity of life and transmigration as well as the assumption that unborn life is ambiguous and not fully formed support the view that abortion is a regrettable necessity (LaFleur, 1992). In Japan, rituals and memorial services (*mizuko kuyo*) are available to women who have experienced abortion or miscarriage (Brooks, 1981) and can facilitate healthy coping and mourning.

Buddhist perspectives also foster the recognition of suffering and difficulty as "givens" as well as the promotion of coping marked by acceptance and a shift in attitude that facilitates resilience (Gaskins, 1999). Although many aspects of Japanese culture are no longer practiced within third- or fourth-generation Japanese American families, the Japanese phrase *shikata ga nai*, translated as "that which cannot be helped," has been used across generations of Japanese descendants in North America to facilitate perseverance (Sakamoto, 2007).

Buddhist sects and traditions vary across Asian countries, often in combination with other indigenous religions (e.g., Shinto practice in Japan). Many other indigenous religious and philosophical systems influence gender dynamics, such as Islam, Hinduism, Taoism, or Christianity. In addition, Japanese Americans and other Asian American who have multiple generations of personal history in North America are less likely to be influenced by Asian religious and philosophical systems than first-generation immigrants. Among contemporary Japanese Americans, for example, 38% identify themselves as Christian, 35% as Buddhist, and 32% as unaffiliated. Whereas 58% of Americans identify religion as important, 39% of Asian Americans identify religion as important to their lives (Pew Research Center, 2013a).

Social and Family Systems

Family values and the social systems that support them vary significantly around the world. Although traditional Japanese family life revolved around an extended family system, rapid change after World War II triggered a shift toward individualism. Post–World War II nuclear family units were predicated on a gendered division of labor in which women are encouraged to serve in full-time housewife roles that complement men's roles as full-time workers (Ochiai, 1997; Tokuhiro, 2010). Women have been typically expected to fulfill roles as professional housewives who manage all domestic, household, and child-rearing responsibilities, thus freeing men to devote long hours to their work (Huen, 2007; Takeda, 2008). However, economic changes after Japan's bubble economy in the 1990s and a long recession have resulted in a reduction in job security, full-time job opportunities, and income levels as well the increased participation of women in paid employment.

The traditional and idealized notion of the good wife and wise mother (*ryosaikenbo*), which defined the adult woman's role as providing moral and educational foundations through domestic caregiving and household management, continues to limit women's and men's views of women's roles (Tokuhiro, 2010). Japanese women continue to carry disproportionate responsibility for child rearing, and many couples delay or give up the idea of having children because of the high costs associated with providing high-quality education for their children. In 2011, 43% of Japanese college-educated women over age 40 did not have children (Hewlett, Sherbin, Fredman, Ho, & Sumberg, 2011).

Over time, Japanese marriage has become an "emotional project" based on romantic relationships rather than an arrangement by two families (Takeda, 2008). The concept of *konkatsu*, or "partner hunting," has been compared with *shukatsu*, the task of job hunting. Underlying this phenomenon is the assumption that marriage is no longer an outcome for everyone but a choice (Yamada, 2010). The challenges of finding a suitable partner are underscored by Yoshida's (2011) qualitative study of Tokyo women, who identified their complex work and social worlds as providing "no chance for romance" (p. 213).

These realities and the desire to circumvent traditional and confining gender roles associated with marriage have contributed to the postponement or delay of marriage, and alternative partnerships and cohabitation have become increasingly common and attractive for Japanese women (Nemoto, 2008; Tokuhiro, 2010; Yoshida, 2011). Psychologists are encouraged to be aware of the diverse forms of partnerships that women may choose and how sociopolitical factors may influence their choices and experiences.

When marriage is not fulfilling, divorce is an option, with one divorce occurring in every three marriages in Japan. However, married women who have fulfilled their social obligations as full-time mothers typically lack financial independence, which limits their ability to seek divorce; most divorced women do not receive financial support for child rearing, and children of divorced parents may be stigmatized (Sugimoto, 2010). Because of systemic factors that support the patriarchal family as well as limited legal support for women's alternatives outside of marriage, *katei-nai-rikon*, or divorce within marriage, is relatively common. In order to maintain appearances within the community, partners may continue to live in the same household but live separate lives (Sugimoto, 2010).

As can be seen from this brief section, even within Japan, substantial diversity related to intimate relationships is present, particularly among young Japanese women. The experiences of Japanese American women also reflect the diversity of experiences associated with their identities as American and Asian American women. Among contemporary Japanese Americans, 64% of those who enter a heterosexual marriage marry a person of non-Japanese descent, with women more likely to marry out than men (Pew Research Center, 2013a). Thus, some of the challenges experienced by Japanese American women in intimate partnerships may involve negotiating cultural differences as well as exploring multiracial identity themes (AhnAllen & Suyemoto, 2011).

Education, Work, and Economics

A comprehensive understanding of gender issues is built on knowledge of social class differences, women's access to schooling, the purpose and goals of women's education, and employment and social opportunities available to women. Although contemporary women of middle-class status in Japan have excellent access to educational opportunities, attaining gender equality in the work force has been elusive. Japan's rankings on gender equality have been low, placing it at 101st out of 135 nations (Hausmann, Tyson, & Zahidi, 2012). A woman's average salary is 70.6% of that of a man, although the discrepancy is shrinking (Huen, 2007).

Among married women, women's labor force participation rate in Japan takes the form of an "M" shape because many women temporarily withdraw from the labor force after childbirth in their late 20s to early 30s and return after completing the most demanding period of child rearing (Huen, 2007). Whereas about three quarters of Japanese college-educated women leave their jobs at childbirth, approximately half as many women do so in countries such as the United States and Germany (Hewlett et al., 2011). In addition to cultural ideologies about the necessity of women's full-time presence in their young children's lives during the first 3 years of life (Tokuhiro, 2010), the M-shape career path is also influenced by the lack of flexibility in corporate work structures, such as extensive and rigid work hours that often preclude a satisfying work–home interface. Other issues include limited access to child-care services, traditional gender beliefs, limited advancement options, and gender biases within companies (Hewlett et al., 2011). Although the number of women participating in the workforce has been increasing, those who reenter the work force after child rearing often experience significant barriers and often are limited to part-time or "nonregular" work status with few benefits. Substantial tax benefits are available to households in which women work part time versus full time, further limiting the financial benefits of full-time employment and pointing to structural supports for traditional family arrangements (Sugimoto, 2010).

Whereas Japanese women have been developing more liberal views of gender roles, a "consciousness gap" (Kelsky, 2001, p. 88) has been observed between men and women, with men having difficulty "catching up" with women's needs and lifestyles (Aono & Kashiwagi, 2011). Consequently, Japanese women may struggle to achieve their ideal lifestyles and career plans while trying to cope with social pressures to be "good wives and wise mothers" (*ryosaikenbo*). Simultaneously, women's ideal lifestyles are becoming more diverse, with some choosing professional housewife roles and others opting for greater freedom, which may be accompanied by the choice to remain single or to adopt alternative intimate relationships (e.g., cohabiting relationships, lesbian intimate relationships). In addition, some women who perceive their Japan-based opportunities as limited explore other options by seeking employment in transnational companies within or outside of Japan or studying and traveling abroad (Kelsky, 2001). These choices may reflect an active social resistance to traditional roles.

Educational backgrounds as well as cultural expectations about the feasibility of balancing work and family are important factors related to the work lives of women in both North America and Japan. For many Japanese women, work-related choices are often associated with less flexibility than is the case for North American women, including Japanese American women. However, concerns about work–family balance, child care, and equality in the workplace are shared across country contexts.

Government, Legal Systems, and Law Enforcement

To conceptualize gender issues effectively, it is important to understand (a) the basic structure of government and to what degree individual rights and choices are protected; (b) the types of laws that support equality or lack of equality; (c) legal guidelines with regard to marriage, divorce, and custody; (d) legal options that are available in response to sexual assault, domestic violence, and sexual harassment; and (e) the degree to which law enforcement systems support women's rights or offer protection.

Within Japan, a variety of laws are designed to support equality among women and men. The Equal Employment Opportunity Law and its subsequent revisions dictate equal treatment of men and women in work settings, methods for resolving grievances, and family leave and sexual harassment policies. When originally enacted in 1986, this legislation eliminated separate categories of "men's" and "women's" work and called on companies to "endeavor" to treat workers equally; however, the law did not establish sanctions for noncompliance and contained loopholes which have resulted in limited positive change in women's work experiences. Companies often responded to mandates by establishing a new version of two tracks: career and noncareer (or ordinary) tracks, which left much of the gendered nature of Japanese employment intact. Given the fact that typical career tracks require a commitment to long and confining work days and work conditions, many women have opted for the greater flexibility afforded by noncareer or ordinary work tracks, which confine them to more traditional and clerical women's work roles (Enns, 2004; Tokuhiro, 2010).

The 1999 Basic Law for a Gender Equal Society identified gender equality in society as a national priority. This law emphasizes the human rights of both men and women, gender neutral social systems and practices, and family life and work balance. Major factors that led the government to establish the Basic Law included declining fertility, an aging population, and international pressure. However, some suggest that this law provides a more acceptable face to the world without substantially changing reality (Huen, 2007).

Violence against women has been another important priority in Japan. In the past, euphemisms were used to depict violence, with rape being referred to as a "violent act" (Kozu, 1999). Sexual harassment was first named in 1989, and the term used to describe this form of gender violence (*sekuhara*) is an English loan word. More recently, however, a 2001 law mandated services for victims of domestic violence and a range of consequences for perpetrators of violence.

As part of these recent efforts, Japan has conceptualized intimate violence in accordance with the United Nations human rights framework and identified domestic violence as a violation of constitutional rights (Enns, 2004).

As seen from the commentary in this section, social policies and legislation often support the expansion of women's roles, but traditional power dynamics and limited enforcement tend to limit the real effects of such policies. For many women, the outward appearance of equality is not matched with the real experiences of their lives, which can contribute to negative internalized attitudes toward themselves and exacerbate the psychological challenges they face.

Adult women from Japan who enter the United States as spouses of Japanese workers (see the case study later in this chapter) may have had limited opportunity to develop their skills in the work world and may appear somewhat traditional. In contrast, younger Japanese women may experience the higher levels of individualism in the United States as freeing. Many Japanese American women whose identities are "American" are likely to expect relatively high levels of equality in the United States but may also experience stereotypes of Asian woman as members of a "model minority," as perpetual foreigners, or as exoticized women (Suzuki et al., 2012; see also Chapter 6, this volume;).

Feminism and Social Justice Movements

Indigenous women's, feminist, and social justice movements have flourished in many regions of the world. Although sharing some broad commonalities, these movements are also shaped by a country's culture and "a complex amalgam of national, racial, religious, ethnic, class, and sexual identities" (Basu, 1995, p. 4). Feminist psychologists working in transnational contexts benefit by developing knowledge of the priorities, strengths, and achievements of local feminisms.

One of the earliest debates within Japanese feminism (in the 1910s) focused on whether the economic independence of women was essential or whether the state protection of motherhood (*boaseihogoronso*), which preserved women's unique child-rearing roles, should be prioritized. Diversity of opinion about liberation is still present in Japan. "Housewife feminism" supports the social change activities of professional housewives and coexists with state feminism and the Gender Equality Bureau of Japan, ecological feminism, and more radical forms of feminism (Enns, 2004, 2011; Tokuhiro, 2010).

The valuing of gender difference within some Japanese feminisms is related to its critique of the constricting and inflexible roles of men in corporate structures, which are seen as offering few rewards, liberation, or life satisfaction. Renowned feminist Ueno (1997) noted that "our primary goal is not to be like men but to value what it means to be a woman" (p. 280). Many Japanese feminists have offered a cultural critique of oppressive corporate work structures, supported alternative paths to liberation, and attempted to "redefine the concept of gender" (Kitagawa, 2007, p. 7). Additional information can be found in a special issue of *Feminism and Psychology*, which explored the "rich tapestry of Japanese feminisms" (Burman & Aono, 2011; Enns, 2011).

For Asian American and Japanese American women, the discrimination against women within North America and the intersections of identity such as race–ethnicity, gender, class, sexual orientation, age, and immigration history are especially important considerations (Enns, 2004; Suzuki et al., 2012). Although a shared Asian American (or pan-Asian) identity has facilitated Asian American women's ability to support shared Asian American feminisms and a unified approach to advocacy and social change, the tremendous diversity among the Asian American women is also noteworthy. Such diversity can become invisible or overshadowed by an overemphasis on shared identity.

Colonialism

Knowledge of the presence, absence, extent, and length of a country's colonial history is crucial for understanding how gender roles and power structures have been shaped. In the wake of a colonial history, members of a culture may carry long-term hostility or internalized negative messages about themselves (Nadal, 2009). In some cases, colonial powers may reinforce social beliefs and related gender inequality or communicate the need to bring a "civilizing" influence to the culture. Furthermore, this "civilizing" influence can involve the distortion of cultural beliefs about gender or communicate the belief that women must be "rescued" from their cultural beliefs through Westernization and Western methods. The presence of a colonial history often influences the forms of feminism that are valued, such as efforts to integrate feminist and anticolonial perspectives (Basu, 1995).

As an extension of feminism's broad focus on human rights and social justice issues, Japanese feminists have often emphasized a range of issues that extend beyond a narrow definition of "women's issues" to encompass concerns related to Japan's colonial and imperial past and Japan's invasion and colonization of some of its East Asian neighbors during World War II (e.g., Korea, Taiwan, China, the Philippines). During the post–World War II era, many of the tensions between Japan and its East Asian neighbors have eased, but intercultural communication challenges remain (Kingston, 2013). Persons of Asian descent who live in Japan are among those who experience the negative long-term effects of colonization, such as women immigrants from other regions in Asia.

A major characteristic of Japanese feminism is feminist scholars' contributions to an analysis of gender and nation in "connecting with other anti-colonial movements and, in particular, allying with the debates about 'comfort women' and the war (and sex) crimes associated with Japanese occupation of South Asian countries in the Second World War" (Burman & Aono, 2011, pp. 496–497). Recognizing that powerful patriarchal interests within their own country have or continue to support forms of abuse related to sex trafficking and cross-national abuse, Japanese feminists have created alliances with women from other Asian countries in order to share resources and challenges practices such as sex tourism and sex trafficking. In general, this trajectory and attention to cross-national collaboration is distinguished from Western feminist movements that have tended to focus primarily on achieving women's reproductive rights and economic and political participation (Enns, 2004).

For Japanese American immigrants to North America, colonialism has been manifested quite differently. The internment of 120,000 persons of first- and second-generation Japanese ancestry during World War II can be viewed as a colonial act of the United States. The long-term economic and psychological consequences of internment have included threats to basic human dignity and a sense of powerlessness as well as the disruption of valued Japanese cultural traditions (Nagata & Takeshita, 2002; Suzuki et al., 2012). Awareness of this historical period is important for understanding the long term effects of discrimination as well as for generating support for fighting against other exclusionary trends and working toward equality for all.

Discrimination, Oppression, and Ethnic Conflict

Ethnic conflicts and power differences between majority and minority groups exist in many countries. These intergroup conflicts often intersect with gender related beliefs and violence as well as with identities associated with religion, race, sexual orientation, or other identities. Women's oppression and abuse may be exacerbated in times of conflict, and the abuse of women may be used to reinforce the power of one ethnic group over another (Norsworthy & Khuankaew, 2004).

Consistent with the theme of intersectionality in Western feminism, Chizuko Ueno (1996) coined the term *fukugosabetsu* to describe the complex interrelationship between multiple forms of oppression and discrimination. *Fukugosabetsu*, which can be translated as "complex discrimination" or "compound discrimination," is useful for explaining the realities and challenges of marginalized women in Japan who are subject to multiple forms of oppression and stigma.

Whereas in the United States "minority groups" often include racial, ethnic, or linguistic minorities, gender minorities, sexuality minorities, age minorities, and religious minorities, there are several unique marginalized groups in Japan that may not fit into the aforementioned categories. *Burakumin* (hamlet people), who represent Japan's largest Japanese social minority group, are ethnically and linguistically indistinguishable from other Japanese people but often face discrimination because they are from areas that were associated with occupations that were once considered "impure," such as professions associated with leather trades and death (Sugimoto, 2010). Although the inferior status of *burakumin* was officially abolished in 1871, individuals from former *buraku* areas continue to report multiple forms of discrimination related to social harassment, housing, education, employment, occupational choice, and marriage (Shirasawa, 1985). Complex forms of discrimination are also experienced by other minority groups within Japan, such as indigenous *Ainu* groups from northern Japan, Korean residents (*Zainichi*), and other foreign (*gaijin*) women who come to Japan as wives and workers (Sugimoto, 2010). For example, foreign sex workers, who are usually from Southeast Asian countries, are often subjected to violence but do not seek help out of fear of being deported.

Japan has shown a high level of acceptance of diverse sexual expression, and sexual expression between men (especially samurai) was seen as an extension of male sexuality; however, lesbians and lesbian sexuality have often remained invisible, and lesbians feel pressured to live double lives. Lesbians may marry men because of economic concerns and the large wage gap that exists between men and women in Japan. Lesbians and bisexual women are also vulnerable to intimate violence, and lesbians and bisexual women in Japan were found to be more likely to experience sexual, physical, and psychological violence by intimate partners than gay and bisexual men (DiStefano, 2009). However, such issues often go unrecognized in both sexual minority communities and Japanese society in general. It should be noted that same-sex marriage is not legalized in any Asian country at this point. Furthermore, in some Asian countries, sexual behavior outside of heterosexual relationships can be criminalized (Kasai & Rooney, 2012).

The brief description within this section points to the complexity of human rights issues that exist even within a country that is often described as relatively homogeneous (Sugimoto, 2010). Within North America, the forms of discrimination experienced by women are also diverse and associated with complex intersections of race–ethnicity, class, sexual orientation, age, and disability. Other stereotypes that support prejudice and discrimination include images of Asian women as exotic or hypersexual, as dangerous or as "Dragon Ladies," as perpetual foreigners, or as members of a model minority that is purported to experience limited discrimination (see Chapter 6, this volume; Suzuki et al., 2012).

PROFESSIONAL RESPONSIBILITY
AND PRACTICE APPLICATIONS

The application of culturally sensitive practice is built on knowledge foundations described in the previous section. In this section, we discuss transnational applications of feminist and gender sensitive assumptions that are relevant to Guidelines 4 through 11. In addition, we briefly describe interventions that are compatible with cultural values.

Transnational Feminist Psychotherapy

The Guidelines speak to the importance of using gender and culturally appropriate interventions characterized by inclusive and unbiased conceptual frameworks as well as implementing interventions and resources that support women's resilience and empowerment within their sociocultural contexts. These criteria characterize feminist approaches, including Japanese feminist therapy approaches, and we encourage those in transnational practice to become familiar with local womanist or feminist approaches, including those that are connected to indigenous traditions. In Japan, Kiyomi Kawano was influential in founding a feminist therapy center called *Nakama* (translated as "companion") and the Society of Japanese Feminist Counseling Practices and Studies. She collaborated with other Japanese feminists in diverse fields, including a sociology professor, community staff, a psychiatrist, an attorney, and a counselor, to create guidelines for providing counseling for women at women's centers in Japan (*joseisenta*, or "center for women"). The guidelines, which were adopted by the Society of Japanese Feminist Counseling Practices and Studies, use the term *counseling* instead of phrases such as *psychotherapy* to reflect the broad range of preparation pathways and settings in which psychological practice occurs.

According to these guidelines, counselors should avoid pathologizing their clients' concerns or assuming that all women's concerns are the objects of or can be resolved through psychological care. Second, whether treatment is long term or short term, individual or group work, it is important for counselors at women's centers to empower women through facilitating their awareness of and maximizing their internal healing capacity. Third, a fundamental foundation of feminist counseling and psychotherapy is gender analysis, which involves the redefinition of the client's presenting issues. In addition, counselors should be knowledgeable of community resources and utilize these resources in order to address women's diverse challenges.

Two final themes in the Japanese guidelines are especially relevant to social change. Counselors are encouraged to make efforts to ensure that the process and accomplishments of feminist counseling are reflected in policies for women. Women's center counselors, psychologists, and psychotherapists are also encouraged to educate and enlighten people in the local community in order to facilitate their understanding of women's issues and to resolve and prevent these issues (Kawano, 1999, pp. 162–167, translated by Machizawa). As is the case in a variety of world regions, Japanese feminist studies have been influenced substantially by grassroots efforts and activism (Burman & Aono, 2011); knowledge of community resources; and alliances between professional mental health workers and paraprofessionals support holistic and comprehensive services. In keeping with the important tradition of grassroots activism and volunteering, much of the therapeutic treatment mandated by Japan's 2001 domestic violence legislation is provided by paraprofessional counselors who receive their training and work within nongovernmental organization (NGO) settings (Hatashita, Hirao, Brykczynski, & Anderson, 2006). Examples of these NGO organizations include the Feminine Life Cycle Institute (Muramoto, 2011), which provides services and training for trauma survivors, and Resilience (http://www. resilience.jp), which provides education and consciousness raising about domestic and dating violence. Similar types of services and collaborations between psychologists, paraprofessionals, and activists are likely to be available in other world regions and offer creative alternatives for enhancing healing and well-being.

Conceptual and Intervention Frameworks

A variety of conceptual frameworks and interventions can be integrated within woman-centered and feminist multicultural frameworks, which serve as a type of umbrella for organizing transnational psychological practice with diverse groups of women. In this section, we briefly address characteristics of these options.

As noted earlier in this chapter, psychology is a growing industry and profession in East Asian countries such as Taiwan, Hong Kong, and Mainland China. North American psychotherapeutic and counseling theories and models have been widely adopted and adapted in these countries, perhaps because Asian therapists often have received their psychotherapy training in the West (Duan et al., 2011). Although psychotherapy effectiveness is strongly influenced by cultural factors (Tseng, 2001), Western frameworks are sometimes applied inappropriately and without sensitivity to cultural nuances (Watters, 2010). It is crucial for transnational feminist psychologists to be aware of clients' diversity and act in clients' best interests by using assessment tools that provide insights about the diverse social identities of clients (see Chapter 2, this volume) and linking assessment information to conceptual options that are respectful of cultural knowledge and traditions. In Japan, for example, cultural values are important for understanding problems such as eating disorders

(Hansen, 2011), depression (Kitanaka, 2011; Watters, 2010), posttraumatic reactions (Muramoto, 2011), and coping with domestic violence (Hatashita, Brykczynski, & Anderson, 2006).

Many Western psychotherapies are characterized as focusing primarily on the individual (often in isolation), a linear cause–effect process of change, verbal expression, and the separation of physical and mental well-being (Sue & Sue, 2008), features that may be inconsistent with more collective orientations to health and change. In contrast, a variety of culture-influenced unique Asian psychotherapies exist (e.g., Daoistic cognitive therapy in China), and are "strongly colored by the philosophical concepts or value systems of the non-Western societies in which they were invented" (Tseng, Kitanishi, Maeshiro, & Zhu, 2012, p. 415). For example, in contrast to more traditional Western therapies, in Japan, *hakoniwa*, or sandtray therapy, is a holistic, whole-body therapy that involves "creating one's world" in the sand. Following an initial nonverbal phase, clients are invited to reflect on and describe their creations, a phase that often elicits feelings, needs, and motivations that can then be more easily articulated. This therapy is based on the integration of Jungian psychology and Buddhist values and supports more nonverbal expression, the integration of mind–body expression, and wholeness supported by one's social-relational context (Enns & Kasai, 2003; Kawai, 1996).

Western psychotherapies were introduced in Japan during the early and midpoints of the 20th century and have been gradually integrated with Japanese cultural values (Iwakabe & Enns, 2012). In addition, some of the indigenous psychotherapies of Japan, which have not been widely practiced in Japan during recent years (e.g., Morita therapy, which emphasizes acting in spite of troubling symptoms and anxieties, and Naikan therapy, which emphasizes self-reflection and gratitude toward significant others), have been introduced and adapted successfully as forms of positive and cognitive behavioral psychologies in North America (e.g., Ishiyama, 2003; Krech, 2002). The contemporary adaptations of these indigenous psychotherapies hold promise for psychotherapy in Japan. Conversely, a variety of popular interventions in the West are influenced by Zen Buddhist assumptions, including acceptance and commitment therapy (Hayes & Lillis, 2012), mindfulness-based stress reduction (Kabat-Zinn, 1991), and dialectical behavior therapy (Linehan, 1993), and may hold potential for working with clients in Japan as well as North America. Finally, active therapies such as yoga and the martial arts, as well as the Zen arts, which consist of calligraphy, *ikebana* (flower arranging), and *sado* (tea ceremony), may also be used as interventions to support stress reduction and personal growth (Enns & Kasai, 2003).

Other approaches that may be compatible with feminist collectivist frameworks have their origin in the relational–cultural model of psychotherapy (Miller & Stiver, 1997), which highlights the role of connections in human growth. This model focuses on major strengths that emerge from close human relationships, and has the potential to be integrated with Japanese indigenous concepts such as *amae* (Bradshaw, 1990; Doi, 1973), which solidifies one's sense of being able to both give and receive care and benevolence from others.

Although the approaches discussed in this section may be most applicable to women living in Japan, they are also beneficial for augmenting psychological practice in North America (e.g., Bradshaw, 1990) with Japanese American women and other Asian American women. For example, Japanese Americans who have retained an appreciation for Japanese and Asian values may find these approaches especially valuable. In addition, those who wish to reclaim aspects of their cultural heritage may also benefit from these alternatives.

CASE STUDIES: SAKI AND KEIKO

In this final section of the chapter, we demonstrate the application of the Guidelines to work with two Japanese women. The first woman (Saki) is middle aged and is married to a Japanese man whose work resulted in a placement in the United States. The types of interventions used in this first case study may also be relevant to work with other Asian American first-generation immigrants. The second woman (Keiko) is younger and has returned to Japan after a sojourn as a student in the United States. The differences between these two women with regard to life stages, values, goals, and transnational experience point to two of the many ways in which psychotherapy might unfold. The following case studies are fictional but informed by clinical practice. Any details related to actual clients have been changed to protect confidentiality.

Case Study 1: Saki

Saki is a Japanese woman in her late 50s who had moved to the United States about 15 years earlier and lived in Los Angeles with her husband and two daughters. She initially visited a neurologist with complaints of memory problems, but the results of the medical and neuropsychological evaluations found no cognitive dysfunction or structural–functional brain abnormalities. Instead, moderately severe depression was noted, and she was referred for individual psychotherapy. She entered psychotherapy with a Japanese psychologist who had been trained in the United States.

During the first several therapy sessions, Saki frequently talked about relational issues with her husband. She stated that her voice was frequently unheard by her husband because whenever she expressed her feelings or thoughts he ridiculed her or said "that is trivial" (*dodemoii*). The therapist noticed that when Saki talked about an upsetting event, she tended to internalize it. For example, one time she talked about their marital argument and a hurtful comment that her husband had made. She concluded, "I made him angry because I asked him too many questions. I think I made him feel that he was being blamed." The therapist considered the potential impact of traditional values on her coping style and how these values might be limiting her views of herself. These actions are consistent with Guideline 1, which emphasizes the importance of taking socialization, stereotyping, and unique life events into account; Guideline 2, which encourages psychologists to consider information about oppression and privilege, and Guideline 9, which calls on psychologists to place problems within their sociopolitical context. The therapist then encouraged Saki to reconceptualize her relational issue as contextual rather than as individual. This approach is consistent with both Guidelines 9 and 7, which recommend practices that promote initiative, empowerment, and expanded alternatives for women. The following is a dialogue between Saki and her therapist:

> *Therapist:* Was it your fault that he [Saki's husband] got angry?
>
> *Saki:* I don't know, but I think he doesn't like when I ask him too many questions. It makes him feel being criticized. He takes it personally.
>
> *Therapist:* Did you ask questions to criticize him?
>
> *Saki:* Of course not. That was not my intention at all! I just wanted to understand his behavior and intention.
>
> *Therapist:* So you just wanted to understand him better.
>
> *Saki:* Exactly.
>
> *Therapist:* So was it your fault that he was upset?
>
> *Saki:* Well, I guess he was angry because he misinterpreted my intention. His parents were really strict and critical when he was a child, so he tends to think that everyone is critical of him.

Over the course of time, the therapist noticed that Saki became more confident and vocal about her needs. For example, when her husband made a joke at her expense, she told him that she found the joke inappropriate and that it hurt her. In addition, she was increasingly able to identify her strengths, such as social skills and empathy. In fact, she had many visitors and was well liked by her friends in different social circles. Initially, she was happy and proud of her transformation. However, she noticed that they had more arguments because "he doesn't like how assertive I am now." It appeared that Saki's transformation was affecting the entire family system, and her husband was experiencing difficulty accepting the "new" Saki.

The therapist suspected that her husband might have perceived Saki's independence and confidence as a threat to his power and authority. On the basis of her knowledge of Japanese culture, the therapist understood that harmonious relationships within the family were extremely important to Saki's well-being. Thus, it was vital to help create a culturally supportive environment that supported Saki's transformation through the use of gender-sensitive and culturally sensitive and affirming practices (Guideline 4) and approaches that are effective for addressing women's concerns (Guideline 6). The therapist showed respect for Saki's collective, relational values and gently explored with her ways to help her family members understand and accept her changes and cope with these changes. Saki also suggested bringing her husband to a therapy session, and thought that the therapist's presence would help them talk through issues in a safe and contained environment.

During the session with both Saki and her husband, the husband admitted that he tended to say hurtful things to Saki when he was upset. He said that when they had a conflict, he often avoided communicating with her out of fear of being too emotional. He also acknowledged that it was difficult for him to balance being a good "boss" in the *kaisha* (company) and being a good husband at home. In the *kaisha*, he was expected to be an independent, confident, authority figure. At home, however, he felt that Saki expected him to listen to her thoughts and often challenged his ideas, which he found difficult to handle. Saki reported that it was helpful to understand the reasons behind his behavior. Saki continued in individual therapy, but she sometimes brought her husband to a session when they had an issue. After one big argument at home, her husband showed up to a therapy session without telling her in advance. Saki was very upset and remained silent throughout the session. After that point, Saki and the therapist set a rule that her husband could only join the therapy session when Saki requested his presence and consented in advance. Saki later reported that it was empowering to know that she had the right to set the rules and boundaries. In this counseling relationship, it was important for Saki to know that the psychotherapy sessions were primarily for her benefit, and that the inclusion of her husband in occasional counseling sessions allowed her to build confidence in her ability to communicate clearly and confidently with him.

As is seen in this case study, Saki had internalized many of the cultural values described earlier in this chapter, and her initial symptoms (memory problems) reflected mind–body expressions that are relatively common among East Asian clients. As someone trained to give *amae* to others and to tie her sense of success to fulfilling family roles and obligations, Saki's ability to express her own feelings was limited. The therapist's knowledge of Japanese culture was central to the timing and application of interventions, such as those related to emotion expression and family involvement. In addition to those described in the case study, Saki's resilience and well-being could be supported through connections to Japanese American social organizations in the community. Saki's well-being might also be enhanced through stress-reduction interventions related to indigenous Japanese traditions (e.g., Zen arts, mindfulness training).

Case Study 2: Keiko

Keiko is a 24-year-old woman from Japan who completed her under-graduate college degree in the United States and then returned to Japan. Her excellent English language skills and her desire for intercultural experiences contributed to her decision to study abroad. While in the United States, she earned a degree with a major in psychology and a minor in ethnic and gender studies. On returning to Japan and having some difficulty readjusting to her country of birth, Keiko sought out counseling from a Japanese psychologist who had received her psychological training in both Canada and Japan and who specialized in working with women.

As an extension of Guideline 1, which focuses on the importance of the unique socialization and life experiences of women across cultural groups, the psychologist helped Keiko explore her concerns, including her feelings that her goals were "out of sync" with her culture. In addition, Keiko disclosed disappointment that her experience as a student in the United States did not offer the advantages that she had hoped for on returning to Japan, especially in the work world. Instead, she felt as though she was being scrutinized for her ability to fit back into a culture that felt confining, especially in terms of gender roles and work.

The psychologist helped Keiko clarify her goals as well as explore her disappointments and the "lack of fit" she was experiencing. Social identity exploration and analysis (see Chapter 2, this volume) was central to their sessions and supported appropriate, personalized assessment (Guideline 8) and the exploration of the subtle biases Keiko faced (Guideline 3). This assessment helped Keiko understand the ways in which her multiple identi-ties and experiences made it difficult for her to move into the traditional pattern of work life in Japan (see the discussion of issues presented earlier in this chapter).

To support Keiko's empowerment (Guidelines 4 and 7), the psychologist briefly disclosed her own challenges moving between cultures and referred Keiko to a support group at a local women's counseling center. Within this support group Keiko was able to interact with other young women who were actively exploring challenges and opportunities facing Japanese women (such as those described in an earlier section of this chapter). Members of the support group offered friendship and helped Keiko focus on ways in which she could realize some of the goals that she feared she might need to give up in Japan. The psychologist also assisted her in negotiating volunteer work in a nongovernmental organization that focused on providing education and raising consciousness about intimate violence in Japan. This experience helped Keiko become more aware of and involved in social change (Guideline 11) and allowed her to make use of her academic learning in psychology and gender studies.

After a frustrating job search, Keiko secured a position providing translation and other services at a hotel that serves many international guests. Although not especially satisfying, the job allowed her to use her English skills on a regular basis. The psychologist and Keiko continued to work on ways that she could find meaning and affirm her strengths and resilience as a Japanese woman. For example, Keiko began taking classes in calligraphy and participating in tea ceremony practices. The integration of these artways with her other activities offered Keiko a new sense of balance and an opportunity to appreciate her Japanese heritage. At the end of therapy, she continued to have questions about her future (e.g., possibilities for intimate relationships), but she felt more confident that she could value what it means to be a Japanese woman in the 21st century.

CONCLUSION

The challenges as well as the rewards of working in transnational contexts are wide ranging. Competence is enhanced through general attitudes that facilitate entry into and learning within new cultural contexts, general intercultural communication skills, and culture-specific knowledge and skills that are relevant to women's realities. As psychologists consider their transnational interactions, some of the following questions are useful for building expertise.

- What concepts and values are central to the cultural context in which I am working?
- To what degree are the psychological theories and research that I endorse compatible with the realities of transnational contexts?
- What modifications or transformations of my worldview, conceptual theories, and interventions will enhance my effectiveness?
- How can local philosophical and indigenous feminisms inform my knowledge of the priorities and strengths of women in a transnational context?

- How can I increase my competence through learning and collaboration opportunities?

As noted throughout this chapter, the "Guidelines for Psychological Practice With Women and Girls" (APA, 2007) offer a positive framework or scaffold for transnational work. In the future, additional research and culture-specific knowledge will be important for filling in the outline and enriching foundations that have been established.

REFERENCES

Abarbanel, J. (2009). Moving with emotional resilience between and within cultures. *Intercultural Education, 20*(Suppl. S1–S2), S133–141. doi:10.1080/14675980903371035

AhnAllen, J. M., & Suyemoto, K. L. (2011). Influence of interracial dating on racial and/or ethnic identities of Asian American women and White European American men. *Asian American Journal of Psychology, 2*, 61–75. doi:10.1037/a0023325

American Psychological Association. (2004). *Resolution on culture and gender awareness in international psychology*. Washington, DC: Author.

American Psychological Association. (2007). Guidelines for psychological practice with girls and women. *American Psychologist, 62*, 949–979. doi:10.1037/0003-066X.62.9.949

Aono, A., & Kashiwagi, K. (2011). Myth or fact: Conceptions and realities of Japanese women/mothers. *Feminism and Psychology, 21*, 516–521.

Arnett, J. J. (2008). The neglected 95%: Why American psychology needs to become less American. *American Psychologist, 63*, 602–614. doi:10.1037/0003-066X.63.7.602

Basu, A. (Ed.). (1995). *The challenge of local feminisms: Women's movements in global perspective*. Boulder, CO: Westview Press.

Bennett, M. J. (2004). Becoming interculturally competent. In J. Wurzel (Ed.), *Toward multiculturalism: A reader in multicultural education* (2nd ed., pp. 62–77). Newton, MA: Intercultural Resources Corporation.

Bradshaw, C. K. (1990). A Japanese view of dependency: What can amae psychology contribute to feminist theory and therapy? *Women & Therapy, 9*(1–2), 67–86. doi:10.1300/J015v09n01_05

Brooks, A. P. (1981). Mizuko kuyo and Japanese Buddhism. *Japanese Journal of Religious Studies, 8*(3–4), 119–147.

Burman, E., & Aono, A. (2011). Editorial introduction: Japanese feminist psychologies. *Feminism & Psychology, 21*, 496–502. doi:10.1177/0959353511422692

Butler, J. E. (2000). Transforming the curriculum: Teaching about women of color. In J. A. Banks & C. A. M. Banks (Eds.), *Multicultural education: Issues and perspectives* (4th ed., pp. 174–193). New York, NY: Wiley.

Clark, K. J., & Wang, R. R. (2004). A Confucian defense of gender equity. *Journal of the American Academy of Religion, 72*, 395–422. doi:10.1093/jaarel/lfh035

DiStefano, A. S. (2009). Intimate partner violence among sexual minorities in Japan: Exploring perceptions and experience. *Journal of Homosexuality, 56*, 121–146. doi:10.1080/00918360802623123

Doi, T. (1973). *The anatomy of dependence*. New York, NY: Kodansha International.

Duan, C., Nilsson, J., Wang, C., Debernardi, N., Klevens, C., & Tallent, C. (2011). Internationalizing counseling: A Southeast Asian perspective. *Counselling Psychology Quarterly, 24*, 29–41. doi:10.1080/09515070.2011.558253

Enns, C. Z. (2004). *Feminist theories and feminist psychotherapies* (2nd ed.). New York, NY: Haworth Press.

Enns, C. Z. (2011). On the rich tapestry of Japanese feminisms. *Feminism & Psychology, 21*, 542–546. doi:10.1177/0959353511422934

Enns, C. Z., & Kasai, M. (2003). Hakoniwa: Japanese sandplay therapy. *The Counseling Psychologist, 31*, 93–112. doi:10.1177/0011000002239403

Enns, C. Z., Kasai, M., & Machizawa, S. (2006, August). Co-mentoring: Applying APA's resolution on culture and gender awareness. In C. Z. Enns (Chair), *Personal perspectives on collaborating and co-mentoring across cultures*. Symposium conducted at the 114th Annual Convention of the American Psychological Association, New Orleans, LA.

Enns, C. Z., & Machizawa, S. (2008, March). *Psychological practice with women and girls: Global perspectives*. Working group conducted at the 2008 International Counseling Psychology Conference, Chicago, IL.

Espín, O. (2005, January). *The age of the cookie cutter has passed*. Keynote presentation delivered at the 2005 National Multicultural Conference and Summit, Hollywood, CA.

Gaskins, R. W. (1999). "Adding legs to a snake": A reanalysis of motivation and the pursuit of happiness from a Zen Buddhist perspective. *Journal of Educational Psychology, 91*, 204–215. doi:10.1037/0022-0663.91.2.204

Gross, R. M. (1993). *Buddhism after patriarchy*. Albany: State University of New York Press.

Hansen, M. G. (2011). Eating disorders and self-harm in Japanese culture and cultural expressions. *Contemporary Japan, 23*, 49–69. doi:10.1515/cj.2011.004

Hatashita, H., Brykczynski, K. A., & Anderson, E. T. (2006). Chieko's story: Giving voice to survivors of wife abuse. *Health Care for Women International, 27*, 307–323. doi:10.1080/07399330500511758

Hatashita, H., Hirao, K., Brykczynski, K. A., & Anderson, E. T. (2006). Grassroots efforts of Japanese women to promote services for abused women. *Nursing & Health Sciences, 8*, 169–174. doi:10.1111/j.1442-2018.2006.00276.x

Hausmann, R., Tyson, L. D., & Zahidi, S. (2012). *The global gender gap report*. Geneva, Switzerland: World Economic Forum.

Hayes, S. C., & Lillis, J. (2012). *Acceptance and commitment therapy*. Washington, DC: American Psychological Association.

Henrich, J., Heine, S. J., & Norenzayan, A. (2010). The weirdest people in the world? *Behavioral and Brain Sciences, 33*(2–3), 61–83. doi:10.1017/S0140525X0999152X

Hewlett, S. A., Sherbin, L., Fredman, C., Ho, C., & Sumberg, K. (2011). *Off-ramps and on-ramps Japan: Keeping talented women on the road to success*. New York, NY: Center for Work-Life Policy.

Hikoyeda, N., Mukoyama, W. K., Liou, L. D., & Masterson, B. (2006). Working with Japanese American families. In G. Yeo & D. Gallagher-Thompson (Eds.), *Ethnicity and the dementias* (pp. 231–245). New York, NY: Taylor & Francis Group.

Hofstede, G. H., Hofstede, G. J., & Minkov, M. (2010). *Culture and organizations: Software of the mind* (3rd ed.). New York, NY: McGraw Hill Professional.

Horne, S. G., & Arora, K. S. K. (2012). Feminist multicultural counseling psychology in transnational contexts. In C. Z. Enns & E. N. Williams (Eds.), *Oxford handbook of feminist multicultural counseling psychology* (pp. 240–252). New York, NY: Oxford University Press. doi:10.1093/oxfordhb/9780199744220.013.0013

Horne, S. G., & Mathews, S. S. (2006). A social justice approach to international collaborative consultation. In R. L. Toporek, L. H. Gerstein, N. A. Fouad, G. Roysircar, & T. Israel (Eds.), *Handbook for social justice in counseling psychology* (pp. 388–405). Thousand Oaks, CA: Sage. doi:10.4135/9781412976220.n27

Horne, S. G., Matthews, S., Brown, D., & DeGroff, S. H. (2009). Not staying home: The experience of Uzbek women crisis counselors and therapists. *Women and Therapy, 32*, 317–337.

Huen, Y. W. P. (2007). Policy response to declining birth rate in Japan: Formation of a "gender-equal" society. *East Asia, 24*, 365–379. doi:10.1007/s12140-007-9026-8

Ishiyama, F. I. (2003). A bending willow tree: A Japanese (Morita therapy) model of human nature and client and change. *Canadian Journal of Counselling, 37*, 216–231. Retrieved from http://cjc-rcc.ucalgary.ca/cjc/index.php/rcc/article/view/233/524

Iwakabe, S., & Enns, C. Z. (2012). Counseling and psychotherapy in Japan. In R. Moodley, U. P. Gielen, & R. Wu (Eds.), *Handbook of counseling and psychotherapy in an international context* (pp. 204–214). New York, NY: Routledge.

Kabat-Zinn, J. (1991). *Full catastrophe living*. New York, NY: Bantam.

Kasai, M., & Rooney, C. (2012). The choice before the choice: Partner selection is essential to reproductive justice. In J. C. Chrisler (Ed.), *Reproductive justice: A global concern* (pp. 11–28). Santa Barbara, CA: Praeger.

Kawai, H. (1996). *Buddhism and the art of psychotherapy*. College Station: Texas A&M University Press.

Kawanishi, Y. (2009). *Mental health challenges facing contemporary Japanese society*. London, England: Global Oriental. doi:10.1163/ej.9781906876005.i-176

Kawano, K (1999). Josei senta ni okeru soudan gyomu gaidorain [Guidelines for counseling practice at a women's center]. In K. Kawano (Ed.) *Feminisuto kaunseringu no mirai* (pp. 157–179). Tokyo, Japan: Shinsuisha.

Kelsky, K. (2001). *Women on the verge: Japanese women, Western dreams*. Durham, NC: Duke University Press. doi:10.1215/9780822383277

Kim, B. S. (2009). Acculturation and enculturation of Asian Americans. In N. Tewari & A. N. Alvarez (Eds.), *Asian American psychology: Current perspectives* (pp. 97–112). New York, NY: Taylor & Francis.

Kingston, J. (2013). *Contemporary Japan: History, politics, and social change since the 1980s* (2nd ed.). Malden, MA: Wiley.

Kitagawa, S. (2007). *Cultural self-understanding and Japanese feminism*. Retrieved from http//utcp.c.u-tokyo.ac.jp/members/pdf/kitagawa_east_asian_feminism.pdf

Kitanaka, J. (2011). *Depression in Japan: Psychiatric cures for a society in distress*. Princeton, NJ: Princeton University Press.

Kozu, J. (1999). Domestic violence in Japan. *American Psychologist, 54*, 50–54. doi:10.1037/0003-066X.54.1.50

Krech, G. (2002). *Naikan: Gratitude, grace, and the Japanese art of self-reflection*. Berkeley, CA: Stone Bridge Press.

LaFleur, W. R. (1992). *Liquid life: Abortion and Buddhism in Japan*. Princeton, NJ: Princeton University Press.

Leung, K., & Bond, M. H. (2004). Social axioms: A model for social beliefs in multicultural perspective. *Advances in Experimental Social Psychology, 36*, 119–197. doi:10.1016/S0065-2601(04)36003-X

Linehan, M. M. (1993). *Skills training manual for treating borderline personality disorder*. New York, NY: Guilford.

Lugones, M. (1987). Playfulness, "world"-travelling and loving perception. *Hypatia, 2*(2), 3–19. doi:10.1111/j.1527-2001.1987.tb01062.x

Mackie, V. (2001). The language of globalization, transnationality and feminism. *International Feminist Journal of Politics, 3*(2), 180–206. doi:10.1080/14616740110053029

Miller, J. B., & Stiver, I. P. (1997). *The healing connection: How women form relationships in therapy and in life*. Boston, MA: Beacon Press.

Mohanty, C. T. (1991). Under Western eyes. In C. T. Mohanty, A. Russo, & T. Lourdes (Eds.), *Third world women and the politics of feminism* (pp. 52–80). Bloomington: Indiana University Press.

Mohanty, C. T. (2003). *Feminism without borders: Decolonizing theory, practicing solidarity*. Durham, NC: Duke University Press.

Muramoto, K. (2011). History and current approaches to violence towards women in Japan. *Feminism & Psychology, 21*, 510–515. doi:10.1177/0959353511422917

Nadal, K. L. (2009). Colonialism: Societal and psychological impacts on Asian Americans and Pacific Islanders. In N. Tewari & A. N. Alvarez (Eds.), *Asian*

American psychology: Current perspectives (pp. 153–172). New York, NY: Taylor & Francis.

Nagata, D. K., & Takeshita, Y. J. (2002). Psychological reactions to redress: Diversity among Japanese Americans interned during World War II. *Cultural Diversity and Ethnic Minority Psychology, 8,* 41–59. doi:10.1037/1099-9809.8.1.41

Nemoto, K. (2008). Postponed marriage: Exploring women's views of matrimony and work in Japan. *Gender & Society, 22,* 219–237. doi:10.1177/0891243208315868

Norsworthy, K. L., & Khuankaew, O. (2004). Women of Burma speak out: Workshops to deconstruct gender-based violence and build systems of peace and justice. *Journal for Specialists in Group Work, 29,* 259–283. doi:10.1080/01933920490477011

Ochiai, E. (1997). *The Japanese family system in transition.* Tokyo, Japan: LTCB International Library Foundation.

Pew Research Center. (2013a). *The rise of Asian Americans.* Washington, DC: Pew Research Center.

Pew Research Center. (2013b). *Second-generation Americans: A portrait of adult children of immigrants.* Washington, DC: Pew Research Center.

Rice, J., & Ballou, M. (2002). *Cultural and gender awareness in international psychology.* Washington, DC: American Psychological Association, Division 52, International Psychology, International Committee for Women.

Sakamoto, T. (2007). The triumph and tragedies of Japanese women in America: A view across four generations. *The History Teacher, 41,* 97–122.

Schwartz. S. J. (2012). An overview of the Schwartz theory of basic values. *Online Readings in Psychology and Culture, 2*(1). doi:10.9707/2307-0919.1116

Shimamoto, S. (2006). Traditional Japanese religious society. In M. Juergensmeyer (Ed.), *The Oxford handbook of global religions* (pp. 133–140). New York, NY: Oxford University Press.

Spickard, P. R. (2009). *Japanese Americans: The formation and transformation of an ethnic group.* New Brunswick, NJ: Rutgers University Press.

Sue, D. W., & Sue, D. (2008). *Counseling the culturally diverse* (5th ed.). New York, NY: Wiley.

Sugimoto, Y. (2010). *An introduction to Japanese society* (3rd ed.). New York, NY: Cambridge University Press. doi:10.1017/CBO9780511781223

Suzuki, L. A., Ahluwalia, M. K., & Alimchandani, A. (2012). Asian American women's feminism: Sociopolitical history and clinical considerations. In C. Z. Enns & E. N. Williams (Eds.), *The Oxford handbook of feminist multicultural counseling psychology* (pp. 183–198). New York, NY: Oxford University Press.

Takeda, H. (2008). The political economy of familial relations: The Japanese state and families in a changing political economy. *Asian Journal of Political Science, 16,* 196–214. doi:10.1080/02185370802204156

Tewari, N., & Alvarez, A. N. (Eds.). (2009). *Asian American psychologist: Current perspectives.* New York, NY: Taylor & Francis.

Tokuhiro, Y. (2010). *Marriage in contemporary Japan*. New York, NY: Routledge.

Tseng, W.-S. (2001). *Handbook of cultural psychiatry*. San Diego, CA: Academic Press.

Tseng, W.-S., Kitanishi, K., Maeshiro, T., & Zhu, J. (2012). Unique psychotherapies developed in Asia. In E. C. Chang (Ed.), *Handbook of adult psychopathology in Asians: Theory, diagnosis, and treatment* (pp. 414–431). New York, NY: Oxford University Press.

Ueno, C. (1996). *Fukugosabetsuron in Sabetsu to kyousei no shakaigaku* [Theory of *fukugosabetsu* in sociology of discrimination and coexistence]. Tokyo, Japan: Iwanami Shoten.

Ueno, C. (1997). Are the Japanese feminine? Some problems of Japanese feminism in its cultural context. In S. Buckley (Ed.), *Broken silence: Voices of Japanese feminism* (pp. 272–301). Berkeley: University of California Press.

Vohra, R. (1999). *China's path to modernization: A historical review from 1800 to the present* (3rd ed.). Upper Saddle River, NJ: Prentice Hall.

Watters, E. (2010). *Crazy like us: The globalization of the American psyche*. New York, NY: Simon & Schuster.

Wilson, J. (2009). *Mourning the unborn dead: A Buddhist ritual comes to America*. New York, NY: Oxford University Press. doi:10.1093/acprof:oso/9780195371932.001.0001

Yamada, M. (2010). *"Konkatsu" genshō no shakaigaku: Nihon no haigūshasentaku no ima* [The sociology of the *konkatsu* phenomenon: Spouse selection in modern Japan]. Tokyo, Japan: Tokyo Keizai Shinposha.

Yoshida, A. (2011). No chance for romance: Corporate culture, gendered work, and increased singlehood in Japan. *Contemporary Japan, 23*, 213–234. doi:10.1515/cj.2011.011

10

INCLUSIVE AND AFFIRMATIVE PSYCHOLOGICAL PRACTICE: UNIFYING THEMES

JOY K. RICE, CAROLYN ZERBE ENNS, AND ROBERTA L. NUTT

The "Guidelines for Psychological Practice With Girls and Women" (American Psychological Association [APA] 2007; hereinafter the Guidelines) reflect 40 years of multicultural and feminist perspectives in psychology and show users, readers, and practitioners how far we have come. They indeed are a very practical and useful foundation for working with diverse groups of women. However, we are just beginning to expand this foundation to ensure that our knowledge base is inclusive of all women. A greater goal is to effect a transformation of psychological practice that centralizes the understanding of women's and girls' multiple diversities. This book is one step forward toward that goal. Repeatedly our authors have spoken of the impossibility of "doing justice" to within-group diversity in one chapter. So filling this gap with additional material, research, and case studies will be an important step for the future. Although this book is a beginning, there are a variety of diversities

http://dx.doi.org/10.1037/14460-010
Psychological Practice With Women: Guidelines, Diversity, Empowerment, C. Z. Enns, J. K. Rice, and R. L. Nutt (Editors)
Copyright © 2015 by the American Psychological Association. All rights reserved.

that we were unable to encompass and centralize. Some include women and aging; the unique developmental experiences of girls; religious diversity; and most important, social class and socioeconomic status (SES).

The theme of *intersectionality* is developed in each and every chapter and points to the importance of attending to the unique life experiences and perspectives of each woman and girl. The rich and varied case studies bring intersectionality to the forefront. We recommend that intersecting perspectives be given more attention and consideration and additional emphasis in all of the various APA practice guidelines.

Social justice has been increasingly emphasized during recent years, and our chapters point out how social justice is relevant to individual psychotherapy as well as to advocacy, teaching, research, supervision, and other applications. The chapters also reveal, however, that bias and oppression continue to have a substantial impact on the lives of girls and women. Interpersonal violence and power differences are frequently discussed in the case studies of diverse women in this book. Unfortunately, the experience of interpersonal violence seems to be shared widely across diverse groups of women. The following section describes 20 themes that embody what we believe are important take-aways for our readers.

UNIFYING THEMES

There is certainly not a one-size-fits-all approach to working effectively with diverse women; however, the rich chapters and case studies in this volume do provide us with some themes and "golden nuggets" for psychotherapeutic practice with women who have multiple and diverse social identities. It is difficult to do justice to all the points made in the book, but here we try to give the reader and the practitioner what we consider the 20 most important highlights and themes of the book.

1. Borderlands

"Living at the borderlands" is a descriptive phrase for living with intersectionality. Identities "intersect," and women with diverse backgrounds learn to negotiate and cope with the ambiguity and contradictions inherent in holding multiple social identities and being able to do so without conflict or distress (Anzaldúa, 1987). Some of these identities may be associated with privilege, honor, and/or power and others with oppression, derogation, and/or powerlessness. Thus, for example, a psychologist working with a Latina needs to understand that the woman or girl lives within a context of intersecting cultures: the U.S. dominant culture, the Latina/o culture, and her specific

Latina/o culture. A useful intervention then would be to assist the client to explore and to identify the areas in which her cultures conflict and the things she has in common with others, thus encouraging a more balanced and interpersonally connected perspective of her multiple social affiliations.

2. Negotiation

Diverse women constantly make tradeoffs between honoring and acting out their many identities, such as being a woman and Black or a lesbian and daughter. Sometimes aspects of these identities conflict, and solutions are not easily negotiated. Sometimes these negotiations depend on varying privileges associated with each identity. One identity may be honored and open for expression because the context is safe; in another situation it is not. For example, a Latina lesbian woman may not reveal her sexual identity in her religious community that strongly prohibits a nonheterosexual orientation. In this context it is not safe for her to discuss her "counternarrative" as a Latina lesbian and member of that church. This kind of maneuvering is both stressful and psychologically draining. The positive, affirming therapist recognizes this particular stress and helps the woman to understand her behaviors and trade-offs and to gain the strength and courage to consider presenting her whole self to others.

In other instances, a bicultural recognition may help a client negotiate dual identities. *Biculturalism* refers to identifying with both the traditional culture of origin and the U.S. culture in terms of values, practices, and behaviors and acquiring the skills to shift back and forth between these two cultures seamlessly (Schwartz & Unger, 2010). By exploring and supporting a bicultural (or a biracial or multiracial) negotiation for their diverse women clients, practitioners can help them increase their confidence and power to find and express their voices in multiple cultures despite the trade-offs they may face and their thoughts of self-doubt and uncertain sense of belonging,

3. Complexity

Every client lives within a multiplicity of interacting social locations and social constructs, despite perhaps being identified primarily with one social identity, such as being "Black." Applying a *biopsychosocial, ecological framework* for therapy helps us appreciate the layers of complexity. Furthermore, the multiple identities that each client represents may be inconsistently manifested and embraced. For example, the various multiple components of identity related to sex and gender, including biological sex, gender identity, gender role, gender expression, gender orientation, and gender behavior, may or may not be consistent with each other within any given individual. Sexual orientation and gender identity also represent *hidden statuses*, and some sexual affiliations may be hidden and only revealed in psychotherapy when the client begins to trust the therapist. Many of the authors in this volume emphasize that when it comes to care and treatment of multicultural people and women of diversity, the greatest implication for professional practice is a compassionate and flexible understanding of the complexities related to culture and intercultural adaptation.

4. Discrimination and Mental Health

Guideline 3 addresses the importance of understanding the impact of bias and discrimination in areas such as health systems, education, workplace, religious institutions, legal system, families and couples, and research methods and language. These are all areas of concern for women with diverse identities. Domination and oppression of multicultural and diverse peoples makes them even more susceptible to internalized oppression and sexual victimization and can negatively impact the client's self-identity, psychological well-being, and relationships with others (Bubar & Thurman, 2004; Sue & Sue, 2012). As but one example, American Indian and Alaskan Native women are more than 2.5 times (5 vs. 2 per 1,000) more likely to be raped or sexually assaulted than other women in the United States (Perry, 2004). The high emphasis diverse women place on community, cohesion in relationships, and concern for their families may preclude disclosure of abuse. Depending on their level of traditionalism, these values often, if not always, come before their own needs.

The therapist also needs to be aware that even the designation *minority* is bound by the nation or culture and the various connotations of this term across cultures. The term *minority* may be perceived as insulting to some marginalized groups who consider it to mean "less than" or "inferior." As Machizawa and Enns note in Chapter 9, in the United States, "minority groups" usually include racial, ethnic, or linguistic minorities as well as gender, sexual, age, and religious minorities. Additionally, however, there are often unique marginalized groups in other cultures that may not fit into those categories, such as one based on caste or historical occupation or even name. The immigrant or transnational client may therefore carry a minority or marginalized status that is invisible or not readily apparent to the therapist who is only educated about and familiar with discrimination and bias against persons with diverse social identities in the United States.

5. Understanding Historical Trauma

Most therapists are aware of how diverse peoples have experienced bias and discrimination in all facets of life, from jobs and housing to education and income disparities to subtle or overt acts of exclusion, isolation, and degradation. Such discrimination ultimately impacts their physical and mental health, and as is emphasized in the Guidelines and in this book, needs to be considered in evaluations of mental health and in treatment and practice. However, many therapists might not also factor in historical or intergeneration trauma. In Chapter 8, on Native women, Peters and colleagues emphasize that *historical trauma* or *intergenerational trauma* (HT/IT) is a key theme in understanding the Native experience as an outcome of societal oppression and socialization. The intergenerational trauma experience of African American women plus the ongoing effects of a history of slavery and discrimination have also generally not been considered in their diagnosis of trauma (Vasquez & Magraw, 2005). Similarly, immigrants from Southeast Asian are sometimes described as experiencing a "historical trauma response" that resembles posttraumatic syndrome symptoms (Sotero, 2006, p. 96). These perspectives on HT are consistent with the emphases of Guidelines 2 and 3, which clarify how discrimination and oppression affect women and girls. The authors point out that HT/IT can also pervade whole communities, even entire societies, and will persist over generations until it is acknowledged and resolved in an appropriate manner (Brave Heart, 2003).

We also encourage practitioners to understand the importance of this phenomenon for other groups of diverse women who have experienced long-term oppression. Diverse women's and girls' experiences are shaped by social, political, economic, and cultural forces imposed by interlocking matrices of domination such as racism and sexism (Collins, 2000), and these experiences shape their psychological development. Thus, the therapist is aware that the client brings to the therapeutic encounter not only her experience of trauma but a layered historical and cultural experience that may go back generations.

An intersectionality construct of identity adds a further layer of complexity to appreciating HT and inheritance. Black women are doubly bound because they must cope with negotiating their shared–common fate and history with Black–African men due to racism and with women due to sexism. A disabled lesbian woman can be said to be triple bound or experience *triple jeopardy* because of facing prejudice about disability, sexual orientation, and gender.

6. Bias

The therapist, even an enlightened or a self-identified "feminist" therapist, comes into the therapy relationship with biases and preconceptions about the client's position that need to be addressed early and constantly analyzed. A practitioner needs to be aware of the strengths and limitations of his or her own training and clinical and other experiences with diverse groups of women, and indeed all clients. Psychologist self-awareness is absolutely key and a necessary first step.

Whereas Guideline 10 recommends referral when appropriate for the client, this guidance is not intended to be a general substitute for obtaining the competence necessary to work with diverse clients, including those whose value systems might differ from the psychologist's faith or other beliefs. Important reflection questions for the psychologist include the following: What are my multiple and intersecting identities, and how are they relevant to my work with others? In what ways are power and privilege associated with my identities, and how might these features influence my work with others? How might my age, sexual orientation, ethnicity, health or disability status, body size, religious beliefs, family history, and geographical orientation be related to my preparedness to work with diverse clients? What am I assuming because of how I was trained? What are the underlying assumptions of the psychological theories I use to assess and conceptualize clients' concerns? Are there elements that are indicative of androcentric, intrapsychic, heterosexist, deterministic, ethnocentric, or monocultural thinking? If I were a woman from another culture, would I think this way?

Exploration of language barriers and misinterpretations is another piece of the ongoing self-awareness and self-analysis that the responsive psychologist considers in working with diverse groups. A bilingual practitioner may have a real advantage not only in building and gaining rapport but also in appreciating language nuances, idioms, cultural constructs, and culturally bound diagnosis.

7. Misidentification

Because diverse women typically exhibit intersecting identities that can be complex and layered, the therapist must resist early assessment decisions about a client's identity or problems. For example, a woman client may identify as Puerto Rican American rather than Latina or Hispanic; a multiracial woman who appears White might see herself as Black. In particular, the status of lesbian, bisexual, or transgender women may not be immediately evident. The self-perception of "disability" can also vary a great deal; a Deaf client may see herself as a member of a linguistic minority rather than disabled. With regard to disability, some clients have practiced *passing* as a way of coping with society's expectations and discrimination, and the therapist may not be immediately aware of the physical problems with which they cope. Passing represents the attempt by some members of marginalized groups to adopt the cultural behaviors and appearances of dominant groups to avoid being discriminated against or perceived as part of marginalized groups. The clinician needs to be aware that the strategy of passing may obscure true social, cultural, racial, and sexual identities. Similarly, behavior that might seem to fit a particular diagnostic category may well be an accepted coping mechanism in the client's culture of origin (see further explanation under No. 9, Diagnosis and Assessment),

8. Labels

No category can encompass the wide diversity of ethnic and racial groups of women, such as Latina, Asian, and Native. Because of this diversity, these women face *multiple stresses* in terms of *multiple roles*, role confusion, and the often conflicting messages and expectations imposed by traditional gender role expectations of women and girls based not only on gender but also on the implicit expectations associated with racial and ethnic identity. Latina, Asian–Pacific Islander American (APIA), and Native women represent very diverse historical, cultural, and sociopolitical experiences. For example, as Gonzalez and colleagues note in Chapter 4, although Latinas share a common history of colonization and oppression, social variables such as geography, social class, and skin color interact to create a diversity of experience, opportunity, and perspective. In appearance, Latinas can have stereotypical White, African, or Asian features. The same caution about generalization applies to Native women. Chapter 8 documents that there are well over 500 legally recognized tribal entities in the United States alone. Further, there are also many more peoples in the United States and its neighboring countries who ethnically identify as Native or Indigenous but who are as culturally distinctive from one another as they are numerous. There are, in addition, distinct multiple and intersecting identities that encompass other variables such as age, ethnicity, sexual orientation, religion, and SES. All contribute to the mosaic of racial, ethnic, and national origins.

Sexual orientation and identity labels may be even more complex and problematic for the therapist. For example, lesbian sexual identity in women might be more fluid than we once thought and may change over time. A woman who engaged in an intimate, even sexual, relationship with another woman while in prison might understand her sexual orientation to be heterosexual and identify as such. A high school student engaged in a period of sexual experimenting with several lesbian experiences may later consider herself bisexual, marry, divorce and then embrace a basically lesbian lifestyle. Thus rather than assuming heterosexuality or even the label "male" or "female," the sensitive clinician will dialogue with the client, beginning early in the therapeutic process, about her perceived status in these areas. Failure to do so can further marginalize clients who then must assume the burden and the risk of deciding if and when it is safe to reveal sexual identity information. Such open respectful dialogue can also help to empower clients and can begin to challenge internalized homophobia. Whereas Guideline 10 recommends referral when appropriate for the client, this is not intended to be a substitute for gaining the competence necessary to work with diverse clients, including those whose value systems might differ from the psychologist's.

9. Diagnosis and Assessment

Not only does the psychologist recognize that labels can be misleading and inappropriate with diverse women, she or he recognizes that a *Diagnostic and Statistical Manual of Mental Disorders* diagnosis represents only one component of the complex, informed, and intuitive thinking that is needed to work effectively with diverse clients. As noted by Guideline 9, comprehensive conceptual frameworks are informed by ingredients such as the many contextual factors that impinge on distress and mental problems—a person's social identities and social locations, developmental factors, a person's life history and coping in response to life challenges, experiences of powerlessness or victimization, competencies and strengths, and health and biological vulnerabilities. All these factors are part of a perspective that embodies a gendered cultural lens and helps us understand how the woman's experiences moderate the expression of psychological symptoms. As one illustration, it is not surprising that gay, lesbian, and bisexual women are more likely to report discrimination than heterosexual women, that such discrimination makes life harder for them, and that such experiences are also associated with negative mental health status (Mays & Cochran, 2001). Likewise, an Asian woman who is deeply angry may be misdiagnosed when she acts contrary to societal expectations that she be meek and quiet. Crosby and Sprock (2004) found a relationship between reliance on stereotyped biases in diagnostic criteria and practitioner overdiagnosis of antisocial tendencies.

In Chapter 2, we ask clinicians to question themselves the following: What are the costs and benefits of applying this label? Does this diagnostic category allow for ways to consider how this person's symptoms are adaptive? How does this diagnostic label inform interventions that can lead to relief and empowerment? How do my client's multiple identities inform how she (or he) experiences distress and empowerment? What is the meaning of my client's symptoms within her ecological context? (APA, 2007; Ballou, Matsumoto, & Wagner, 2002; Yakushko, Davidson, & Williams, 2009).

In choosing a culturally responsive tool, the practitioner seeks to utilize evidence-based practices that can be culturally adapted. She or he also needs to be familiar with the validity and reliability of an instrument with diverse communities and the methods used to translate the instrument and to provide results to clients in a culturally responsive manner. Also as noted in this book, assessment of the client's verbal and literacy dominance and preferences is critical before choosing the language of the formal assessment. With diverse clients, language difficulties can stem from the fact that English is not the person's first language but may also be related to education, lack of exposure, anxiety, cognitive deficits, or even traumatic brain injury.

Therapists must readily appreciate that when they take on diverse clients with complex and multilayered identities (e.g., Pacific Asian disabled mother; Black bisexual adolescent), they often must be prepared to deal with a family system, multiple additional resources, and sometimes advocacy for the client. For example, treatment for women with disabilities is usually multifaceted and can involve a combination of neuropsychological testing, family psychology, hypnotherapy, cognitive rehabilitation, relaxation techniques, biofeedback, community resources and support groups, referral to other providers of services such as physical and/or occupational therapy, and assistance in obtaining disability compensation. These realities exemplify the need for comprehensive assessment followed by treatment of the whole woman.

10. Social Identity Analysis

One of the first steps in working with diverse women involves developing a *social identity analysis* with the client. The goals of social identity analysis are to form a clear picture of the unique mosaic of identities and experiences that impact distress and wholeness. The information gained contributes to a comprehensive assessment of a person's strengths and concerns and increases both the client's and therapist's awareness of social expectations and roles. In addition, social identity analysis helps clients reframe or redefine distress, which helps to motivate and empower them. There are many tools that a therapist can utilize effectively to assess social identity. Some of the better-known are the ADDRESSING (Hays, 2008) and RESPECTFUL (D'Andrea & Daniels, 2001) frameworks and visual maps and genograms (McGoldrick, 2011; see also Chapter 2, this volume). Client and therapist can complete these assessments mutually. Thoughtful, respectful follow-up questions about themes, events, or people that clients have identified as personally relevant can provide useful foundations for ongoing discussion.

Further, as Williams notes in Chapter 3, when doing a social identity analysis for a particular woman client, one needs to ask, Who is the comparison group? Is the conceptualization of Black and African American women's and girls' experience centered in their phenomenology? Or rather, is it considered in juxtaposition or opposition to Black–African descent men or boys, or other women or girls of color, or White women or girls and White men or boys? And of course, that question can be applied to women and girls of other ethnicities and races. Social class can make the relevant comparison more layered. For example, the negative effects of perceived discrimination on Latinas' mental health are stronger for those in Latinas in lower SES circumstances when compared with their higher SES peers (Flores et al., 2008).

The foundation of a social identity analysis is to emphasize the strengths and resilience of the client. Several approaches are available and discussed in Chapter 2, including the strengths-based therapy model (Jones-Smith, 2014; Smith, 2006). This approach employs the use of multidimensional strength assessment procedures, which involve identifying emotional, character, creative, educational, analytical–cognitive, financial–economic, survival, social support, and community strengths in multiple domains such as relationships, family, work, and home. Closely related to strength assessment is *reframing*, or identifying underlying forms of resilience and strength, even when symptoms appear to be signs of pathology. It also involves looking at social as well as intrapsychic causes: "What is going on around you, and how are your problems an adaptive response to these circumstances?" Such analysis also leads the client to think about her personal power or lack of power and how to reclaim her power, thus moving from self-blame to proactive action. Thoughtful and well-constructed assessments and conceptual frameworks provide the basis for ethical, inclusive, and effective psychotherapy with clients.

11. Social–Familial Context

The various case studies in the book repeatedly point to how the therapist must consider the client's problems in relation to a multitude of factors such as her family and significant others and their ethnicity, immigration, cultural values, and more. A communal perspective instead of a Western individualistic perspective is needed (Enns, 2004), and family-oriented assessment tools can be useful as documented in Chapter 2.

Diverse women may be strongly influenced by cultural norms that feminists and many contemporary U.S. women would consider to be the product of patriarchal influences. For example, *marianismo* is a set of norms that generally guides Latina female gender-role behavior in traditional families (Castillo, Perez, Castillo, & Ghosheh, 2010). Latinas are expected to model their behavior after the Virgin Mary and to be loyal, self-sacrificing, humble, passive, submissive, yielding, docile, chaste, and spiritually superior as well as to accept restrictions on social activities and privileges (Stevens, 1973). In traditional Asian families, women are expected to be obedient, dutiful, silent, and deferent to authority figures within and outside the family (Suzuki, Ahluwalia, & Alimchandani, 2012). These expectations can present a paradox for the therapist who desires to respect the cultural heritage of the woman client while reinforcing empowerment, autonomy, direct communication, and the kind of independent decision making and action we have come to associate with a "mentally healthy" person in our culture. Appreciating the potential positive aspects of a "servant-leader" stance—self-esteem, courage, sacrifice for others, family unity and harmony—is critical to understanding the stance of the client. Also important is understanding that in some instances, the closeness of the family may act as a protective factor to diverse women who experience discrimination outside the family. If this posture, however, is accompanied by verbal or physical violence or abuse by significant others in or outside the family, the therapeutic paradox becomes more problematic. With such revelations, the therapist may need to sensitively help the client to confront experiences that are abusive and not acceptable even when culturally sanctioned and prevalent. Many of the case studies present diverse women and girls who have experienced abuse and violence, and the therapist is confronted with how not only to help the client but also how to involve the impacted family in this effort.

Thus, it is imperative that the clinician also understand the impact of the client's personal changes on the family and the family's direct influence, be it supportive or not, and also to consider the wisdom of bringing family members into therapy. The therapist may attempt to enlist family members in an effort to help the client by exploring cultural expectations that contribute to conflict experienced by the client and family. The therapist shows respect for the woman client's collective, relational values and can sensitively explore ways to help her family members understand and accept her changes and to cope with these changes in a safe, accepting environment. In some instances, however, the family members and spouse are resistant to change, and the woman client may believe she must stay in an unsupportive family environment. Further, divorce may not be perceived as a viable option for transnational or immigrant women brought up in cultures that essentially prohibit it. The therapist then has a difficult situation of helping a woman in an unhappy marriage live a separate, fulfilling life. Alternative partnerships and families, however, have become increasingly common and attractive and are receiving increased acceptance across cultures and nations (Rice, 2001, 2006). Psychologists and other clinicians are encouraged to be aware of the many forms of partnerships and families in which diverse women live and how sociopolitical and economic factors may influence their choices and experiences.

12. Affirmative Healing

Although this book documents the historical and contemporary bias and discrimination daily experienced by women of diverse identities, all the authors emphasize how the therapist must look beyond the stated difficulties and impediments that the woman client articulates or implies. The bedrock of this approach is sometimes described as positive, empowering, and feminist. It means that the therapist is constantly addressing the strengths, resources, creativity, and resilience of the woman client. *Empowerment feminist therapy* embodies such an approach by centralizing the client's experience within a sociocultural and political context (Worell & Remer, 2003). The Guidelines also underpin this approach. Professional practices that support diverse women and girls' optimal development and well-being are encouraged by Guidelines 3 and 4, and specific culturally relevant, gender appropriate practices and community-based applications are stressed by Guidelines 6, 7, 8, 9, and 10.

Affirmative healing also means appreciating how groups of diverse women have attempted to revitalize and to live their cultural heritage, sometimes in the midst of American culture or in opposition to it. Their efforts to teach their children about their traditions and values, to value bilingualism, and to be sensitive to the needs of a much larger extended family and community can be seen by the therapist as a source of strength and a demonstration of courage and resilience. These efforts may also represent a kind of *retraditionalization* (Peters, 2011) as, for example, when Native women gather together and work to reclaim and revitalize what is left of their long, rich traditions for their children. It is certainly a strength-based approach and response to the conflicts of assimilation.

13. Violence and Abuse

Every woman in every culture, across epochs and eras, has implicitly or explicitly faced the prospect of gender-based violence and abuse. Thousands of studies have documented this unfortunate scenario, and although in modern times we have made progress in openly identifying, prohibiting, and curbing violence and abuse toward women and girls, the road ahead is a long one. Thus, it is no surprise that the case studies in this book often reveal a component of perpetrator abuse or sexual violence against the client that must be addressed as part of therapy. Because women with minority statuses have less perceived and actual power in many cases, they are particularly vulnerable. Abuse is an ongoing problem for women with disabilities, as noted by Banks (2007), and needs to be assessed carefully and integrated with safety planning. Therefore, another takeaway is the great importance of assessing these issues early in therapy and with women and girls of any background, whether abuse or violence are revealed by the client or not, a procedure that often is not common for many practitioners (Harway & Hansen, 2004).

Experience of abuse may be far more subtle than having been raped or physically assaulted, and the therapist learns to listen and appreciate the many potential "microaggressions" that a woman of diversity may experience in her daily life. These can range from smirks and put-downs about her language, appearance, and immigration status to nativist comments, marginalization, and innuendo about her lack of acculturation (Falicov, 2012).

14. Body and Beauty

Given the great emphasis in our modern society on upper middle class and popular media definitions of female beauty—being White, blond, young, athletic, and slender to the point of being anorexic—it may not be easy for diverse women to feel positive about their body and self-image. For example, the large, dark Black woman, the transgender masculine-appearing woman, and the woman with a cane will all have to internalize an image of beauty that is based on norms different from what is promulgated by the media and deal with conflicting messages about what it means to be female. This central theme of a societal definition of femaleness is one that can be explored in therapy, helping clients to understand the ways in which their appearance and bodies will be perceived as threatening or unattractive to other women and girls and to men and boys. However, in keeping with a strength-based and resilience approach, psychologists and therapists will also help diverse women affirm their inherent beauty by developing a counter narrative and internalizing its messages of self-worth and attractiveness.

15. Suspicion of Psychotherapy

Sometimes it may be difficult to convince a client to seek therapy because of cultural biases and prohibitions about psychotherapy and suspicion of Western ideas and methods of dealing with personal and familial problems. Because of these negative perceptions, counseling and psychotherapy may be underutilized. As but one example, APIAs underutilize mental health treatment, despite the fact that Asian American women between the ages of 15 and 24 and over 65 have the highest suicide rates of all racial–ethnic groups (National Center for Health Statistics, 2011). That reality is also why it is so important to establish rapport, believability, and trust with diverse women clients and cement the therapeutic relationship as quickly as possible. That means educating oneself about diverse women's beliefs, values, and culture, expressing positive appreciation of difference and communal values, showing sensitivity to abuse and oppression, and practicing active listening for nuance and difficulties of persons with minority status who are negotiating life tasks in a majority culture.

16. Enlisting Community Resources

This theme is closely related to prior themes of respecting communality and promoting empowerment. The client needs to be helped by others who have traversed her path and by the rich array of resources and people in her community. Qualities that make up a strong sense of community, such as a shared emotional connection, reciprocity and reinforcement of needs among members, and feelings of trust and belonging, can be very empowering for clients (Wright, Perez, & Johnson, 2010). Psychologists and other practitioners are encouraged to maintain awareness of religious and spiritual resources within the community that are accessible to and supportive of women of diversity. It is also critical to determine the actual accessibility of resources, including the availability of transportation, childcare, and health services.

Within today's 21st-century context, community also includes an "e-community" of online resources, helpers, and experts around the world. Social network groups, such as Wise Latina and Disabled Women, can be found on the web and can also be helpful for clients. The therapist is only one resource, and it is important for the therapist to help diverse women use their existing and potential "social capital." Social cohesion can be reinforced in therapy and can play a large part in developing a sense of personal empowerment among diverse women.

Therapists can assist lower income clients who are trying to manage the complexity of one or more systems (e.g., immigration, justice, education, housing, social welfare) by educating them about what they should expect to experience and by helping them seek out the right resources, services, and advocates to navigate the complexities of those systems. Finally, any services or service providers to whom a psychologist might refer lesbian, gay, bisexual, or transgender clients should also be screened for their knowledge and skills in working affirmatively with such clients.

17. Gaining Competence

We may not always be trained to help women of diverse backgrounds effectively in psychotherapy. For example, despite the high therapy utilization rate for lesbians, Matthews in Chapter 5 notes that research has found that mental health professionals are not always prepared to work with them. Guideline 10 addresses how the self-aware therapist assesses his or her competence and own bias and values in working with a client or deciding to make a referral or gain competence. Categorical refusal to work with lesbian, bisexual, or transgender women is not endorsed or implied by this guideline. The same could be said for working with women with disabilities, women from different cultures, and classes and situations that are much different than those of the practitioner. One can use ongoing self-education, continuing education, consultation, and collaborations with local resources to gain the competence necessary to work effectively with diverse clients.

18. Out of the Armchair

"The personal is political" is an axiom of feminist, liberatory, and affirmative empowering practice. It also implies some involvement in social activism or advocacy. Many clinicians resist doing this. It is so comfortable once we have established a good working relationship with clients just to go on assessing, affirming, listening, and suggesting options, secure in the confident belief that we are truly helping them. But how much more could we be offering if we just took a little step outside the practice of psychotherapy to assist not only our clients but also the much larger group of people to which they belong? This commitment comes under the category of social activism (Guideline 11) and is emphasized and explained by many of the authors in the book. Psychologists are encouraged to provide psychological services through prevention, education, and social policy interventions from local to national levels (APA, 2007). Social activism does not have to be a large scary step like testifying in a courtroom or participating in an especially impactful project such as helping to set up a local community intercultural center. It could be as simple as making a call or signing a petition. Affirmative psychologists, for example, can help empower women with disabilities by supporting accommodations in the workplace or by writing letters to employers attesting to the need for financial or other workplace assistance.

19. How to Use Therapy Guidelines

The Guidelines were developed to inform the practice of professionals working with girls and women by contextualizing girls' and women's experiences and promoting culturally competent practice. However, it must be remembered that they are aspirational, not mandatory. Second, any one set of guidelines (e.g., gender, disability, multicultural, sexual orientation) needs to be used in a complementary fashion with other sets. Additional information is needed to enhance the application of the Guidelines with diverse groups of women. This view is consistent with an intersectional approach. If a complexity approach is ever widely recognized and practiced, separate guidelines for each of these social constructs or identities will become outdated, and a set of guidelines for working with diversity of any kind may be adopted by APA and be even more useful to practitioners.

Third, guidelines change. We live in a constantly changing world. Gay marriage is now accepted in much of the Western world. Social class is increasingly being recognized as perhaps a more potent divider than race (Hardaway & McLoyd, 2009; Sawhill, 2013). As the population significantly ages and demands scarce resources, ageism may turn out to be a more divisive form of bias in modern times than sexism or racism. So any set of guidelines will reflect our changing culture and the influence of a global perspective. While this book has attempted to expand the 2007 Guidelines by bringing in some cross-national concerns and issues, psychotherapy guidelines may never be truly international in their application.

20. Transnational Applications

The women clients with whom psychologists work may live (or may have lived) in various countries of origin but may also be recent immigrants to another country or part of a diasporic community. The word *transnational* used in this book is meant to highlight the complex interactions among nation, gender, sexuality, race, and other identities that these women and girls may live and experience. Four central assumptions embedded in the Guidelines are relevant to psychologists and practitioners working in a transnational context. These assumptions emphasize (a) recognizing and valuing diversity and multiple identities, (b) exploring the unique privileges and oppressions experienced by diverse groups of women, (c) attending to power dynamics across cultures and contexts, and (d) addressing institutional and systemic variables as well as working toward social change (Rice & Ballou, 2002).

Working successfully and effectively in a transnational context requires substantial expansion of traditional, Western psychological theories and research based on "WEIRD" people—people from Western, Educated, Industrialized, Rich, and Democratic contexts or cultures. A critical analysis of Western perspectives includes the need to evaluate these perspectives on psychotherapeutic practice, feminism, and gender issues (APA, 2004; Rice & Ballou, 2002). There may be important differences in therapist–client relationships, for example, boundaries, expectations, time constraints, payment options, and limitations for counseling; and national differences in ethical codes related to practice (Duan et al., 2011).

To enhance the applicability of the Guidelines to transnational and multiple contexts, Chapter 9 considers how aspects of the Guidelines that seem particularly consistent with Western individualistic values can be reinterpreted or modified for practice in other contexts. For example, popular Western interventions that are influenced by Zen Buddhist assumptions, such as acceptance and commitment therapy, mindfulness-based stress reduction, and dialectical behavior therapy, can be adapted for working with clients in Japan as well as North America. Other alternative therapies, such as yoga, the martial arts, and the Zen arts, may also be used as helpful interventions for stress reduction and personal growth (Enns & Kasai, 2003). As technology, communication, and travel combine to foster a more global perspective, psychologists increasingly will transform their profession and its practices to encompass all peoples and women of diversity.

CONCLUDING COMMENTS

We introduced this book by highlighting the transformative potential of social justice practices in psychology and the Guidelines. In this final chapter, we have summarized 20 key attitudes and practices explored by the authors of this edited volume. Together, these practices and viewpoints provide important lenses for enacting transformative processes in psychology. In addition, the complex and informative case studies contributed by the chapter authors reveal the challenges and rewards of practicing affirmative and inclusive psychological practice.

By focusing on the lives and experiences of women with complicated and multiple identities, we believe that authors have gone beyond informing readers about competent practice with women who are typically identified as "diverse." The chapter contents also inform psychologists about the types of attitudes and frameworks that facilitate uncovering, identifying, and working effectively with the diversities of *all* women and girls, including those whose lives appear, at least on the surface, as "typical." We are hopeful that the contents and values communicated by this book's authors will serve as a catalyst for additional exploration and expansion of the work presented in this volume. When intersectionality comes to be recognized as an anchor concept in better understanding diversity, then our teaching, research, and practice will all be changed and transformed. And as mentioned earlier, the practice guidelines of various professional organizations and helping professions will also become more inclusive and centered on the basic concept of unraveling multiple layers of social location and identity that go far beyond a simplistic appreciation of the effects of race, gender, ethnicity, disability, sexual preference or class. If this happens in our lifetimes, we will be gratified that psychological practice with women and girls has truly been transformed.

REFERENCES

American Psychological Association. (2007). Guidelines for psychological practice with girls and women. *American Psychologist, 62,* 949–979. doi:10.1037/0003-066X.62.9.949

Anzaldúa, G. (1987). *Borderlands/la frontera: The new Mestiza.* San Francisco, CA: Spinsters/Aunt Lute Book Company.

Ballou, M., Matsumoto, A., & Wagner, M. (2002). Toward a feminist ecological theory of human nature: Theory building in response to real-world dynamics. In M. Ballou & L. S. Brown (Eds.), *Rethinking mental health and disorder: Feminist perspectives* (pp. 99–141). New York, NY: Guilford Press.

Banks, M. E. (2007). Women with disabilities, domestic violence against. In N. A. Jackson (Ed.), *Encyclopedia of domestic violence* (pp. 723–728). New York, NY: Taylor & Francis.

Brave Heart, M. Y. H. (2003, January). The historical trauma response among natives and its relationship with substance abuse: A Lakota illustration. *Journal of Psychoactive Drugs, 35*, 7–13.

Bubar, R., & Thurman, P. J. (2004). Violence against Native women. *Social Justice, 31*(4), 70–86.

Castillo, L. G., Perez, F. V., Castillo, R., & Ghosheh, M. R. (2010). Construction and initial validation of the marianismo beliefs scale. *Counselling Psychology Quarterly, 23*, 163–175. doi:10.1080/09515071003776036

Collins, P. H. (2000). *Black feminist thought*. New York, NY: Routledge.

Crosby, J. P., & Sprock, J. (2004). Effect of patient sex, clinician sex, and sex role in the diagnosis of antisocial personality disorder: Models of underpathologizing and overpathologizing biases. *Journal of Clinical Psychology, 60*, 583–604. doi:10.1002/jclp.10235

D'Andrea, M., & Daniels, J. (2001). RESPECTFUL counseling: An integrative model for counselors. In D. Pope-Davis & H. Coleman (Eds.), *The interface of class, culture and gender in counseling* (pp. 417–466). Thousand Oaks, CA: Sage. doi:10.4135/9781452231846.n17

Duan, C., Nilsson, J., Wang, C., Debernardi, N., Klevens, C., & Tallent, C. (2011). Internationalizing counseling: A Southeast Asian perspective. *Counselling Psychology Quarterly, 24*, 29–41. doi:10.1080/09515070.2011.558253

Enns, C. Z. (2004). *Feminist theories and feminist psychotherapies* (2nd ed.). New York, NY: Haworth Press.

Enns, C. Z., & Kasai, M. (2003). Hakoniwa: Japanese sandplay therapy. *The Counseling Psychologist, 31*, 93–112. doi:10.1177/0011000002239403

Falicov, C. (2012). Immigrant family processes: A multidimensional framework. In F. Walsh (Ed.), *Normal family processes: Growing diversity and complexity* (4th ed., pp. 297–323). New York, NY: Guilford Press.

Flores, E., Tschann, J. M., Dimas, J. M., Bachen, E. A., Pasch, L. A., & de Groat, C. L. (2008). Perceived discrimination, perceived stress, and mental and physical health among Mexican-origin adults. *Hispanic Journal of Behavioral Sciences, 30*, 401–424. doi:10.1177/0739986308323056

Hardaway, C. R., & McLoyd, V. C. (2009). Escaping poverty and securing middle class status: How race and socio-economic status shape mobility prospects for African Americans during the transition to adulthood. *Journal of Youth and Adolescence, 38*, 242–256. doi:10.1007/s10964-008-9354-z

Harway, M., & Hansen, M. (2004). *Spouse abuse: Assessing and treating women, batterers, and their children* (2nd ed.). Sarasota, FL: Professional Resources Press.

Hays, P. A. (2008). *Addressing cultural complexities in practice* (2nd ed.). Washington, DC: American Psychological Association.

Jones-Smith, E. (2014). *Strengths-based therapy: Connecting theory, practice and skills.* Los Angeles, CA: Sage.

Mays, V. M., & Cochran, S. D. (2001). Mental health correlates of perceived discrimination among lesbian, gay, and bisexual adults in the United States. *American Journal of Public Health, 91*, 1869–1876. doi:10.2105/AJPH.91.11.1869

McGoldrick, M. (2011). *The genogram journey: Reconnecting with your family.* New York, NY: Norton. doi:10.1037/e579162012-002

National Center for Health Statistics. (2011). *Health, United States, 2011: With special feature on socioeconomic status and health.* Hyattsville, MD: Author.

Perry, S. W. (2004). *American Indians and crime: ABJS statistical profile 1992–2002.* Washington, DC: Bureau of Justice Statistics, U.S. Department of Justice, Office of Justice Programs. doi:10.1037/e311672005-001

Peters, W. M. K. (2011). *The indigenous soul wound: Exploring culture, memetics, complexity and emergence.* (Doctoral dissertation). Retrieved from ProQuest Dissertations and Theses. (Order No. 3474460)

Rice, J., & Ballou, M. (2002). *Cultural and gender awareness in international psychology.* Washington, DC: American Psychological Association, Division 52, International Psychology, International Committee for Women.

Rice, J. K. (2001). Family roles and patterns: Contemporary trends. In J. Worell (Ed.), *Encyclopedia of women and gender* (pp. 411–423). San Diego, CA: Academic Press.

Rice, J. K. (2006). Presidential address: What is family? Global changes in family structure and lifecycle. *International Psychology Bulletin, 10*(4), 4–12.

Sawhill, I. V. (2013). Family structure: The growing importance of class. Brookings Monthly Institute. *Economic Studies Bulletin, January/February*, 1–6. Retrieved from http://www.brookings.edu/research/articles/2013/01/family-structure-class-sawhill

Schwartz, S. J., & Unger, J. B. (2010). Biculturalism and context: What is biculturalism, and when is it adaptive? *Human Development, 53*, 26–32. doi:0.1159/000268137

Smith, E. J. (2006). The strength-based counseling model. *The Counseling Psychologist, 34*, 13–79. doi:10.1177/0011000005277018

Sotero, M. M. (2006). A conceptual model of historical trauma: Implications for public health practice and research. *Journal of Health Disparities Research and Practice, 1*, 93–108.

Stevens, E. P. (1973). Marianismo: The other face of machismo in Latin America. In A. Decastello (Ed.), *Female and male in Latin America* (pp. 88–109). Pittsburgh, PA: University of Pittsburgh Press.

Sue, D. W., & Sue, D. (2012). *Counseling the culturally diverse: Theory and practice* (6th ed.). Hoboken, NJ: Wiley.

Suzuki, L. A., Ahluwalia, M. K., & Alimchandani, A. (2012). Asian American women's feminism: Sociopolitical history and clinical considerations. In C. Z. Enns & E. N. Williams (Eds.), *The Oxford handbook of feminist multicultural counseling psychology* (pp. 183–198). New York, NY: Oxford University Press.

Tokuhiro, Y. (2010). *Marriage in contemporary Japan.* New York, NY: Routledge.

Vasquez, H., & Magraw, S. (2005). Building relationships across privilege: Becoming an ally in the therapeutic relationship. In M. P. Mirkin, K. L. Suyemoto, & B. F. Okun (Eds.), *Psychotherapy with women: Emphasizing diverse contexts and identities* (pp. 64–83). New York, NY: Guilford Press.

Worell, J., & Remer, P. (2003). *Feminist perspectives in therapy: Empowering diverse women* (2nd ed.). Hoboken, NJ: Wiley.

Wright, C. V., Perez, S., & Johnson, D. M. (2010). The mediating role of empowerment for African American women experiencing intimate partner violence. *Psychological Trauma: Theory, Research, Practice and Policy, 2,* 266–272. doi:10.1037/a0017470

Yakushko, O., Davidson, M. M., & Williams, E. N. (2009). Identity salience model: A paradigm for integrating multiple identities in clinical practice. *Psychotherapy: Theory, Research, Practice, Training, 46,* 180–192. doi:10.1037/a0016080

INDEX

Clinton, Bill, 112
Code switching, 62, 100–101
Cognitive–behavioral therapy (CBT), 216
Cohen, B., 93–94
Collaboration, in transnational practice, 229–230
Collectivism, 232, 233, 245
Collins, P. H., 59, 60
Colonialism, 240–241
Colorado, 118
Comas-Díaz, L., 8, 44, 94
"Coming out to others" (identity development stage), 115
"Coming out to self" (identity development stage), 115
Community
    Black, 63
    Deaf, 172
    disability, 172
    sense of, 270
Community-based interventions, 217
Community-based participatory programs, 204, 217
Community-centered approaches, 202–203
Community genograms, 40, 42
Community health workers, 96
Community resources, 24
    in case study, 71, 72, 100
    and empowerment, 4–5
    enlisting, 269–270
    for Latinas, 96
    for lesbian, bisexual, and transgender women, 123–124
    for Native people, 216–219
    for women with disabilities, 177–178
Community violence, 63
Competence, of therapists, 121, 270
Compulsory heterosexuality, 112
Conceptualization
    challenges of, 32–34
    of disability culturally competent care, 160
    with empowerment feminist therapy, 94
    of positionality, 228
    and theoretical frameworks, 47
    of women with disabilities, 163

Confucianism, 234
Coping
    by Black/African descent females, 59, 67
    and spirituality, 43–44
Counseling theories, 228–229
Counselors for Social Justice, 33
Crawford, M., 4
Critical race feminism, 53–54
Crosby, J. P., 264
Crossroads: The Psychology of Immigration in the New Century (APA Presidential Task Force on Immigration), 97
Cubans, 89
Culturagram, 40
Cultural adaptation, of theoretical frameworks, 94
Cultural frame-switching, 90–91
Cultural genograms, 40, 92
Cultural sensitivity, 23, 201
Cultural values, 85–87

D'Andrea, M., 36
Daniels, J., 36
Daniels, J. A., 171–173
DAT (disability-affirmative therapy), 174–175
Deaf community, 172
DeBruyn, L. M., 197–198
Defense of Marriage Act, 118
Deloria, Ella, 195
Denner, J., 89–90
Depressive symptoms, 88–89
Diagnosis, 24
    challenges of, 32–34, 264–265
    in the Guidelines, 11
    of Native people, historical trauma and, 197
Diagnostic and Statistical Manual of Mental Disorders (5th edition; DSM–5), 32–34
Diagnostic labels, 32, 34
Diamond, L. M., 116
Díaz-Lázaro, C. M., 93–94
Dimensions approach, 33
Dion, K. K., 137
Dion, K. L., 137

Disabilities. *See also* Women with
  disabilities (WWD)
  defined, 159
  pathologization of, 162–163
  self-perception of, 262
  in social model of disability, 162
Disability-affirmative therapy (DAT),
  174–175
Disability community, 172
Disability identity development, 175–177
Disabled Women on the Web, 178
Disableism, 162
Discrimination, 22–23
  ableism as, 161–162
  effects of, 260
  toward Latinas, 87–88
  toward lesbian, bisexual, and trans-
    gender women, 117–118
"Dis" Discourse method, 66
Disorders of sexual development
  (DSDs), 113
Diversity, 4, 22
  among Native tribes, 206–207
  among women, 10, 12–13
  defined, 4
  in transnational practice, 230–232
Drabble, L., 110
DSDs (disorders of sexual development),
  113
DSM–5 [*Diagnostic and Statistical Manual
  of Mental Disorders* (5th edition)],
  32–34
Dubois, W. E. B., 58
Dunbar, N., 89–90
Dunn, D. S., 173–174
Dupont, I., 144
Duran, B., 197
Duran, E., 197

East Asian women. *See* Transnational
  practice
EBTs (evidence-based treatments),
  201–202
Ecograms, 40
Ecomaps, 40
"E-communities," 270
Education
  continuing, for therapists, 270
  and transnational practice, 236–238
  for women with disabilities, 166–167

EFT (empowerment feminist therapy),
  93–94, 268
Eibach, R. P., 8
Employment
  and transnational practice, 236–238
  of women with disabilities, 167–168
Empowerment, 4–5, 23–24
Empowerment feminist therapy (EFT),
  93–94, 268
Empowerment-focused interventions, 65
Enculturation, 116–117
Equal Employment Opportunity Law
  (Japan), 238
Espín, Oliva, 8
"Ethical Principles of Psychologists and
  Code of Conduct" (APA), 121
Ethnic conflict, 241–242
Ethnoviolence, 62–63
Evidence-based practice, 92
Evidence-based treatments (EBTs),
  201–202
Externalizing, 45

La facultad (term), 44–45
Familial capital, 96
Familismo (term), 86, 90
Family maps, 40
Family systems, 235–236
Family trees, 40
Fassinger, R. E., 115
Federal Crime Control Bill (1994), 199
"Feeling different" (identity development
  stage), 115
Feldman, S. I., 175
Femininity
  masculinity vs., 232, 233
  and sexual orientation, 114
Feminism(s)
  of Black women, 58, 60
  Confucian or Buddhist vs. Western,
    234
  critical race, 53–54
  in development of the Guidelines,
    9–10
  in Japan, 239–241
  and social justice movements,
    239–240
  transnational, 225, 243
  and women with disabilities, 161, 173
Feminist therapy, 11, 92–93

Language
  and assessment, 264–265
  brokering of, 90
  in psychological practice with
    Latinas, 94–95
  use of, among women with disabilities,
    172
  use of English in intercultural
    communication, 228
Larance, L. Y., 64, 66, 67, 74
Latinas, 81–102
  advocacy for, 96–97
  case study of, 97–101
  community resources for, 96
  cultural values in gender socialization
    of, 85–87
  future research on, 102
  impact of discrimination and bias on
    health of, 87–89
  intersecting identities of, 83–85
  psychological practice with, 91–95
  strengths and assets of, 89–91
  in United States, 82–83
Legal system(s)
  Native persons affected by, 199
  and transnational practice, 238–239
  women with disabilities in, 169
Legislation, 118. *See also specific legislation*
Lesbian(s). *See also* Lesbian, bisexual,
    and transgender women
  among Native women, 195
  and disabilities, 169
  identity as, 263
  and identity development, 115–116
  in Japan, 242
  therapists' preparation to work with,
    270
  use of therapy by, 110
Lesbian, bisexual, and transgender
    women, 109–130
  of Asian–Pacific Islander descent, 136
  avoiding stereotypes of, 113–114
  of Black/African descent, 61–62
  case study of, 124–130
  identity components related to sex
    and gender, 111–112
  identity development in, 114–117
  and minority stress, 117–119
  psychological practice with, 119–123
  resources and advocacy for, 123–124

Lev, A. I., 113
Liddle, B. J., 112–113
Liu, W. M., 143
Lopez, N., 90

Mackie, V., 227
Maeshiro, T., 245
Manifest destiny, 194
Marecek, J., 4
Marianismo (term), 85–86, 266
Marianista (term), 86, 87
Marriage
  in Japan, 235–236
  same-sex, 118
Masculinity, 232, 233
Mattering maps, 40, 42
Matthews, C. R., 116–117, 124
Mattis, J. S., 43
Mays, V. M., 117–118
McNulty, K., 168
Media coverage, 62–63
Memes, 198
Memetics, 198
Mending the Circle, 210
Mending the Sacred Hoop, 217–218
Menses, 201
Mental health
  of Asian–Pacific Islander Americans,
    140–141
  effect of discrimination on, 117–118,
    260
  of Latinas, 88
  positive, 43
Mental health resources, 24
Meyer, I. H., 117
Meyer, O. L., 143
Miller, A. D., 118
Miller, Jean Baker, 143
"Minority," as label, 260
Minority groups
  generalizations of, 263
  in international contexts, 242
Minority stress, 117–119
Misidentification, by therapists, 262–263
Model minority, 137–138
Mohatt, G. V., 202
Mona, L. R., 161
Monism, 193–194
Mukherjee, D., 166–167, 169
Multiculturalism, 10

Psychological practice, 4, 91. *See also*
    Unifying themes in practice
    with Asian–Pacific Islander Ameri-
        can women (case studies,
        techniques, issues), 135–157
    with Black African American
        women and girls (case study,
        techniques, issues), 53–80
    with Latino women and girls
        (case study, techniques,
        issues), 81–108
    with lesbian, bisexual, and trans-
        gender women and girls
        (case study, techniques,
        issues), 109–134
    with Native women and girls
        (case studies, techniques,
        issues), 191–224
    with transnational women
        (case studies, techniques,
        issues), 225–256
    with women with disabilities
        (case study, techniques,
        issues), 159–190
Psychotherapy. *See also specific therapies*
    Asian, 245
    biopsychosocial, ecological framework
        for, 259
    comprehensive conceptual frameworks
        for, 264
    suspicion of, 269
Publication Manual (APA), 172
Purdie-Vaughns, V., 8
Pyke, K. D., 139

Quiroga, S. S., 143
Qureshi, M. E., 65–66

Race-related medical conditions, 165
Raffaelli, M., 85–86
Ramos, B., 89
RCT. *See* Relational–cultural theory
Realization stage (disability identity
    development), 177
Referrals, by therapists, 121–122
Reframing, 44–45, 266
Rehabilitation Institute of Chicago, 178
Reis, J. P., 166–167
Relational–cultural theory (RCT), 143
    in Asian psychotherapies, 245–246
    in case study, 149

Religious belief systems
    in case study, 73–74
    and transnational practice, 234–235
Religious institutions, 168–169
Remer, Pamela, 8–9, 37, 47, 93–94
*Report of the Task Force on Appropriate
    Therapeutic Responses to Sexual
    Orientation* (APA Task Force on
    Appropriate Therapeutic Res-
    ponses to Sexual Orientation), 120
Research models, 170–172
*Resolution on Culture and Gender
    Awareness in International
    Psychology* (APA), 226
RESPECTFUL framework, 36, 38
Respeto (term), 87
Re-storying, 40, 42
Retraditionalization, 217, 268
Rich, Adrienne, 112
Riggle, E. D. B., 118
Rodriguez, M. A., 143
Roosevelt, Franklin, D., 176
Rostosky, S. S., 118
Russell, G. M., 118

Salley, B. B., 161
Same-sex marriage, 118
Sandtray therapy, 245
Savin-Williams, R. C., 111–112
Schmidt, S. R., 210
Schriempf, A., 173
Self-awareness
    of bias, 261–262
    of different cultural norms, 201
    of disability conceptualization, 166,
        173–175
    of sexual/gender identity, 120
    of therapists, 23, 91–92, 120, 166,
        173–175, 201, 261–262
    and transnational practice, 227–229
Servant-leadership, 86, 266–267
SES. *See* Socioeconomic status
Settles, I. H., 55–56
Sex, biological, 111
Sex trafficking, 241
Sexual behavior, 111–112
Sexual identity
    of Black/African descent females,
        60–62
    defined, 112
    labels of, 263–264

Sexuality, of Black/African descent
    females, 60–62
Sexual orientation
    in case study, 71
    defined, 111
    efforts to change, 120
    as hidden status, 259–260
    labels of, 263–264
Sexual victimization, 260
Shaw, A., 56
Simpatía (term), 86–87
Smith, John, 209
Social activism
    in the Guidelines, 10–11
    by therapists, 271
Social capital, 96, 270
Social context, 22
Social–familial context, 266–267
Social identities
    development of, 37–38
    in different contexts, 35
    of therapists, 36, 46
Social identity analysis, 34–42, 265–266
    acronyms for, 35–37
    in case study, 249
    defined, 34
Social justice, 258
Social justice movements, 239–240
Social model of disability, 162, 173
Social support, 72
Social systems, 235–236
Society of Japanese Feminist Counseling
    Practices and Studies, 243
Socioeconomic status (SES)
    of Asian–Pacific Islander Americans,
        137–138
    and community resources, 270
    and disabilities, 162
    and impact of bias, 88, 89
    of Native individuals, 200–201
Sociopolitical context, 24
Sokoloff, N. J., 144
Soul wounding, 196–198
Sovereign status, 199, 209
Spiral dynamics, 193, 198
Spirita (term), 44
Spirituality
    of Black/African descent females, 67
    in case study, 207–208

    in Native worldview, 193, 196
    and soul wounding of Native people,
        196–198
    as strength, 43–44
    for women with disabilities, 168–169
Sprock, J., 264
Standards of Care (World Professional
    Association for Transgender
    Health), 110
Stereotypes
    of Asian–Pacific Islander Americans,
        137–138, 151
    of Asian women, 242
    and diagnosis/assessment challenges,
        264
    and gendered racism, 7–8
    of Japanese American women, 239
    of lesbian, bisexual, and transgender
        women, 113–114
    of Native women, 209
    of women with disabilities, 169
Stevens, E. P., 85
Stevens-Watkins, D., 64
Strength-based therapy model, 43, 266
Strengths
    assessing, 42–44
    of Latinas, 89–91
Stress
    from intersecting minority statuses,
        61–62
    and violence toward Black/African
        descent females, 64
Sue, D., 136
Sue, D. W., 136
Suicide, among Asian–Pacific Islander
    Americans, 140
Szymanski, D. M., 115, 129

Task Force on Evidence-Based Practice
    in Psychology (APA), 92
Tegart, G., 175
Teitelman, A. M., 64
TF-CBT (trauma-focused cognitive–
    behavioral therapy), 209–210
Theoretical frameworks, 46–47, 94
Therapeutic alliance, 23–24
    with Asian–Pacific Islander
        Americans, 145
    and language, 95

Therapists
    biases of, 261–262
    competence of, 121, 270
    misidentification by, 262–263
    self-awareness of, 23, 91–92, 120,
        166, 173–175, 201, 261–262
    social activism by, 271
    social identities of, 36, 46
    and work with LGBT clients, 110
Tillman, K. H., 88
Tollrian, R., 198
Transformation, of psychological
    practice, 4
Transgender (term), 112
Transgendered individuals. *See also*
    Lesbian, bisexual, and transgender
    women
    in Native cultures, 195
    therapy during transition for, 122–123
Transnational feminism, 225, 243
Transnational practice, 225–251
    applications of the Guidelines in,
        272–273
    case studies of, 246–250
    collaboration in, 229–230
    and colonialism, 240–241
    cultural dimensions in, 232–233
    diversity in, 230–232
    education and work opportunities in,
        236–238
    and ethnic conflicts/power differences,
        241–242
    and feminist and social justice
        movements, 239–240
    and government/legal systems,
        238–239
    philosophical/religious belief systems
        in, 234–235
    positionality and self-knowledge in,
        227–229
    psychological practice as, 243–246
    social and family systems in, 235–236
Trauma, 62–64. *See also* Historical trauma
    intergenerational, 196–198
    and posttraumatic stress disorder, 65,
        179–182
Trauma-focused cognitive–behavioral
    therapy (TF-CBT), 209–210
Traumatic brain injury, 179–182

Tribal court systems, 199
Tribal enrollment, 207
Trocki, K., 110
Tseng, W., 245
Two-Spirit people, 195
Tyler, K. M., 64

Ueno, C., 239–240, 241
Uncertainty avoidance, 232
Unifying themes in practice, 257–273
    affirmative healing, 267–268
    bias, 261–262
    body image, 269
    borderlands, 258–259
    community resources, 269–270
    complexity, 259–260
    diagnosis and assessment, 264–265
    effects of discrimination, 260
    historical trauma, 260–261
    labels, 263–264
    misidentification, 262–263
    negotiation, 259
    social activism, 271
    social–familial context, 266–267
    social identity analysis, 265–266
    suspicion of psychotherapy, 269
    therapists' competence, 270
    therapy guidelines in, 271–272
    transnational application, 272–273
    violence and abuse, 268
United States, 82–83
Upadhyay, W. S., 174
U.S. Census Bureau, 82, 136
U.S. Department of Justice, 199, 200
Utsey, S. O., 65

Validation, Challenging and Requesting
    (VCR) model, 65–66, 70
Vasquez, Melba, 97
VCR (Validation, Challenging and
    Requesting) model, 65–66, 70
Verdinelli, S., 93–94
Violence
    against Black/African descent females,
        62–64
    interracial, 200
    against Japanese women, 238–239
    against Native women, 199–200
    against women and girls, 268
Violence Against Women Act, 199, 218

ABOUT THE EDITORS

Carolyn Zerbe Enns, PhD, is a professor of psychology and a contributor to the ethnic studies and the gender, sexuality, and women's studies programs at Cornell College, Mount Vernon, Iowa. Her scholarly interests include multicultural, feminist, and transnational perspectives on psychotherapy and pedagogy. She has written approximately 60 articles and chapters that focus primarily on gender, pedagogy, and feminist theory and psychotherapy. Dr. Enns is the author of *Feminist Theories and Psychotherapies* and coeditor of *Teaching and Social Justice* and the *Oxford Handbook of Feminist Multicultural Counseling Psychology*. She has received the Heritage Award for contributions to feminist practice (American Psychological Association [APA] Society for the Psychology of Women), the Distinguished Leader for Women in Psychology Award (APA Committee on Women), the Florence L. Denmark/ Mary E. Reuder Award for contributions to the international psychology of women (APA Division of International Psychology), and the Woman of the Year Award and the Foremother Award (Section for the Advancement of Women, APA Society of Counseling Psychology).

Joy K. Rice, PhD, is a clinical psychologist and emerita professor at the University of Wisconsin–Madison. She is a recipient of the Educational Press

Association Distinguished Achievement Award and the Denmark/Reuder Award for Outstanding International Contributions to the Psychology of Women and Gender. Her 4-decade career has focused on women and their issues and concerns nationally and globally in the areas of marital and family studies and gender and cross-cultural issues in psychotherapy. Dr. Rice is the coauthor of *Women and Leadership: Transforming Visions and Diverse Voices* and "International Perspectives on Women and Mental Health" in the 2010 *Handbook of Feminism and Women's Rights Worldwide*.

Roberta L. Nutt, PhD, ABPP, is training director of the counseling psychology doctoral program at the University of Houston, Texas. She formerly served as founder and training director of the counseling psychology doctoral program at Texas Woman's University and director of professional affairs of the Association of State and Provincial Psychology Boards (ASPPB). She is past president of American Psychological Association (APA) Divisions 17 (Counseling Psychology) and 43 (Family Psychology), is past chair of the Texas State Board of Examiners of Psychologists, holds fellow status in APA and seven of its divisions and ASPPB, and is American Board of Professional Psychology certified in counseling psychology and family psychology. She has published numerous articles, chapters, and books on women's and gender issues in psychology.

Drs. Nutt, Rice, and Enns coauthored the 2007 "APA Guidelines for Psychological Practice With Women and Girls" and were corecipients of the 2008 Woman of the Year Award from the APA Section for the Advancement of Women in Counseling Psychology for "significant contributions and promotion of the status of women in psychology, leadership and activism on behalf of women, and research that has significantly advanced knowledge of women's concerns in counseling psychology."

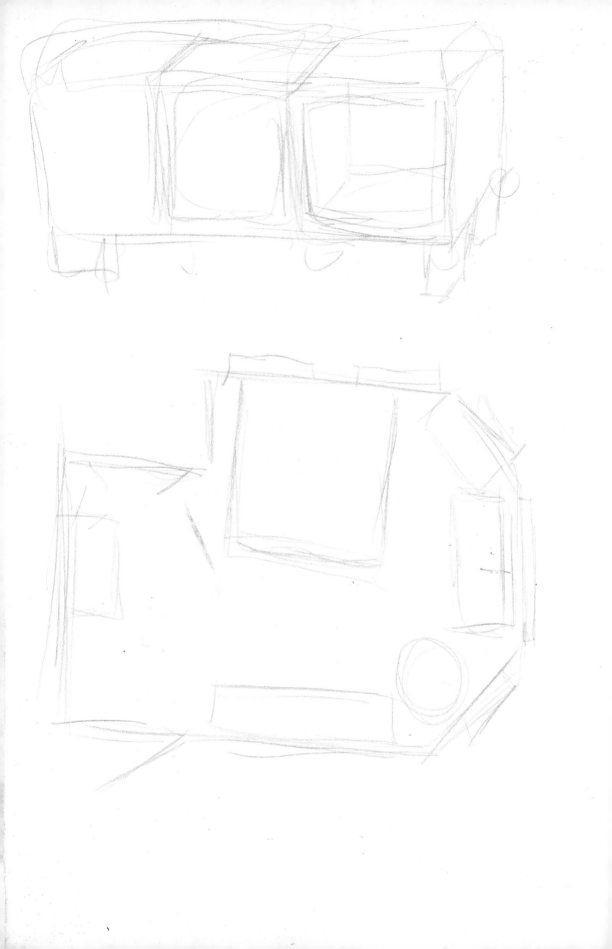